To Take Shape and Meaning

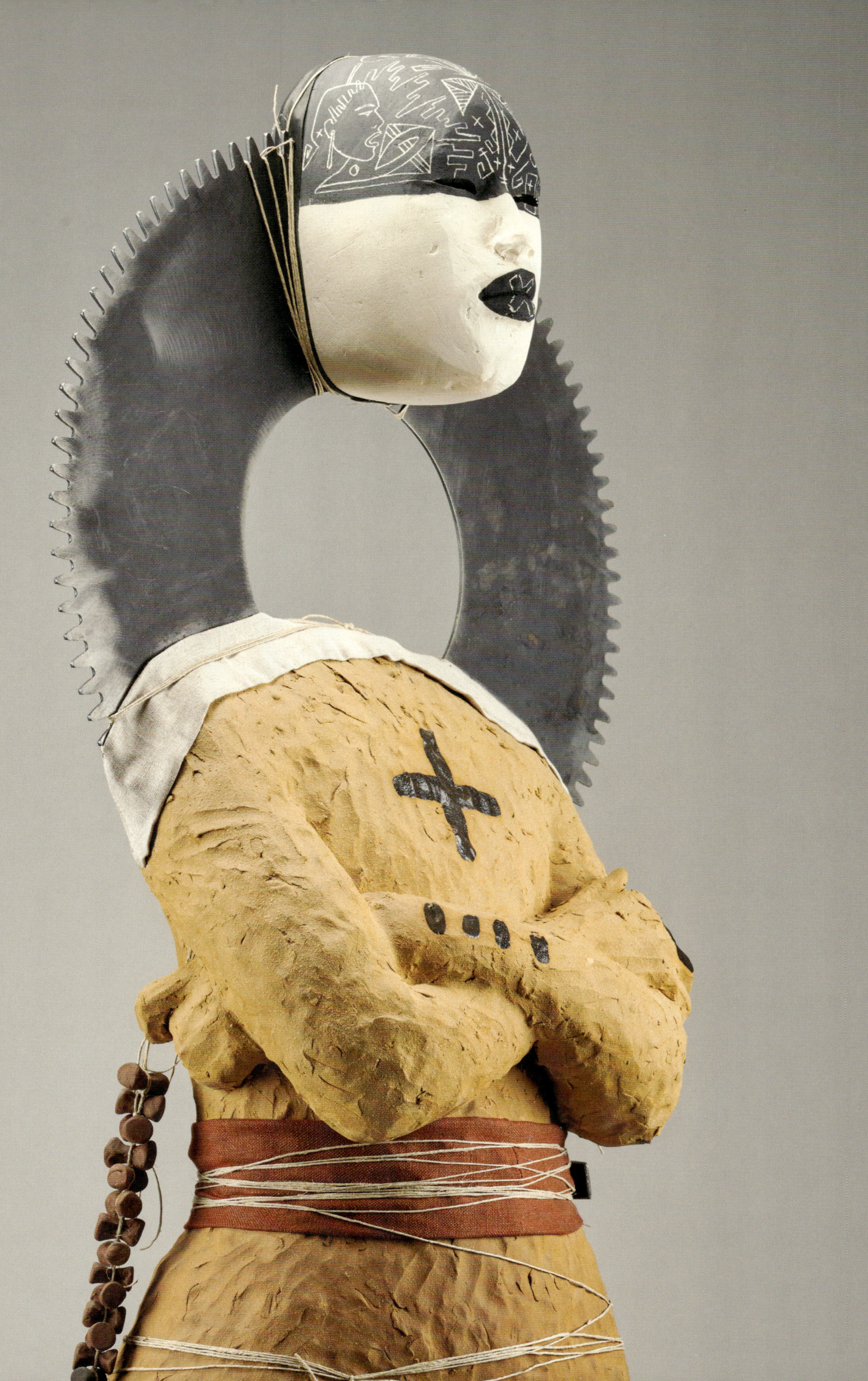

To Take Shape and Meaning

Form and Design in Contemporary American Indian Art

Nancy Strickland Fields

with Rose B. Simpson

and Stephen Fadden

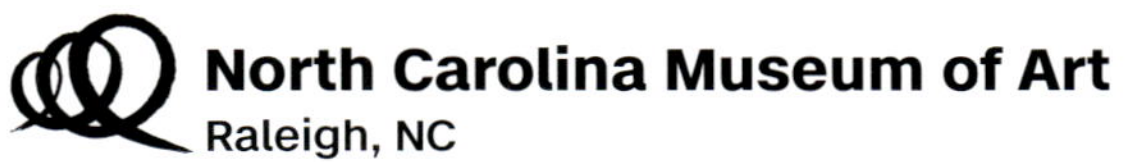

North Carolina Museum of Art
Raleigh, NC

Published by the North Carolina Museum of Art on the occasion of the exhibition *To Take Shape and Meaning: Form and Design in Contemporary American Indian Art*, March 2–July 28, 2024

Organized by the North Carolina Museum of Art

To Take Shape and Meaning: Form and Design in Contemporary American Indian Art is made possible at the North Carolina Museum of Art by the Hartfield Foundation and Libby and Lee Buck.

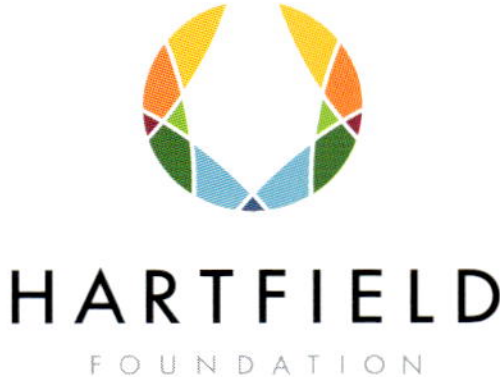

The exhibition and catalogue are also made possible, in part, by the North Carolina Department of Natural and Cultural Resources; the North Carolina Museum of Art Foundation, Inc.; and the William R. Kenan Jr. Endowment for Educational Exhibitions. Research for this exhibition was made possible by Ann and Jim Goodnight/The Andrew W. Mellon Foundation Fund for Curatorial and Conservation Research and Travel.

The North Carolina Museum of Art is an agency of the North Carolina Department of Natural and Cultural Resources, D. Reid Wilson, secretary. Operating support is provided through state appropriations and generous contributions from individuals, foundations, and businesses.

North Carolina Museum of Art
2110 Blue Ridge Road
Raleigh, North Carolina
ncartmuseum.org

Designer: Dan Ruccia
Editor: Laura Napolitano
Photo Editor: Sean Livingstone
NCMA Photography: Christopher Ciccone
Director of Collections and Exhibitions
Management: Meghan Olis
Curatorial and Exhibitions Assistant: Denice Celley

Printed in the United States of America through Porter Print Group, Bethesda, Maryland

Library of Congress Cataloging-in-Publication Data
Names: Fields, Nancy (Nancy Strickland) To take shape and meaning. | Simpson, Rose Bean. Of an artist. | Fadden, Stephen, 1954– Creating a future of hope. | North Carolina Museum of Art. organizer, host institution.
Title: To take shape and meaning : form and design in contemporary American Indian art / Nancy Strickland Fields ; with Rose B. Simpson and Stephen Fadden.
Description: Raleigh, NC : North Carolina Museum of Art, [2024] | Summary: "This exhibition catalogue features 3-D works by contemporary Indigenous artists from throughout the US, including North Carolina. Sections on place of being, rootedness, genealogy, encoded commentary, and revival and evolution highlight how American Indian artists use their art forms to retain meaning and in true tradition continue to evolve culture"—Provided by publisher.
Identifiers: LCCN 2023040760
ISBN 9780882599137 (hardcover)
Subjects: LCSH: Indian art—United States—21st century—Exhibitions.
Classification: LCC N6538.A4 T6 2024 | DDC 704.03/97—dc23/eng/20230912
LC record available at
https://lccn.loc.gov/2023040760

FRONT COVER: Senora Lynch (Haliwa-Saponi), *Woodland People Bowl*, 2003, red and white clay, H. 20 × Diam. 15 in., Collection of Bobby Brayboy

This stunning ceramic vessel, poignantly coded with allegorical meaning, embodies the intent behind *To Take Shape and Meaning*. Centrally featured in the composition are hummingbirds, dogwood flowers, and turtles. The dogwood flowers represent a new beginning, renewal, birth—a time to **take shape**. The turtles represent survivance, perseverance, spirituality—the longevity of wisdom and **meaning**. The hummingbirds represent the ancestors Native peoples honor—those who have continued the traditions and pushed the boundaries of art making from time immemorial. Lynch is not only a talented artist but also a beautiful and wise soul. Her art serves as an honorable introduction from North Carolina to three-dimensional contemporary Native art from around Turtle Island.

BACK COVER: Jamie Okuma (Luiseño/Shoshone e-Bannock/Wailaki/Okinawan), *Adaptation II*, 2012, shoes designed by Christian Louboutin, leather, glass beads, porcupine quills, sterling silver cones, brass sequins, and chicken feathers, each H. 8⅝ × W. 3¼ × D. 9³⁄₁₆ in., Lent by the Minneapolis Institute of Art, Bequest of Virginia Doneghy, by exchange

FRONTISPIECE: Rose B. Simpson (Santa Clara Pueblo), *Root I* (detail), 2019, ceramic, glaze, linen, jute string, steel, and leather, H. 70 × W. 20½ × D. 16 in., Rennie Collection, Vancouver

Contents

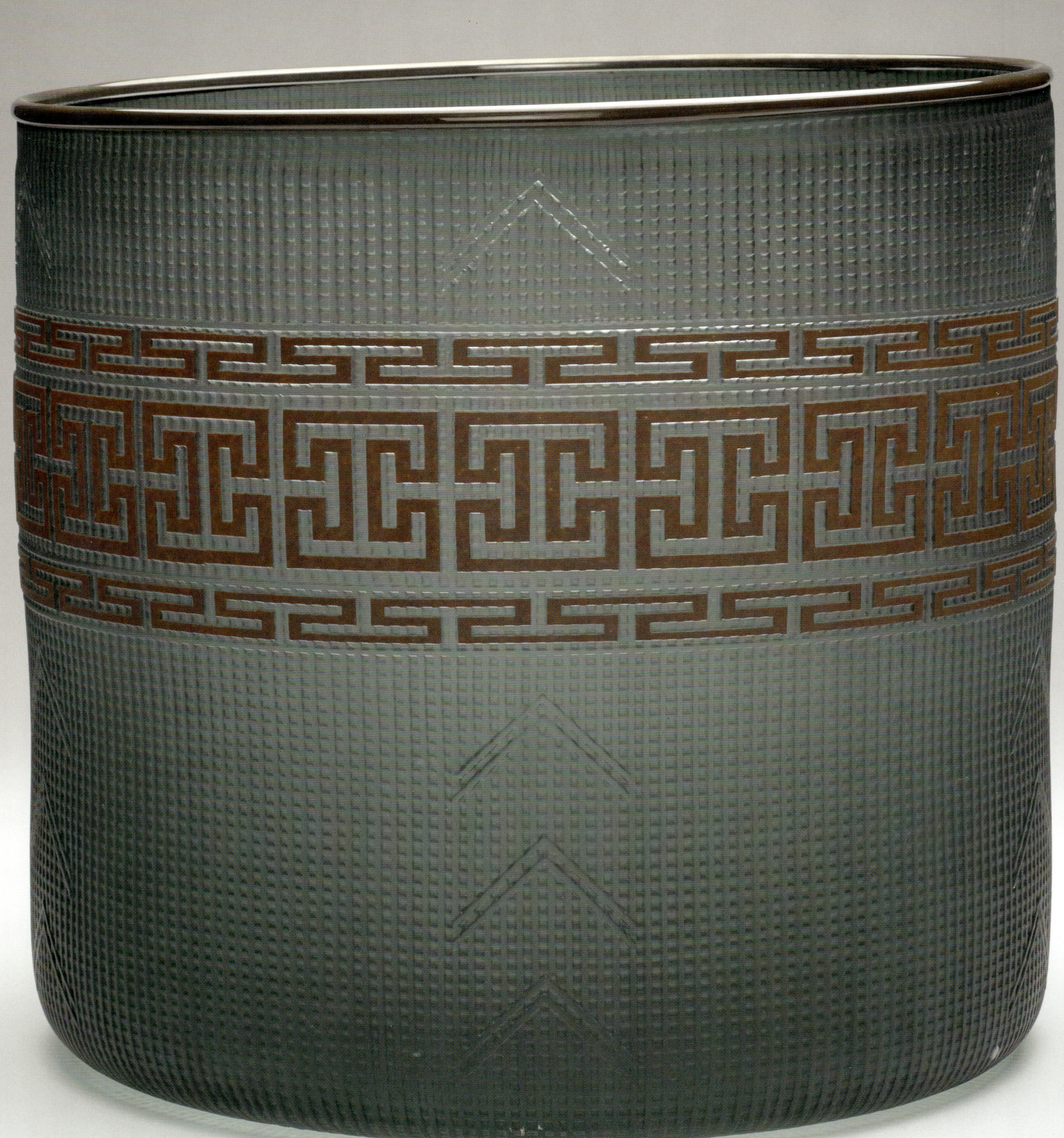

Director's Foreword

Over the last four years, we have been fortunate to work with Nancy Strickland Fields (Lumbee), director and curator of the Museum of the Southeast American Indian at the University of North Carolina at Pembroke, on the reimagining of our collection galleries to highlight multiple, diverse histories, voices, and perspectives and on the present exhibition, *To Take Shape and Meaning: Form and Design in Contemporary American Indian Art*, the first at the NCMA to focus exclusively on American Indian artists. This exhibition, curated by Fields in collaboration with Linda Dougherty, the NCMA's chief curator and senior curator of contemporary art, brings together over seventy contemporary American Indian artists from across the country working in three dimensions and a rich array of media. Presented both inside and outdoors in the Ann and Jim Goodnight Museum Park, the show calls attention to traditional and contemporary practices and offers insight into the process of giving objects form and life to fulfill functional and cultural roles within Native tribes and cultures.

This catalogue includes essays by Fields, artist Rose B. Simpson (Santa Clara Pueblo), and art historian and storyteller Stephen Fadden (Mohawk). The written words on the pages that follow are a part of the creative process of this project, which aims to shed light on the histories, experiences, and purposes reflected in the artworks in the exhibition, underscoring points of continuity while also celebrating uniqueness.

I wish to express the Museum's gratitude to the artists, authors, curators, NCMA staff, and the Hartfield Foundation and Libby and Lee Buck for making this exhibition possible. And I would like to echo Fadden's hope that "with shared cultural understandings, encoded in the stories we remember and tell, we can co-create a shared future."

Valerie Hillings, PhD
Director, North Carolina Museum of Art

Large detail of image on page 161

Acknowledgments

Land Acknowledgment

The state of North Carolina is situated on the ancestral homelands of many American Indian tribes who have lived in this place, cared for these lands, and traveled throughout the region for thousands of years. Tribes spoke different variants of Algonquian, Iroquoian, and Siouan languages. We honor them as the first stewards of this place and acknowledge, with sorrow and remorse, the violent history of their dispossession and forced removal.

We respectfully acknowledge the Coharie, Eastern Band of Cherokee, Haliwa-Saponi, Lumbee, Meherrin, Occaneechi Band of the Saponi, Sappony, and Waccamaw Siouan and honor the enduring presence, vibrance, and diversity of contemporary Indigenous communities.

I would like to extend my sincerest gratitude and appreciation to the North Carolina Museum of Art for the extraordinary opportunity to curate this exhibition. An exhibition of this caliber at the NCMA is a dream come true not only for me but for countless Native peoples throughout North Carolina. This is our ancestral home. Having ourselves and Native brothers and sisters represented in this space honors our peoples and affords us an opportunity to share who we are through the most intimate of our expressions, our art. Privileging our languages, traditions, allegories, creative processes, and identities allows us to share with the public a special window into the Native world.

I honor Museum Director Valerie Hillings for her commitment to present a Native exhibition at the NCMA that gives the public the opportunity to learn about our traditions, cultures, and values. I would also like to express a very heartfelt thank you to Linda Dougherty, chief curator and senior curator of contemporary art, for her invitation to curate this exhibition and belief in the importance of Native art. I owe a huge debt of gratitude to Blakely Kralovec, former manager of exhibitions, and Meghan Olis, director of collections and exhibitions management, who worked tirelessly to bring the many aspects of this exhibition together.

I would like to thank my daughter Kasey and my granddaughter Kynlee for their encouragement and inspiration throughout this process. A very special thank you goes to Harlen Chavis for the countless hours of conversation about Native art and history that helped me through the curatorial journey. Most importantly, I would like to offer my most sincere thank you to each artist for participating in this exhibition. Your vision, creativity, and art make the project significantly meaningful and groundbreaking. This exhibition celebrates all you are, all you do, and all that you create **to give shape and meaning**.

In the language of my ancestors,

Hawuh Kurii
Nya-we
Kenah

Nancy Strickland Fields (Lumbee)
Guest Curator, *To Take Shape and Meaning*

This exhibition developed from numerous conversations I had with our guest curator, Nancy Strickland Fields, whom I met through her position as director and curator at the University of North Carolina at Pembroke's Museum of the Southeast American Indian. Her deep knowledge of and boundless enthusiasm for contemporary American Indian art is incredibly inspiring and engaging. This groundbreaking show and publication are the result of her vision and guidance.

Because of Nancy's tremendous generosity, this exhibition has been a truly collaborative process from the onset and a unique opportunity for us to work together—a process we hope to repeat again in the future. Foremost, we would like to express our gratitude to the Hartfield Foundation and Libby and Lee Buck for their generous support of this ambitious project.

We would like to thank all of the artists in the exhibition for their wholehearted cooperation every step of the way and for numerous exhilarating conversations that made this endeavor so successful and enjoyable from beginning to end. We extend our sincerest gratitude to all of the lenders, whose support and generosity made this exhibition possible. We also want to express our heartfelt thanks to our colleagues at other institutions and galleries, their staff members, and the numerous individuals who assisted us with many aspects of the show. We greatly appreciate insightful, thought-provoking, and poetic essays contributed to the catalogue by Rose B. Simpson (Santa Clara Pueblo) and Stephen Fadden (Mohawk).

At the North Carolina Museum of Art, coordinating and presenting this exhibition and catalogue called on the expertise of every department. Director of Collections and Exhibitions Management Meghan Olis and former Manager of Exhibitions Blakely Kralovec have been an integral and indispensable part of this project from its inception, coordinating virtually every aspect of the exhibition, and they have handled every task with diplomacy, efficiency, good humor, and their amazing organizational skills. Denice Celley, curatorial and exhibitions assistant, provided crucial support gathering information for the exhibition and the catalogue. Jamie Powell, institutional gifts officer, gave invaluable insight and feedback, resulting in a successful grant award.

Associate Registrar Angie Bell-Morris capably and patiently handled the myriad details associated with multiple loans and varied shipping and installation requirements. Kathryn Briggs, senior exhibition designer, came up with creative solutions and innovative designs to present all of the work in the best possible way. Graphic Designer Dan Ruccia designed a catalogue that perfectly realizes the theme of the exhibition. Laura Napolitano, editor and manager of book publishing, patiently and gracefully provided a critical eye for detail and articulate editorial comments and revisions that guaranteed a successful catalogue. Manager of Digital Imaging Christopher Ciccone captured the perfect image for numerous works in the catalogue. Sean Livingstone, project associate, navigated gathering external images and all necessary rights and reproductions with ease.

Rachel Woods, director of museum park operations, and Ben Bridgers, manager of Park collection and exhibitions, skillfully oversaw the installation of Rose Simpson's work in the Museum Park. Ian Larson, chief art handler, and Rand Esser, head preparator, expertly coordinated and led the exhibition installation, with the assistance and input of Megan Salazar-Walsh, exhibitions conservator. Felicia Ingram, manager of interpretation, accessibility, and diversity, worked closely with us to create innovative interpretation elements throughout the exhibition. Director of Marketing and Communications Lizzie Newton and her staff enthusiastically and effectively helped us promote this project. We extend our heartfelt thanks to everyone who helped make *To Take Shape and Meaning* possible.

Linda Johnson Dougherty
Chief Curator and Senior Curator of Contemporary Art

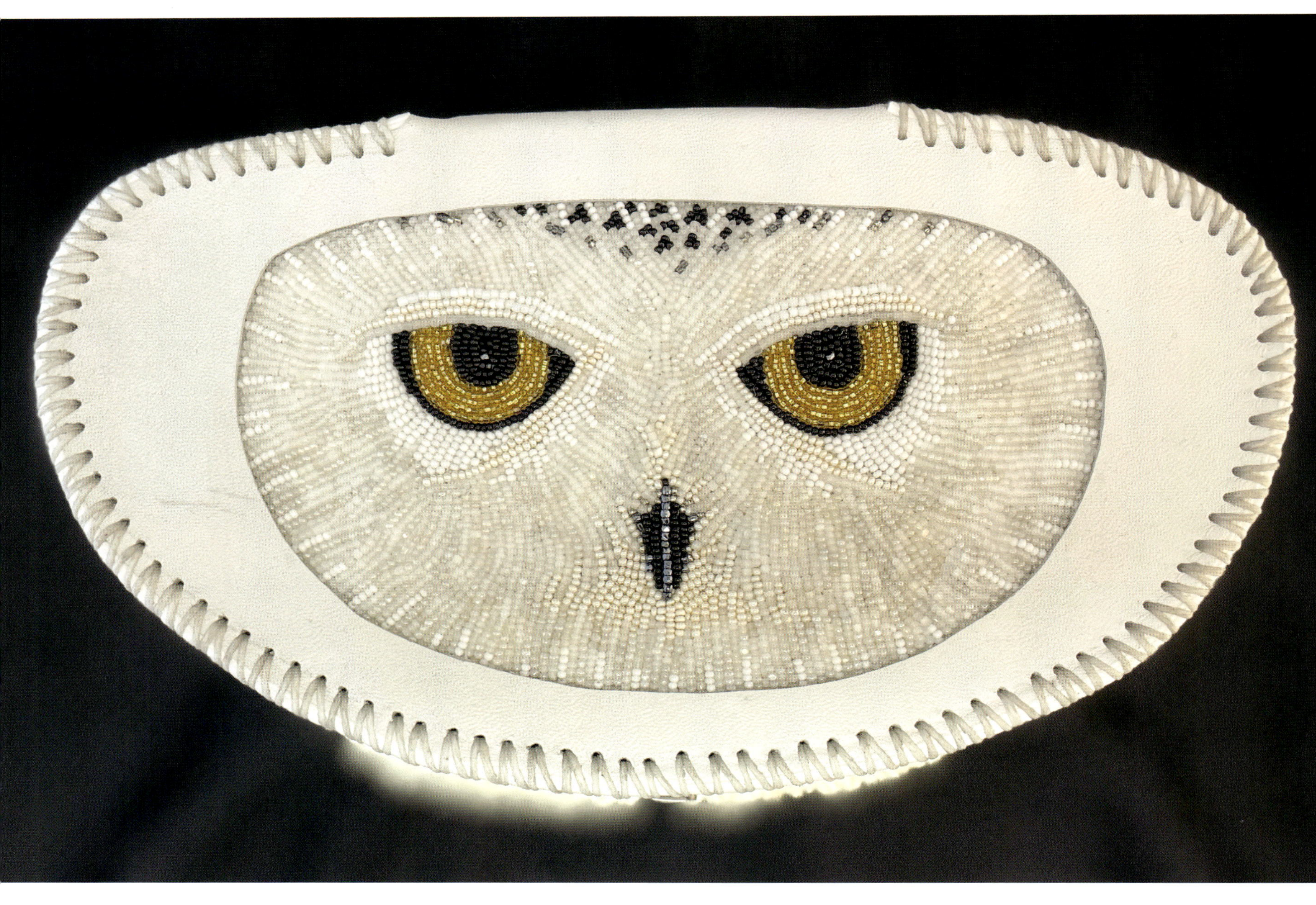

Detail of image on page 105

Lenders to the Exhibition

Allan Houser Inc.
Marcus Amerman
Venancio Aragon
Ashville Art Museum
Keri Ataumbi
Audain Art Museum
Martha Berry
Birmingham Museum of Art
Joanna Underwood Blackburn
Bobby Brayboy
Jackie Larson Bread
Millie Bridwell
Brooklyn Museum
Joyce Chelberg
Steven Chrisjohn
Kelly Church
Vivian Garner Cottrell
Leslie A. Deer
Denver Art Museum
Orlando Dugi
Eiteljorg Museum
Tom Farris
Sue Fish
Cliff Fragua
Bill Glass Jr.

Dorothy Grant
The Gutierrez Collection
Barbara Harjo
Heard Museum
Emil Her Many Horses
Kenneth Johnson
Jontay Kahm
Renferd Koruh
Kouri + Carrao Gallery
Mina Levin and Ronald Schwarz
Longyear Museum of Anthropology, Colgate University
Maine Historical Society
Dallin Maybee
Michigan State University Museum
Minneapolis Institute of Art
Wanesia Misquadace
Katrina Mitten
Museum of the Cherokee Indian
Museum of the Southeast American Indian
Nasher Museum of Art, Duke University
National Cowboy & Western Heritage Museum

Native American Studies Center, University of South Carolina Lancaster
Jane Osti
Philbrook Museum of Art
Private collection
Private collection, North Carolina
Rankin Museum of American Heritage
Rennie Collection
The Robert and Barbara Buker Collections
School for Advanced Research
Rose B. Simpson
Preston Singletary
Richard Zane Smith
Laura Walkingstick
Jodi Webster
Billy Welch
Margaret Roach Wheeler
Wheelwright Museum of the American Indian
Dennis Michael Wilkins
Ken Williams Jr.
Holly Wilson

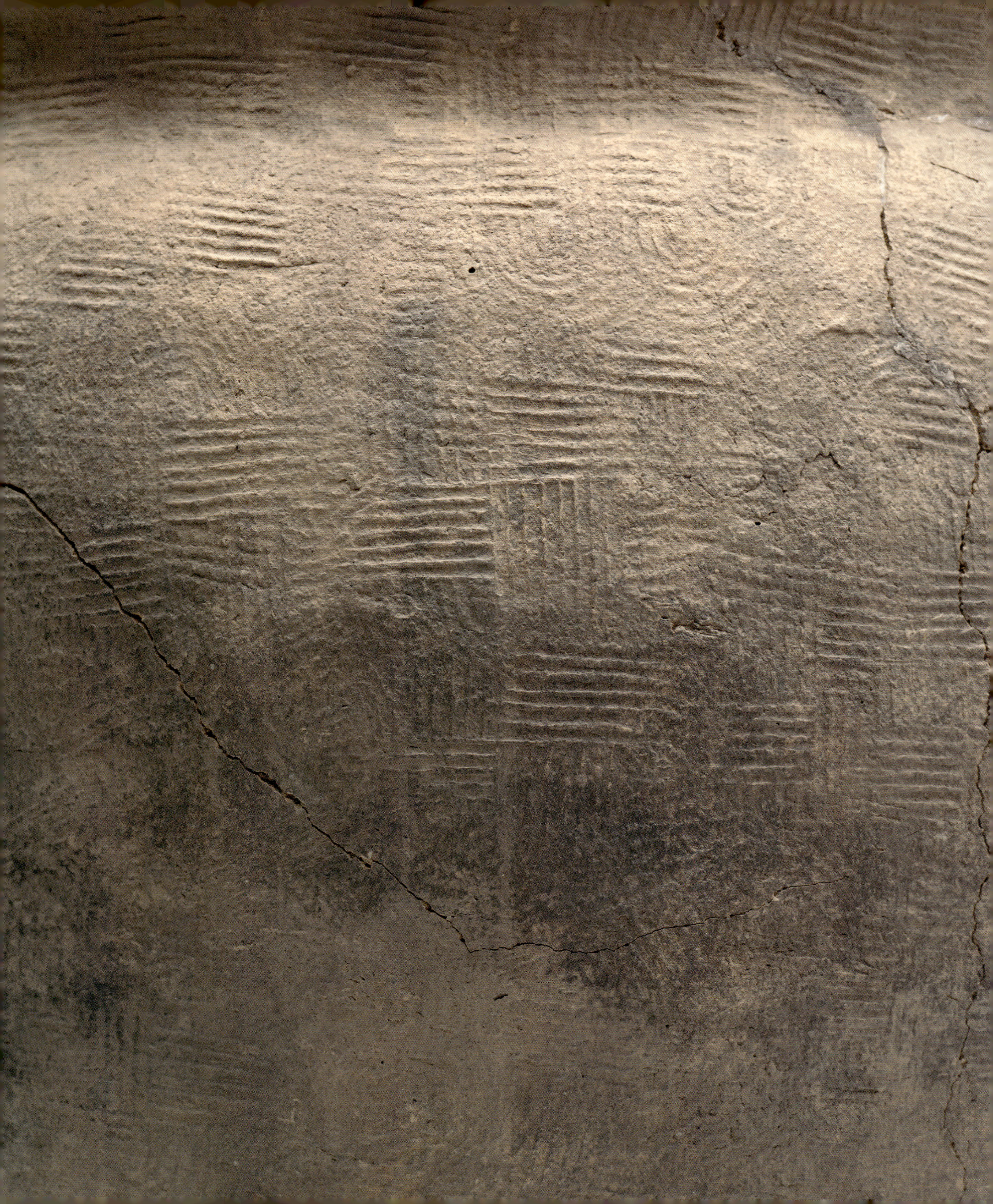

To Take Shape and Meaning

Nancy Strickland Fields
Lumbee

In a Mississippian Indian village near present day Mt. Gilead, North Carolina, an adolescent girl went to the Little River and collected clay with her grandmother. It was late spring. The ground and water had warmed in the earlier months. Her grandmother squatted on her flat feet and used a small hoe to scoop clay from a family clay deposit near the riverbank. She used the hoe to roll the viscus clay on top of itself in uniform spools of wet earth hued with orange and gray and sparkled with minerals. Her brown, strong hands collected each spool, and she placed them neatly on end in a wide-open pot made of the same earth. The girl watched in silence. Enhancing the silence was the gentle sound of water rolling over rocks and pushing toward the Pee Dee River, water that would soon reach Winyah Bay in the Atlantic, transforming from fresh to salt. A breeze passed over them, releasing the faint smell of smoke in her grandmother's clothing from the morning fire. The sunlight created dancing mirrored sparkles across the river water and reflected brilliant silver strands in her grandmother's black hair. **And the clay filled the pot.**

The grandmother and the girl took the pot and sat it next to another waiting at the river's edge. The grandmother took several of the clay rolls and placed them in this other pot. She then bent the pot down to the river to cover the clay with water. Fingers first, she dipped her hand in the pot and stirred the soaked clay, separating it from its rolls. The clay released small pebbles, fragments of mussel shells, twigs, and a tiny bone. Next, she poured the clay over a cane mat sieve and poured water over the sieve, working her hand back and forth to remove any remaining debris. She placed the clay back into the pot and repeated the process until all she had collected was cleaned. While the grandmother did this work, the young girl collected her own scoop of clay. She removed debris and rinsed the clay in her cupped hands with water. She emulated her grandmother's process. Her grandmother noticed her granddaughter and praised her with encouraging words and the loving look that only a grandmother can give.

After their work the two walked back to the village. The clay in the pot was placed in the corner of the house to dry. The two went outside, and the grandmother sat on the ground next to another pot of clay ready for use. With two hands she reached in and grabbed a large lump of clay. She slabbed it onto a large, tablet-shaped stone and began rolling it out with her flat hands, making long, uniform, cylindrical-shaped strands. Her hands moved back and forth along the length of the strands with the knowledge of her ancestors. The granddaughter grabbed a handful of clay and repeated the woman's motions. Her grandmother smiled at her. The grandmother took another large lump of clay and worked it into a disk. Her mind wandered to

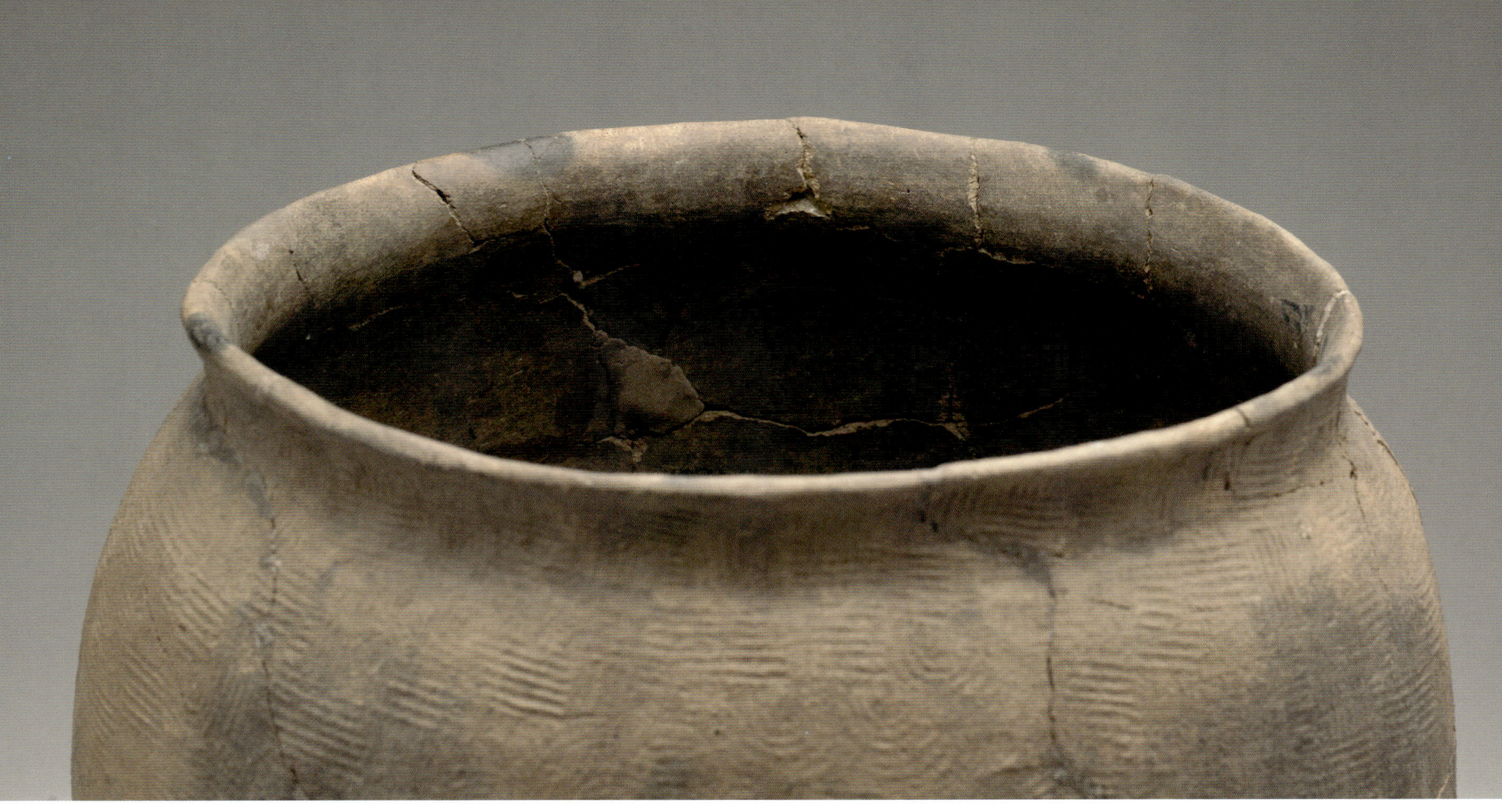

her own grandmother's hands performing the same work. She could remember how her hands looked forming a disk for the base of a pot. As she had done so many times, she searched her memories of her grandmother to find the instructions for the form she wanted to create. Entranced in memory, the grandmother achieved the size disk that would form the base of the pot. She took one of the strands and laid it along the edge of the disk. She took another strand and coiled it on top of the other, repeating until she had built the size pot she wanted. She used a stone and wooden paddle to smooth the walls of clay **to give it shape. And the clay built the pot.**

The grandmother began to sing in a low voice. The granddaughter knew the song, and she quietly sang with her. The girl used a found stick to slap the clay she had shaped into a small pot that nestled in her hand. The older woman admired her granddaughter's skill and smiled approvingly at her. The grandmother sat up on her knees and carefully placed her arm inside the pot to position her hands along the inside and outside of the walls to work out air bubbles and imperfections in the design. Her mind's eye fixed on the design and scale of the pot. She sat back and took a break. Her granddaughter marveled at the size of the pot, the smoothed clay, the beauty of what her grandmother had created. The woman looked at the pot critically. She inspected it closely, using her stone and water to smooth lines, fingerprints, and bubbles. To the granddaughter, this seemed to take forever. The grandmother leaned in and

away from her creation to make sure every aspect of the pot was perfect. Once she was satisfied, she picked up another paddle wrapped with rope, and using her stone for pressure, she carefully impressed the pot with the design on the paddle. Her movements were graceful and methodical. Careful not to compromise the form of the pot, she artfully imprinted the clay **with meaning.**

After hours of working, the pot was complete. The granddaughter and grandmother stood together and admired the masterpiece. The pot was beautiful and stately, and now it had to dry. Pleased with her work, the older woman led the girl away to prepare a meal.

A couple of days later, the grandmother built a fire with her granddaughter. It was time to finish the pot. The woman placed it against burning pieces of wood in the roaring fire. She opened her hand for her granddaughter to hold and began to pray. The grandmother watched the pot, and when the time was right, she used a stick to gently rotate the pot on its side in the fire. And she prayed. She continued this process throughout the afternoon and into the night, holding vigil with her granddaughter against the glow of the fire. When the firing was complete, the grandmother removed the pot from the smoldering coals and left it to cool.

At dawn, with her granddaughter in tow, she took the pot to her son. It was a gift. He looked at the pot and then to his mother. The son broke down in tears. He wept uncontrollably in his mother's arms. The granddaughter clung to her father's leg for comfort. He welcomed his mother into the home, carrying the pot with both arms close to his chest. The son began to pray. He turned the pot over onto its opening. He took a club and bashed a hole into the bottom of the pot, releasing its spirit. The grandmother watched. The granddaughter watched. The hole was clean and in the center. The pot had been sacrificed. He turned the pot right side up. The granddaughter's mother walked over and handed her husband a bundle wrapped in leather, and he laid it next to the pot. The mother's brother walked over carrying a small child. She was gone. Grieving and weeping, the father took the child and held her close to his chest. Tears filled everyone's eyes. He tenderly placed the child in the pot. He then placed the bundle with the child. The top was covered with a shroud. The pot was lowered into the earthen ground of the floor in the home, completing the meaning of the pot. **And the clay filled the pot.**

The exhibition *To Take Shape and Meaning: Form and Design in Contemporary American Indian Art* is more than a gathering together of art by Native America's most renowned artists. Each work expresses traditions and evolutions of form and design that are encoded with Indigenous meaning. This exhibition offers unique insight into American Indian culture and identity. For most American Indian peoples, the process of creating art is the same process that gives life to all objects—it breathes meaning and purpose into the existence of the object. For the grandmother, who was an artist (even if imagined), the method she had of collecting the clay, the rites she possessed to create the pot, the songs she sang, the prayers she whispered, the knowledge she passed down to her granddaughter, the ritual she shared with her son and his family—all were involved in the purpose of the pot.

Each object featured in the exhibition pushes past aesthetics and relates knowledge, information, a message—this art was created with intent and meaning. Each object has a spirit, a life. The works hold intimate parts of the artists, not only through their creation but also through the cultural aspects assigned by tradition and carried out by the artists and the functionality, purpose, and role of the objects within Native communities. Many of these objects perform and fulfill specific functions within their communities, such as the Apache burden basket used in a girl's sunrise dance. While much is revealed in allegories encoded in art, there is also privileged knowledge only shared among those who are entitled to understand the meaning and engage with the object's purpose. Native art has the ability to visually communicate complex ideas and cultural

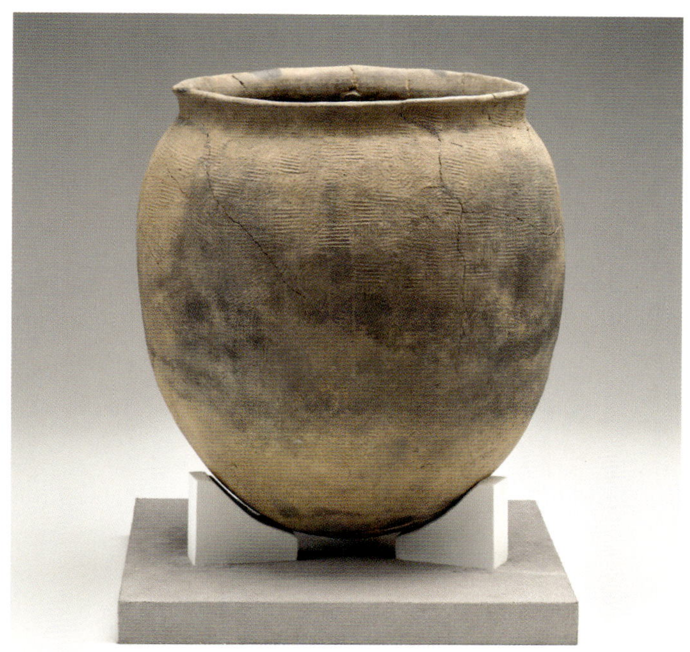

representations and to reveal the interests and passions of an artist. Moreover, Native art has the power to connect with viewers in meaningful ways and the power to share these elements.

This exhibition features three-dimensional works that are rooted in traditional American Indian art forms. Beautiful baskets fashioned from rivercane, vessels made of clay, and textiles woven from fiber represent indigenous environments that reflect Native homelands. They are formed with materials employed for millennia to create objects of use and meaning. Baskets woven of printed paper, cars transformed into vessels, and portraits made of dice reveal transitions of place, experiments in materiality, and meanings blended from present-day and traditional beliefs. These objects capture the constant progression of Native culture and identity and express the reality that Native peoples are not static but ever evolving within a modern world they help to define. *To Take Shape and Meaning* brings together a wide range of Indigenous world views, ideas, experiences, traditions, cultures, and media, and the continuities of Indigenous arts—collective and individual expressions of Native America. This exhibition is a celebration of all these things: the brilliance, mastery, knowledge, and significance of American Indian peoples.

PAGES xii, 2, AND 3: Details of image on page 18

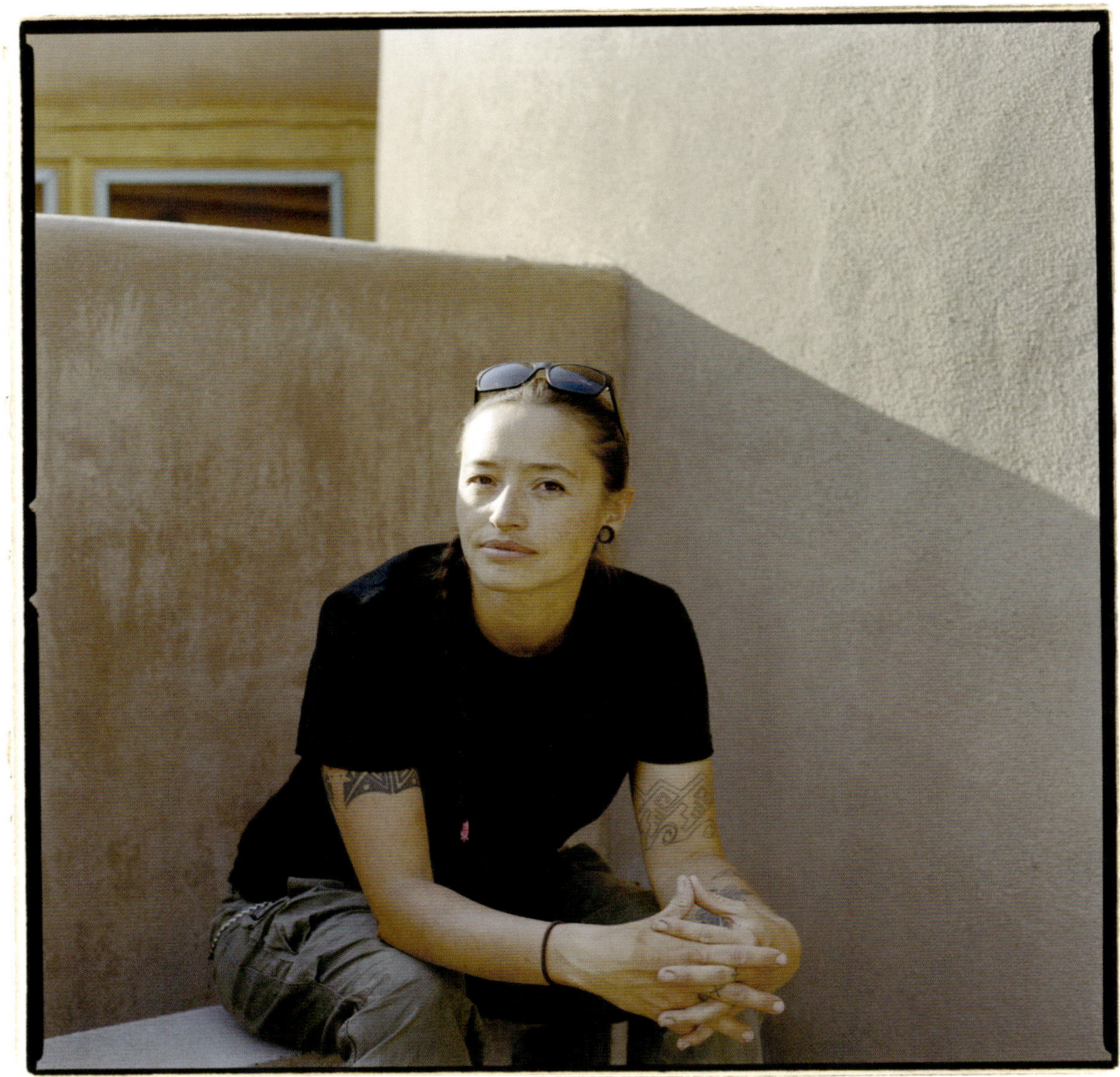

Rose B. Simpson

Of an Artist

Rose B. Simpson
Santa Clara Pueblo

I.

I LIVE IN A ONE-BEDROOM HOUSE that my great-grandfather built for his wife, Rose. I was close to my great-grandmother, and I like to think she enjoyed our shared name.

In the night my daughter curls her small body under my arm, and I listen to her breath tell me her dreams have arrived. On a shelf across from the bed is where I put the photos of loved ones who have gone home to the ancestors. My great-grandmother Rose, her daughter Rina, and my uncle Cleo are some of the faces that will watch us sleep.

My mother sleeps in the house to the north, my brother, his wife, and children are next door, my cousin and his family are directly upwind. The creek flows east from Tsikumu Pin in the western Jemez Mountains and will merge with Posongeh (the Rio Grande) heading south along the base of Ku-Seng Pin nestled in the Sangre de Cristo mountain range. There are layers of ancestral life and building sites, old stones and gardens all throughout these hills and valleys. Our relations, grandmothers and grandfathers, their handwork is everywhere in pot sherds and obsidian points. Our community still lives in this bowl—still here. With the strong Earth below and the basket of stars above, I cradle my child. And the two of us are cradled by my family living and passed, who are cradled by place, culture, history, and hope.

Now imagine this image as a traditional clay pot. This pot has pattern on the inside, fingerprints on the outside. The contrast in the lines becomes the chapters of a story, the nesting of landscape, the integration of beliefs. This pot becomes not just a metaphor but also a prayer. It is a powerful thing, that which has the capacity to nurture not just our bodies but also our dreams. It is a deeply delicious aesthetic.

And there is a basket above. There is a crisp sound as the fibers bend but do not break. It allows movement through—prayer out to the larger universe, light and weather back in, but it holds us together.

There is a weaving on the bed, rising and falling as the child's breath deepens. Her little hand grasps the fraying edge. This tapestry is the color of earth, the fibers still an identifiable source energy—it is plant, it is animal, the lines in the designs are not straight, as it is made by hand, but they step, step, step, build, build, build. There is warmth and embrace, simultaneously holding a story and embedding it into a lived experience.

It makes sense, doesn't it.

II.

I find aesthetics fascinating.

The way that I observe aesthetics is through a feeling—a hypersensory awareness. Maybe this sense lives deep below, or maybe above, because it doesn't just exist through the eyes, ears, nose, lips, or hands. Maybe the feeling is found in my belly, the soft spots of my upper arms, the space three feet behind my heart that grows like unseen wings up around my neck and out from my shoulders. I know what I like. I know how to feel that "yum" ten thousand ways. As an artist this path of "yum" is my choice maker, and I am the tracker. The more I engage, the stronger the muscle of discernment. I say to myself, *This, not that. Oh yes, this ...* and so on as my investment evolves within the constant yumformation feedback loop.

But to make these decisions, I must invest deeply in the guidance of my feelings, and because of this I know exactly how important dissociation can be when a psychological or emotional challenge feels insurmountable. I know very well the part of myself that wants to shut down the yum-compass because to know what feels good is also to know what doesn't. Maybe it's lived experience, genetic memory, or a story of genocide; identifying that yum can be inextricably embedded in trauma. It often is, and I personally have compassion in the moment where I might choose a cheap, smooth, mass-produced/heartless "yum" as a safer step. To decide with feeling is to feel it all, from delicious to excruciatingly painful.

And to put it in perspective, this is done in our postmodern world where, it seems, the constant need for greater ease has run our intentionality empty. We often access the aesthetic reward at the very first level of perception, rarely requiring us to involve ourselves any further. I know this in myself; I understand why an easy aesthetic might be desirable. For example, I grew up with parents whose vehicles were often breaking down. Some of the experiences of breaking down were scary, cold, dark, and stressful—the outcomes uncertain. Because of this, I invested in learning how cars work and how to fix them, as I didn't like the powerless feeling of having a nonfunctional vehicle. I now have a fairly strong skill set in this regard, but if I can afford a reliable vehicle over one that is prone to "adventure," I might choose this route, as it may not hammer my senses with more of that trauma.

Under the influence of sugars, plastics, and a barrage of imagery emanating from a screen in my palm, however, my choosing becomes lazy and my yum-compass tends to lose north. My life patterns become robotic as basic survival is increasingly cheap and cheapened and I see youth devaluing the ability to use their bodies to craft, create, innovate (and even play) while promoting values growing from deep in a mystery-less, Google-able, cyber-dimensional maze. What happened to wonder? What happened to the ability to navigate discomfort and to discern via intuition?

I have noticed in myself that I will inherently first choose the easy route, but I know from experience that sometimes the hard work or mystery makes for a much more informed and fulfilling experience. So again, I consciously work the muscle of agency to pull forth the aesthetic experiences that I have learned bring higher quality moments, clearer visions, and crisper feelings.

I believe we are experiencing a time of deep human transformation, and our ability to imagine must be balanced with the capacity to craft—to innovate with a grounded materiality. We look to examples of craft, of functional form to guide us back to ourselves. We look to descriptions and rhythm embedded in design to teach us how to listen through what is felt. Deep and intense perception becomes story, story turns into tools, and tools create the stuff of this world.

III.

Here we are driving our future. Here we are building what is to be.

Here we are laying all that we have learned in our lives—all that we have inherited from our ancestral links—we are carefully laying it out on the ground in front of us. Look—there are patterns. See the way we hold the spoon when we stir a batter or a stew, where on our internal shelf we might place our victimry. Look—there are tools. See the stone we pray with, maybe the way a hip might shift to affect the room. Look—there are stories; some feel of truth, some elaborate manipulations, all with much to teach. Look—there is that high school buddy and that one thing they said in the car that snowy day, and look—there is the glint of sunlight from the creek winding through the ponderosa, Grandma set in the grass with her feet in the cold water, pants rolled up, beer in hand. She's smiling. Look—there is our face growing older in the mirror. Look—it's changing. The dirt road is now paved. And now it has potholes. Look—there are our hands, still holding all we have ever done in the scars and creases. They are open for all we will ever do. Look—there's

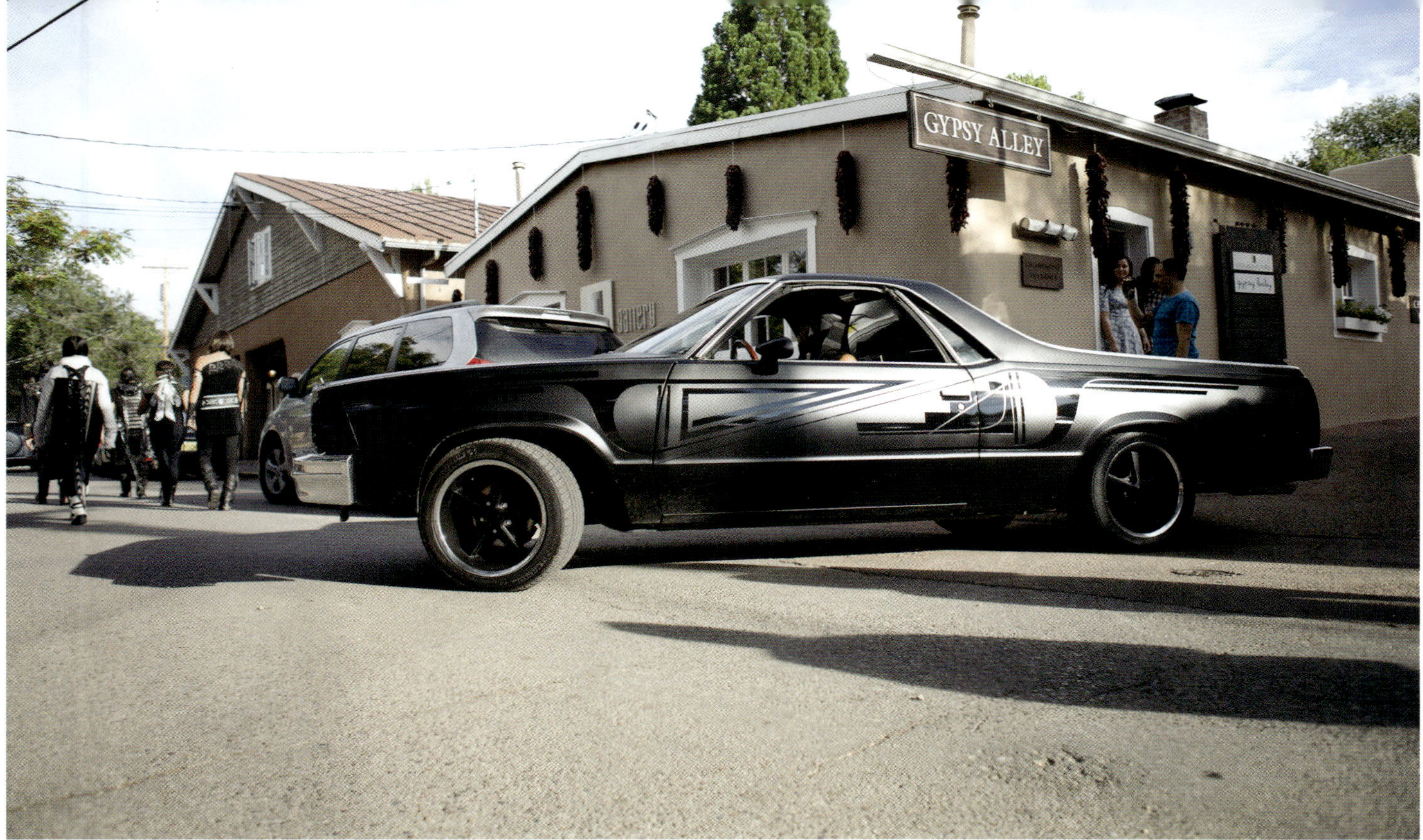

Rose B. Simpson driving *Maria* during a performance at the Denver Art Museum, 2014

space for more. Look, with all we can muster, look. Look with so many layers of perception, look! Look without categorizing good and bad, just hold witness and feel.

Life is movement through choosing. We choose to engage, we choose to appreciate, we choose to witness, to deny, to judge. We are the makers of choices. These choices become the materials of reality. The more self-aware we are, the clearer, stronger, healthier our creative process.

IV.

Hey, friend. How goes it? Like not just *I'm fine. You?* but how do the feeling-things of your days sit in that spot at the base of your palm where hand turns to wrist? Cuz that's where it flows through, all that you do. And because of this, there's knowing.

Tell me. When you tell me of you, it helps me to know me. And that, my dear, feels like love. Maybe they call that empathy, but it's us, in it, always, together. Near and far like breathing.

I am thinking of you dearly. I am sending tenderness to your steps. I am imagining that the experiences that grace your day are sweet and satiating. I am believing that you aced that last challenge and you are proud of yourself and you are standing, ready, for the next beautiful level to show you new perspective. A goot one! The kind you look back on and think *I can't believe I did that, but I got through, and I feel amazing*. That kind.

I'm picturing you standing somewhere outside—somewhere where there's a prickle of sun, just a little bit. And maybe just a little breeze; not so much that the wind makes that roar in your ear—just enough that it feels like the wind is sniffing around, noticing you. And you notice back. And you wonder if that was someone you once knew or an ancestor adjusting your shirt because they know you so, so well. I'm imagining that you close your eyes and turn your head slightly to the side, a slight shake to let a couple unnecessary, grouchy thoughts tumble out your ear, and then when you open your eyes, there it is—something beautiful. And it is framed simply by the edges of your vision, and you want to keep it forever, but there's no way, and no photo will do, so you take its breath, and it becomes you.

It's kind of funny, isn't it. This love thing. It's yummy. It tickles.

Hey, let's try something. Let's keep this feeling running, hey? Let's roll everything through this meter, see how it keeps feeling. Right now I'm catching some gratitude, the kind that is enamored with all that is. The kind that brings the heart to writhe.

I am excited to see you there, friend, in the learning wonder, where all of this, all of this, is an aesthetic experience. Let's build, witness, build, witness, build.

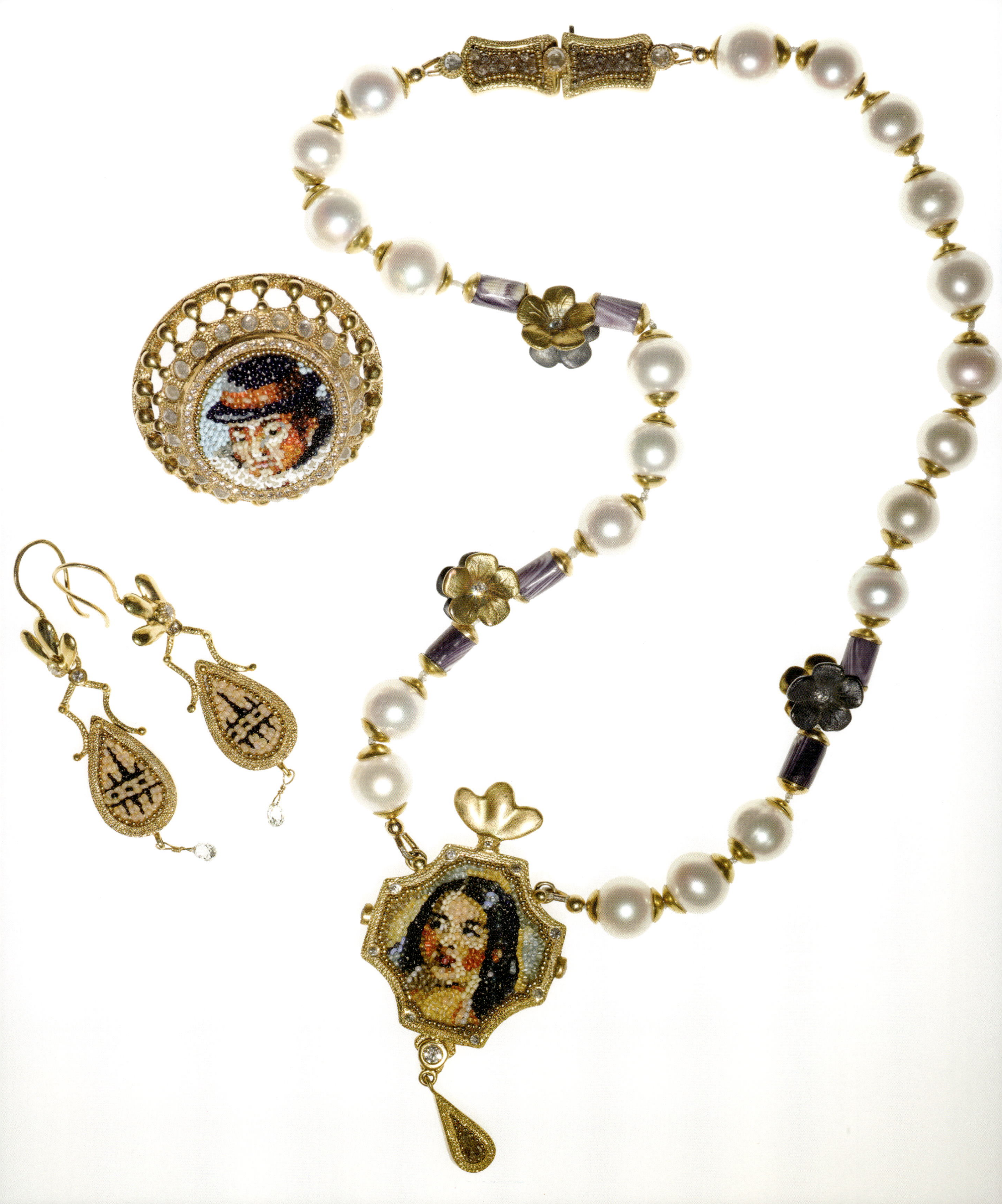

Creating a Future of Hope

Stephen Fadden

Mohawk

To Take Shape and Meaning ALIGNS with a significant trend in the ways that galleries and museums are now presenting the cultural and personal histories of Indigenous peoples and their art. History tends to be perceived by many as a passive and objective study of the past. This viewpoint encompasses only one-third of the totality of history. We study the past, and in doing so we can better comprehend the present. This drives us to the most important aspect art history can illuminate, which is the creativity that all people, not only artists, share. With our knowledge about past and present, we can create a future. That awareness is most empowering when we understand that our shared futures depend on the decisions we make today and on our plans to bring them to completion for future generations through choices we commit to with a strong sense of conscience.

This project invites viewers to look deeper into the histories (plural) and the present of America's Indigenous peoples and their creativity. *Indigenous* seems the more appropriate term, since the term *Native American* is a bit more homogenizing, used to make blanket legislation and assumptions about tribes who are culturally and historically distinct from one another. In the past those tribes did not necessarily identify as one race or ethnicity with other tribes, while their histories were sometimes intertwined with those of other Indigenous groups and imperially minded societies, with varied consequences.

Until the twentieth century, artistic media were commonly conceptualized in a purely physical sense by Western societies. Typically, for a work to be considered fine art, it had to be made of precious materials; one of a kind, static, and monumental in intent; and created by academically trained men. The transformative, spiritual properties of media were rarely, if ever, considered. It was thought art represented the individual efforts of the artist.

Among Indigenous peoples, the medium selected has spiritual powers on its own, and in some ways the creation is a transformative co-creation between the artist and the spirit of the materials. Therefore, many works are comprised of conglomerate (read mixed) media that historically would have been considered common and profane to Eurocentric high art aficionados and artists. When we view the creative works of Indigenous peoples, who for so long relied on oral traditions for cultural continuity, we might ponder the art of history in an ephemeral-eternal sense, two forces that seem to contradict each other. Our memories, our languages, and the physical manifestations of cultural thought and spirit that we now consider

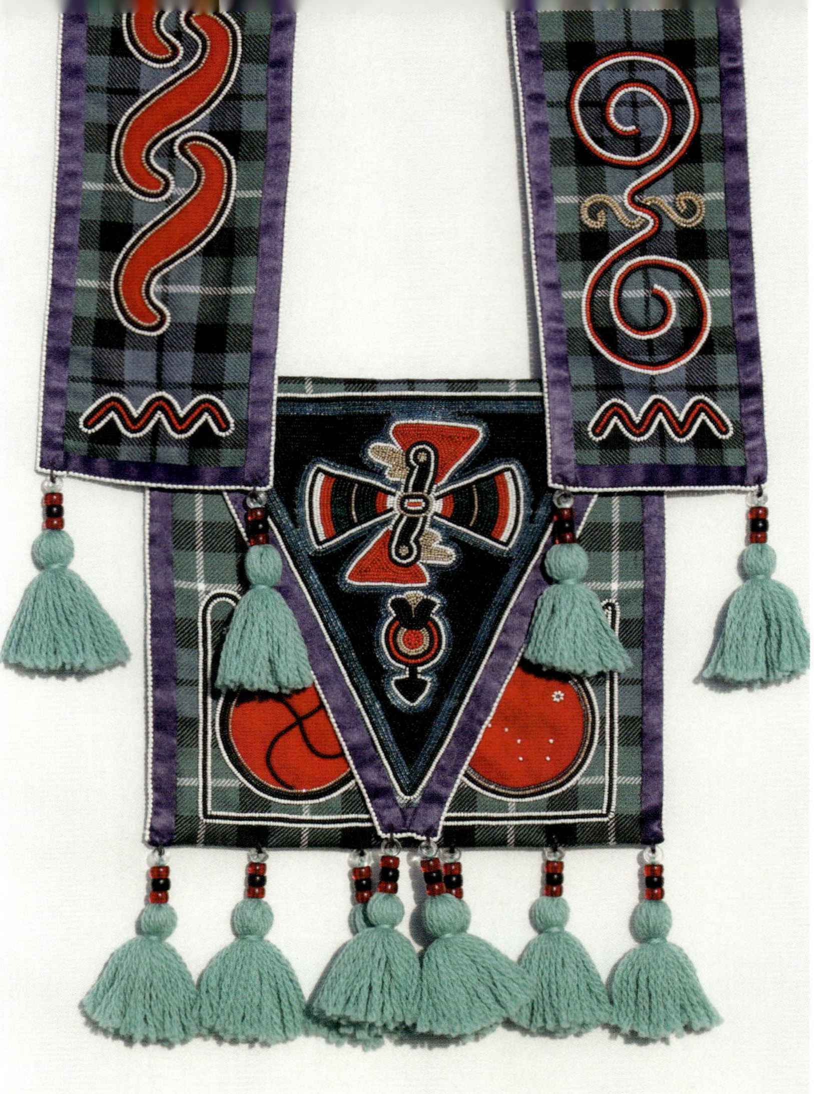

to be art rely on the most important traditional medium for oral traditions, storytelling. Art and storytelling fulfilled educational purposes in preliterate societies. The ephemerality of the spoken word—our personal and tribal stories—encoded in creative works carries those memories into the future.

The selection of works explained within this essay illustrates how we have opportunities to learn more about the tribal and artistic histories as well as the personal stories of the artists represented. In so doing, we discover the intracultural and intercultural richness given physical form in the creation of art.

Consider the work titled *Maria* (pp. 78–79) created by Rose B. Simpson, a multimedia artist known most for her figural pottery but who also is an automobile restoration artist, yes, an automobile artist. Through her restoration of a 1985 El Camino, Simpson has completed a cross-cultural transformational act. She pays homage to the well-known potter from San Ildefonso Maria Martinez, who became renowned for her revival of black-on-black pottery. One of Martinez's creations also is featured in this exhibition (p. 163). The bowl, which is a collaborative effort with her husband, Julian, features the black-on-black style. Among those who collect pottery created by Indigenous peoples, when someone says, "It's a Maria," no one questions

"Maria who?" Her name and fame are synonymous with her art, much the same way as for cubist artist Pablo Picasso. When some says, "It's a Picasso," no one asks, "Picasso who?" However, the El Camino, an object that was mass produced and made of mundane materials, would not fall within the rubric of fine art. Adding the matte black design on the glossy black exterior body allows the car to become a vessel, much like Martinez's pots, for carrying history. The transformation is complete as a vintage car, restored by a contemporary artist, honors and creates history all at once.

When the Highlands Met the Mounds (above and p. 89), created by beadwork artist Martha Berry, captures another instance of intercultural contact and transformation. Many Scottish Highlanders fought alongside Indigenous allies in European conflicts, such as Queen Anne's War, that took place on North American soil. While the Scots are the original ethnic group of Scotland, they are not considered an Indigenous group per the United Nations' declaration that uses the term. How-ever, like the tribes they fought alongside, they are peoples known for their clannishness, courage and valor, and love of dance. The Scots and America's Indigenous peoples were driven from their lands by British authorities and viewed as

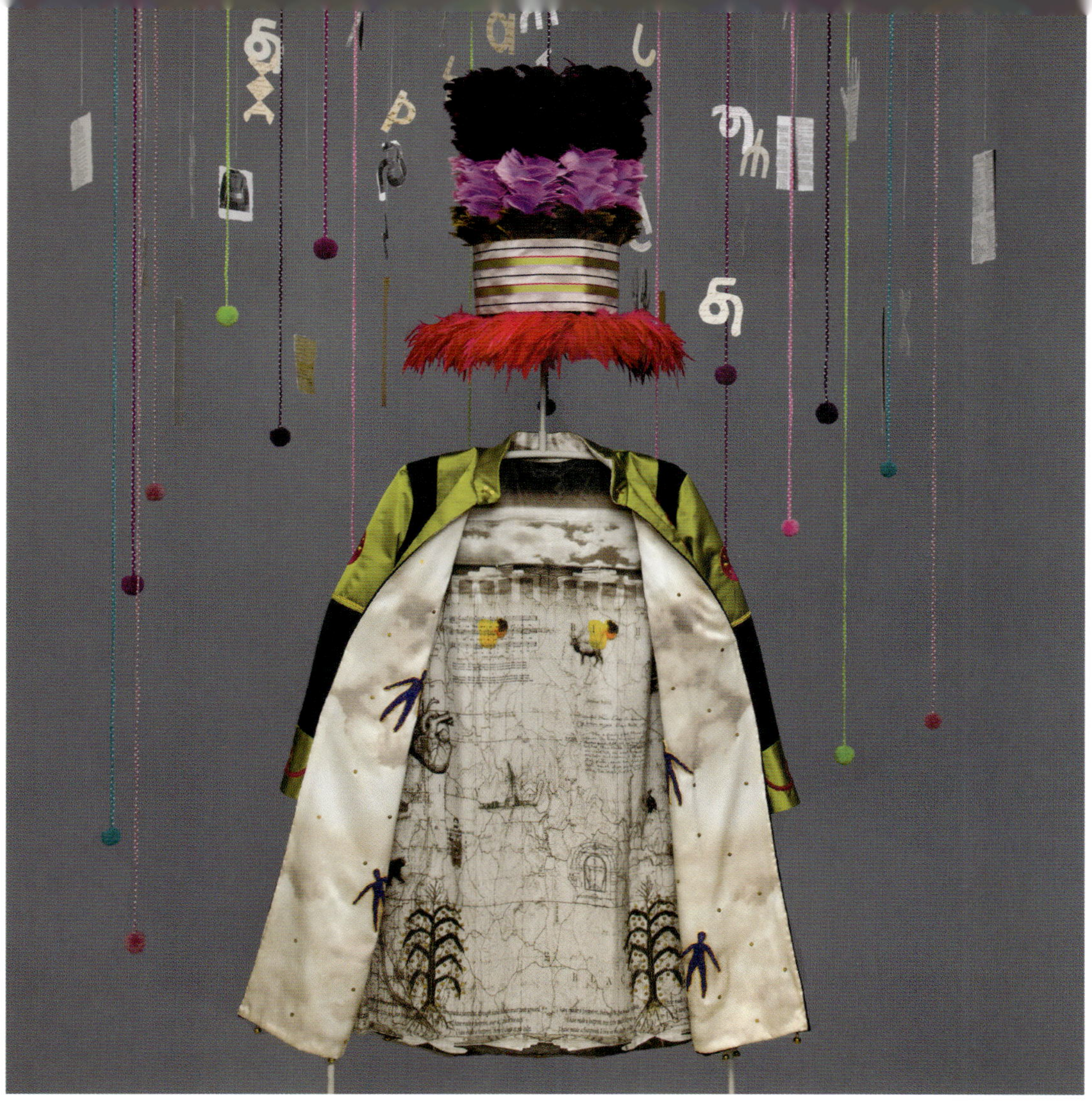

disposable military allies or mercenaries for the crown. The Highlanders fought alongside and traded with tribal groups, who, as a result of mutual respect, adopted some of the Scots' attire. For example, the Mohawks took up the kilt, the Glengarry bonnet with tartan ribbon, and even the jig from the Highlanders. The Cherokee adopted the bandelier bag, originally used to carry musket balls, wadding, and powder, as a bag that could, but not necessarily, be used for munitions.

Anita Fields's *To Know Your People Are Beautiful* Osage wedding coat (above and pp. 38–39) heralds the transformations in wedding customs and attire undergone by the Osage. By the twentieth century, women's attire in preparation for and during marriage had gradually become replaced with military jackets and hats. The coats and hats replicate those given to the Osage by dignitaries from Washington, DC, who were visiting the tribe. While the clothing retains the original tailored look, this coat in particular features the documents written by United States government agents, traders, and journalists and brought to the tribe during various visits. In contrast, the Indigenous cultural symbols displayed on this coat and others like it more appropriately portray love, prosperity, and peace rather than military achievement and dominance through warfare.

Ring from Pocahontas Jewelry Set (p. 8) is a collaborative work by Keri Ataumbi and Jamie Okuma, who both have works in the exhibition. Pocahontas, the daughter of Powhatan, was captured and held for ransom in 1613 by English colonists during the hostilities that erupted between the English at Jamestown, Virginia, and the Powhatan Confederacy. During her captivity she was coerced into or converted to Christianity and baptized as Lady Rebecca. In 1614 she married tobacco planter John Rolfe. They moved to England in 1616, and an engraving by Simon de Passe, completed that same year, was probably one of the first portraits of an Indigenous woman from North America. In an effort to get more English businesspeople to invest in New World colonies and moneymaking ventures, she was presented as an example of a civilized savage who had become dignified in English society. Ironically, she would become Disney-fied in the United States in the 1990s in a cartoon that speaks to fantasies about her life more than to the reality of the life she lived—once again her image was exploited for capital gain. The ring represents to this viewer a beautifully rendered beaded portrait of Lady Rebecca/Pocahontas, set in gold and adorned with a mix of media that illustrates Old World valuables juxtaposed against New World values.

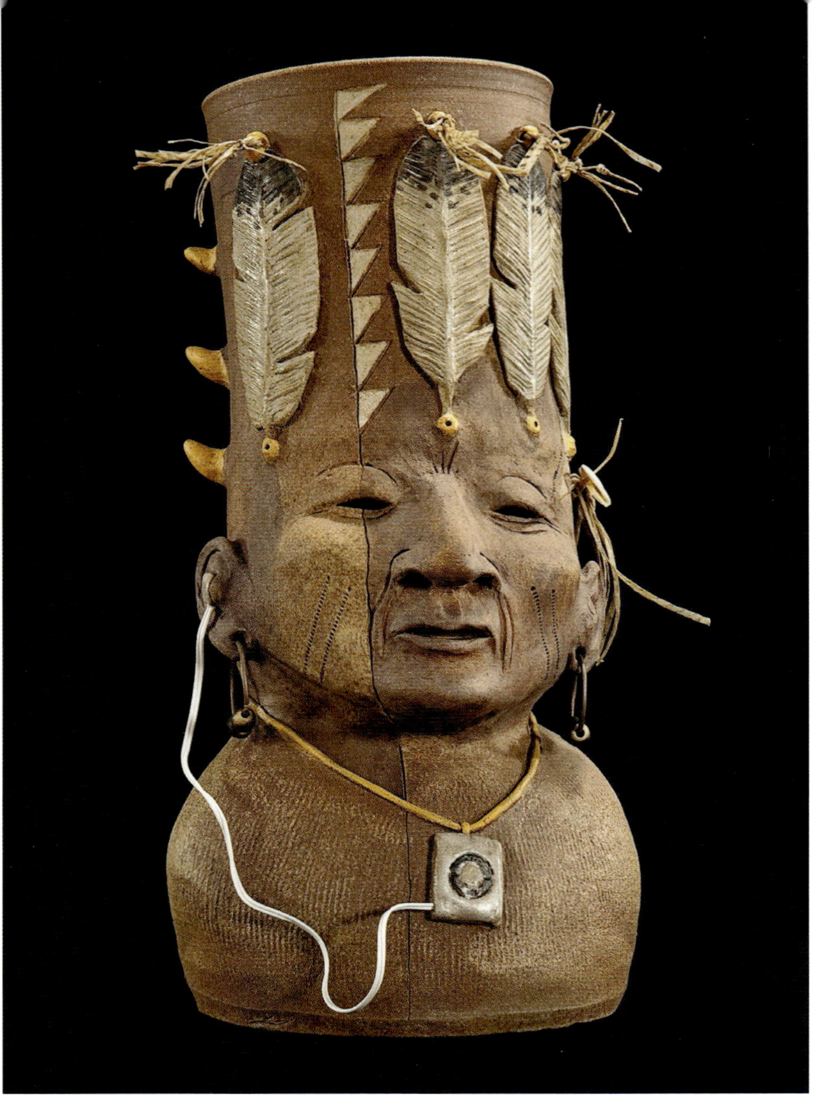

Peter B. Jones's *New Indian Portrait Jar* (above and p. 139) examines the transformation of Indigenous peoples, who for hundreds of years passed stories and songs from generation to generation by word of mouth. This is the intergenerational exchange of knowledge that so many tribes are trying to revitalize in the wake of technocratic transfusions of media. The spoken and sung words, presented in face-to-face contexts, have been interrupted by cell phones, media players, and earbuds. We see this temporal juxtaposition represented in the clay sculpture itself. Pierced ears have long been a body modification among Indigenous groups the world wide, albeit for tribal identity rather than fashion. Jones represents this older tradition of tribal identity in his work. However, our attention is drawn more to the earbuds and media player, which signify the ways our tribal identities have been somewhat compromised by the array of mass media that competes for our attention. In light of the many people who have become plugged in to technology and confuse communication electronics with communication, we might wonder what will become of the endangered languages and oral traditions that Indigenous peoples could be losing.

One of the most poignant ways a person's actions in the present can assist in the creation of a future is embedded in the works of Alan Houser. The bronze titled *As Long as the Waters Flow* (opposite), similar in style to his works in this exhibition, recalls an oft-used line in treaties between the tribes and the United States, suggesting that the agreements would last in perpetuity. While the tribes remembered their commitments to the treaties, the United States government's memory was very short. This bronze seems to represent continuity in a different sense, as we view an Apache woman in traditional attire, draped in a wavelike manner from her body, illustrating the forward-thinking continuity of cultural beliefs and practices as carried by Indigenous women. The Apache, like many other tribes before European contact, are matrilineal, and family lineage, like that river of life, flows through them. Houser, like the headwaters of a great river, set his students on artistic journeys, as he taught the importance of retaining cultural memory through art to early generations of students at such places such as the Institute of American Indian Arts (IAIA) in Santa Fe, New Mexico. In a very real way, through the creative works of Houser, his students, and the array of Indigenous artists and teachers featured here, some of them with IAIA lineage, the stories continue to be told as we bring the words and wisdom of our elders and teachers to new generations of artists. Through

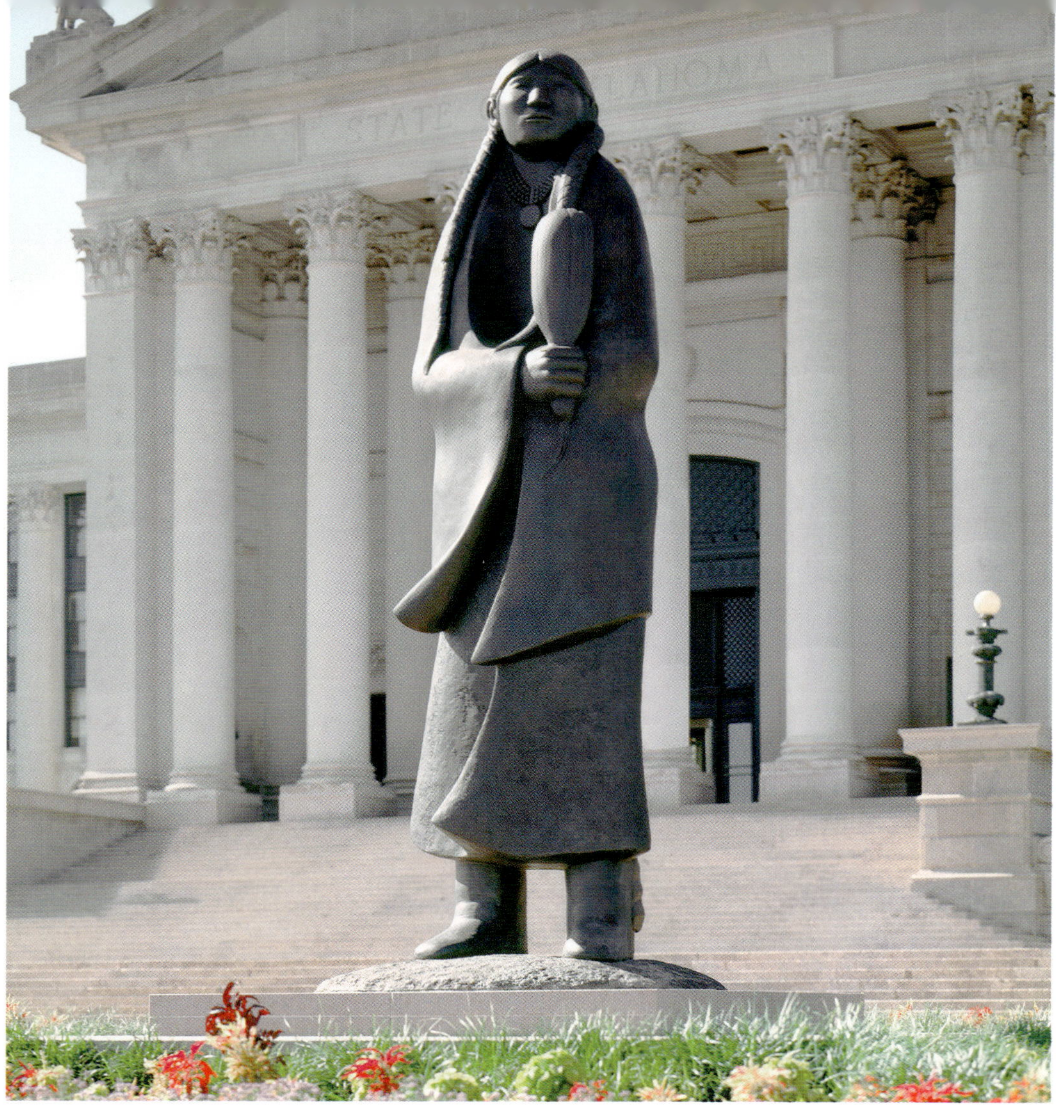

our art we not only recognize and honor our collective cultural pasts but we consider the potentials for tomorrow. And we do this in the midst of rapid technological and cultural transformation. In a world of swiftly changing realities, our art anchors us to our creative traditions.

Exhibition goers have a choice in the ways they experience this art and the other works in *To Take Shape and Meaning*. The objects can be looked at passively purely for their visual aesthetics, appreciated for their styles, techniques, colors, forms, and lines, while viewers remain somewhat cognitively and emotionally removed from the subject matter. Visitors can also take the initiative to learn about the cultures and histories of the artists, tribes, and objects presented to more fully understand the inseparability of Indigenous histories, artistic traditions, and storytelling. Most often, the stories are more enlightening and engaging, even when the memories might be painful, than the bleached narratives of the past. Ultimately, *To Take Shape and Meaning* is an exhibition of hope in the present, as we consider the possibility that with shared cultural understandings, encoded in the stories we remember and tell, we can co-create a shared future.

PAGE 8: Keri Ataumbi (Kiowa) and Jamie Okuma (Luiseño/Shoshone e-Bannock/Wailaki/Okinawan), *Pocahontas Jewelry Set*, 2014, antique glass, 24-karat electroplated beads, buckskin, 18-karat yellow gold, sterling silver, wampum shell, freshwater pearls, rose- and brilliant-cut diamonds and diamond beads, and diamond briolites, dimensions variable, Minneapolis Institute of Art

PAGE 10: Detail of image on page 89

PAGE 11: Detail of image on page 39

PAGE 12: Detail of image on page 139

ABOVE: Alan Houser (Fort Sill Apache), *As Long as the Waters Flow*, 1988, bronze, H. 168 × W. 56 × D. 56 in., Oklahoma State Capitol Art Collection

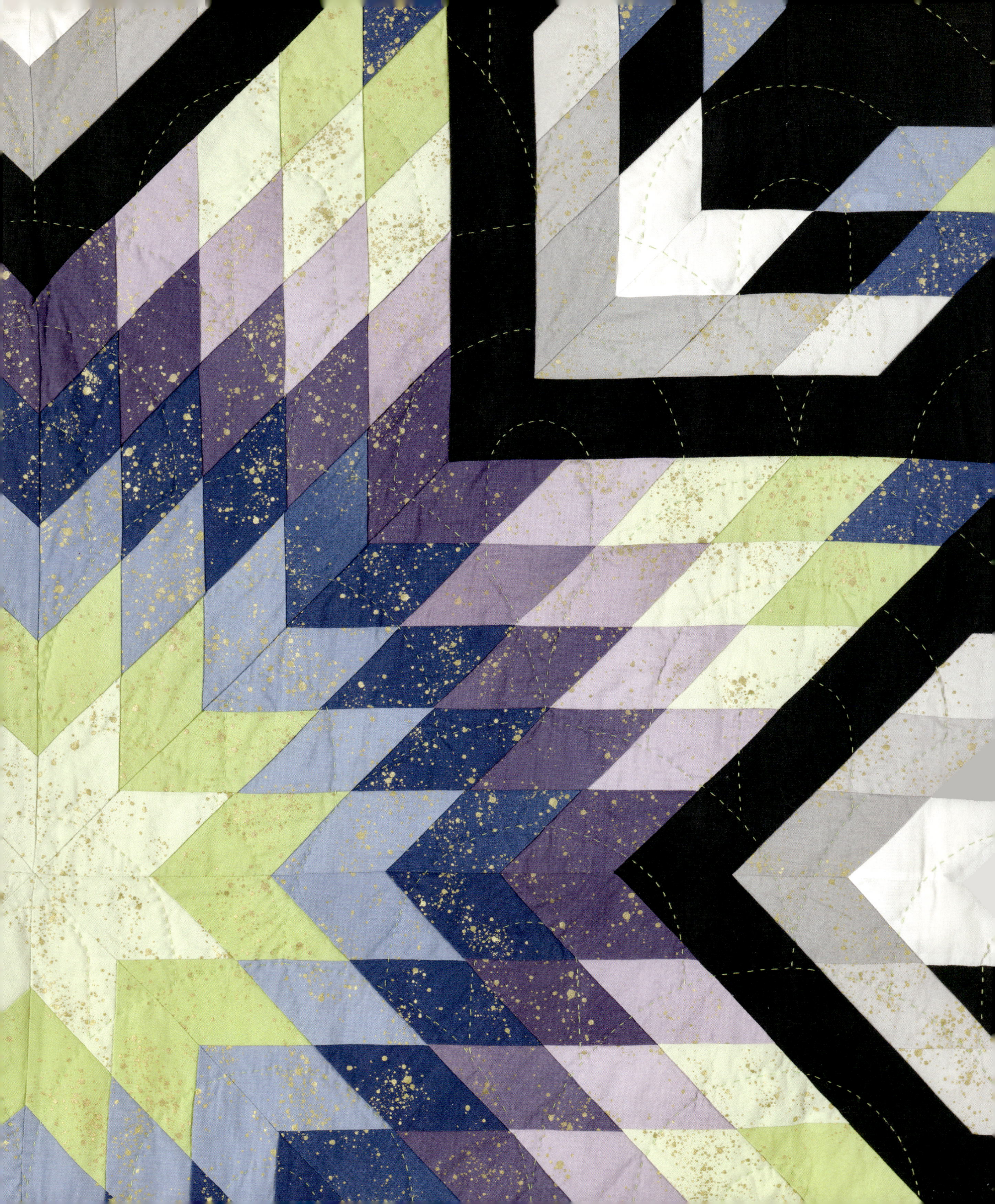

Place of Being

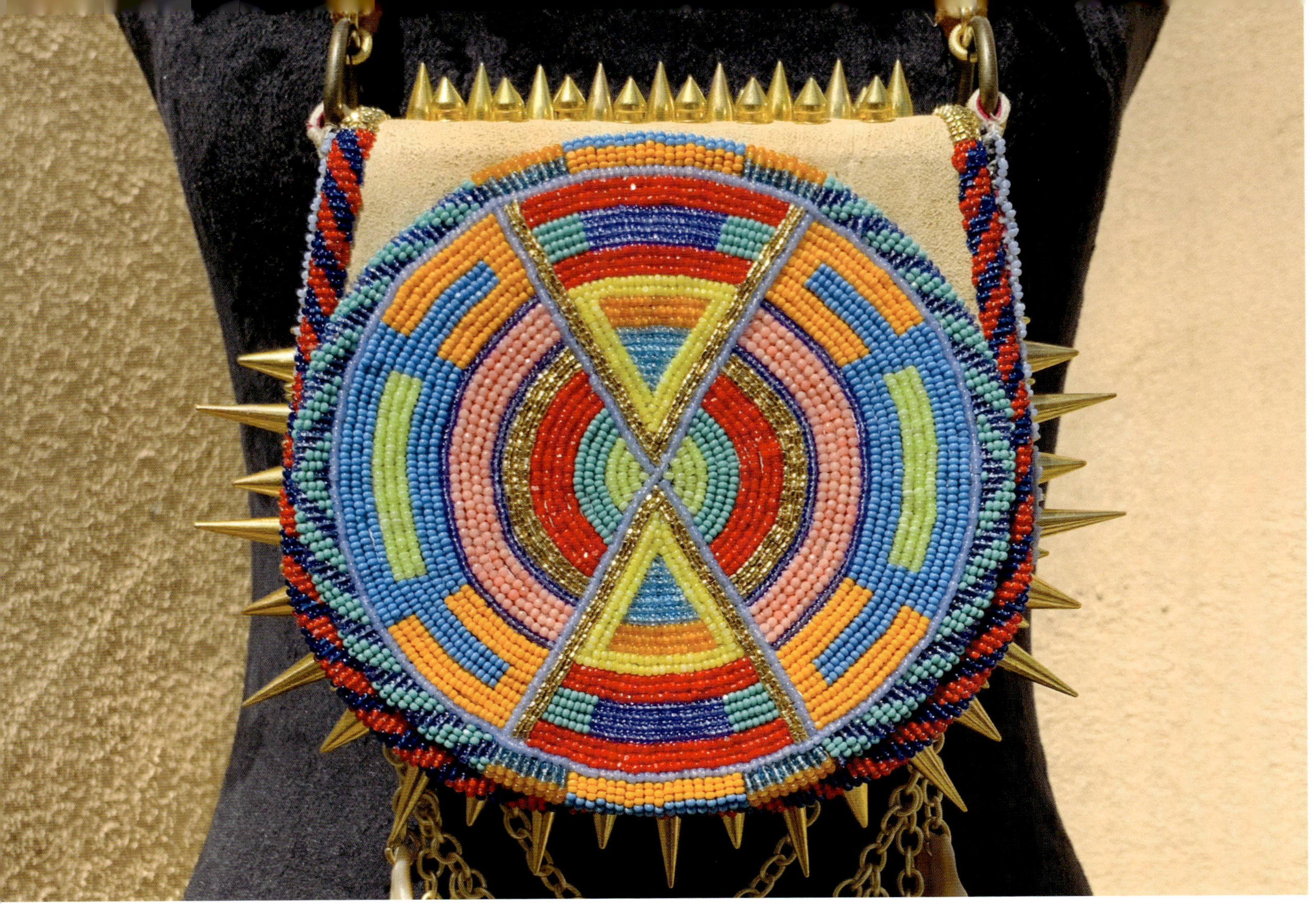

ELIAS JADE NOT AFRAID BEADS A STORY about the Crow **place of being** (Crow: Basawe, "Our Land") in his work *Beaded Spiked Neck Pouch Bag* (above). Situated among geometric patterns are two elegant isosceles triangles intersecting at their apexes. The point of connection centered among the light blue–colored beads creates a fluidity of lines reaching across the plane of a glistening glass-cut bead circle. Filling the space at the top of the inverted triangle is the Creator's knowledge—the Creator's instructions for humans to follow to live a good life. The intersecting apexes symbolize the connection to humans—the receiving of the Creator's knowledge and instruction. The space filling the triangle below represents the place on earth where humans share this knowledge among one another. In essence, these isosceles triangles are forever in transmission of knowledge and communication between humans and the Creator, a prayer between the spiritual and physical worlds.

Place of being is an existence that holds together the spiritual and physical worlds. For Native peoples objects that express places of being hold sacred importance and facilitate different roles within societies. These objects are often created with assigned functions that operate in systems of philosophy, religion, culture, and identity. Baskets, pottery, beadwork, carvings, textiles, among countless other objects, are often created with a purpose to convey the meaning of concepts surrounding place of being.

The materiality of these works can also reflect the natural environments that produce grasses, reeds, wood, clay, and the animals that offer fur, skin, and bone. Intimate knowledge of landscapes and ecologies inform the time and place to collect materials, such as the season to gather birch bark for weaving or the time of day to dig clay. In balance with this knowledge is the awareness of origin stories as well as belief systems exclusive to the connection with the spirit world.

Place of being accounts for change and evolution. Transitions in cultural values, materials used, and places resulting from removal or relocation are apparent in contemporary art. Representation of this existence can reflect collective identity as well as individual agency, creative ideas, and artistic skills. For instance, Navajo weaver Sally Black demonstrates her nation's affinity for Blue Bird flour by depicting the company logo in baskets woven with sumac and traditional techniques. The brand is so embraced by Navajo people as the critical ingredient in

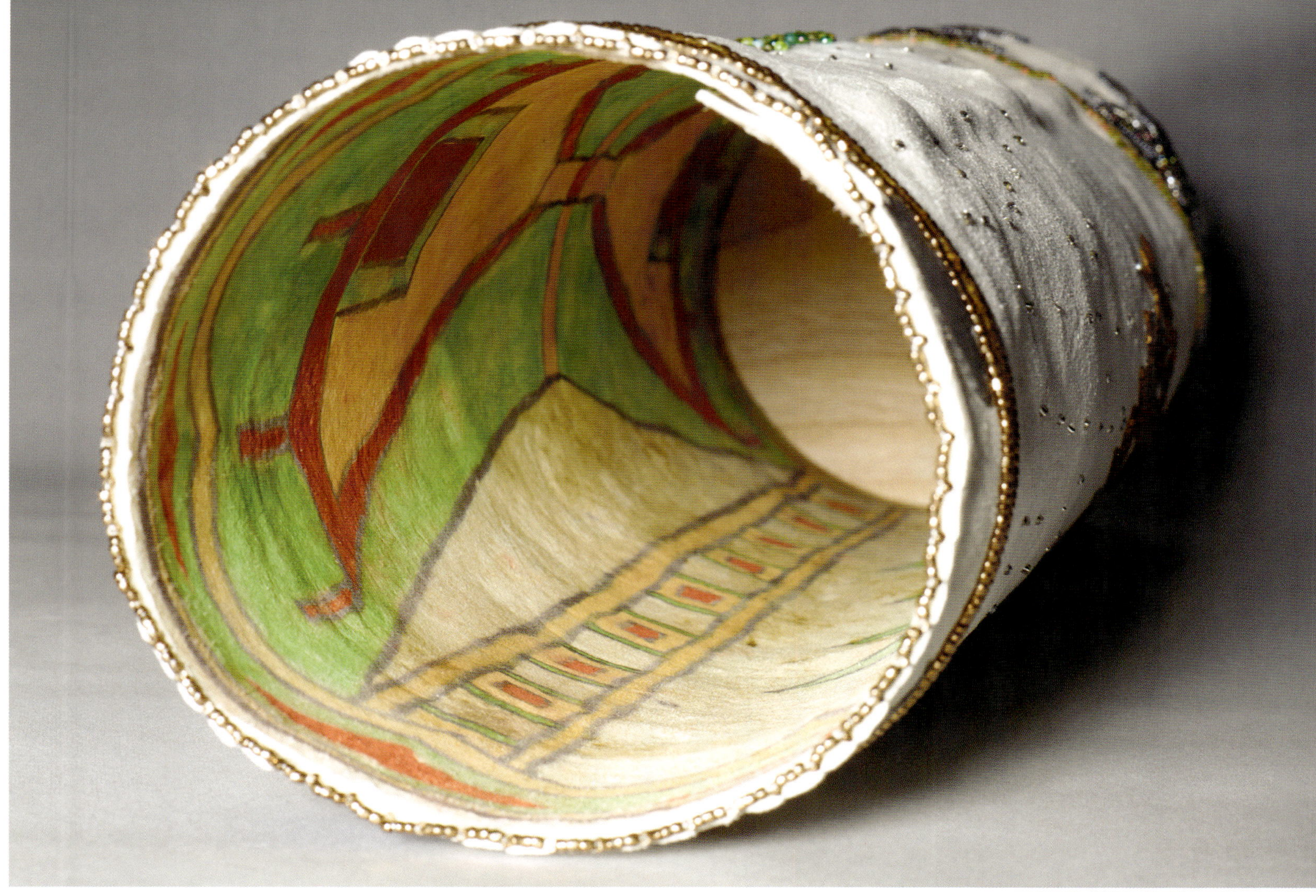

fry bread that it has become synonymous with Navajo identity. Not Afraid adorns his beaded purse with gold-toned spikes to reflect his personal interest in punk culture. These examples articulate some of the many facets of place of being: philosophy, individuality, humanity, spirituality, world view, culture, physical place, and identity.

PAGE 14: Detail of image on page 32

OPPOSITE: Elias Jade Not Afraid (Apsaalooké Nation), *Beaded Spiked Neck Pouch Bag*, 2023, glass seed beads, pink coral faceted beads, smoked and brain-tanned deer hide, Italian leather, bull elk ivory, and vintage brass chain, dimensions variable, Private collection

ABOVE: Detail of image on pages 36–37

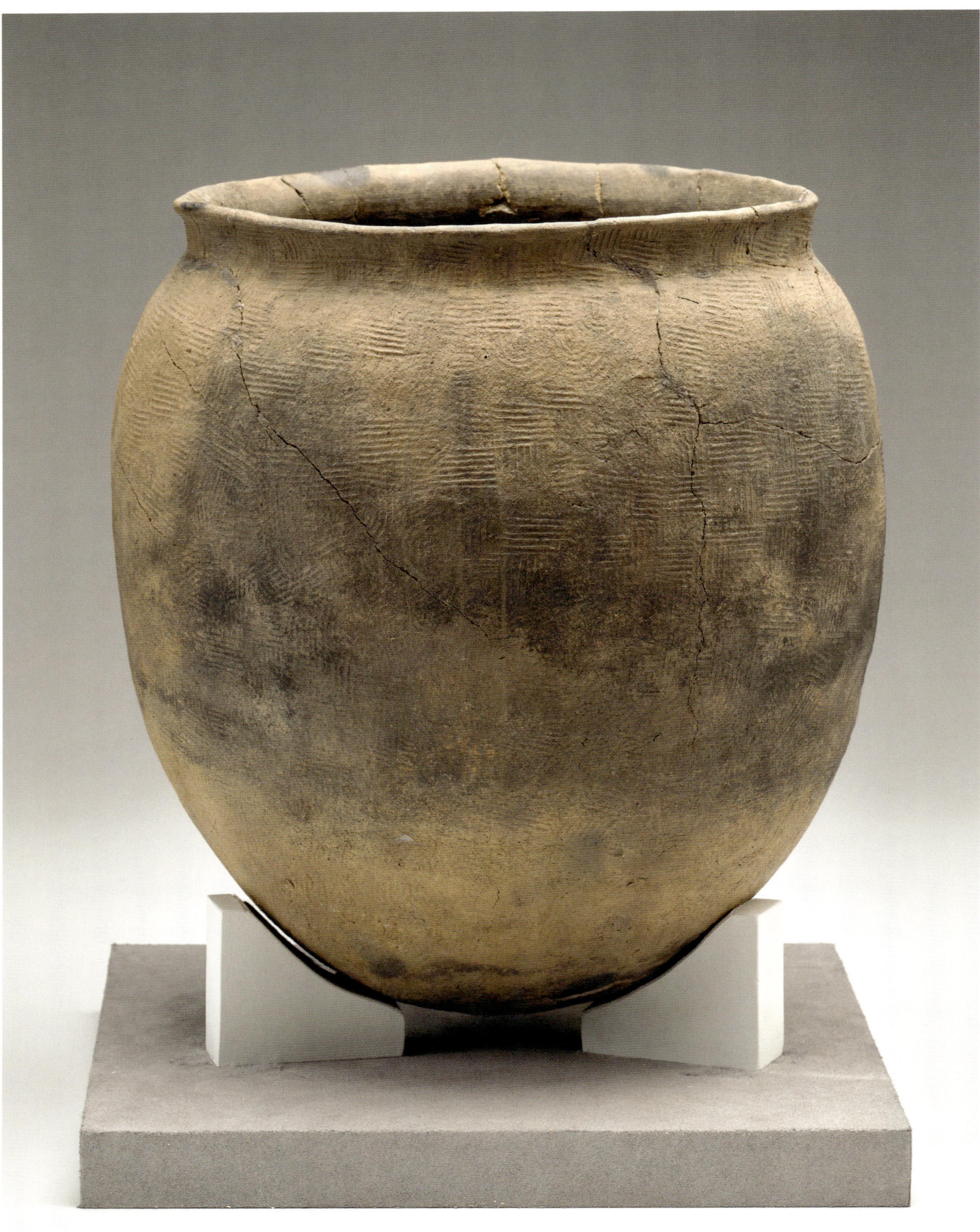

Peedee Artist
Storage Vessel, 1100
Earthenware
H. 20 × W. 15 × D. 15 in.
Collection of the Rankin Museum of American Heritage

Senora Lynch
Haliwa-Saponi, born 1963
Woodland People Bowl, 2003
Red and white clay
H. 20 × Diam. 15 in.
Collection of Bobby Brayboy

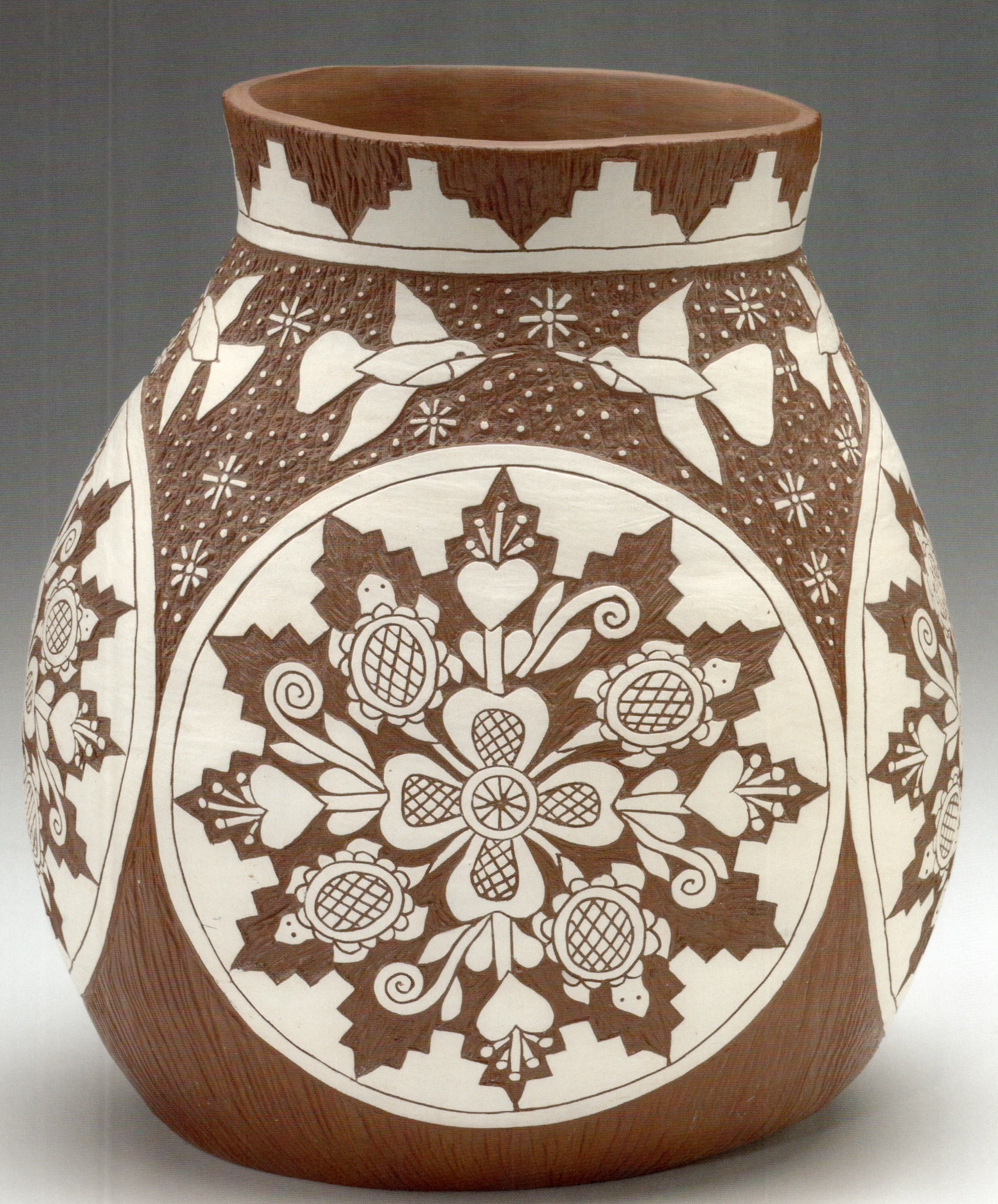

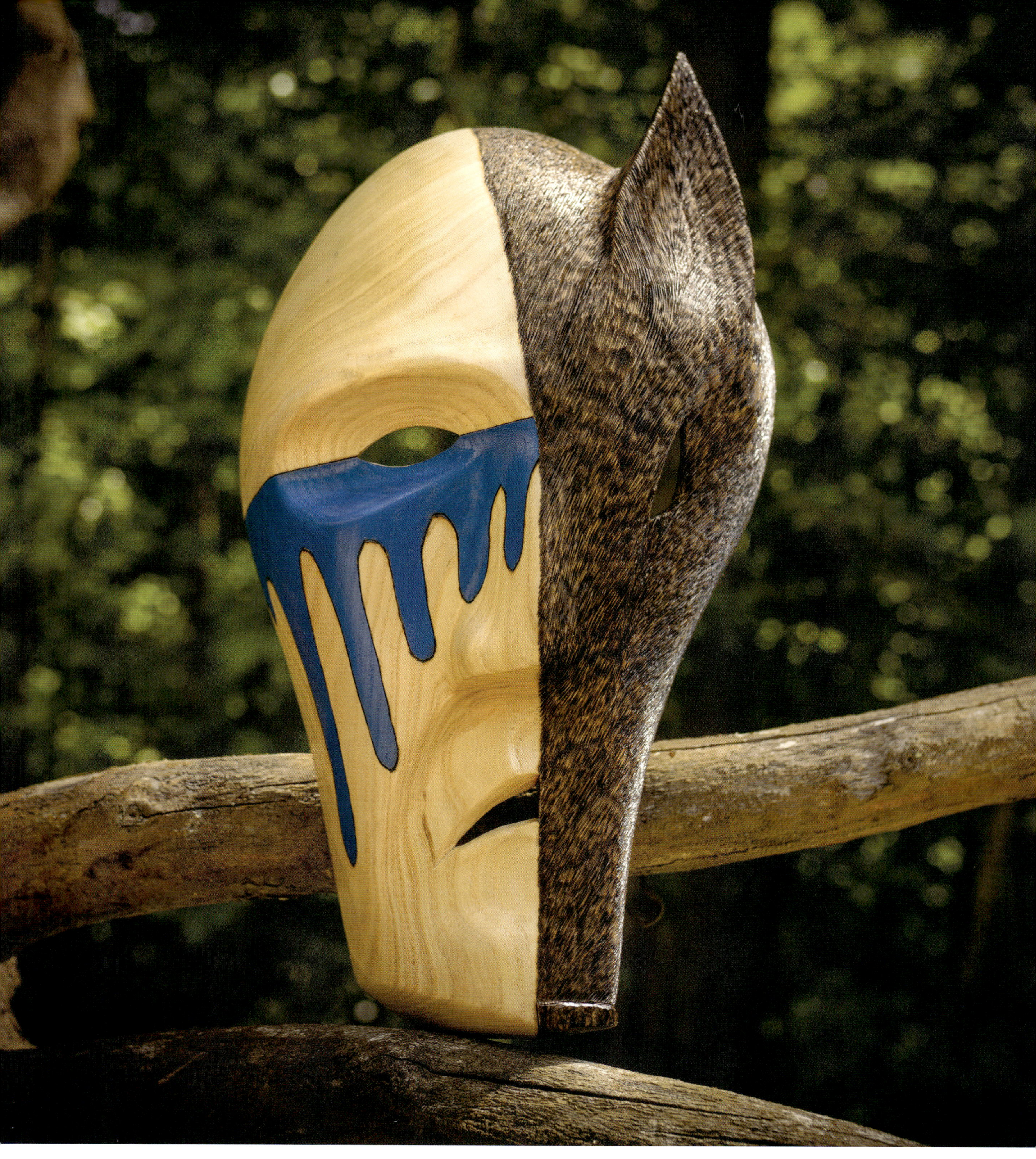

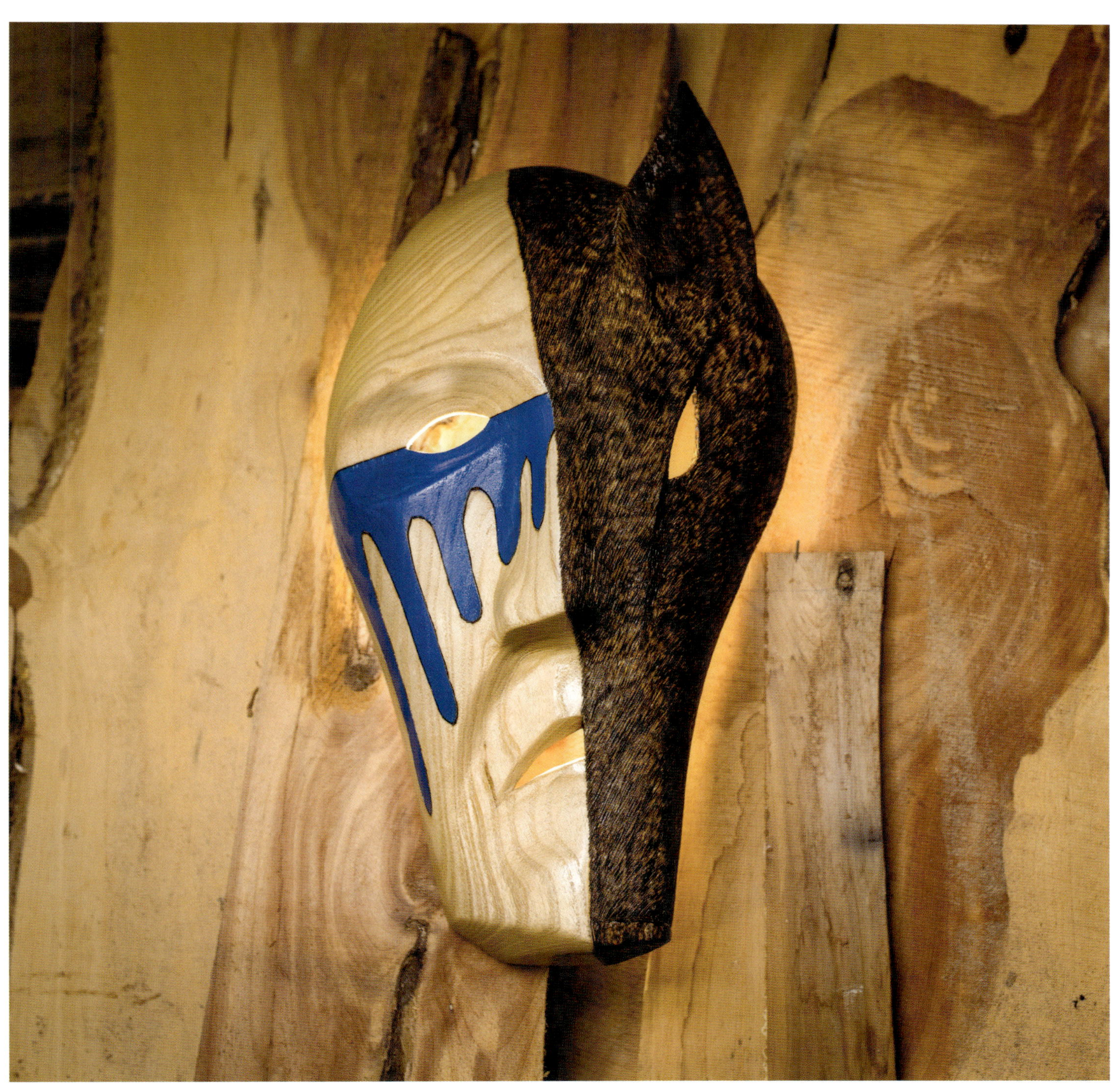

Billy Welch
Snowbird Cherokee, born 1967
Shapeshifter Mask, 2023
Walnut and stain
H. 12 × W. 7 in.
Courtesy of the artist

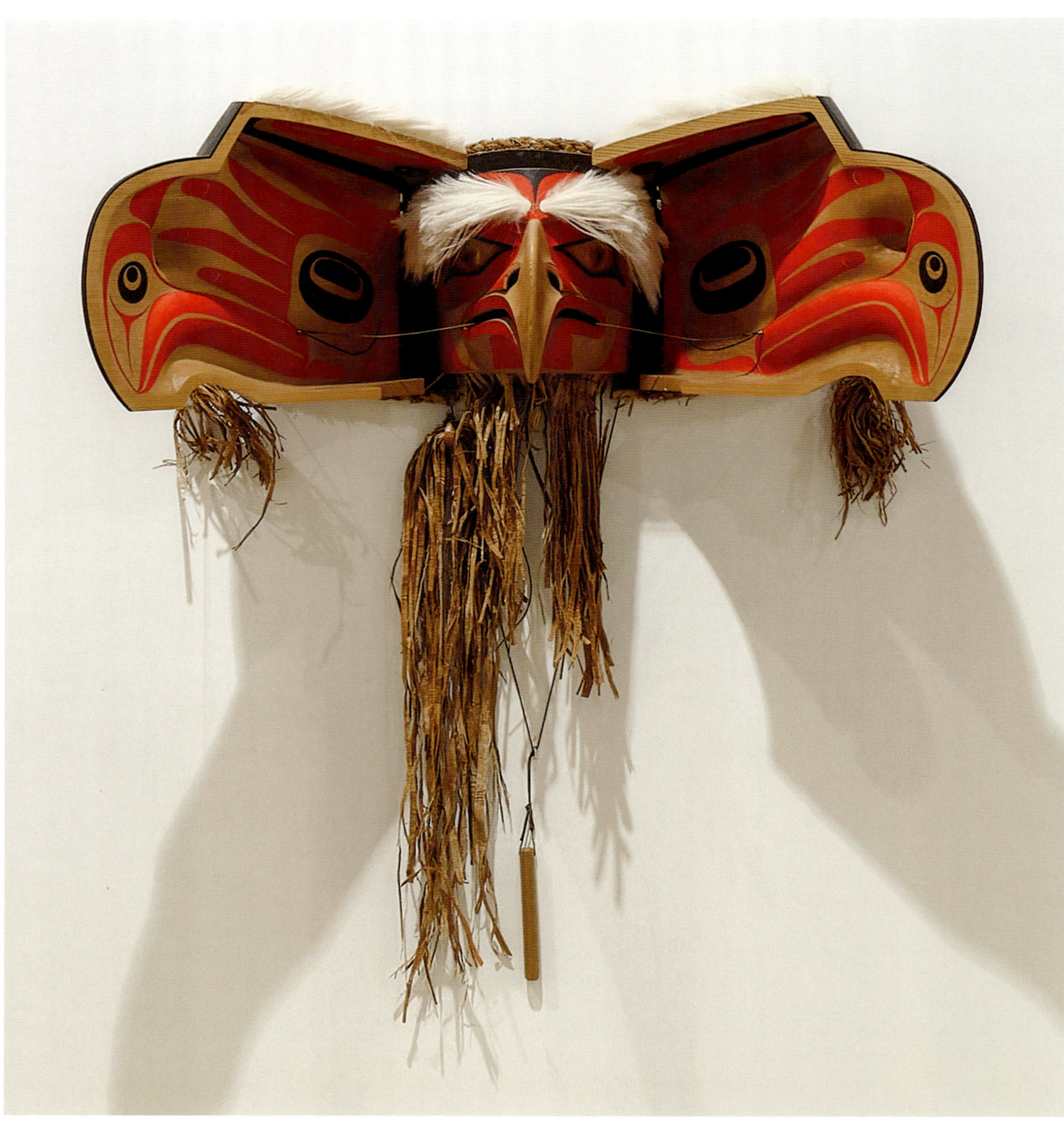

ABOVE
Robert Davidson
Haida, born 1946
Eagle Transformation Mask, 1998
Red cedar, pigment, cedar bark, and hair
H. 15 × W. 35⅜ × D. 23 in.
Audain Art Museum Collection,
Gift of Patricia and S. Bruce McLaughlin

OPPOSITE
Steven Chrisjohn
Oneida
Moundbuilder Necklace, 2022
Serpentine, sterling silver, and copper
H. 11 × W. 6¼ in.
Courtesy of the artist

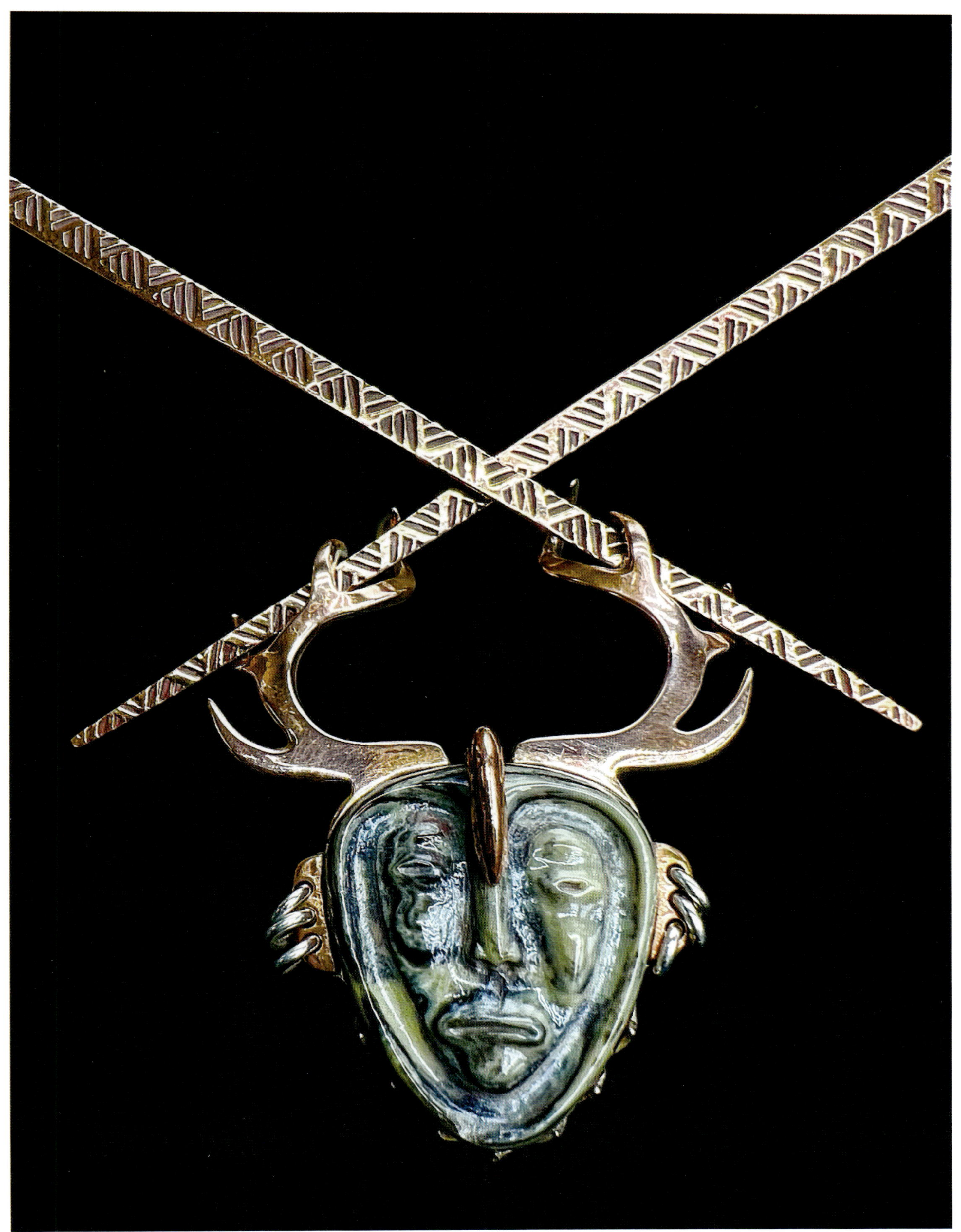

Place of Being

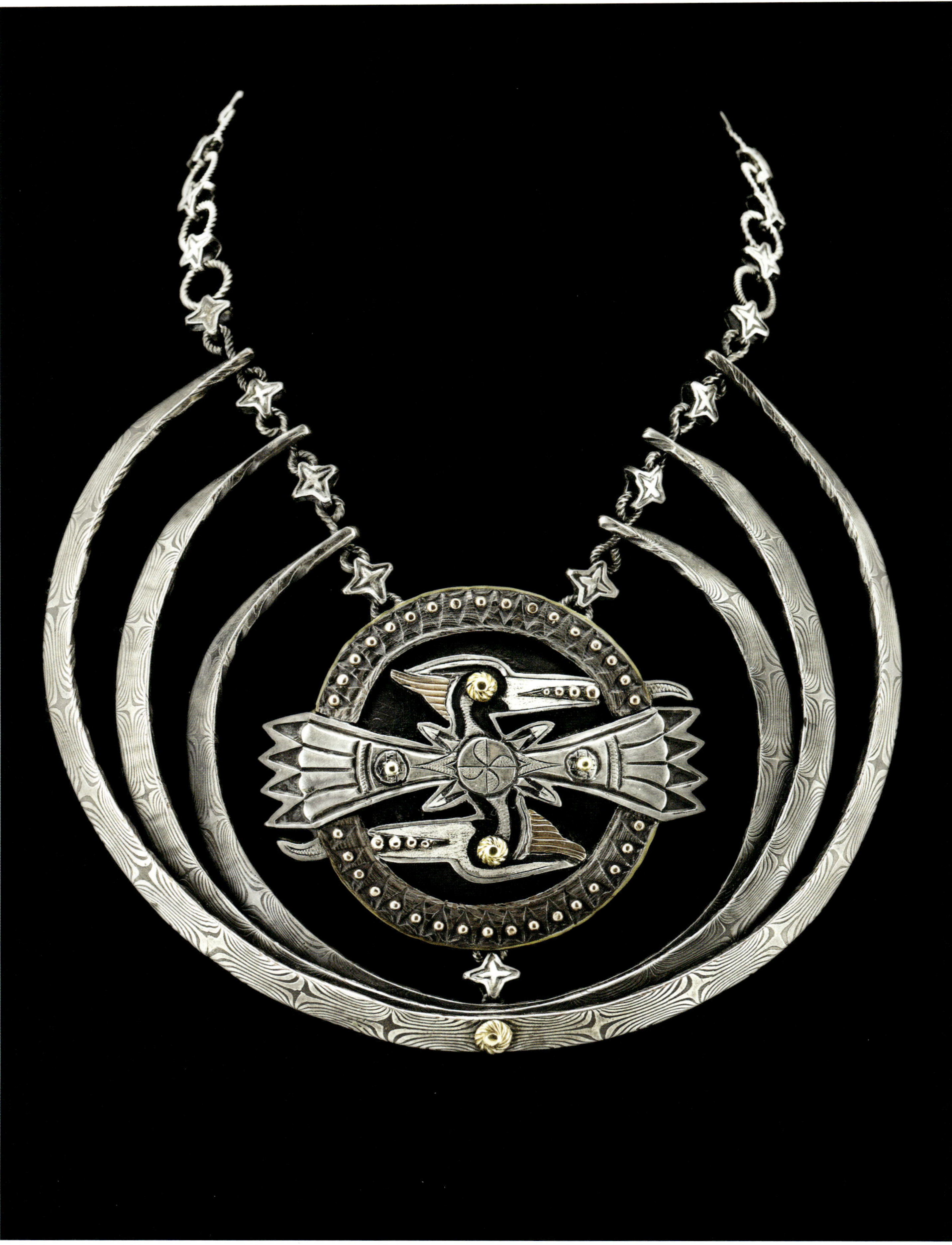

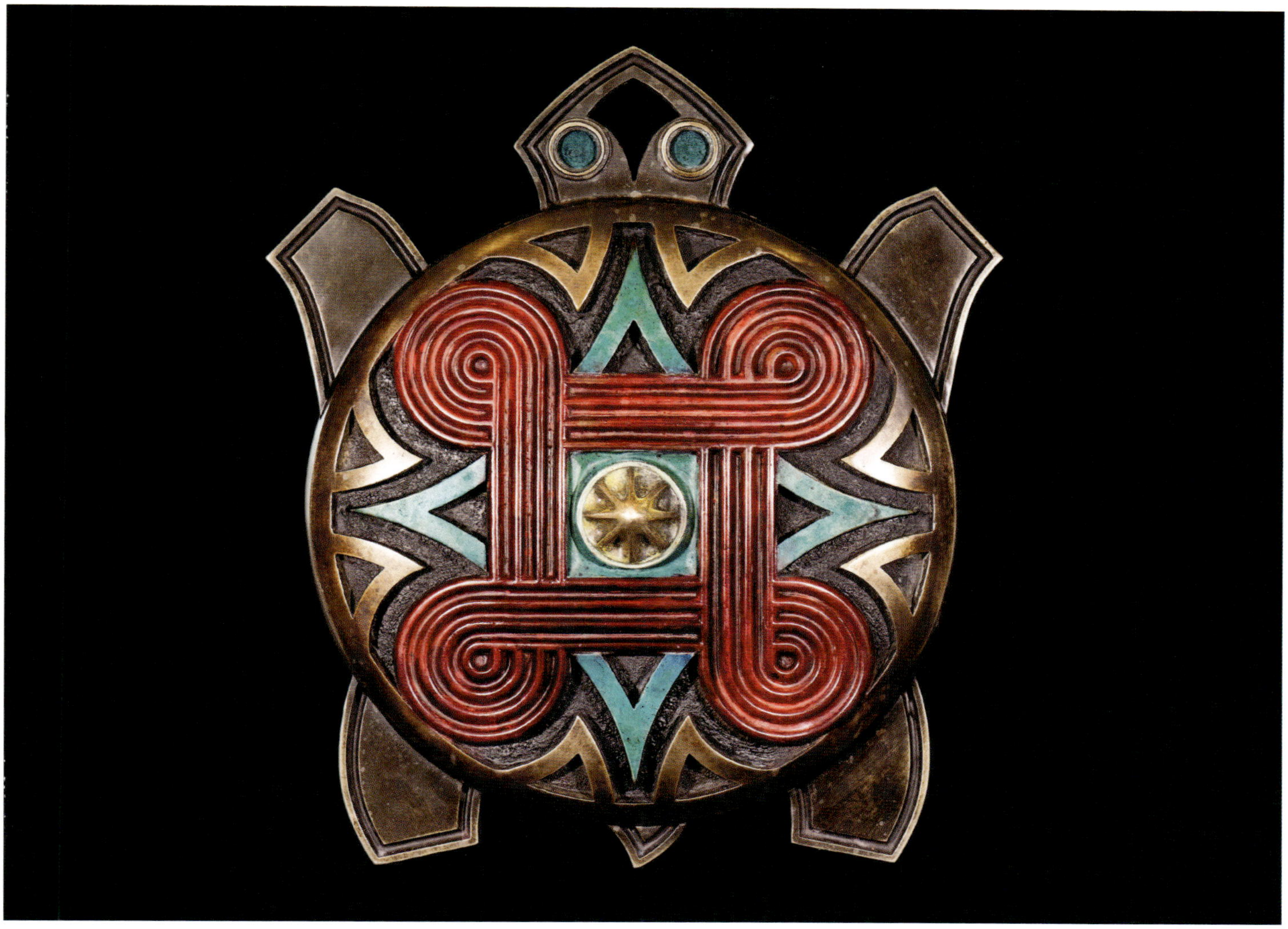

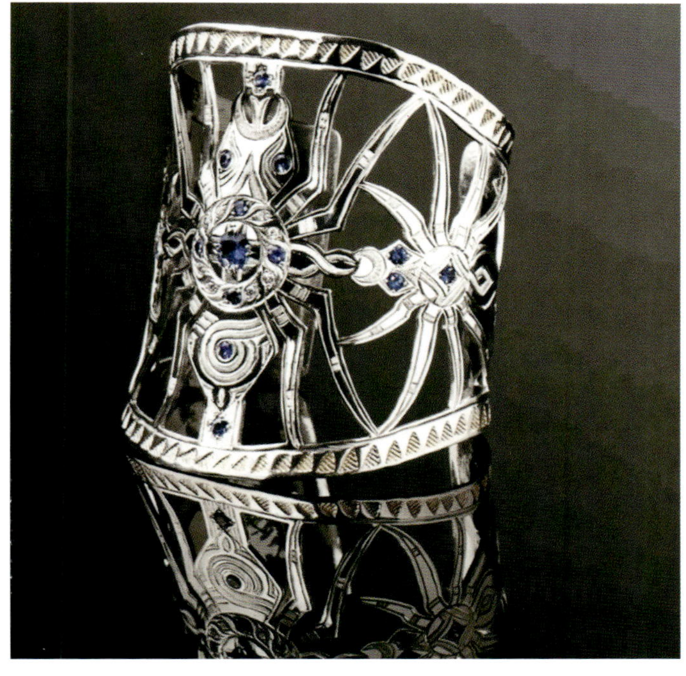

Kenneth Johnson
Muscogee/Seminole, born 1967

CLOCKWISE FROM LEFT
Songs of the Fourth World, 2022
Silver, copper, 18K red and yellow gold,
and Mokume Gane layered metal
H. 13 × W. 6 × D. ⅜ in.
Courtesy of the artist

"Mother Earth" Turtle, 2023
Silicon bronze cast
H. 20 × W. 17 × D. 3½ in.
Courtesy of the artist

Sun Spider Cuff, 2023
Palladium, 24K gold, and sapphire
H. 2½ × W. 2½ × D. 3 in.
Courtesy of the artist

Marcus Amerman
Choctaw, born 1959
Warriors of Snaketown, 2010
Glass
H. 14¾ × W. 8 × D. 8 in.
Courtesy of the artist

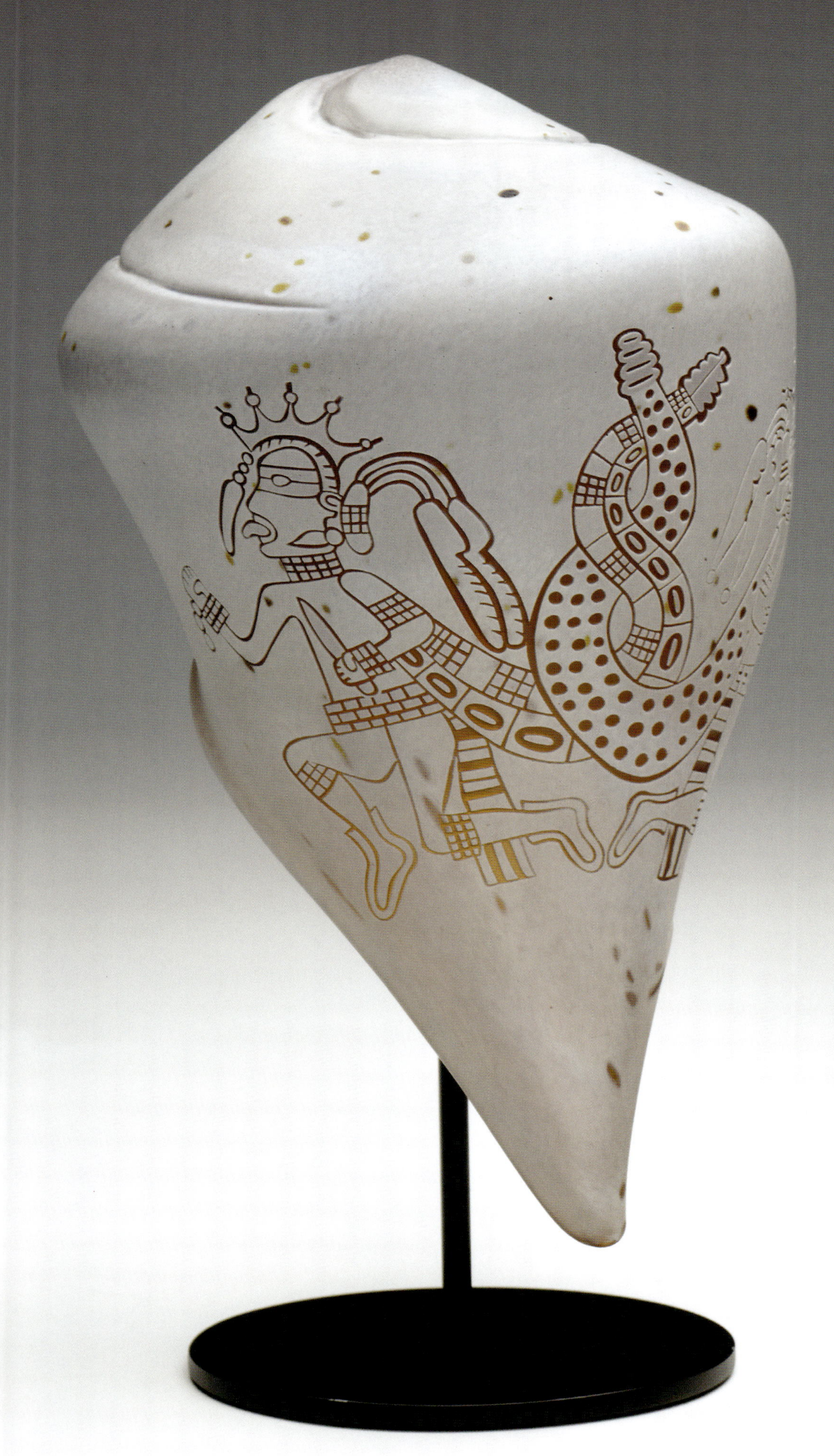

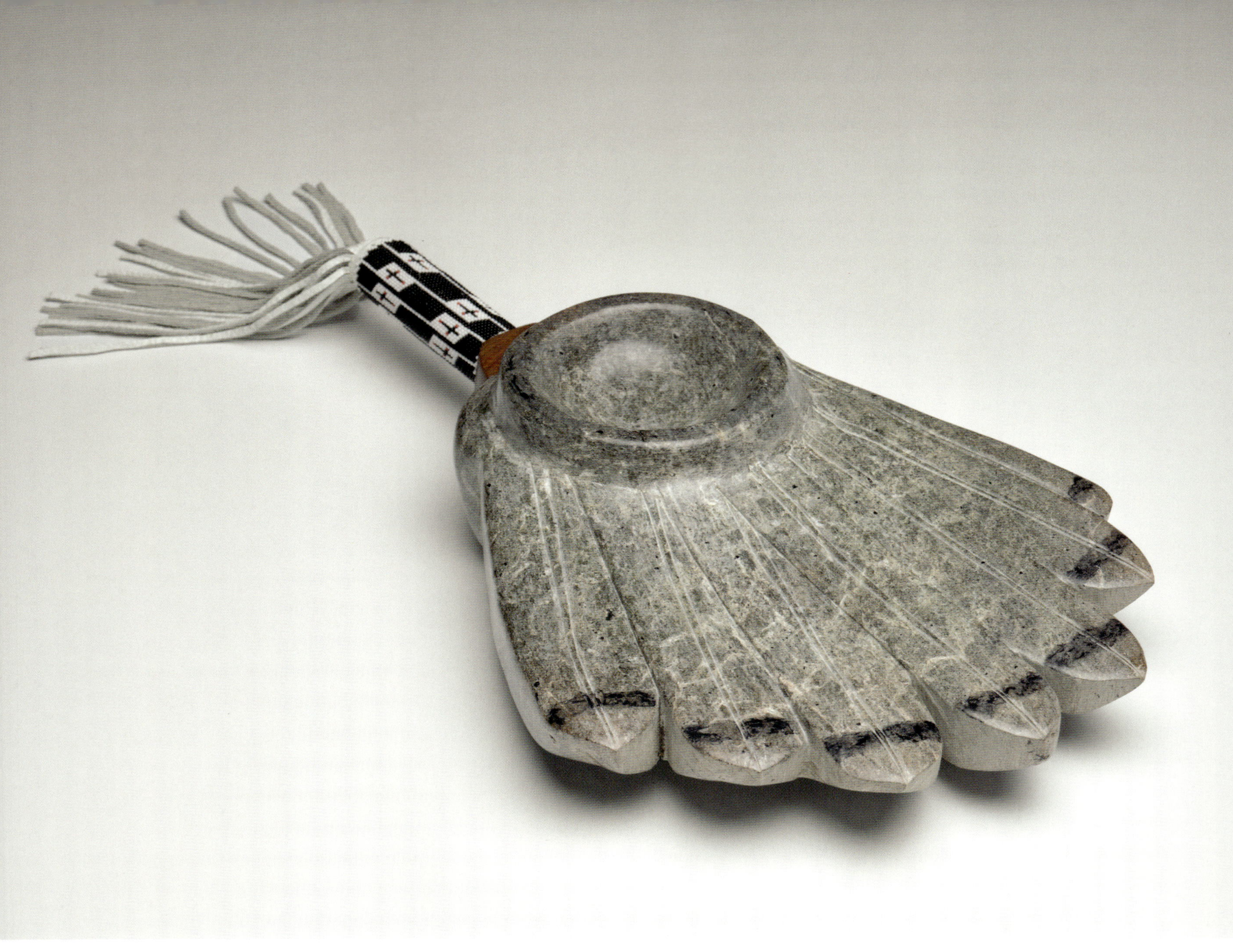

ABOVE
Dennis Michael Wilkins
Lumbee
Fan Bowl, no date
North Carolina soapstone, wood, and beads
H. 4 × W. 11 × D. 25½ in.
Courtesy of the artist

OPPOSITE
Elias Jade Not Afraid
Apsaalooké Nation
Apsaalooké Rosette Earrings, 2023
Smoked deer hide, antique glass seed beads,
ermine tails, and vintage brass connectors
H. 7 × W. 2¾ in.
Private collection, North Carolina

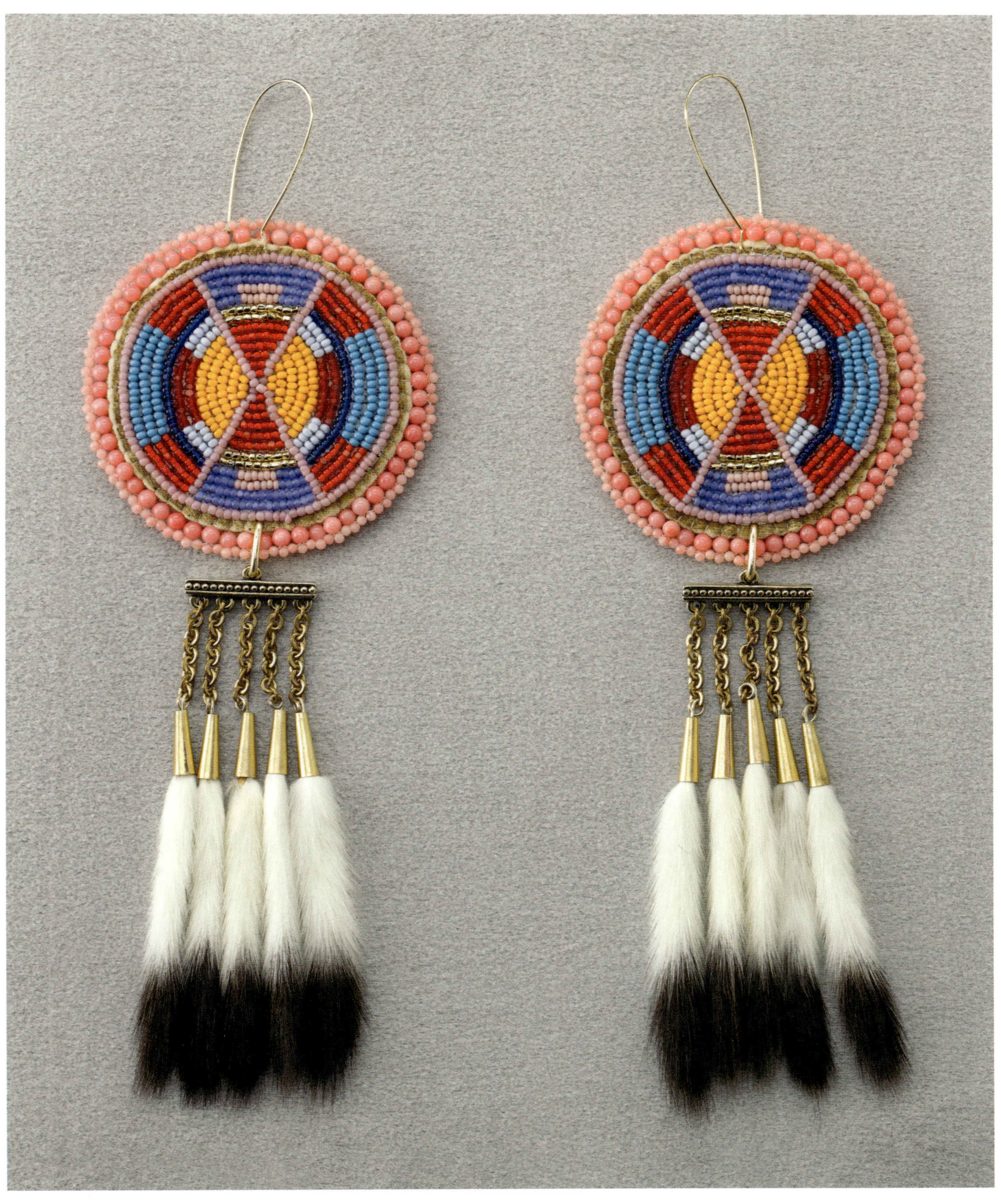

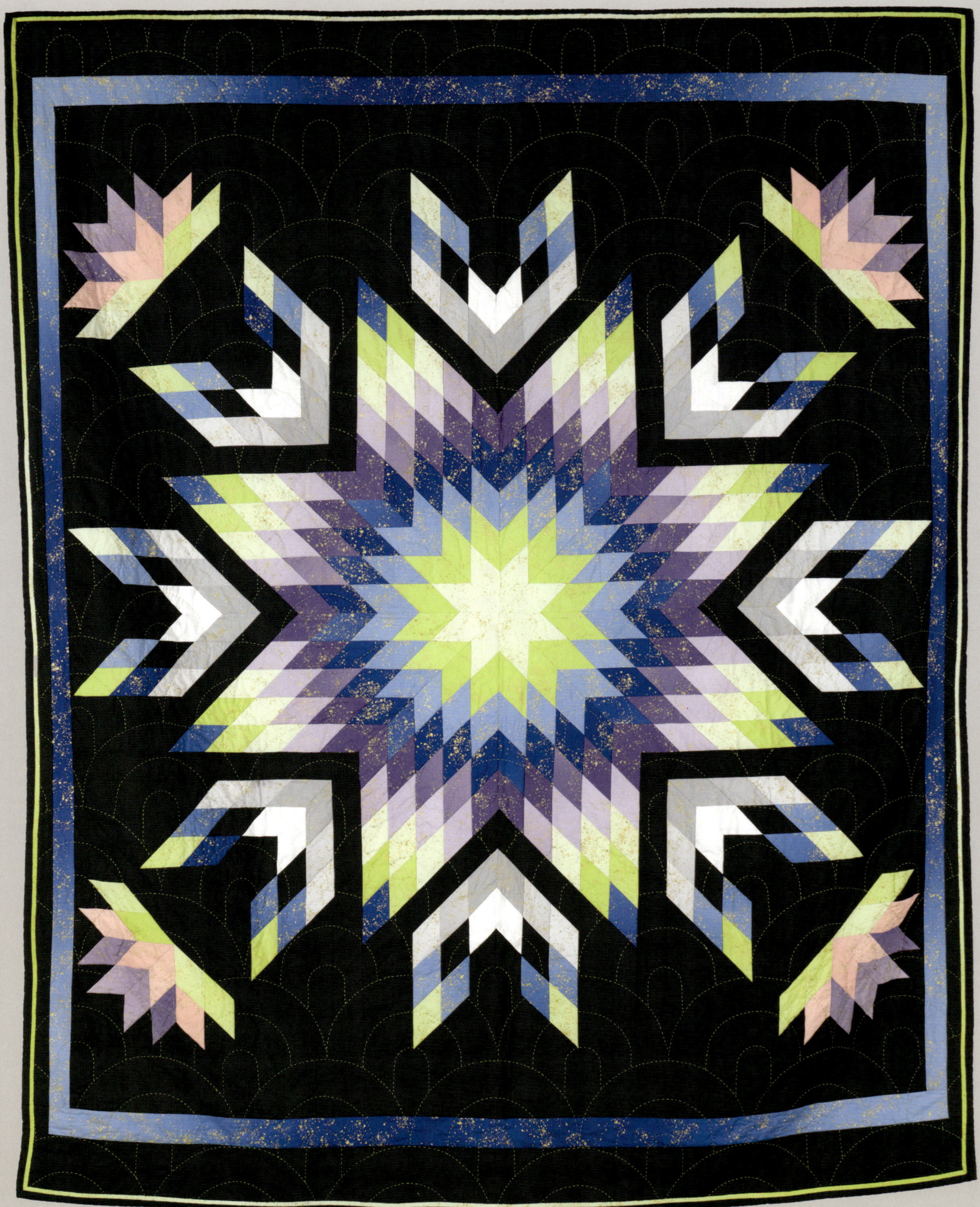

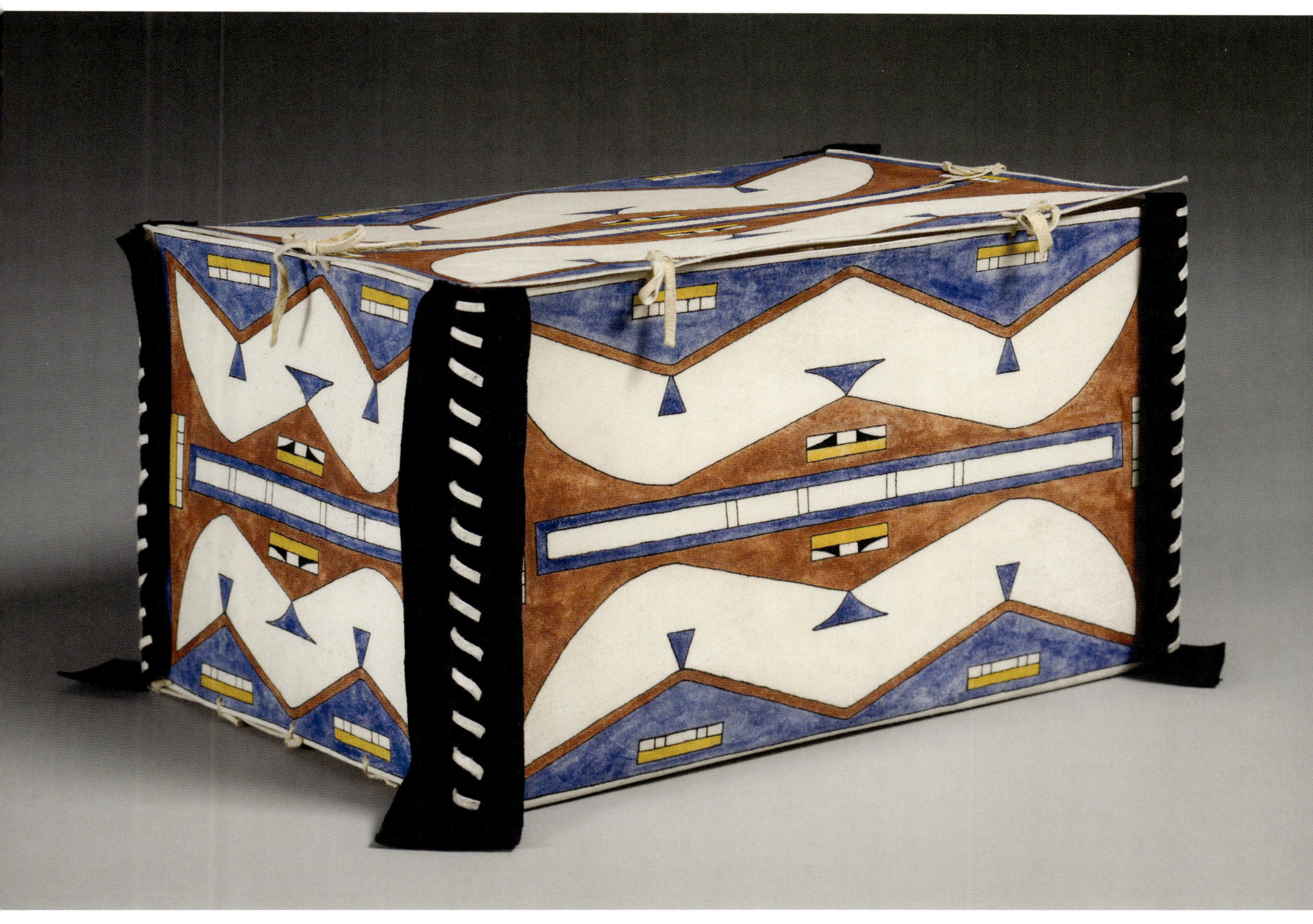

Millie Bridwell
Cheyenne River Sioux
Star Quilt, 2023
Cotton
H. 79 × W. 70 in.
Courtesy of the artist

Debra Box
Southern Ute, born 1956
Box, 2010
Cowhide, pigment, and wool
H. 10½ × W. 20 × D. 13 in.
Denver Art Museum: Native Arts acquisition fund,
2010.497

Kelly Church
Ottawa/Pottawatomi/Matchi-be-nash-she-wish, born 1967
blueberry time, 2015
Black ash, Rit dye, and sweetgrass
H. 10 × W. 11 × D. 11 in.
Courtesy of the artist

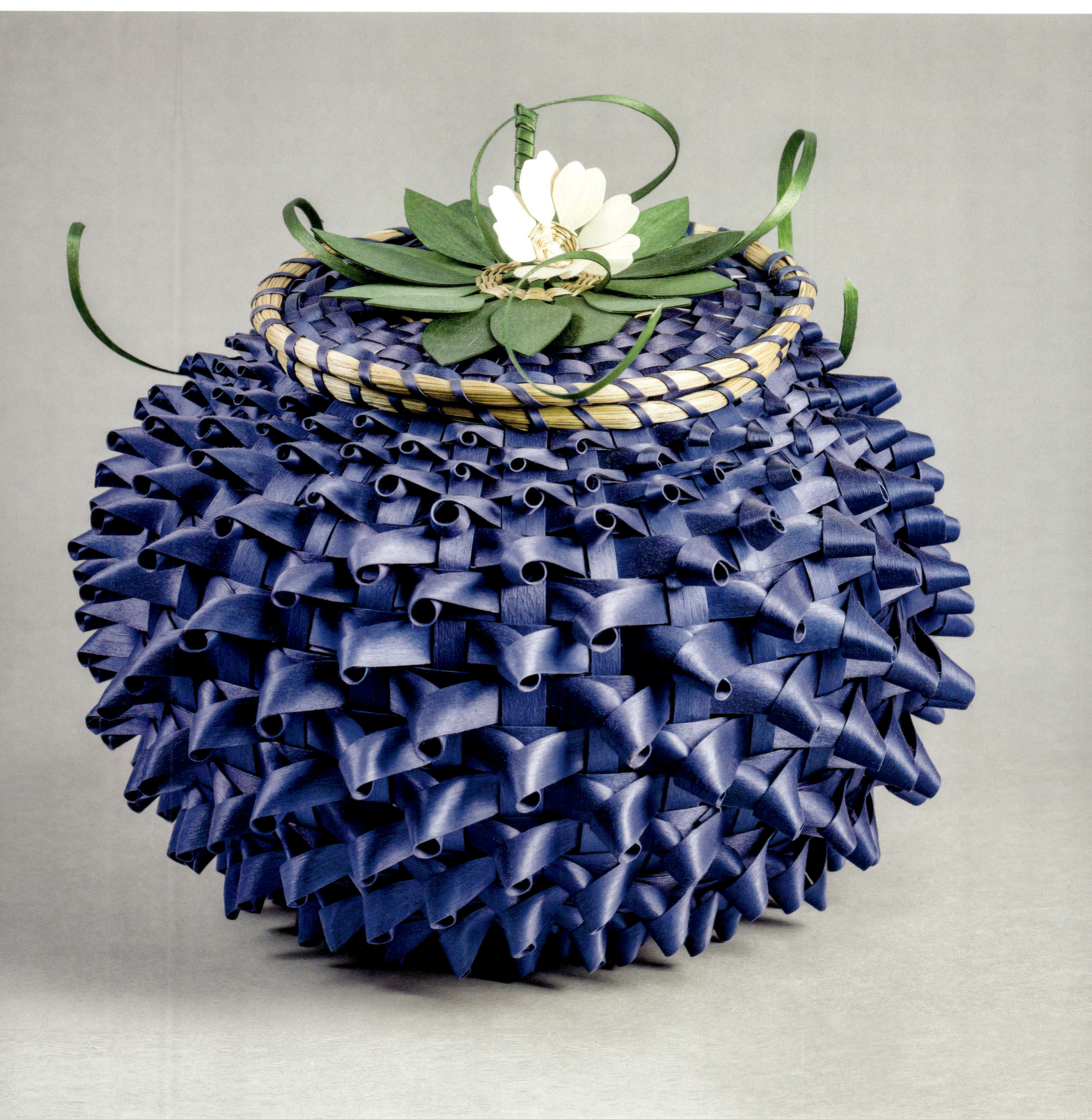

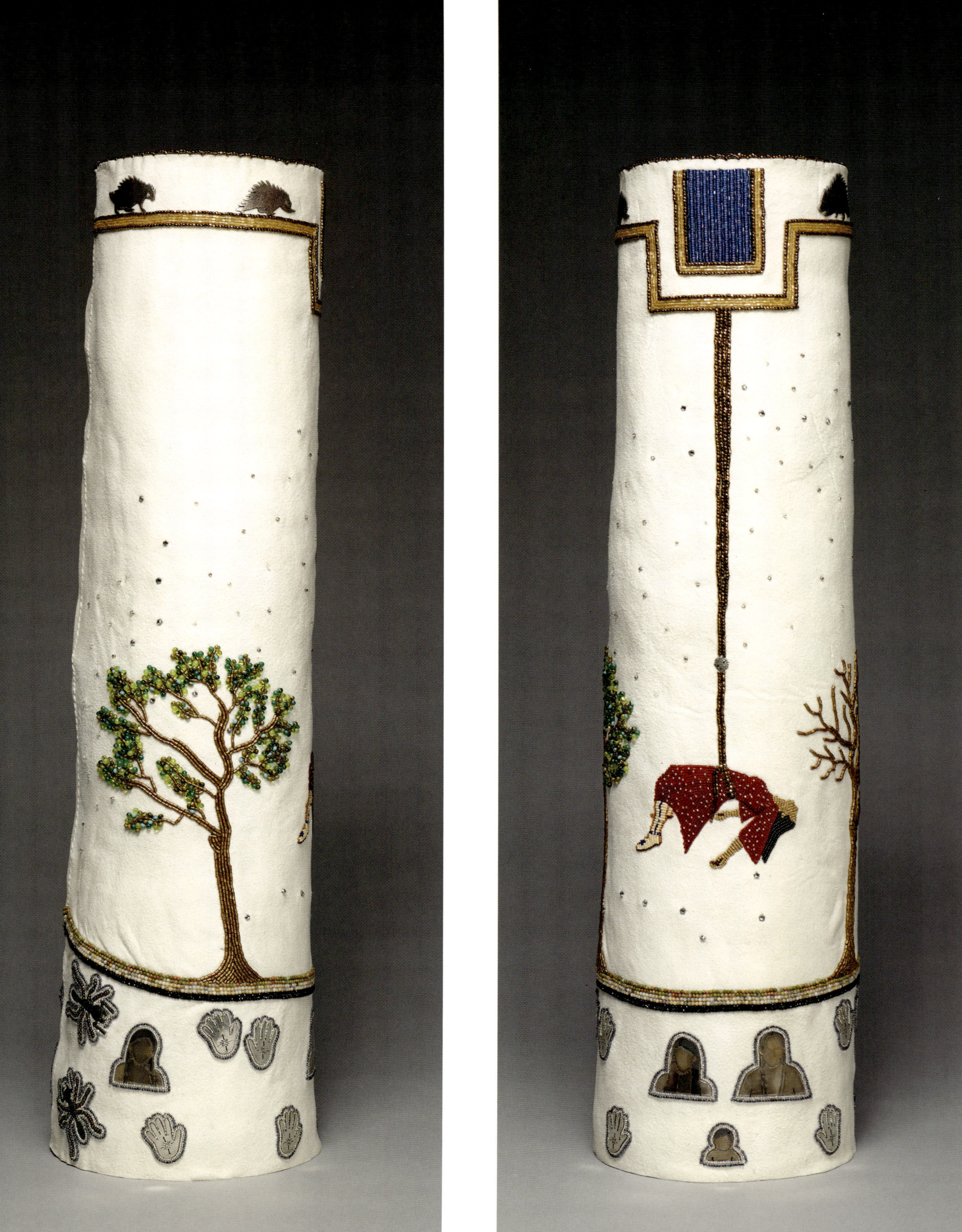

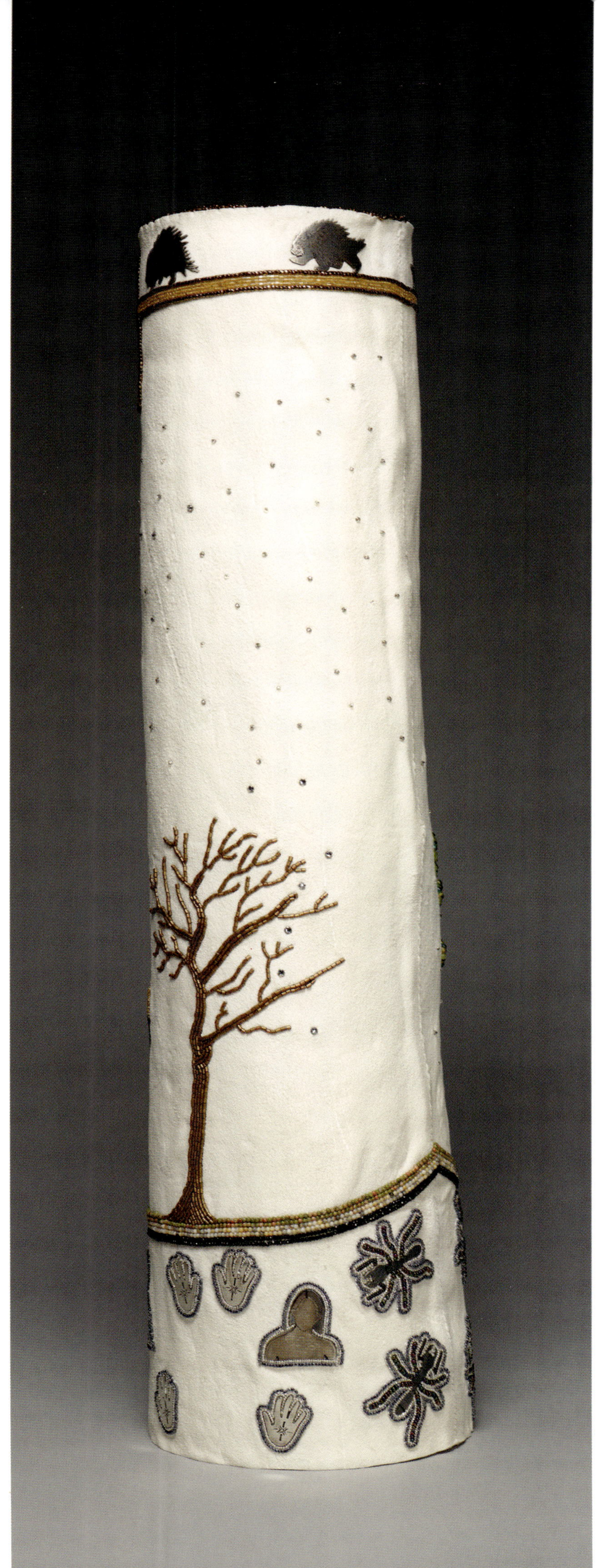

Teri Greeves
Kiowa, born 1970
"Between Worlds" Beaded Parfleche Vessel, 2016
Rawhide and beads
H. 23 × Diam. 7 in.
Collection of the Art Fund Inc.
at the Birmingham Museum of Art;
Gift of Martha Pezrow, AFI.105.2016

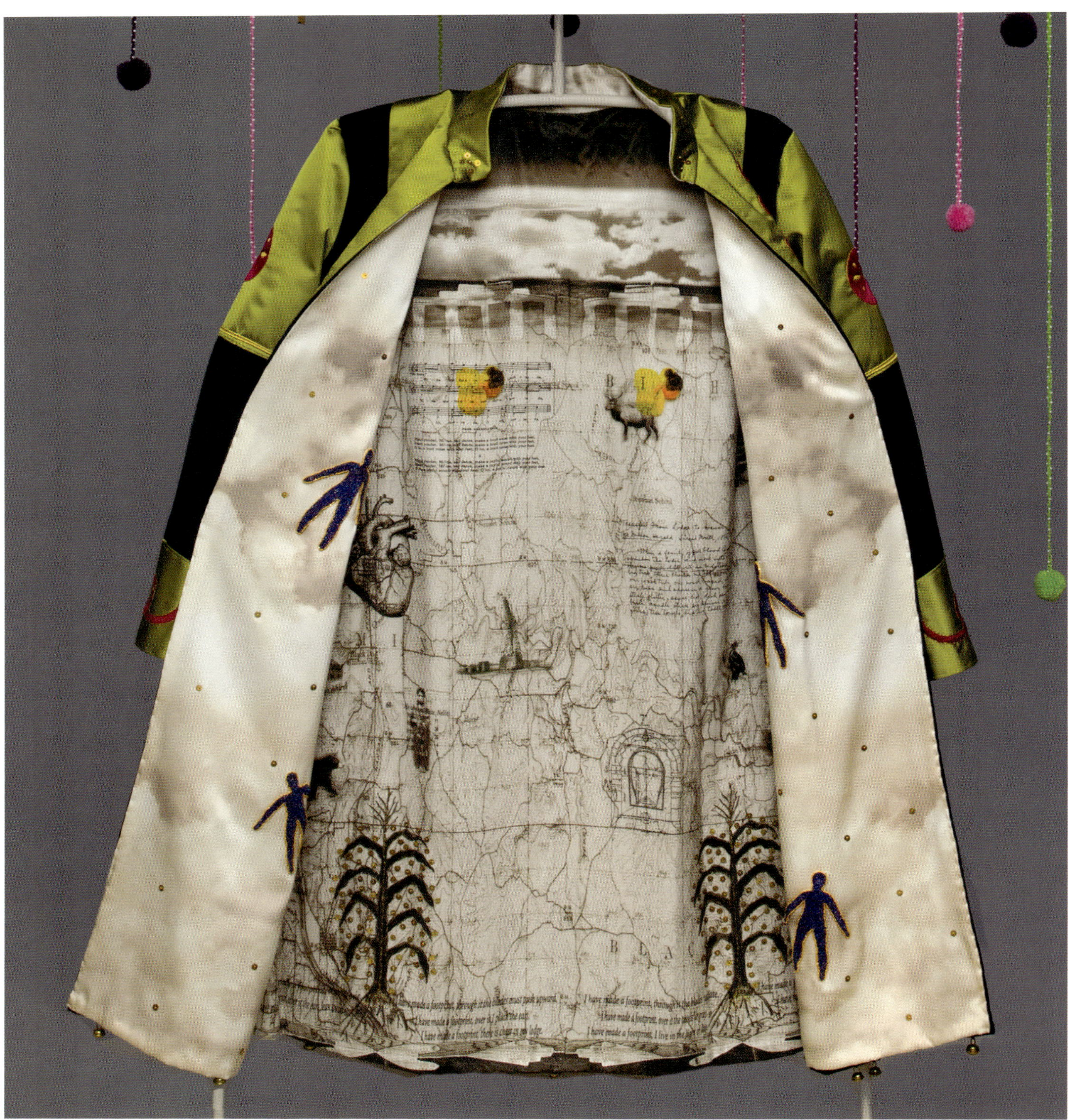

Anita Fields
Osage, born 1951
To Know Your People Are Beautiful, 2019
Contemporary Osage wedding coat with deconstructed images of historical
documents written by US government agents, traders, and journalists
H. 120 × W. 60 × D. 60 in.
Eiteljorg Museum, Museum purchase from the Eiteljorg Contemporary Art Fellowship

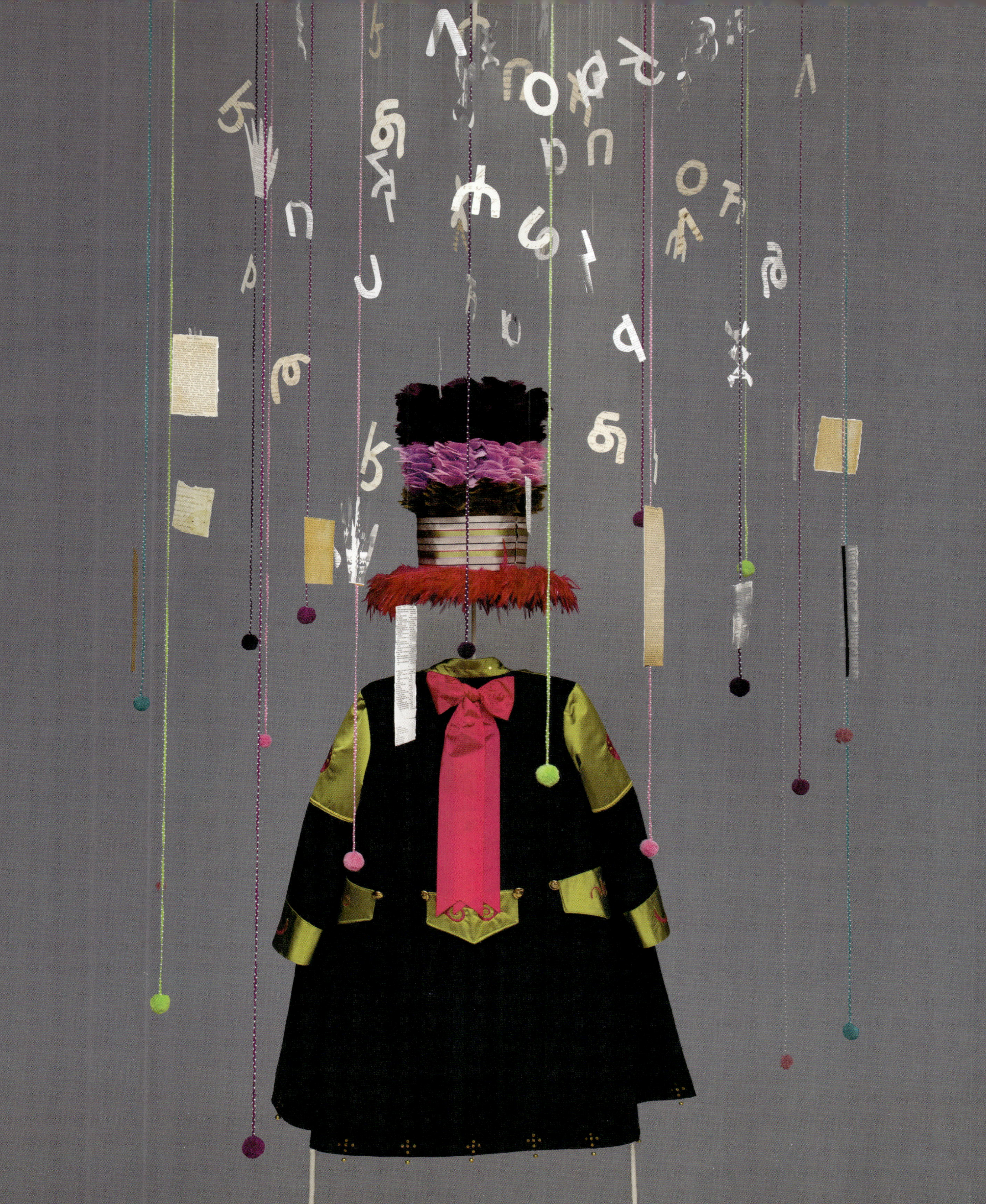

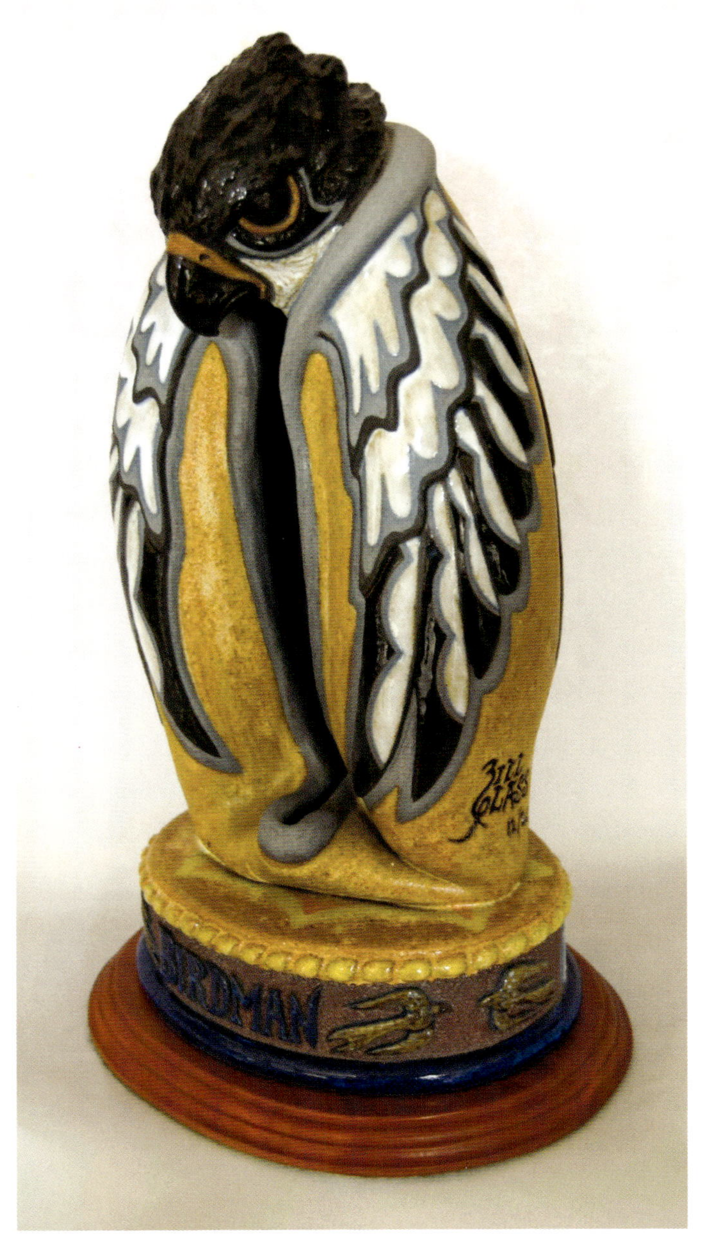

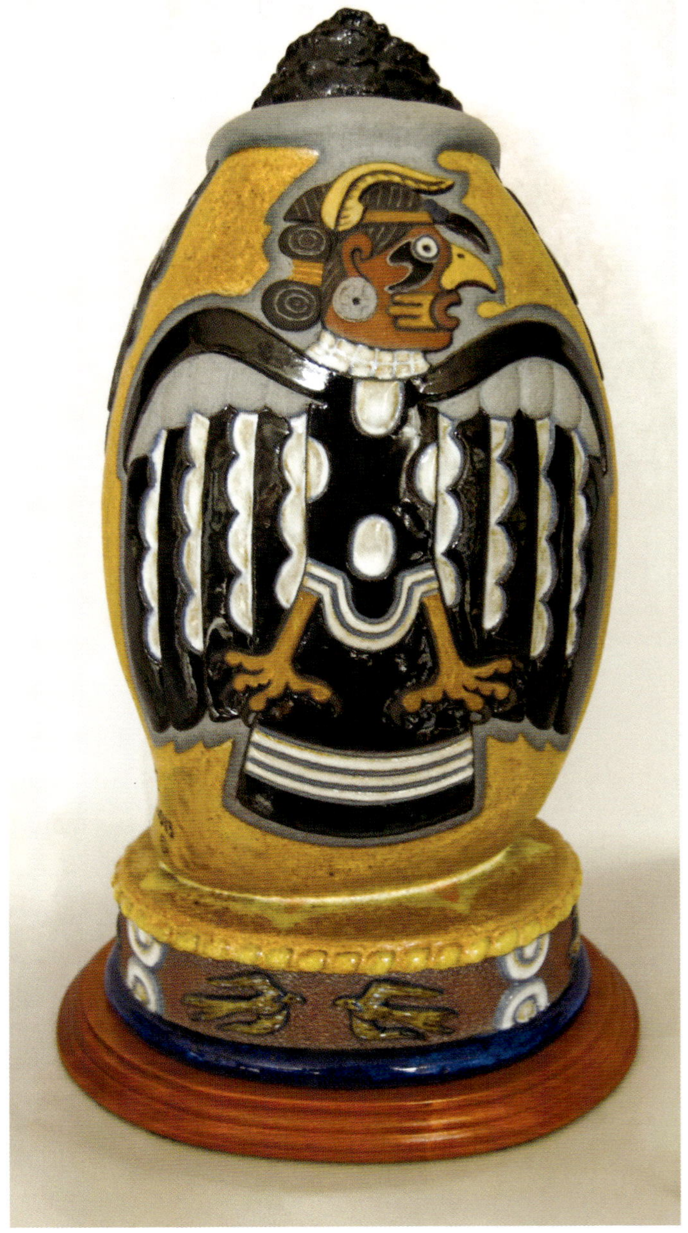

Bill Glass Jr.
Cherokee Nation of Oklahoma, born 1950

ABOVE
Birdman, 2013
Lizella clay and glazes fired at Cone 6 oxidation
H. 14 × W. 7½ × D. 6 in.
Courtesy of the artist

OPPOSITE
Southeast Images, 1996
Lizella clay and glazes fired at Cone 6 oxidation
H. 7¼ × W. 9 × D. 9 in.
Courtesy of the artist

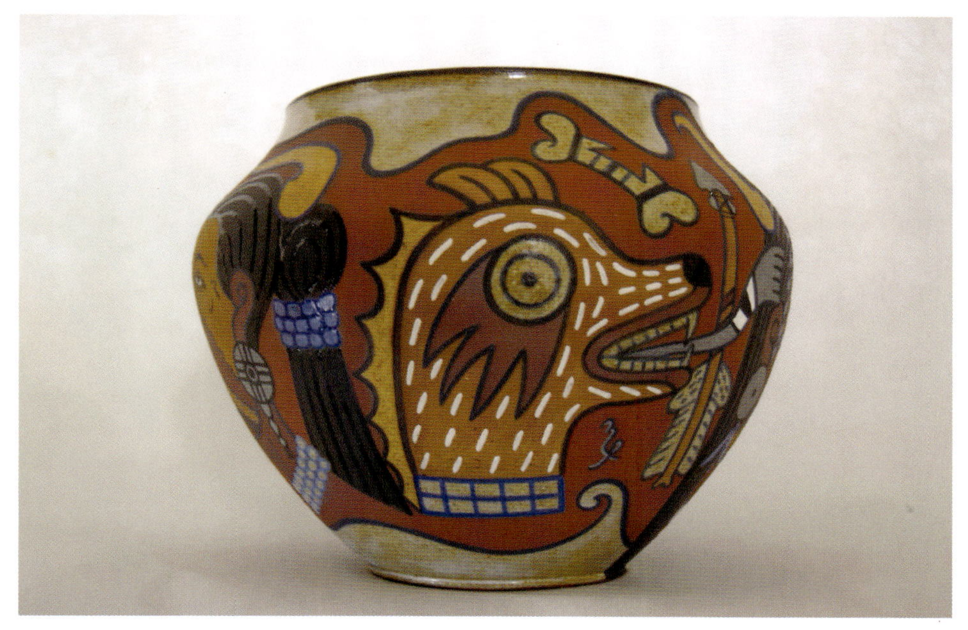

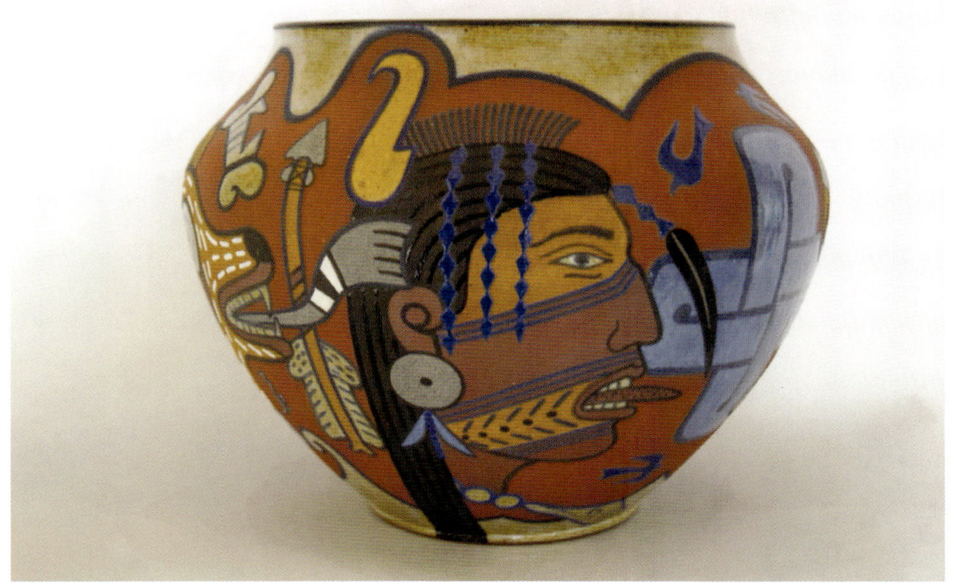

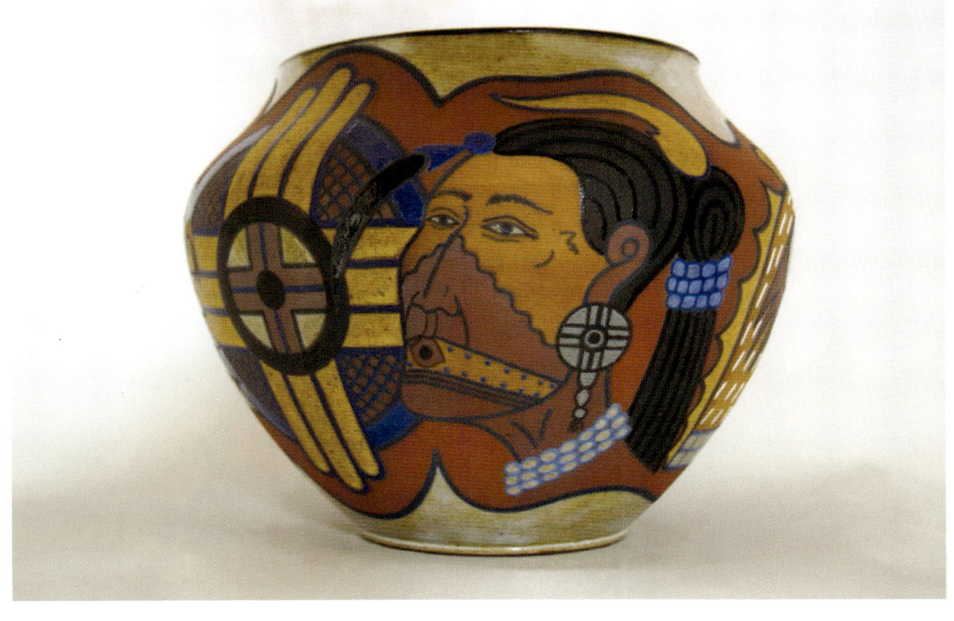

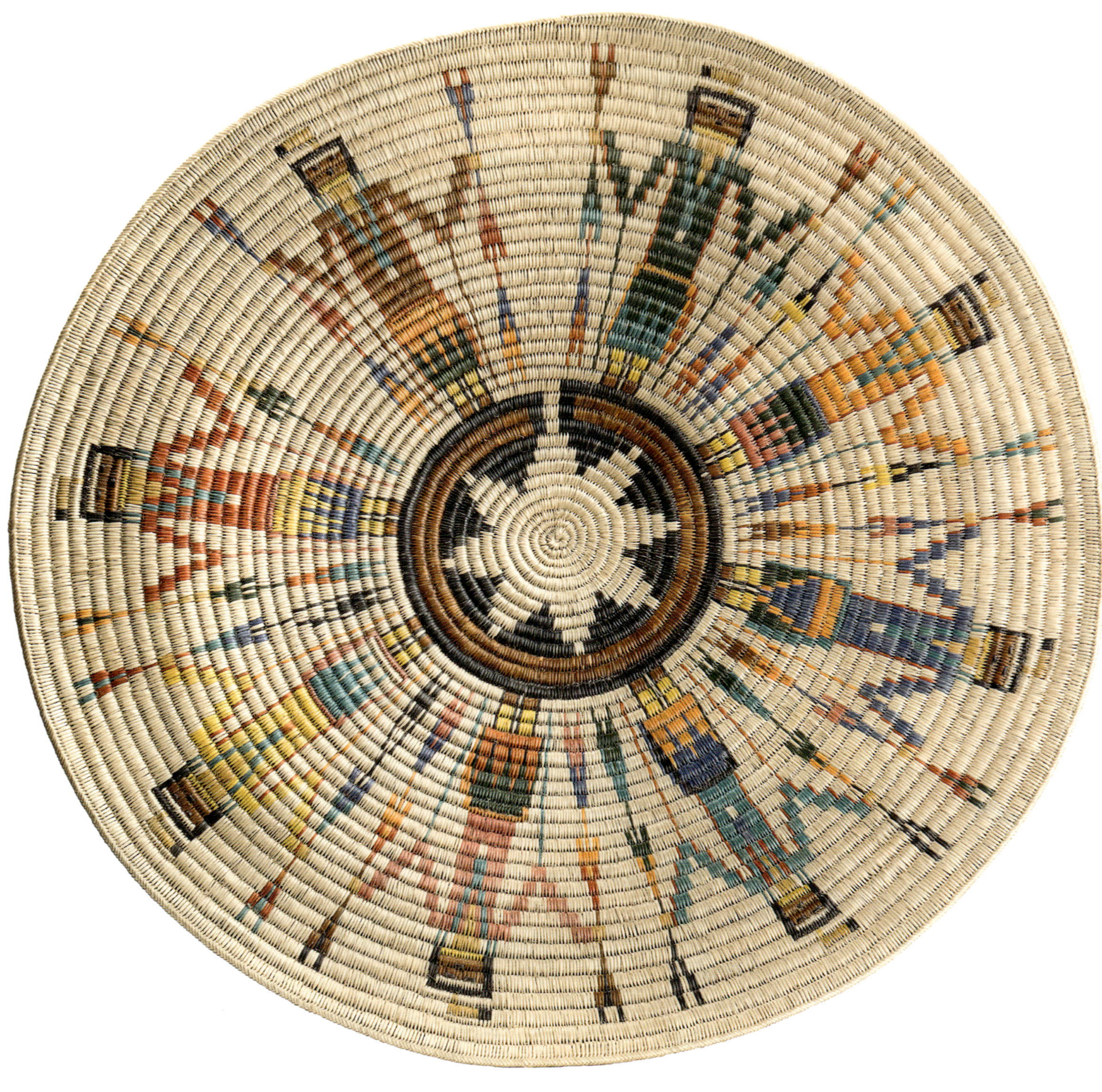

ABOVE
Sally Black
Navajo, born 1959
Untitled, 1979
Coiled sumac, vegetable dyes,
and commercial dyes
H. 4 × Diam. 41¼ in.
Heard Museum Collection, NA-SW-NA-B-20

OPPOSITE
Evalena Henry
San Carlos Apache, born 1939
Burden Basket, 1983
Willow or sumac, leather, twine, and tin cones
H. 13¾ × W. 16¾ in.
Courtesy of the School for Advanced Research,
Indian Arts Research Center purchase for the
permanent collection, 1983

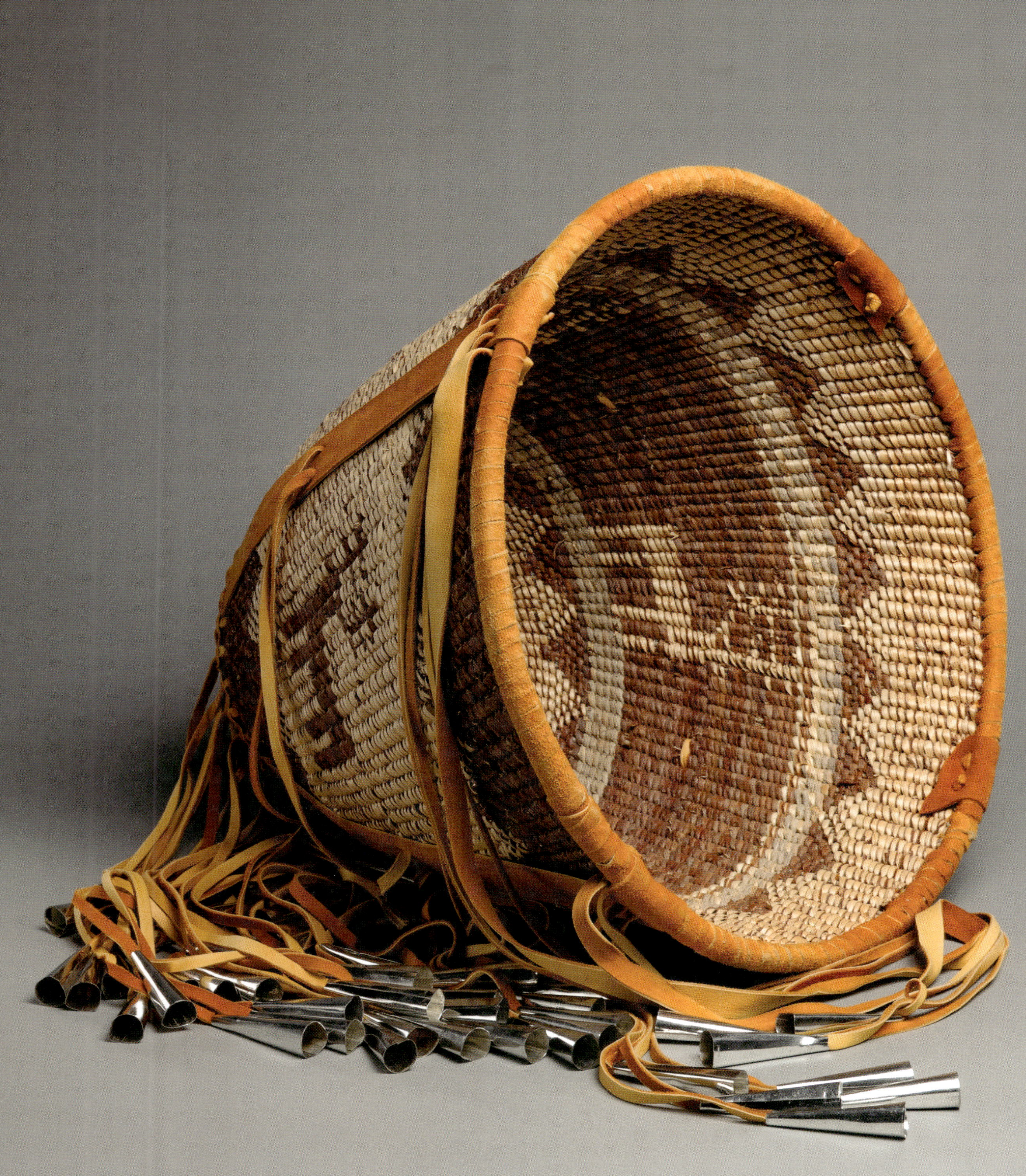

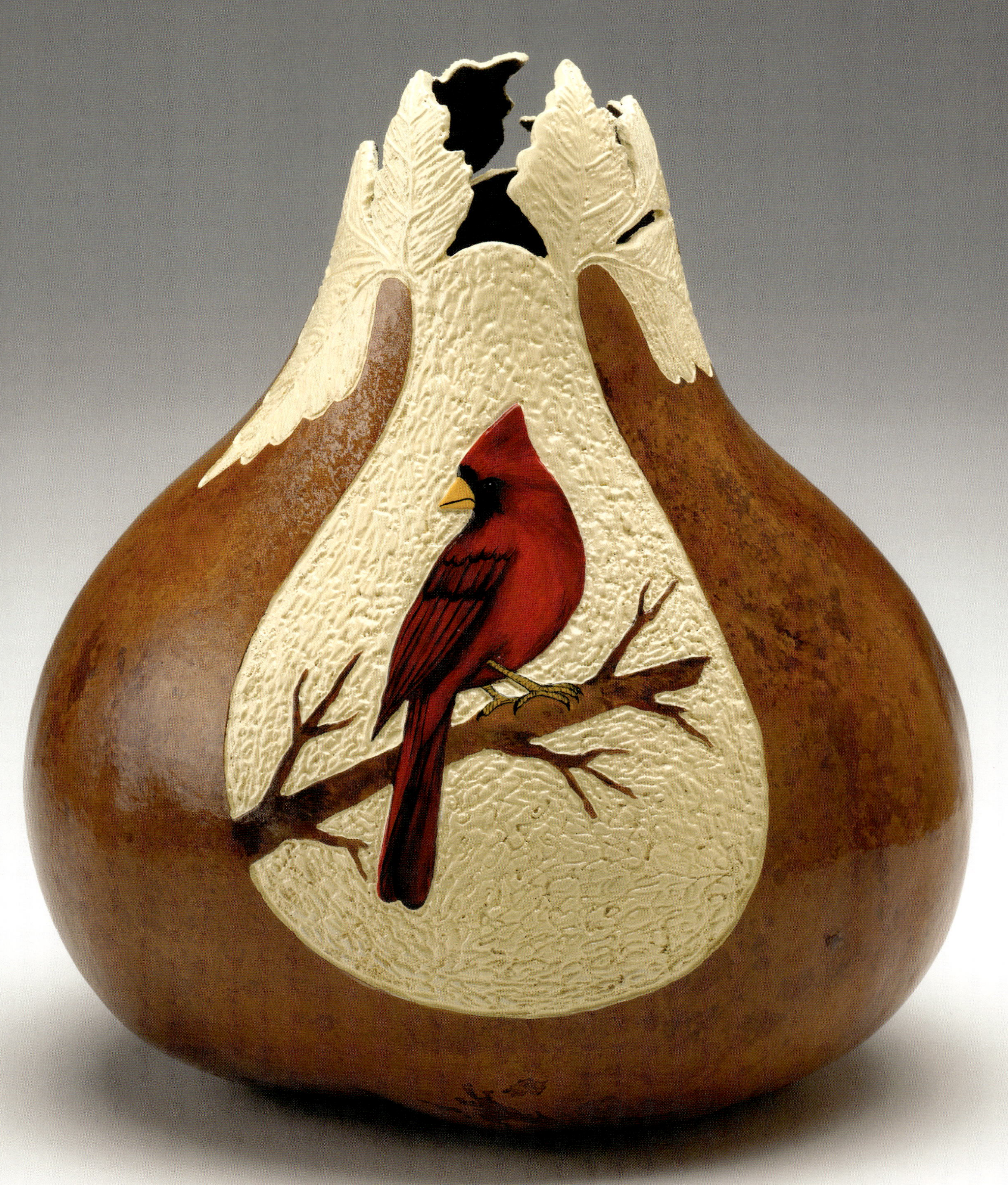

Chalmers Locklear
Lumbee
Cardinal Gourd, 2014
Acrylic on gourd
H. 11 × W. 9½ in.
Collection of the Museum of the Southeast American Indian

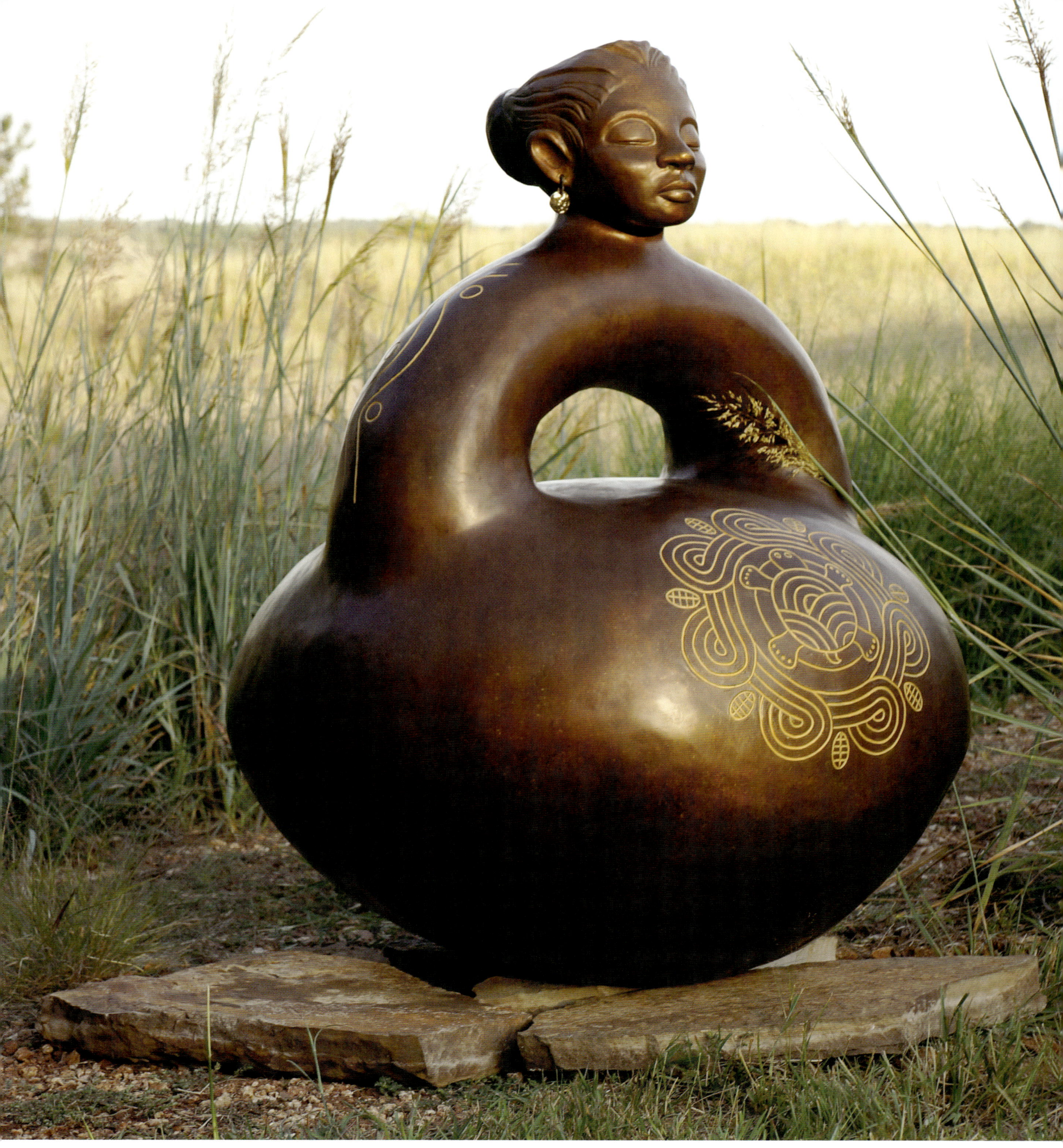

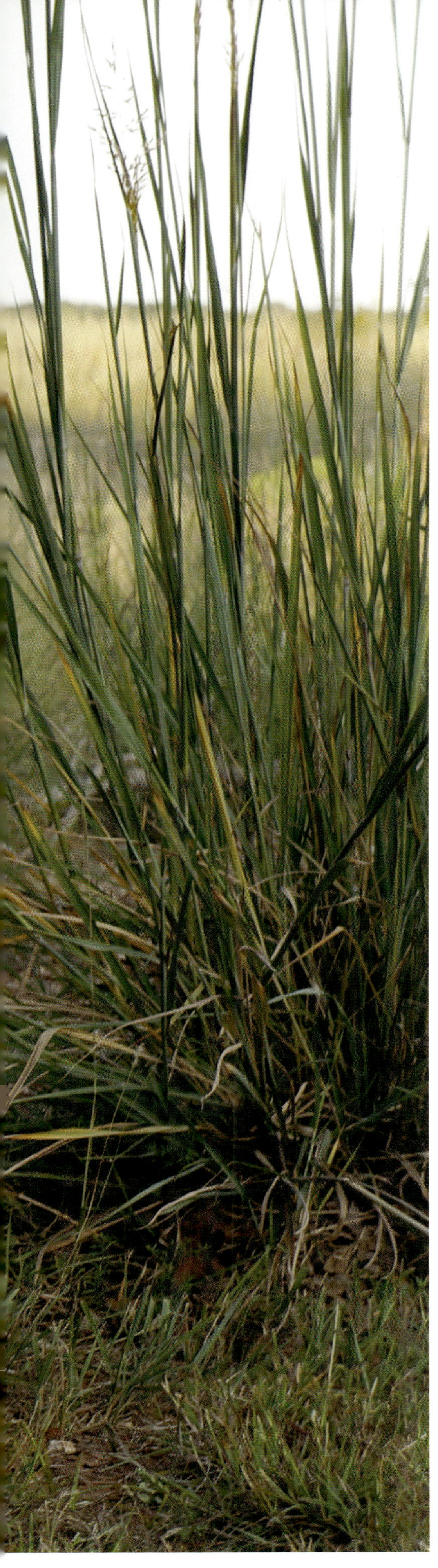

Joanna Underwood Blackburn
Chickasaw Nation
Water Jar, 2017
Bronze
H. 46 × W. 48 × D. 48 in.
Courtesy of the artist

Margaret Roach Wheeler
Chickasaw/Choctaw, born 1943
Chikasha Issoba, Chickasaw Horse, 2015
Handwoven cotton, glass beads, copper, and handmade brass bells
H. 37 × W. 25 × D. 25 in.
Courtesy of the artist

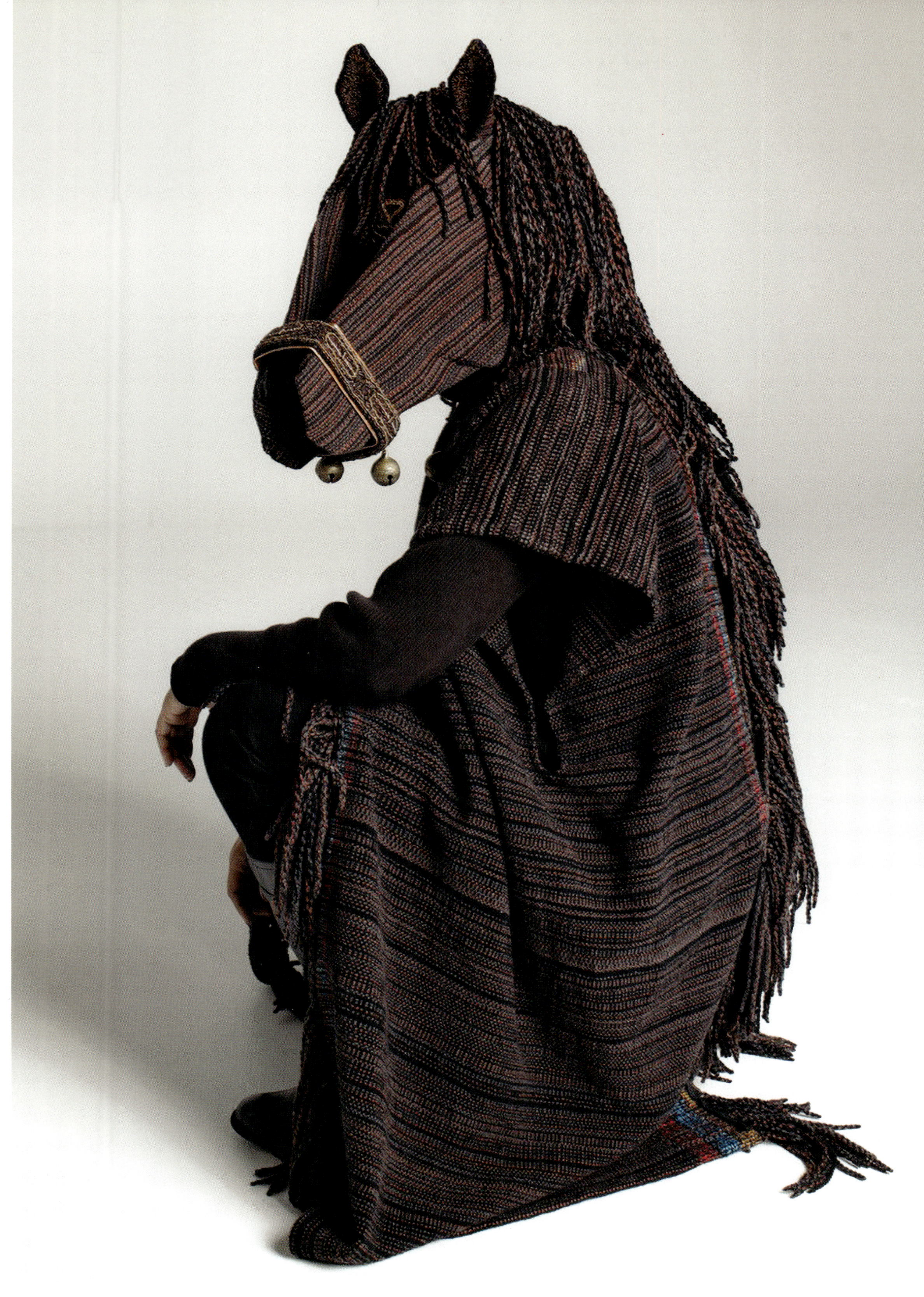

49

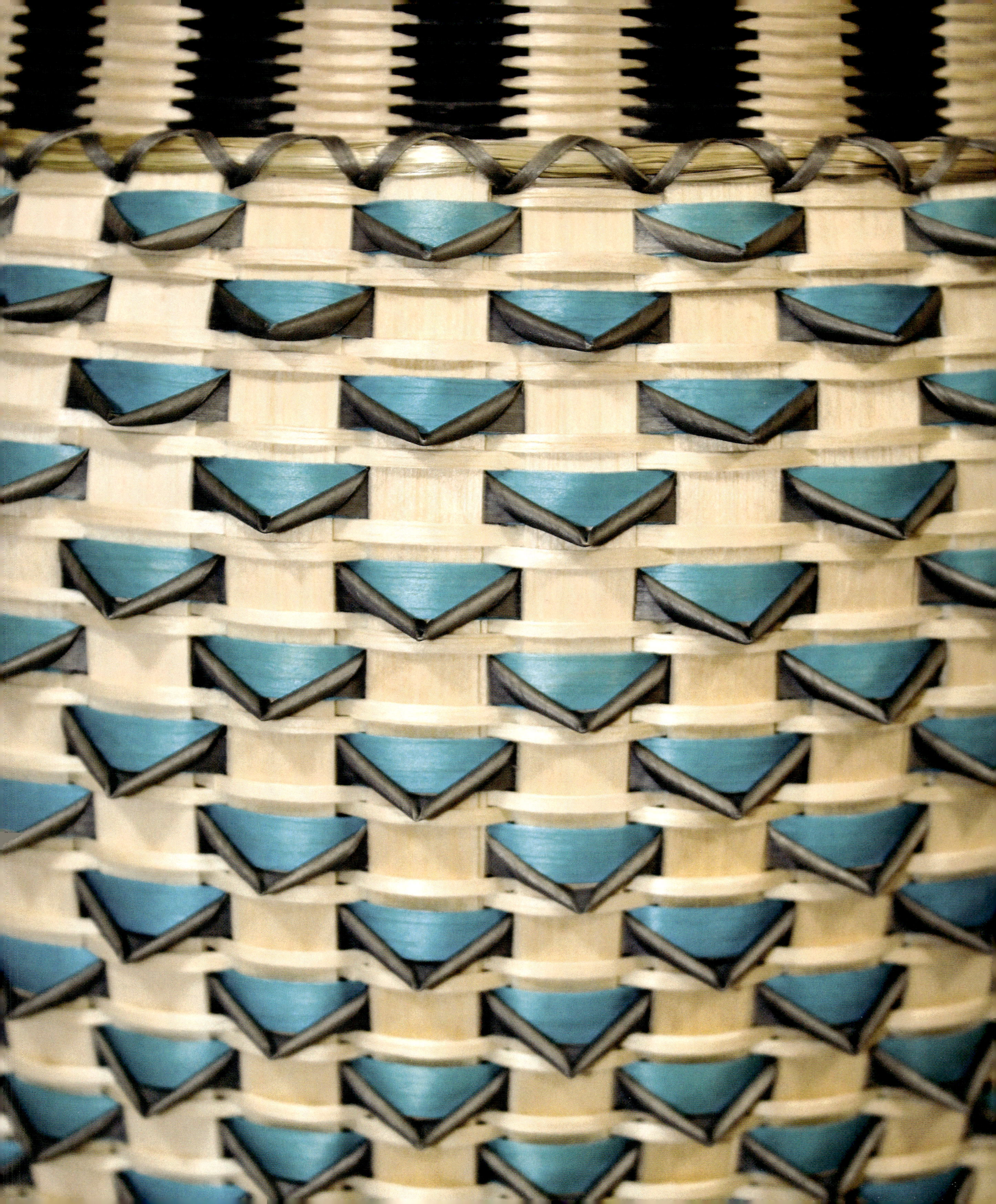

Rootedness

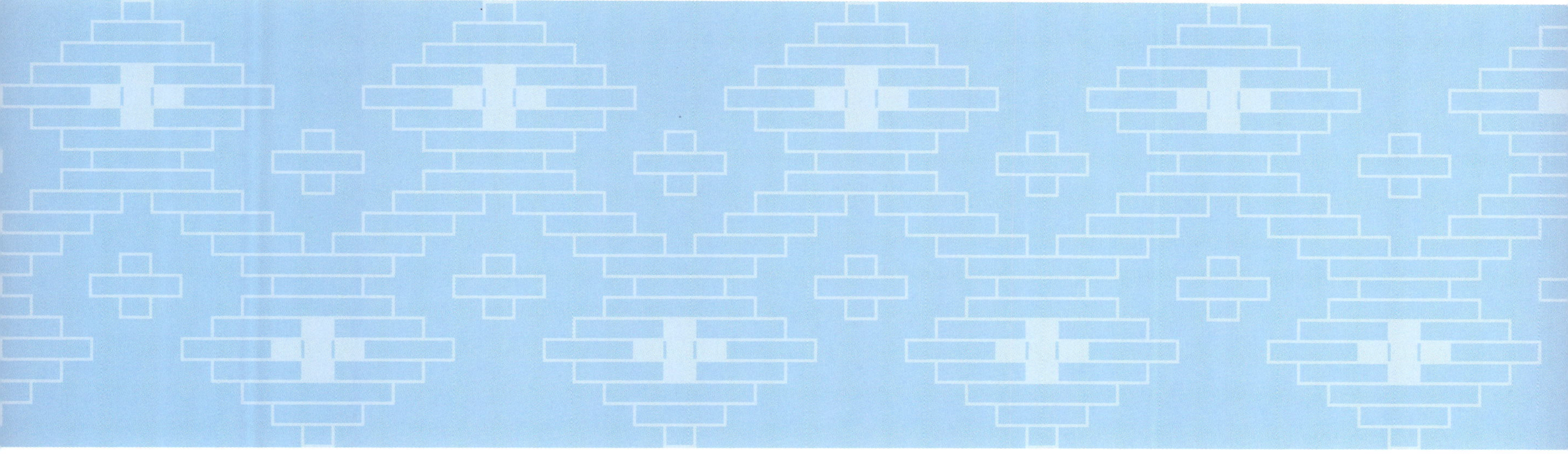

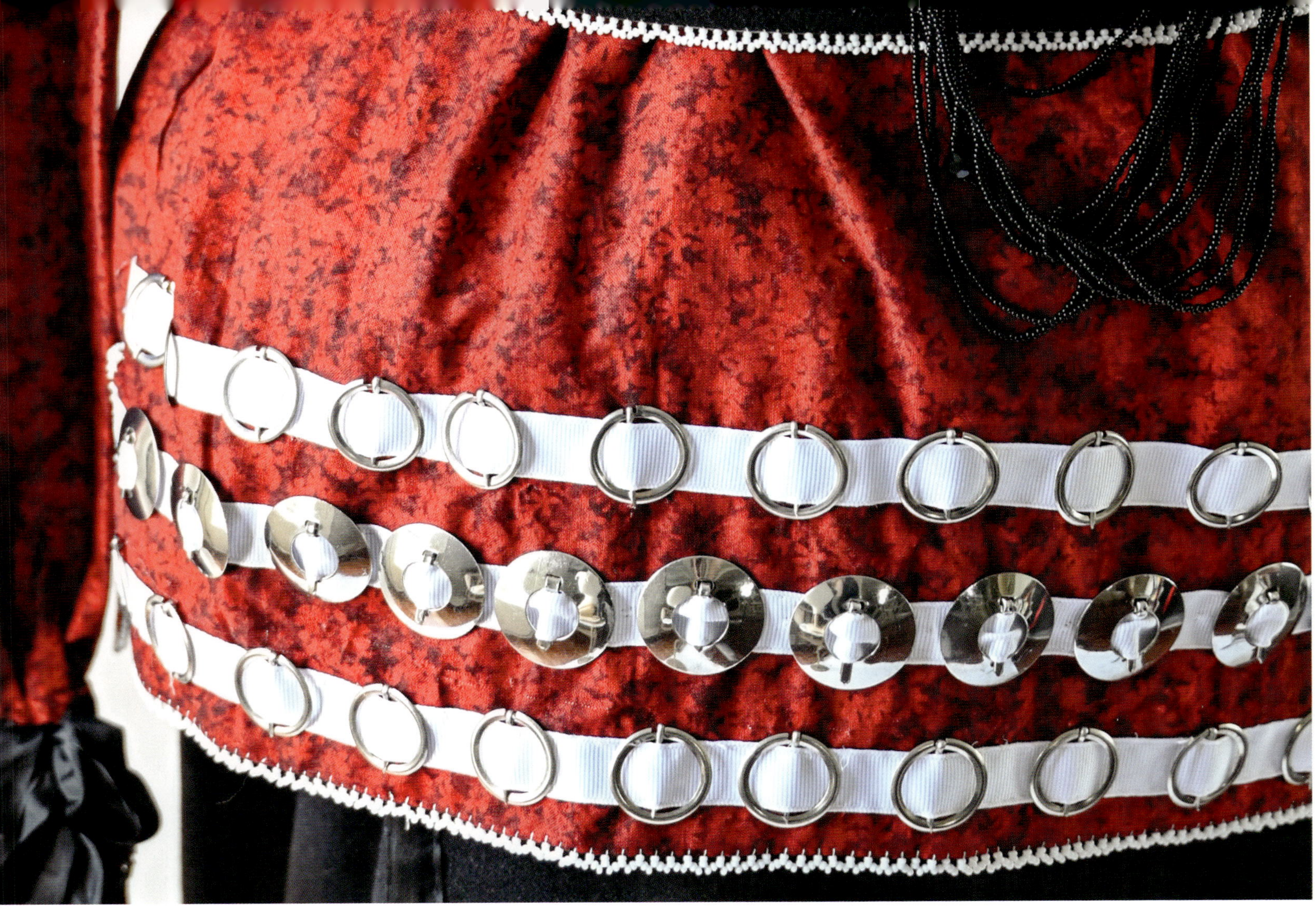

UNTIL THE MID-NINETEENTH CENTURY, impenetrable stands of rivercane stood dense along the rivers in the Southeast United States. Living among them were hundreds of thousands of Indigenous societies organized in both chiefdoms and smaller bands of communities. For many Southeastern tribes, rivercane (Chickasaw: *bokoshi oski*) was an essential material used in everyday life. It was the staple material in creating fishing poles, housing materials, blowguns, and arrows, among countless other uses. Mats made of rivercane were used to cover floors for seating areas in homes and council houses and for beds to sleep on. Beautifully woven mats were part of death rites in burials. During the mound-building eras, rivercane baskets were used to construct mounds that still hold sacred meaning, their vestiges prevalent across the Southeastern landscape today.

The ancient technique of weaving rivercane into mats and baskets dates back thousands of years in the Southeast. Native people split rivercane into thin strips, tinted them various hues of brown with natural dyes made of black walnut, bloodroot, yellowroot, and other botanical materials, and wove them into intricately encoded patterns containing cultural meanings. Chickasaw/Choctaw weaver Sue Fish designs her baskets with patterns that relate knowledge about the Chickasaw world view and cultural understandings. For example, the diamond pattern in many of her works represents the diamondback rattlesnake present in the Mississippi homelands.

Found throughout this exhibition are artistic traditions of rootedness that convey deep ancestral knowledge defined by a sense of belonging, connectedness to kin, keen understanding of the landscapes from which artists originate, and the spiritual framework that holds it all together and gives meaning to every aspect of their existence. This is all rooted together in an interdependent foundation of being. Rootedness, a sense of belonging to a culture, to a uniquely defined people, is expressed in the visual languages designed in art among Native peoples throughout the Americas. These visual languages, then and now, underpin the process of teaching and passing down cultural knowledge. Like the interlocking root systems of rivercane, the intersecting of belief, identity, spirituality, and other cultural hallmarks are deeply embedded in Native art to create a sense of belonging and connectedness that solidifies bonds between people and world views. This rootedness strengthens Native societies through artistic traditions that preserve core cultural meanings across time and place.

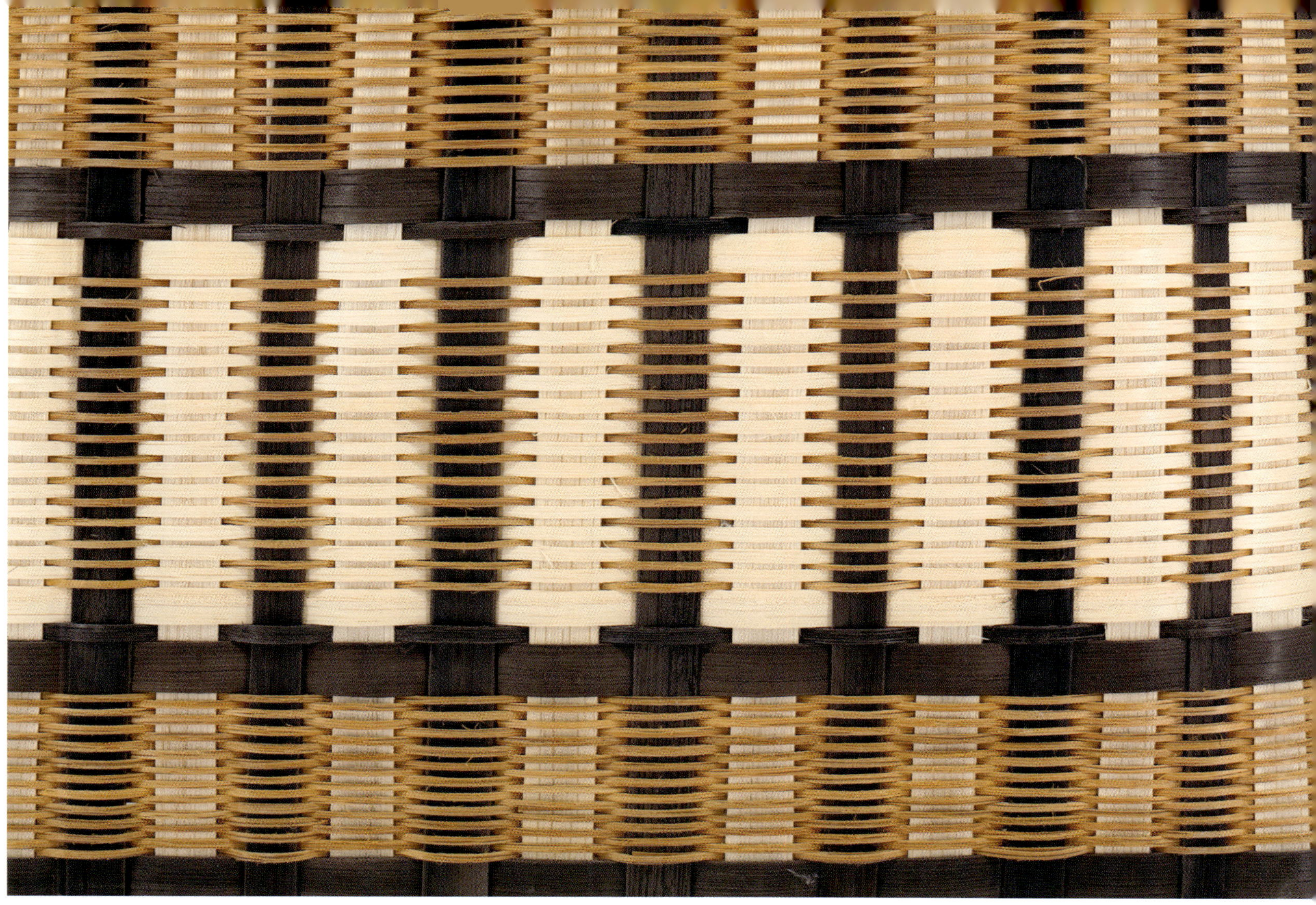

The sense of **rootedness** in art took on significant importance during the Indian removal period, when people were displaced or **unrooted** from their homelands. They took with them their cultural knowledge—knowledge that was informed by place and environment—to vastly different landscapes, ones that often did not reflect their history nor provide the materials needed to create their traditional art forms. Not only did absence from homelands threaten the continuation of basketry but during the nineteenth and twentieth centuries, Southeastern basketry was under further risk of extinction because of the lack of rivercane among removal lands in Indian Territory (present-day Oklahoma). Without rivercane, it was almost impossible to create baskets and mats; weaving techniques and pattern meanings were in jeopardy of being lost forever. Those who remained in their homelands faced the growing pressure of free-range cattle, who feasted on the entire plant quickly and efficiently, pushing rivercane to near extinction in the Southeast. Worsening the crisis were United States assimilation policies designed to terminate Indigenous traditional arts.

Against all odds Native people throughout the Southeast found ways to preserve their traditions by secluding their practices. They reduced the presence of the designs to continue the utilitarian tradition of basketmaking. Many Native people convinced outsiders the meaning of the designs was decorative and cultivated a commercial market for their art. Although a great deal was lost forever, the people themselves losing part of their culture and identity, efforts to preserve the traditions were effective. Even with the scarcity of rivercane, dedicated modern weavers have adapted to commercial materials and reclaimed and restored their traditions for future generations. In doing so they have regained and strengthened their ancestral rootedness.

Basketry is only one example of how the understanding of **rootedness** is represented in art and is essential to the continuation of Native traditions. Rootedness expresses the intent of shape and meaning in American Indian art and provides the foundation for artistic expression, evolution, belonging, and continuum among all Indigenous art.

PAGE 50: Detail of image on page 59

OPPOSITE: Detail of image on page 70

ABOVE: Detail of image on page 61

Inupiaq, born 1972
Baleen Basket with Polar Bear Head Finial, no date
Baleen and ivory
H. 4 × W. 3 × D. 3 in.
Private collection, North Carolina

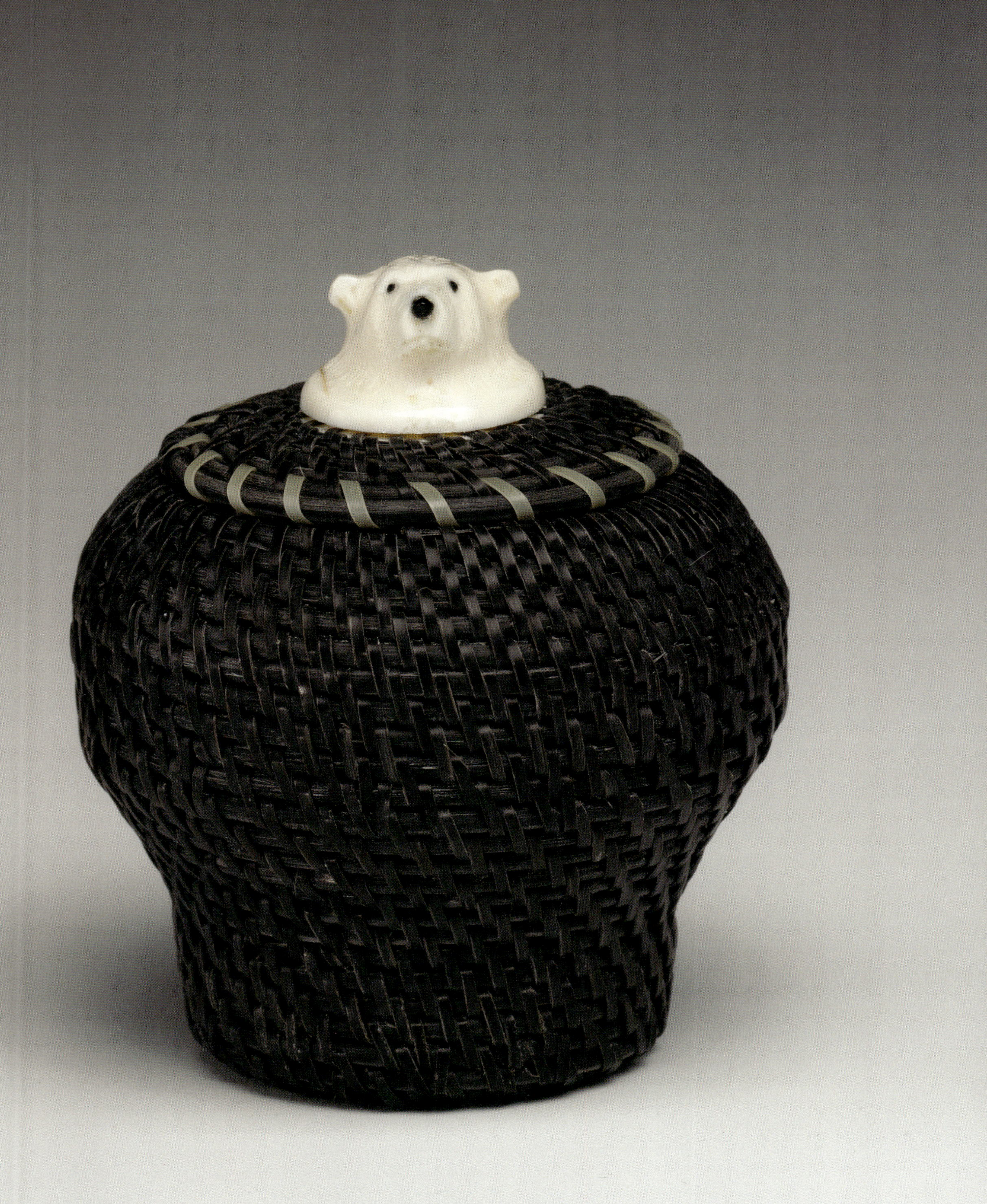

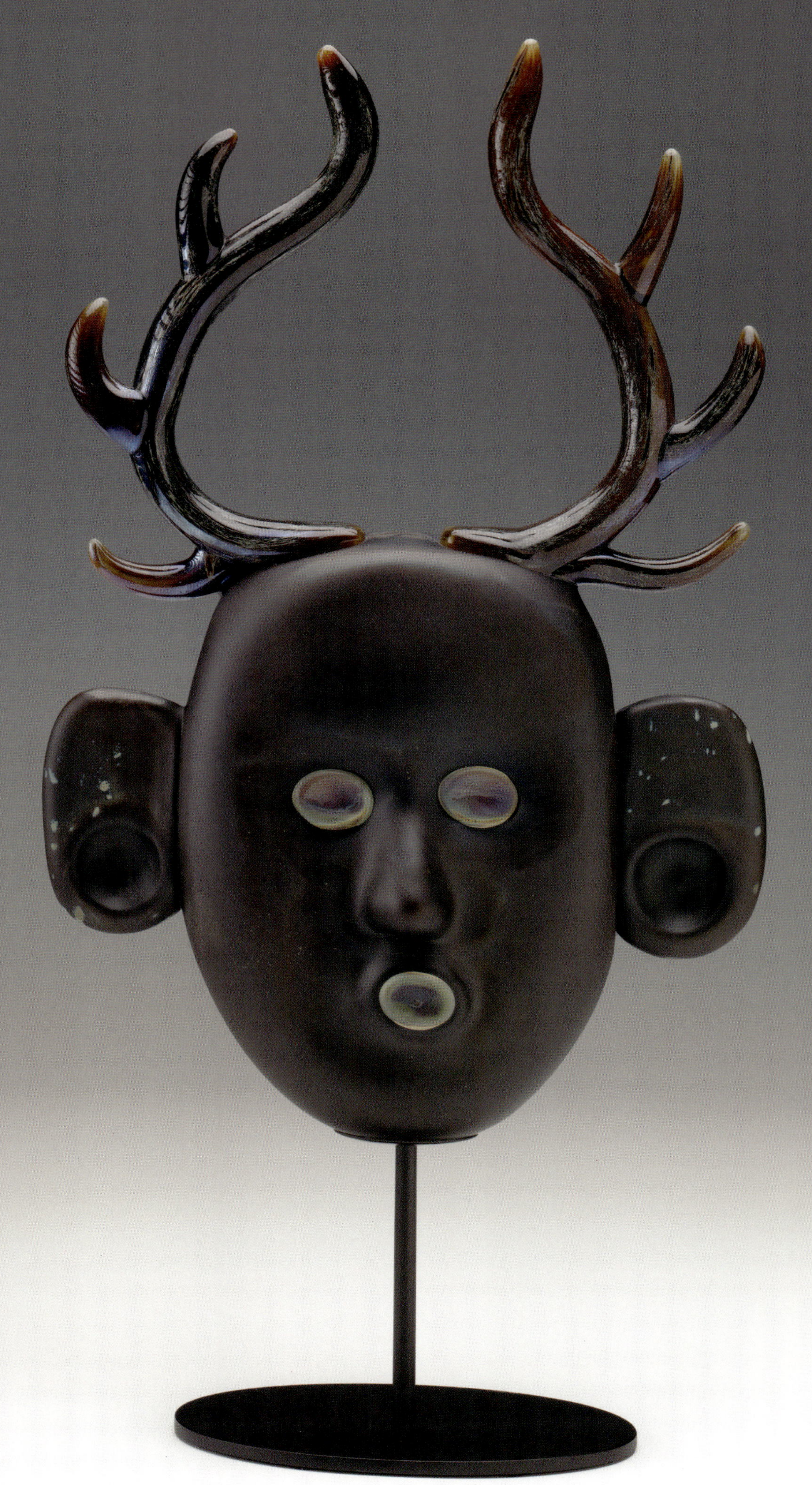

Marcus Amerman
Choctaw, born 1959
Preston Singletary
Tlingit, born 1963
Deerman of the Hopewell, 2010
Glass
H. 24½ × W. 12 × D. 5 in.
Courtesy of the artists

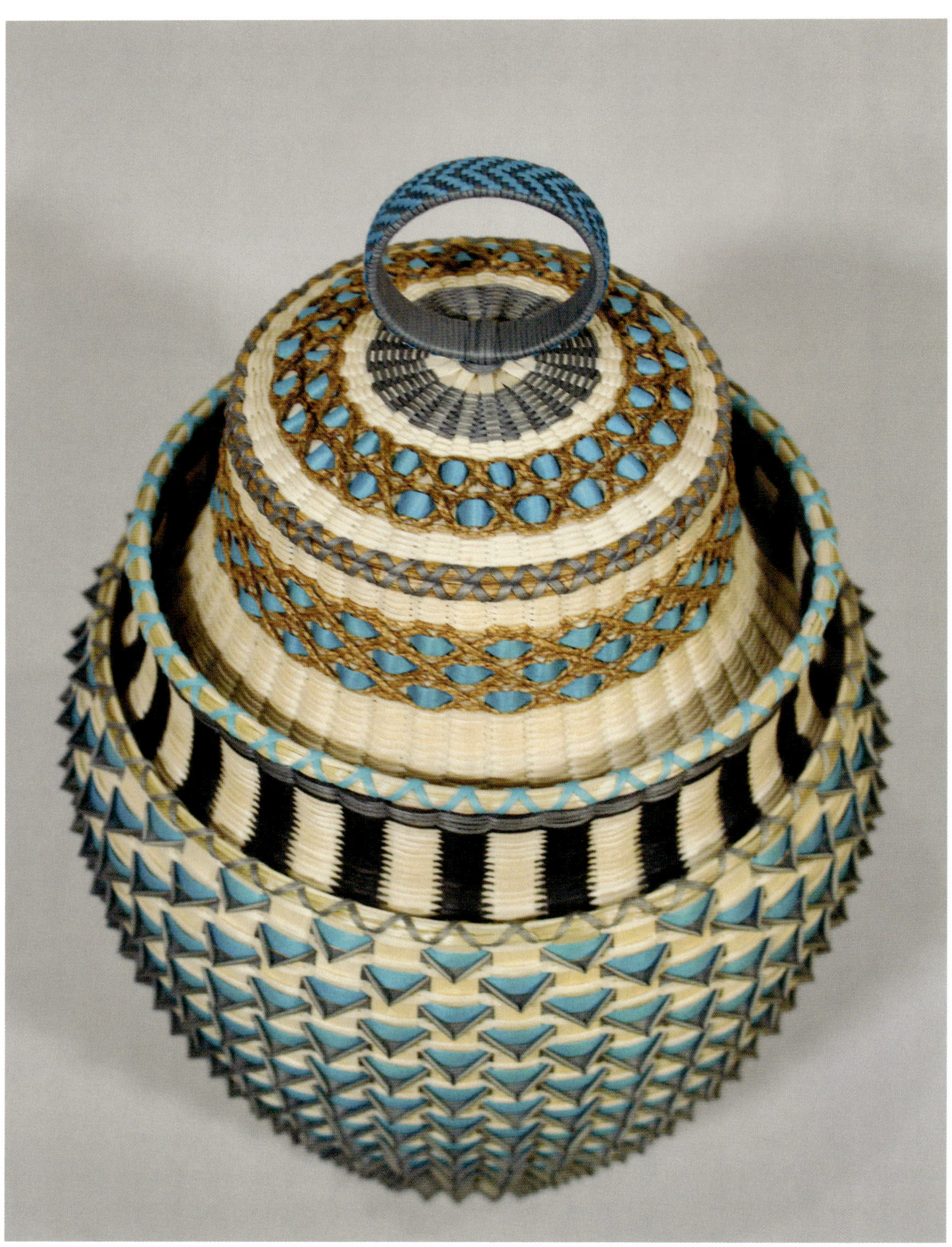

Jeremy Frey
Passamaquoddy, born 1978
Quilted Cedar, 2020
Black ash, cedar bark, sweet grass, and synthetic dye
H. 19 × W. 10 × D. 4 in.
The Robert and Barbara Buker Collections

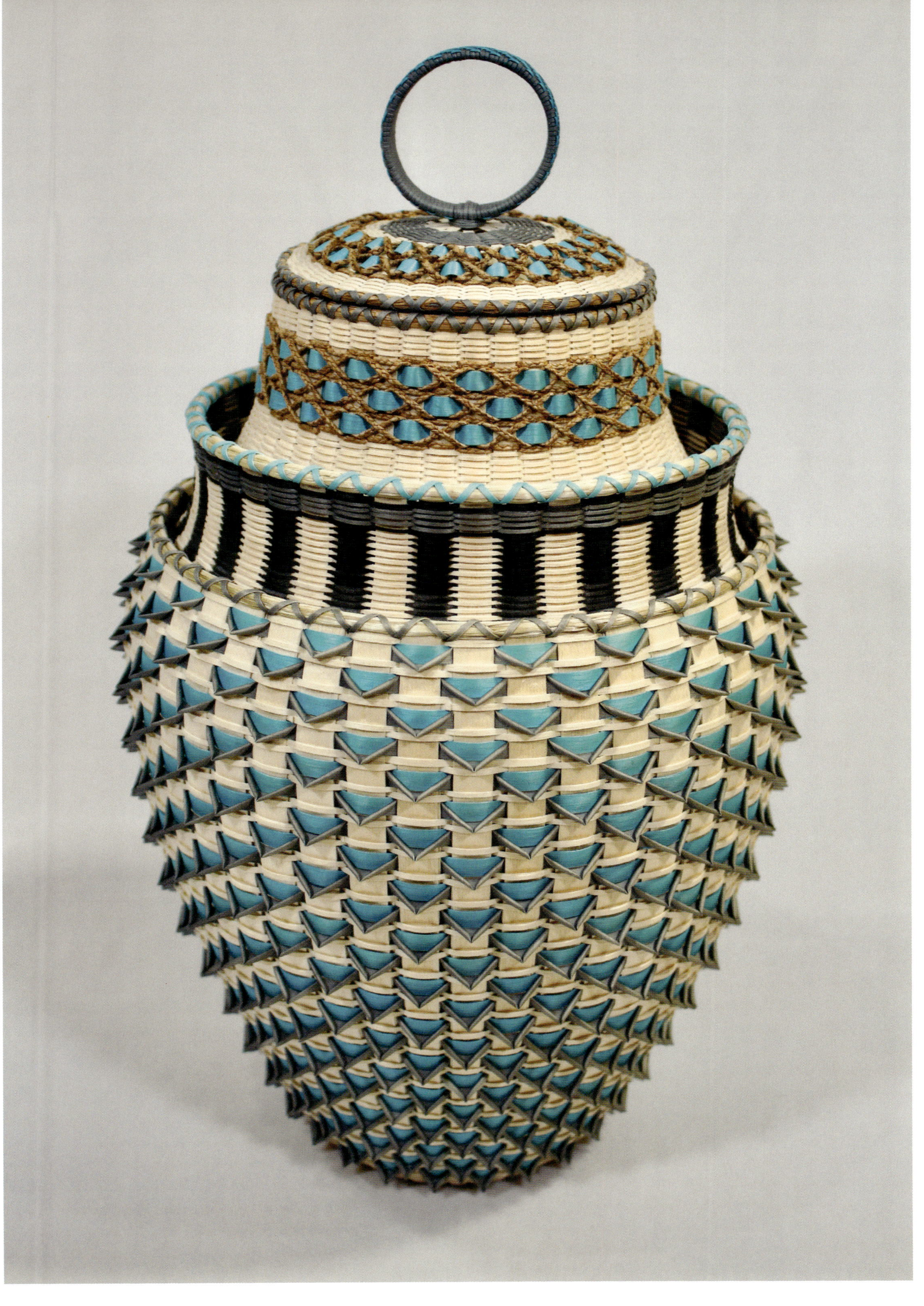

Maidena Welch Wildcatt
Cherokee, born 1951
Basket, circa 1990–2000
White oak, bloodroot, and butternut root
H. 14 × W. 14 × D. 6 in.
Museum of the Cherokee Indian, Maidena Welch Wildcatt Collection, 2011.599

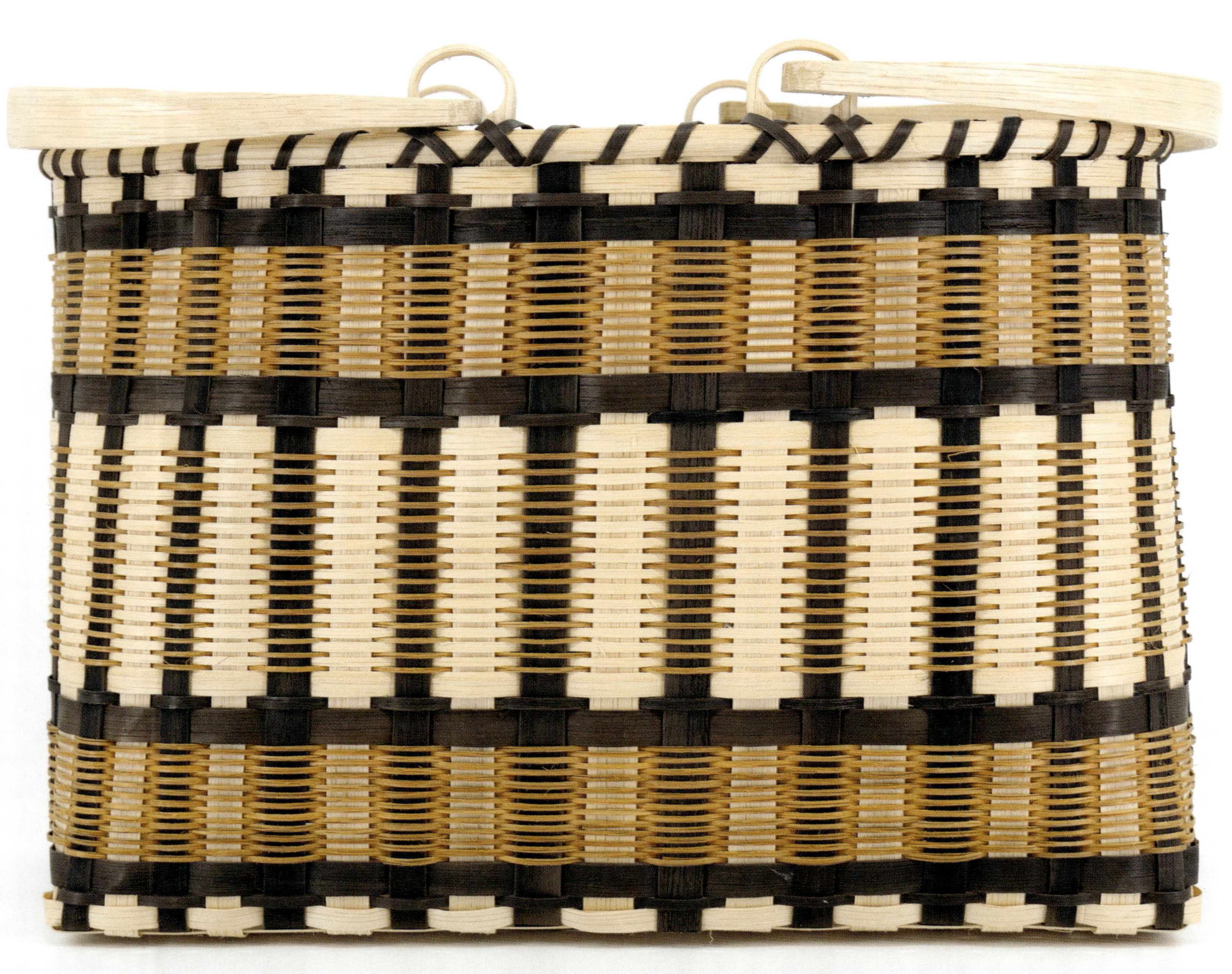

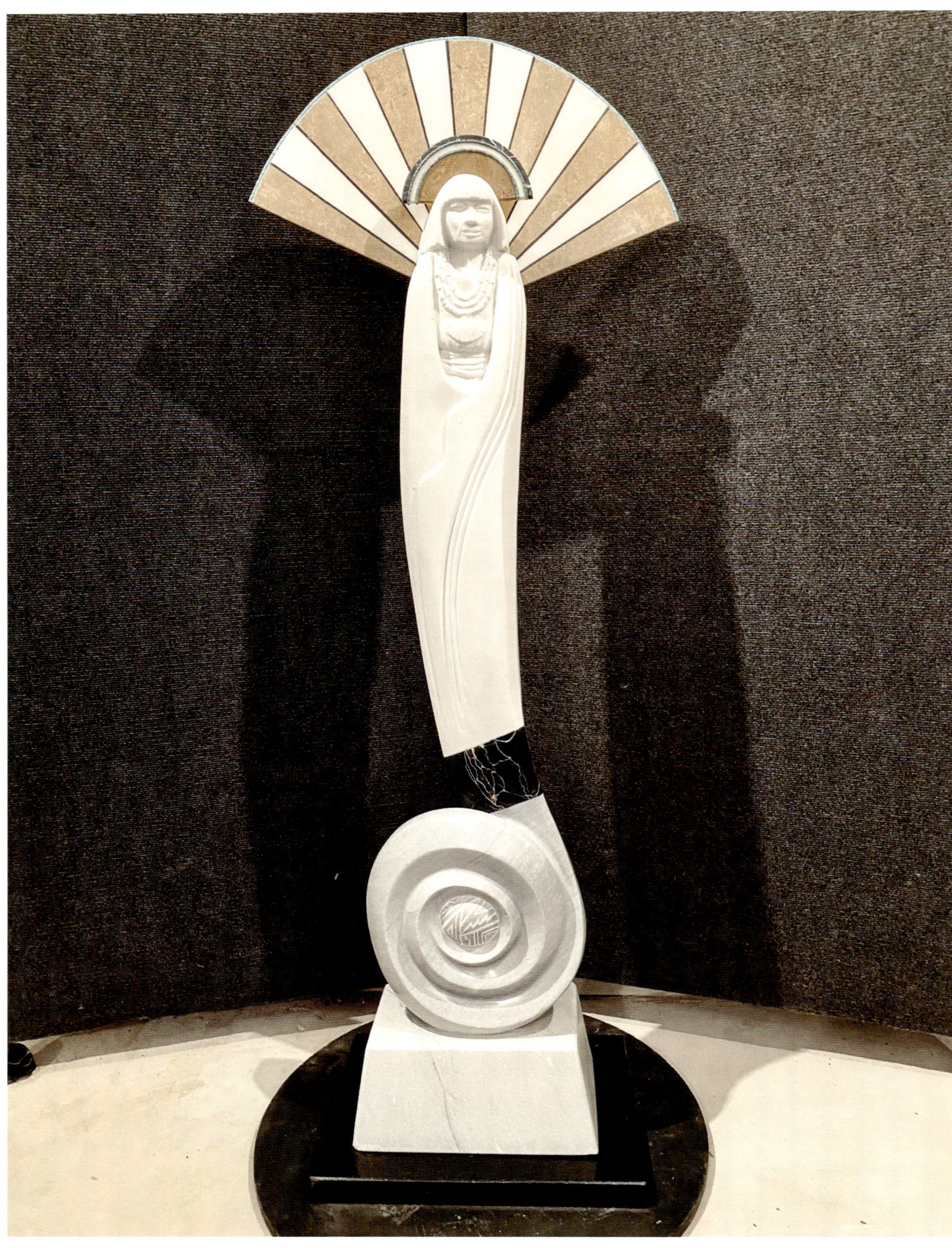

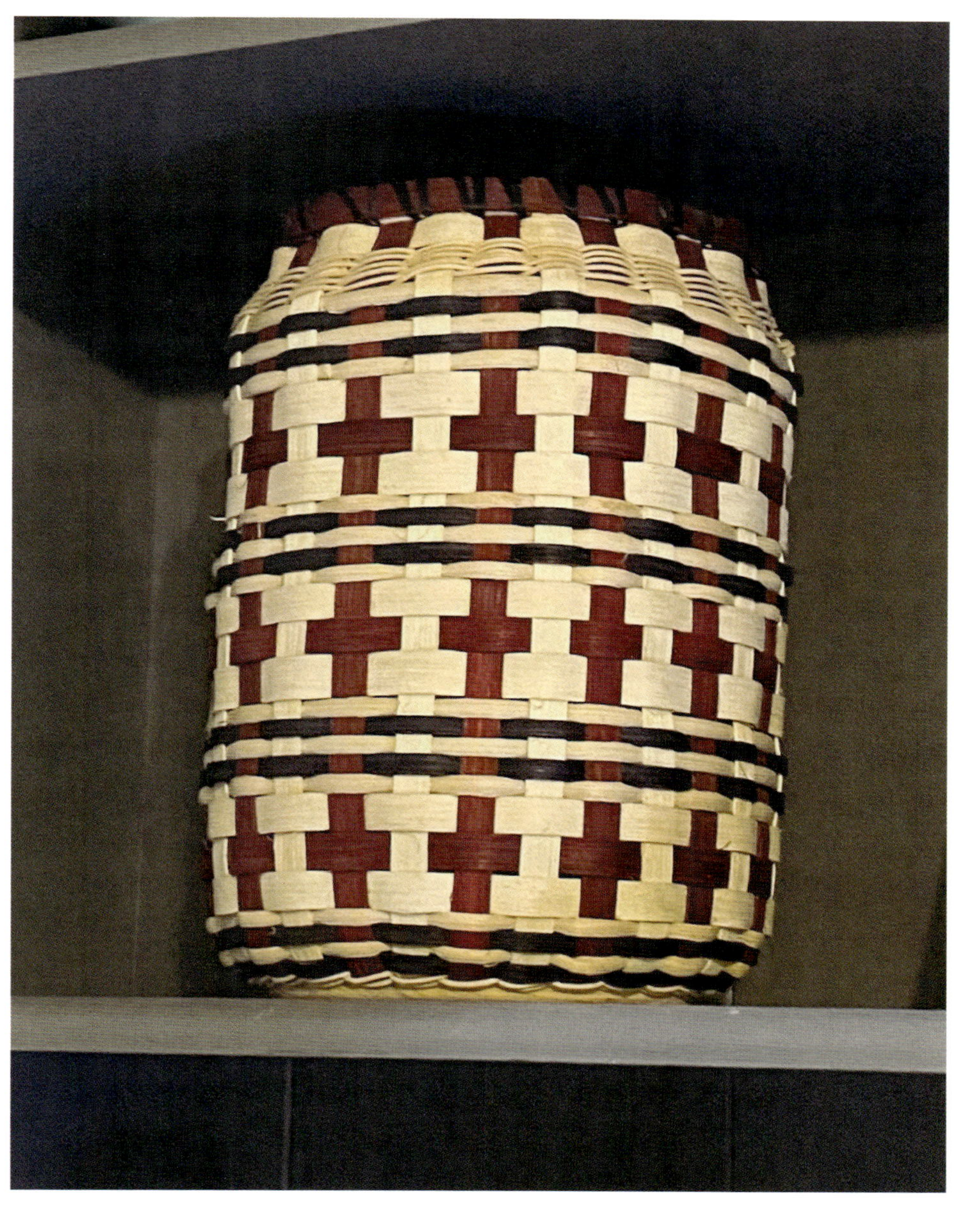

OPPOSITE
Cliff Fragua
Pueblo of Jemez, born 1955
Earth Song, no date
Marble and turquoise
H. 56¾ × W. 21½ × D. 12 in.
Courtesy of the artist

ABOVE
Sue Fish*
Chickasaw/Choctaw, born 1957
Crosses for COVID, 2020
Reed and dye
H. 15 × W. 8 in.
Private collection
** The exhibition includes a similar work by this artist.*

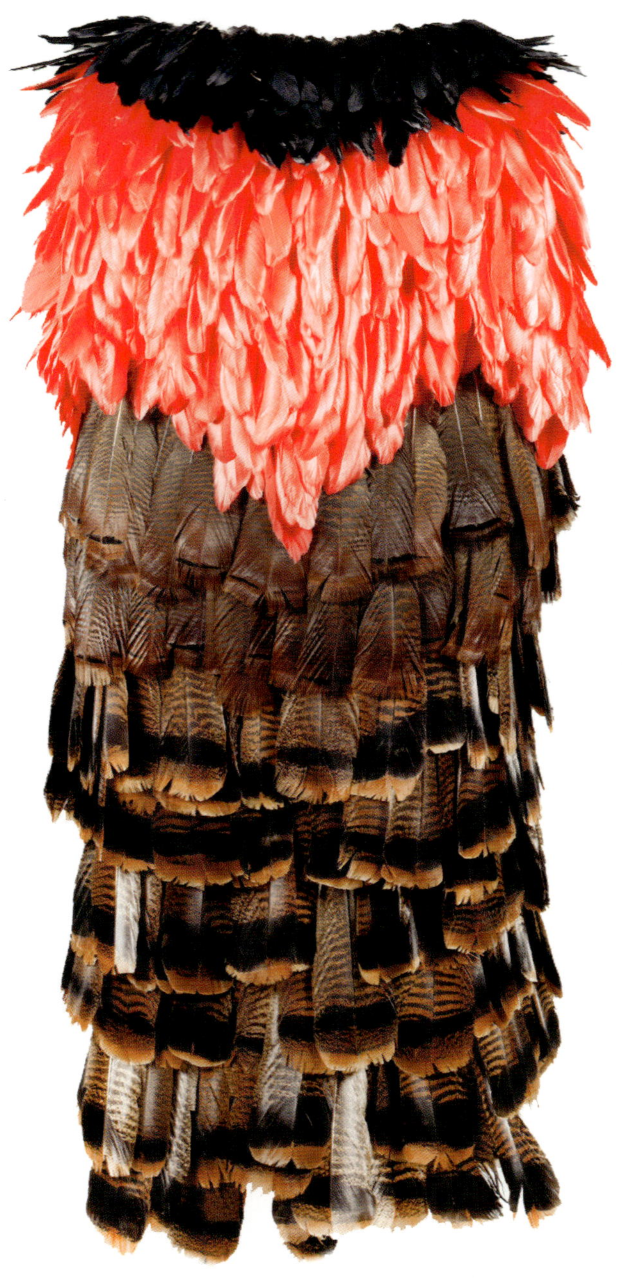

Lisa Rutherford
Cherokee Nation, born 1958
In Times of War (War Chief's Mantle), 2015
Hemp netting, tanned deerskin, wild turkey
feathers, and dyed domestic goose feathers
Dimensions variable
Eiteljorg Museum, Harrison Eiteljorg Purchase
Award, 2015 Indian Market & Festival

Vivian Garner Cottrell*
Cherokee Nation
Rivercane Basket, no date
Rivercane
Dimensions variable
Courtesy of the artist

* *The exhibition includes a similar work by this artist.*

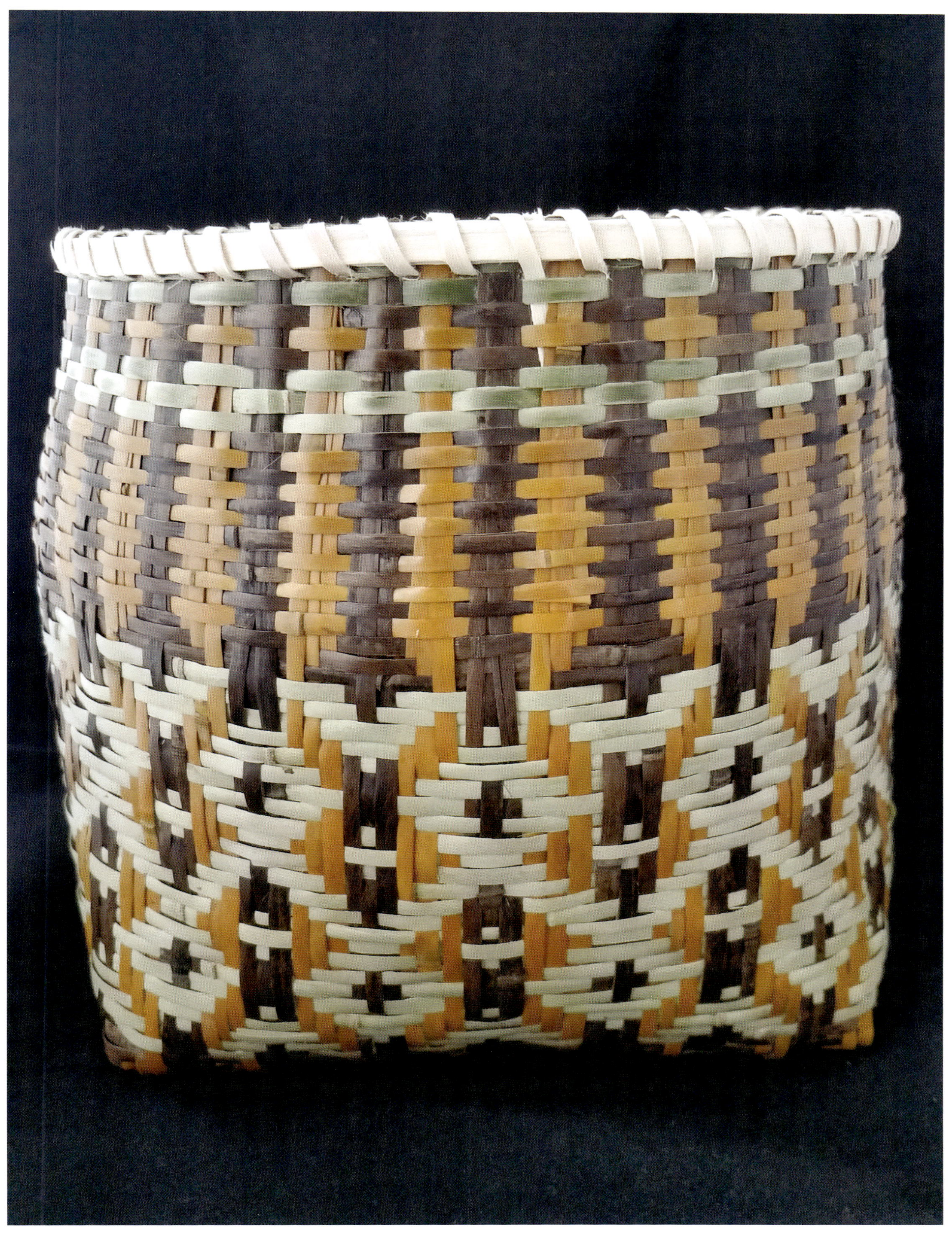

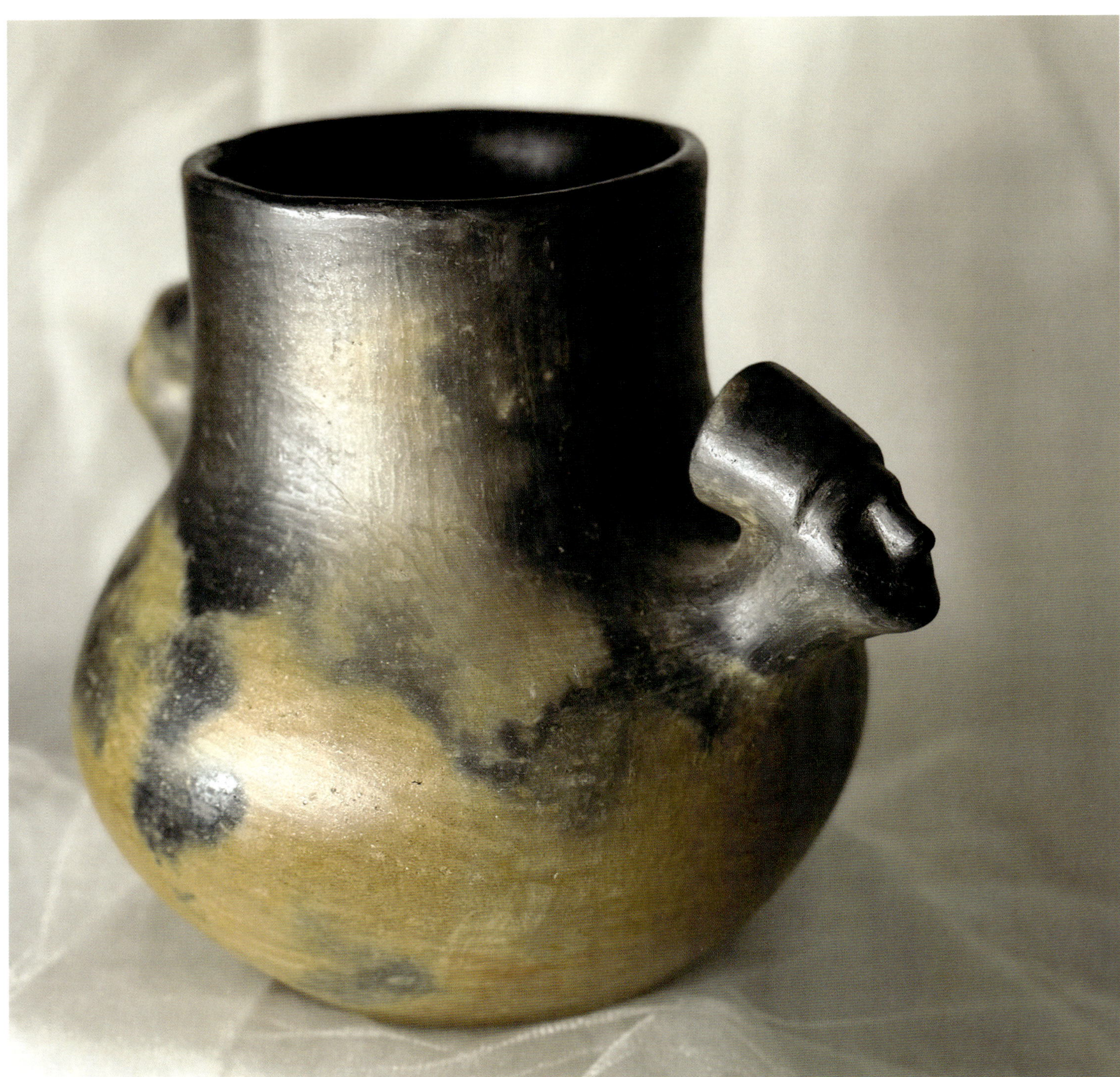

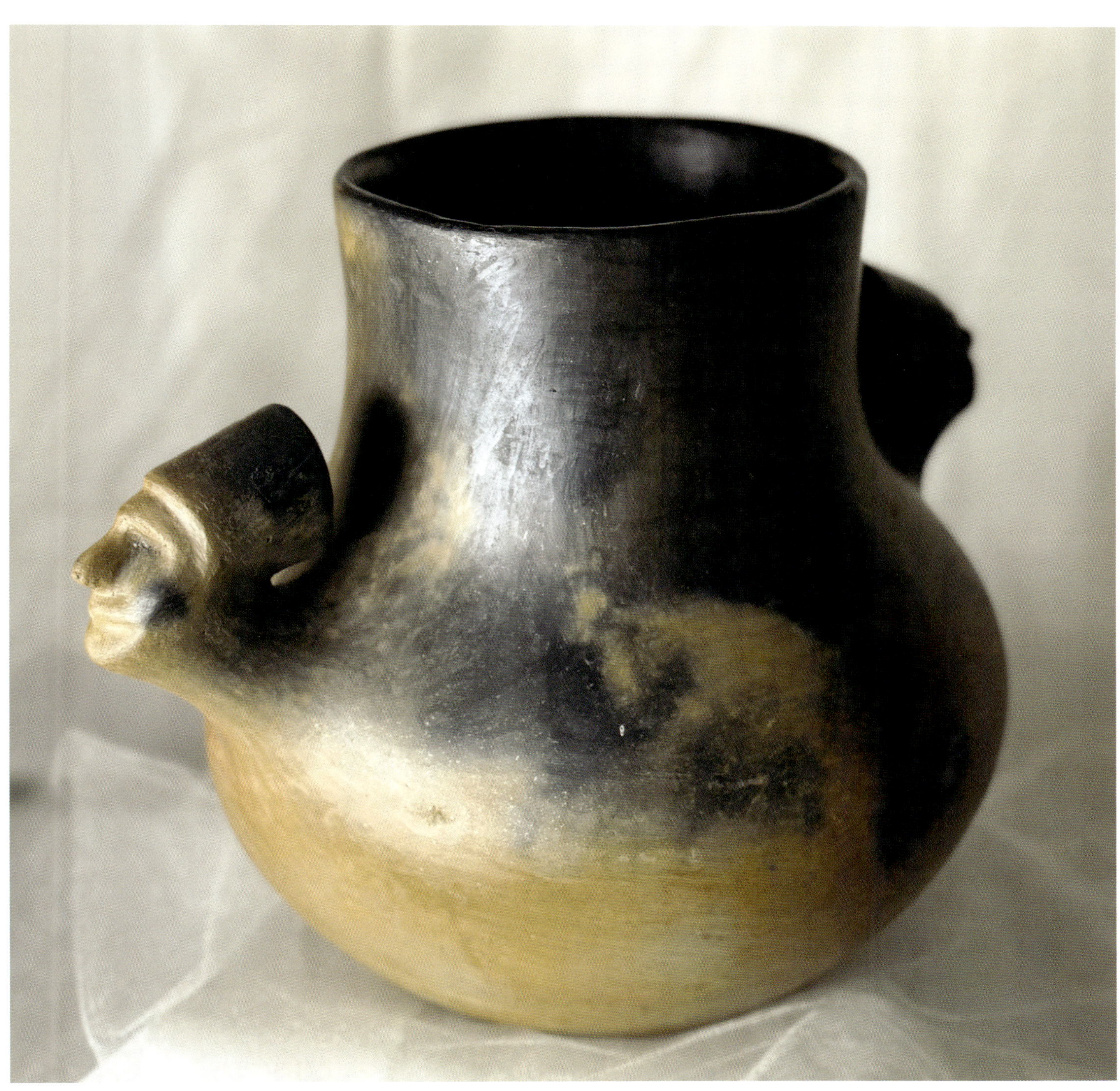

Georgia Harris
Catawba, 1905–1997
Indian Head Jar, no date
Earthenware
H. 8½ × W. 10½ × D. 7½ in.
Collection of the Native American Studies Center,
University of South Carolina Lancaster

Rhonda Holy Bear
Lakota, born 1959
The Last Lakota Horse Raid, 1991
Wood (basswood), native-tanned and commercial leather,
glass beads, pigment, cotton cloth, hair, dentalium shells,
abalone, German silver, metal cones, brass tacks, and beads
H. 30 × W. 13 × D. 9 in.
Collection of Joyce Chelberg

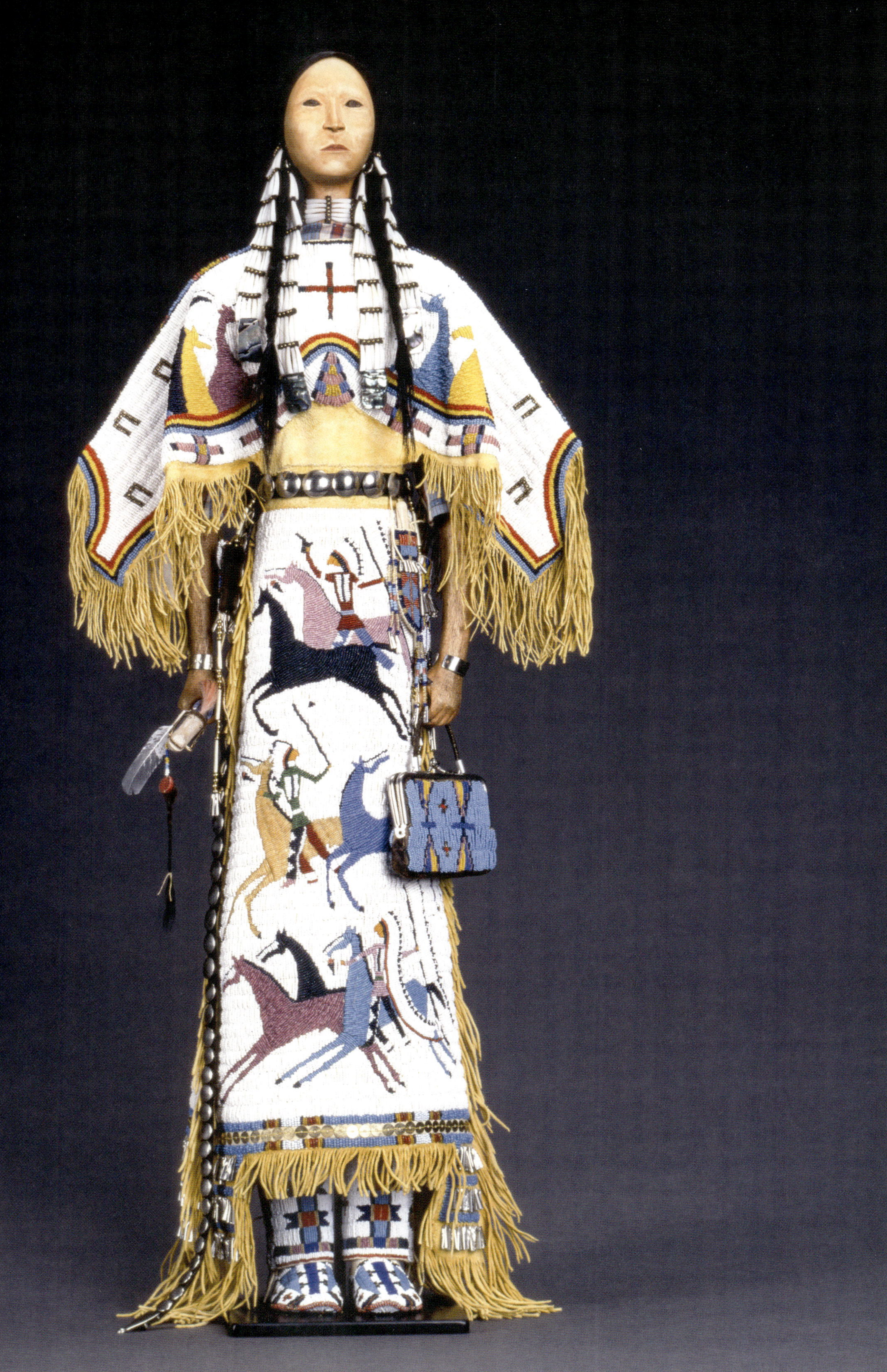

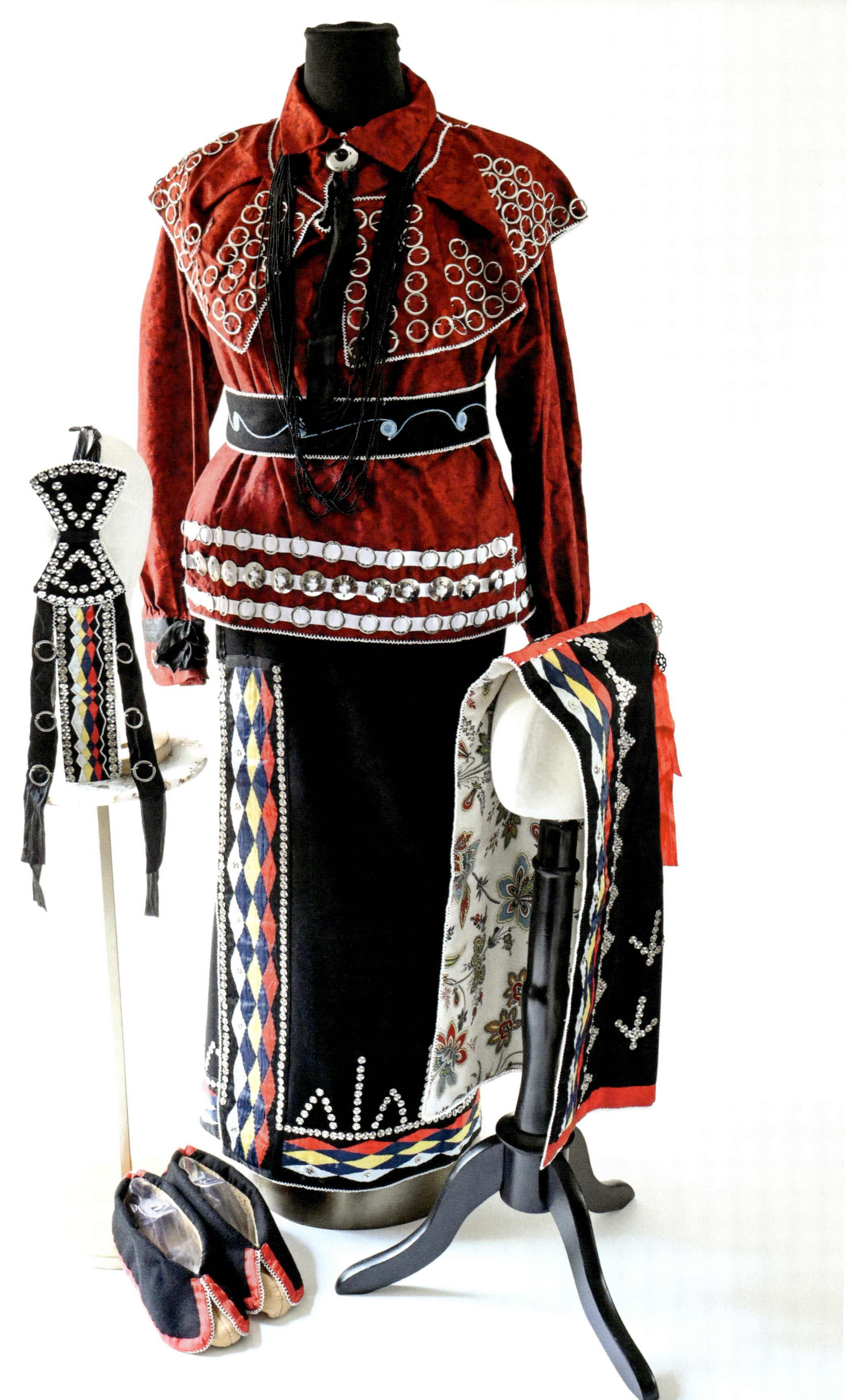

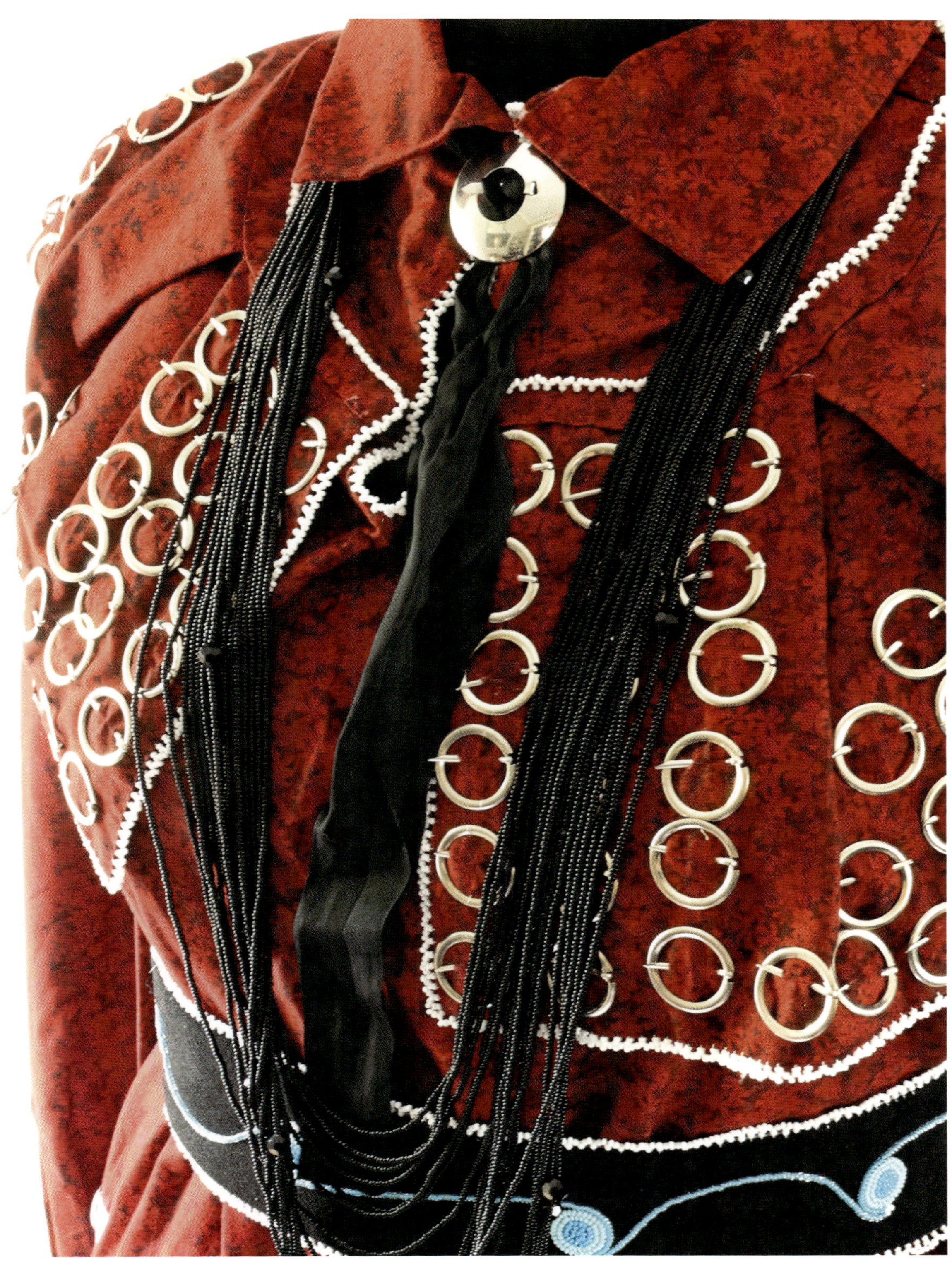

Katrina Mitten
Miami Tribe of Oklahoma, born 1937
She Shimmers, 2022
Wool, silk ribbon, trade silver, sterling silver, brain-tanned and smoked
deer hide, cotton print fabric, and size 11 Czech seed beads
Dimensions variable
Courtesy of the artist

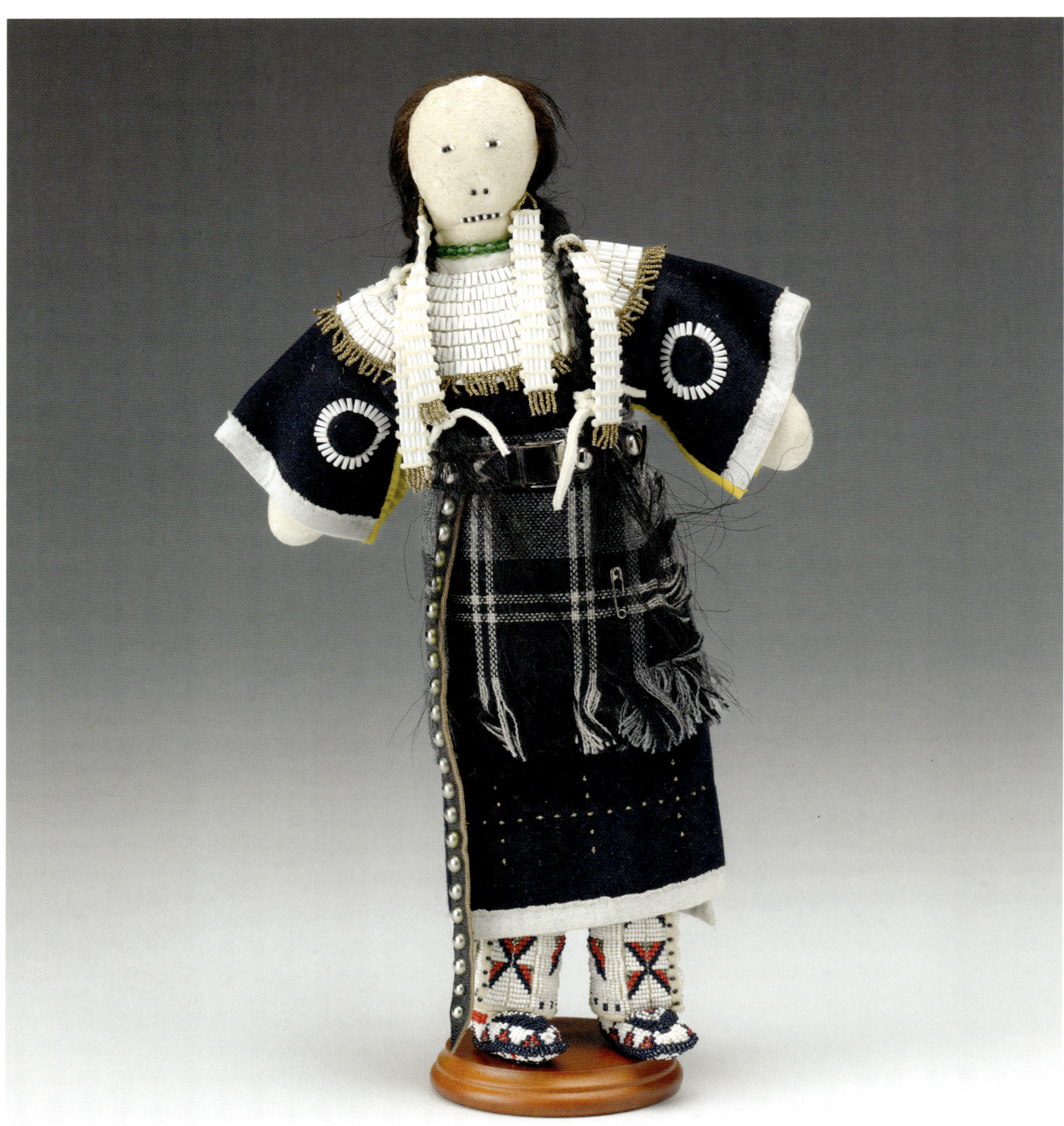

Emil Her Many Horses
Oglala Lakota

Traditional Doll, 1989
Size 13 seed beads, tanned deer hide, wool cloth,
bugle beads, silver metallic beads, and buffalo hide
H. 14 × W. 8 × D. 8 in.
Courtesy of the artist

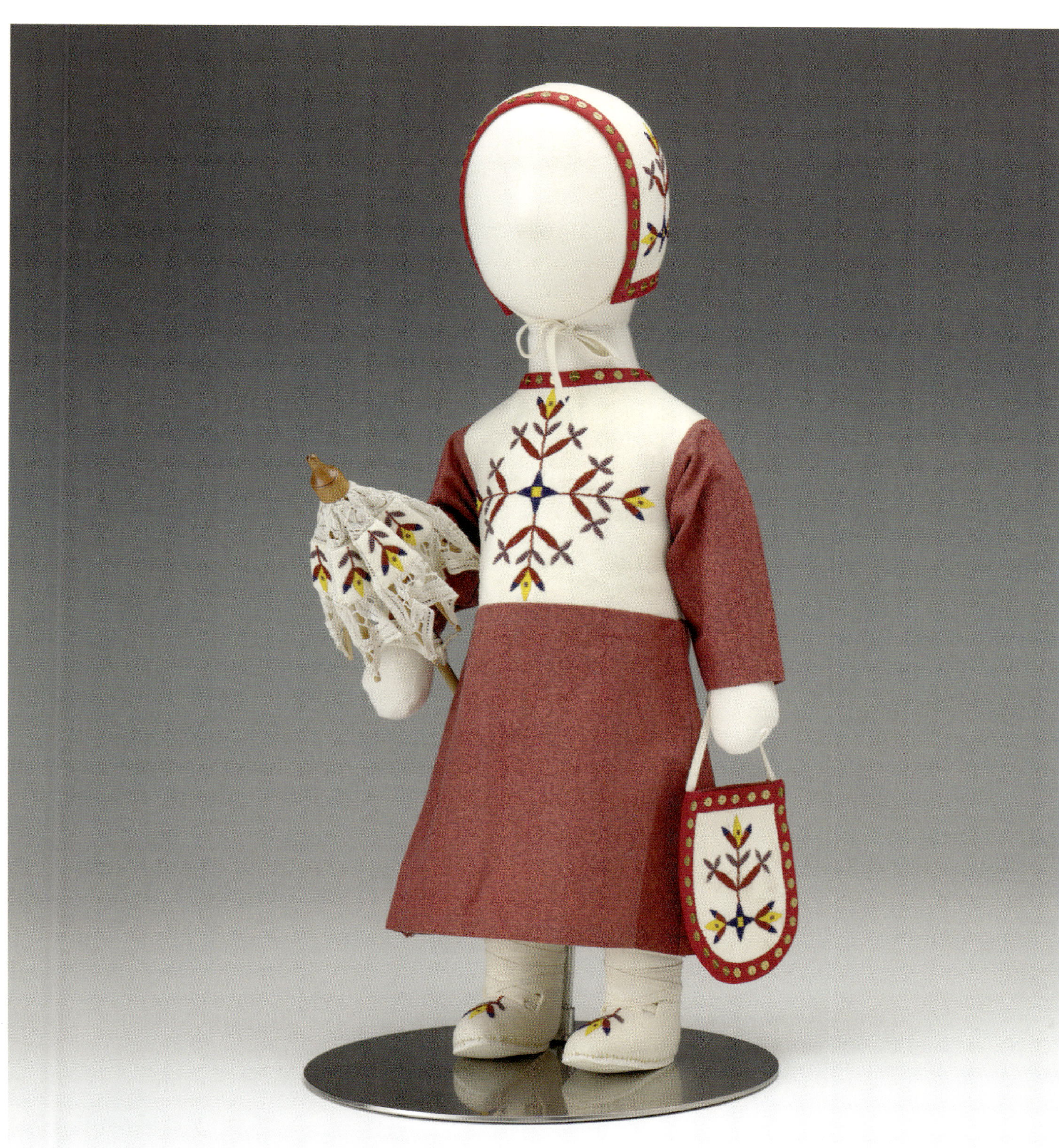

Grandma's Favorite, 2022
Size 13 cut-glass beads, tanned hide, cotton cloth,
and brass sequins
H. 28 × W. 11 × D. 11 in.
Courtesy of the artist

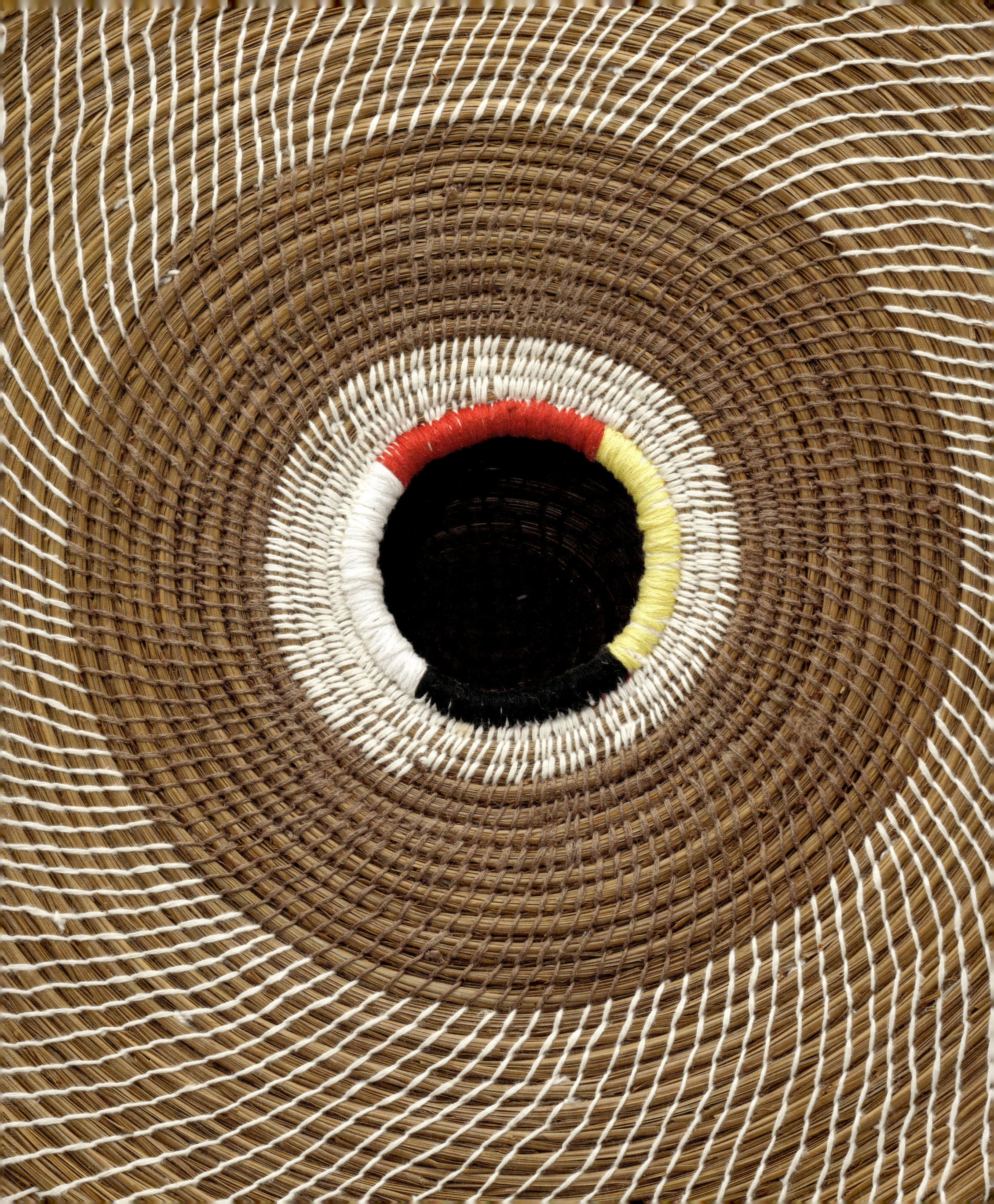

Genealogy

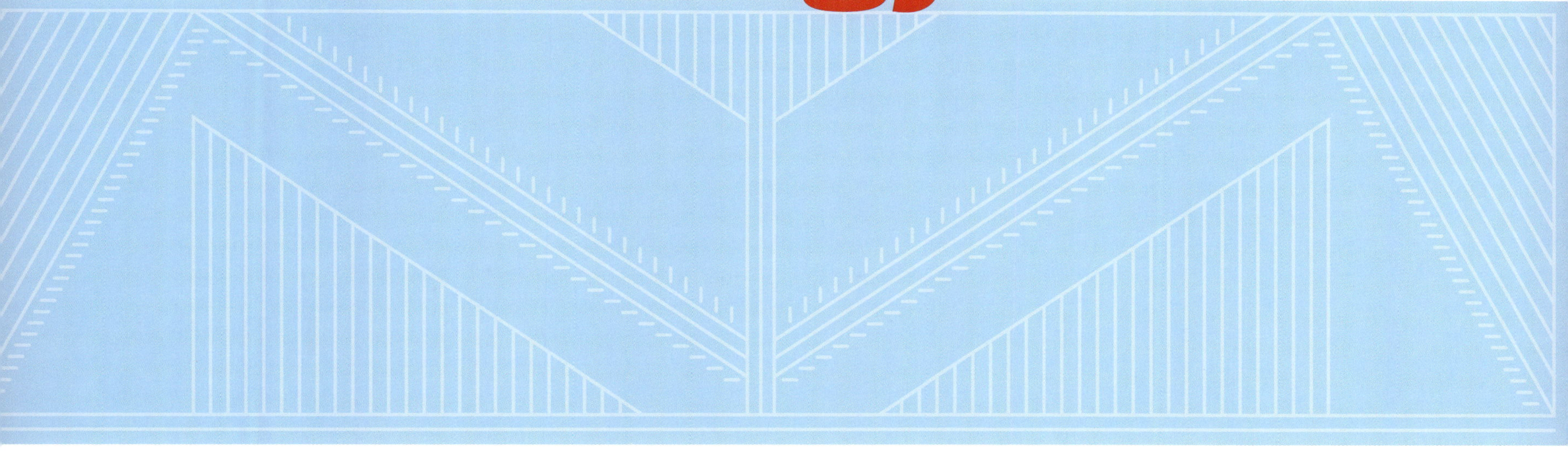

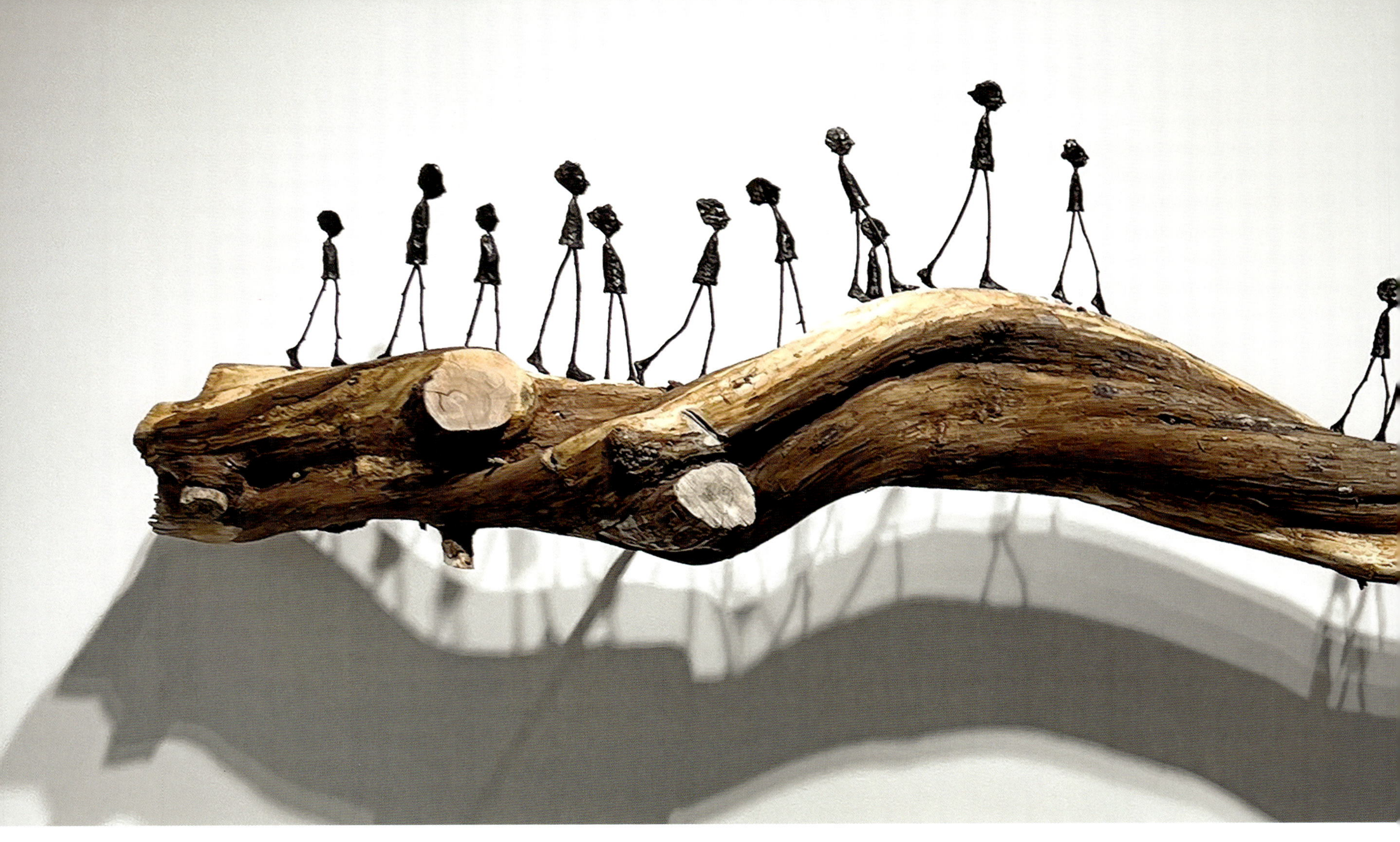

THE GENEALOGY REPRESENTED in this exhibition follows kinship among ancestors and descendants, mentors and mentees, teachers and students, mothers and daughters, partners, and families. **Genealogy** is fundamental to the process by which artistic and cultural knowledge is taught and shared. The artistic fingerprint of one person can be found present in the work of those they inspire. There is intimacy with, a driving focus around, and a respect for someone who shares or influences another's work. These connections leave semblances, traits, and homages to experiences and relationships in the resulting beautiful and compelling works of art. Coming together to learn about traditional and even nontraditional practices is critical to cultural survival and evolution. Native artists who have reached a pinnacle in their skill understand and honor the responsibility to pass this knowledge on to others. Genealogical bonds and relationships inform the evolution of process, materials, tools, and representation within systems of Indigenous kinship traditions.

Harlen Chavis Jr. (Lumbee) has a strong connection to his ancestors' art. Cultural objects from his people's past are easily found on his ancestral land in rural Maxton, North Carolina. Fragmented pieces of aged green copper; shards of incised pottery; and bone, clay, and glass trade beads are scattered about the landscape, which is dotted with ancient mounds. A former welder by trade, Chavis is inspired by his ancestors. He spends considerable time researching mound-building cultural materials like shell gorgets, copper accessories, and ceramic jewelry to energize his work. He has translated his welding skills into jewelry making to create beautifully engraved copper pieces that reflect his ancestors' ancient past (p. 85). "I regard ancestral art as heirlooms. When I create this work, I feel that I am immortalizing them, I am privileging their designs and materials that continues to represent our Indigenous identity and culture. Through my art, I feel that I am activating blood memory, which allows me to honor who I am and where I come from. I am in essence walking in their footsteps by both living on the same land and continuing their legacy of art making. I am a continuation of their story. They inspire me every day, and I hope my art makes them proud."

A strong, creative, intellectual maternal lineage flows through mother Roxanne Swentzell and daughter Rose B. Simpson. They've descended from a long line of Kha'po Owingeh (Santa Clara Pueblo) potters, including Swentzell's grandmother Rose and her mother, Rina. Both Swentzell and

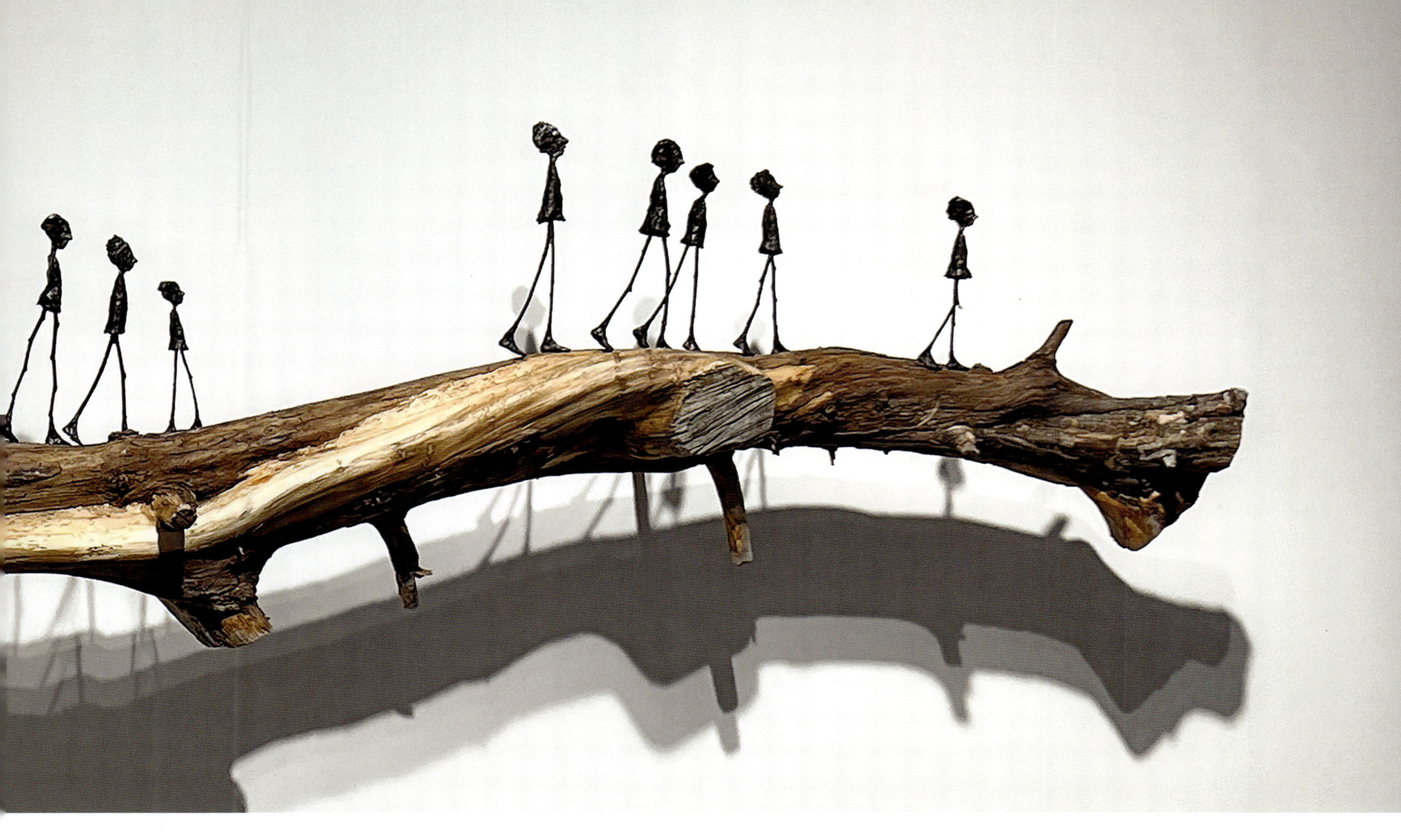

Simpson have used their command of clay to move from traditional forms of Kha'po Owingeh pottery to sculpt figurative and human forms that are intentionally imprinted with personal, political, and social commentary. Swentzell was given clay as a child to help her communicate better with her family. Now she uses her voice found in clay to create expressive figures that communicate directly with the viewer (p. 94). This conversation invites ideas and questions about topics such as consumerism, motherhood, femininity, and Kha'po Owingeh sacred values.

The cerebral and emotional underpinning of her work carried forward to her daughter. Simpson uses her work to express similar ideas, yet it also holds a strong conviction for female empowerment. Simpson's work extends beyond clay to include other media, such as metal. Perhaps her most unexpected yet beautifully connected piece to ceramics is the El Camino car she transformed into the artwork *Maria* (pp. 78–79). It is a touching tribute to famed P'Ohwhoge Owingeh (San Ildefonso) potter Maria Martinez. Simpson's initial use of the car to harvest crops made a moving correlation of the bed of the truck to a vessel, essentially a utilitarian pot. This inspired her to completely restore the car and paint it in the signature shiny-on-matt-black finish revitalized by Maria and her husband, Julian Martinez.

This allows viewers to make the direct association between Martinez's pottery (p. 163) and the car itself as a vessel.

There are many more examples of **genealogy** in *To Take Shape and Meaning*. Look for the genealogical fingerprint in the accessories and gowns of partners Kenneth Williams Jr. (Northern Arapaho/Cattaraugus Seneca) and Orlando Dugi (Navajo) (pp. 87 and 116), the glass sculptures of good friends Preston Singletary (Tlingit) and Marcus Amerman (Choctaw) (pp. 29, 57, 144, and 160–61), and the weavings of mother and daughter Kelly Church and Cherish Parrish (Ottawa/Pottawatomi/Matchi-be-nash-she-wish) (pp. 35 and 93).

PAGE 74: Detail of image on page 82

ABOVE: Large detail of image on pages 96–97

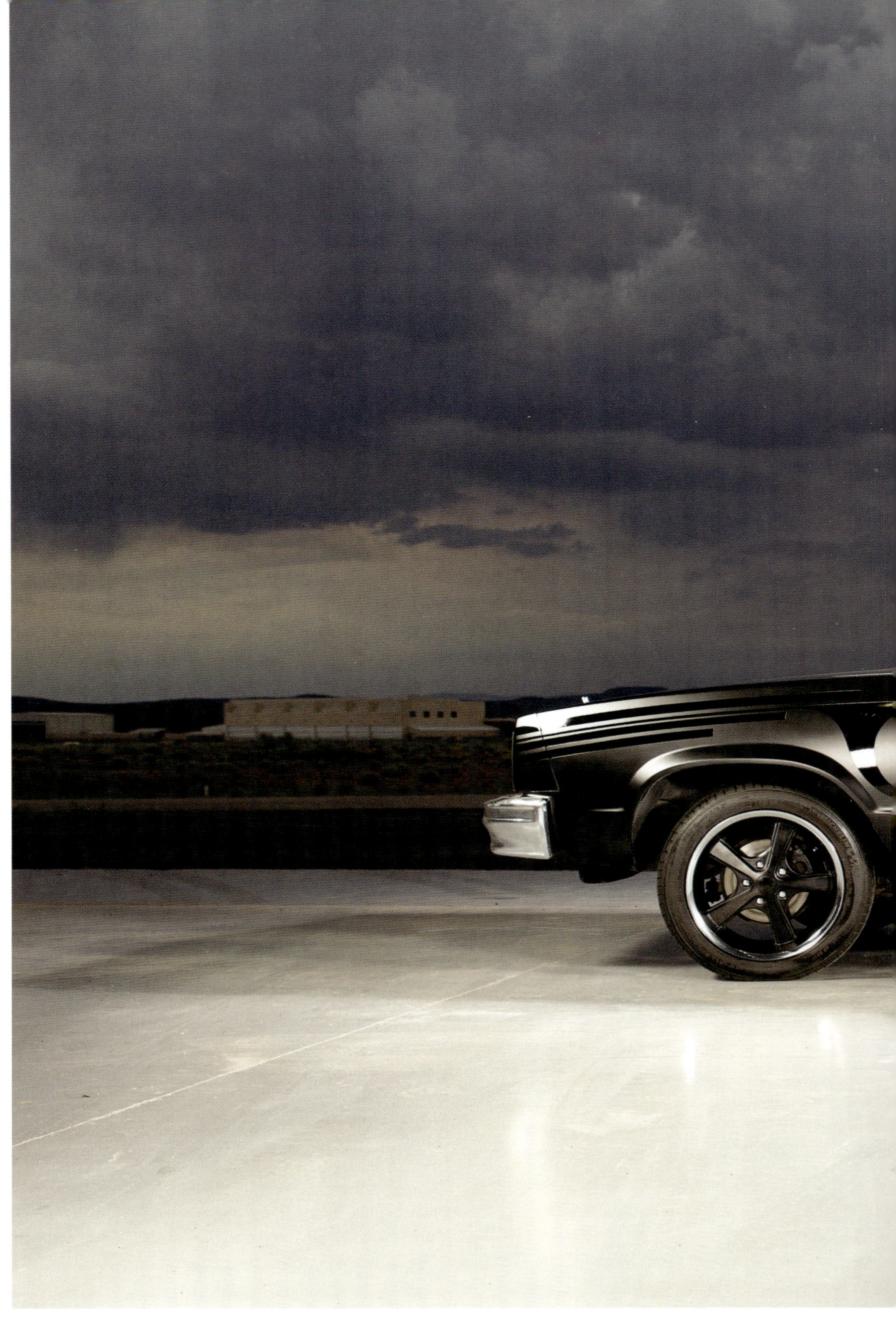

Rose B. Simpson
Santa Clara Pueblo, born 1983
Maria, 2014
1985 Chevy El Camino
H. 54 × W. 72 × D. 202 in.
Courtesy of the artist

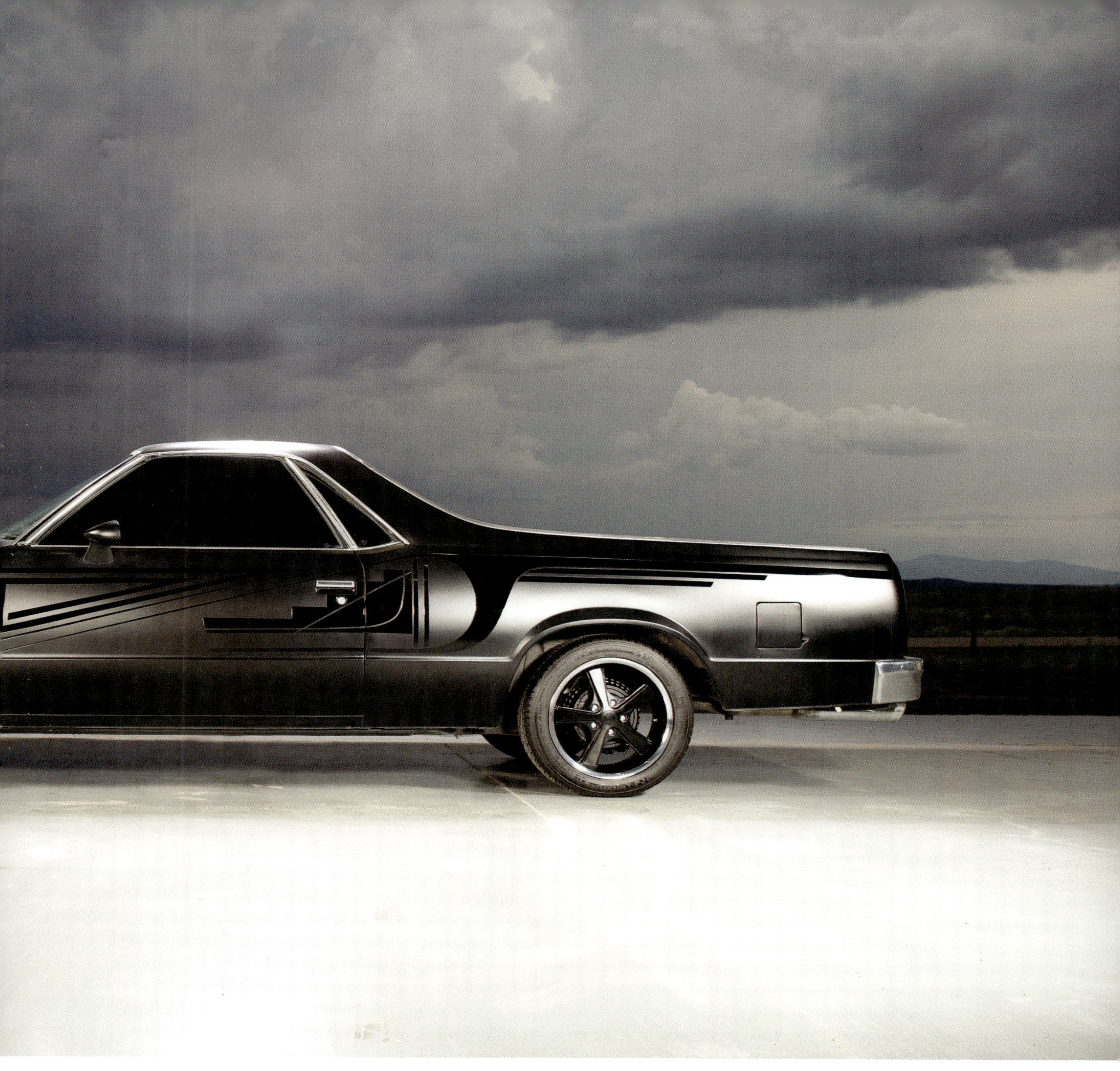

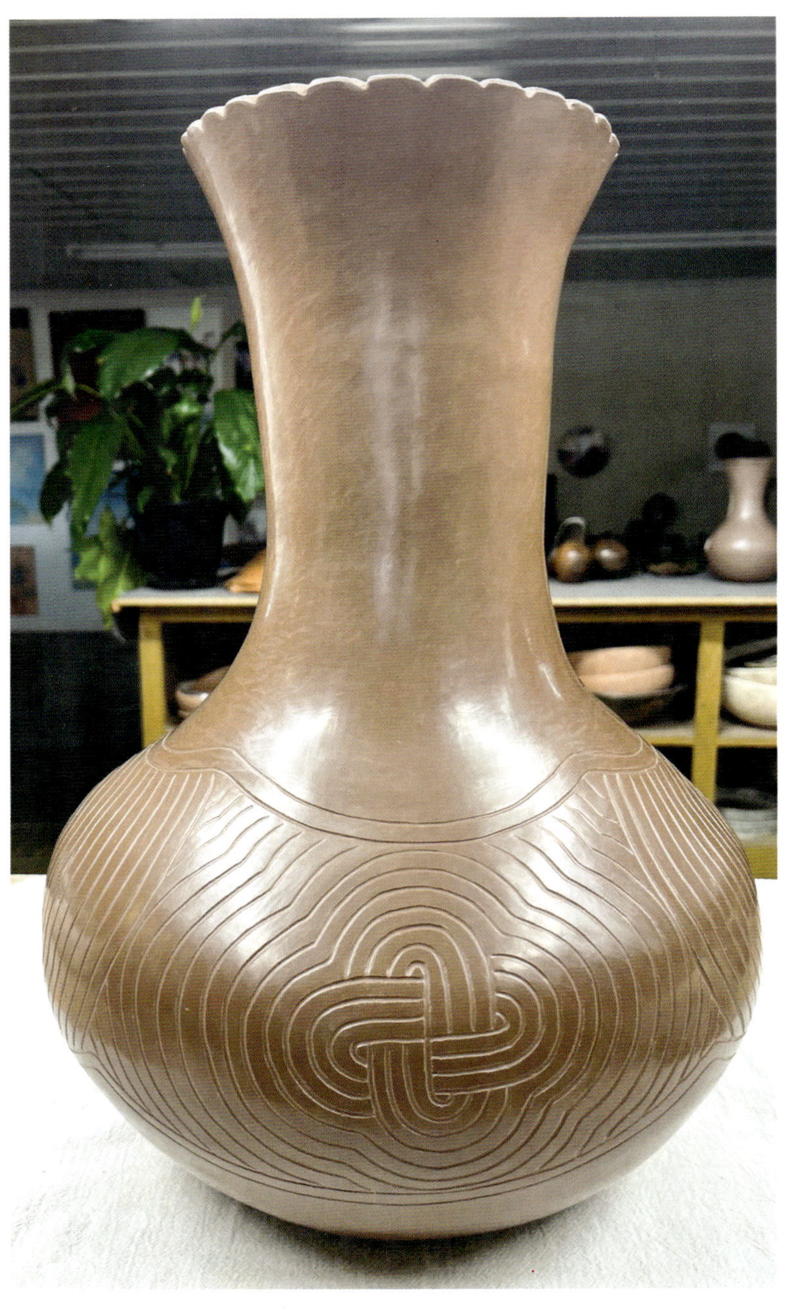

ABOVE

Jane Osti
Cherokee, born 1945
Pot, 2023
Ceramic
Dimensions variable
Courtesy of the artist

OPPOSITE

Richard Zane Smith
Wyandot Nation of Kansas, born 1955
tribute to my ancestors, 2022
Hand-dug and processed Oklahoma clay painted
with clay slips
H. 17½ × Diam. 13 in.
Courtesy of the artist

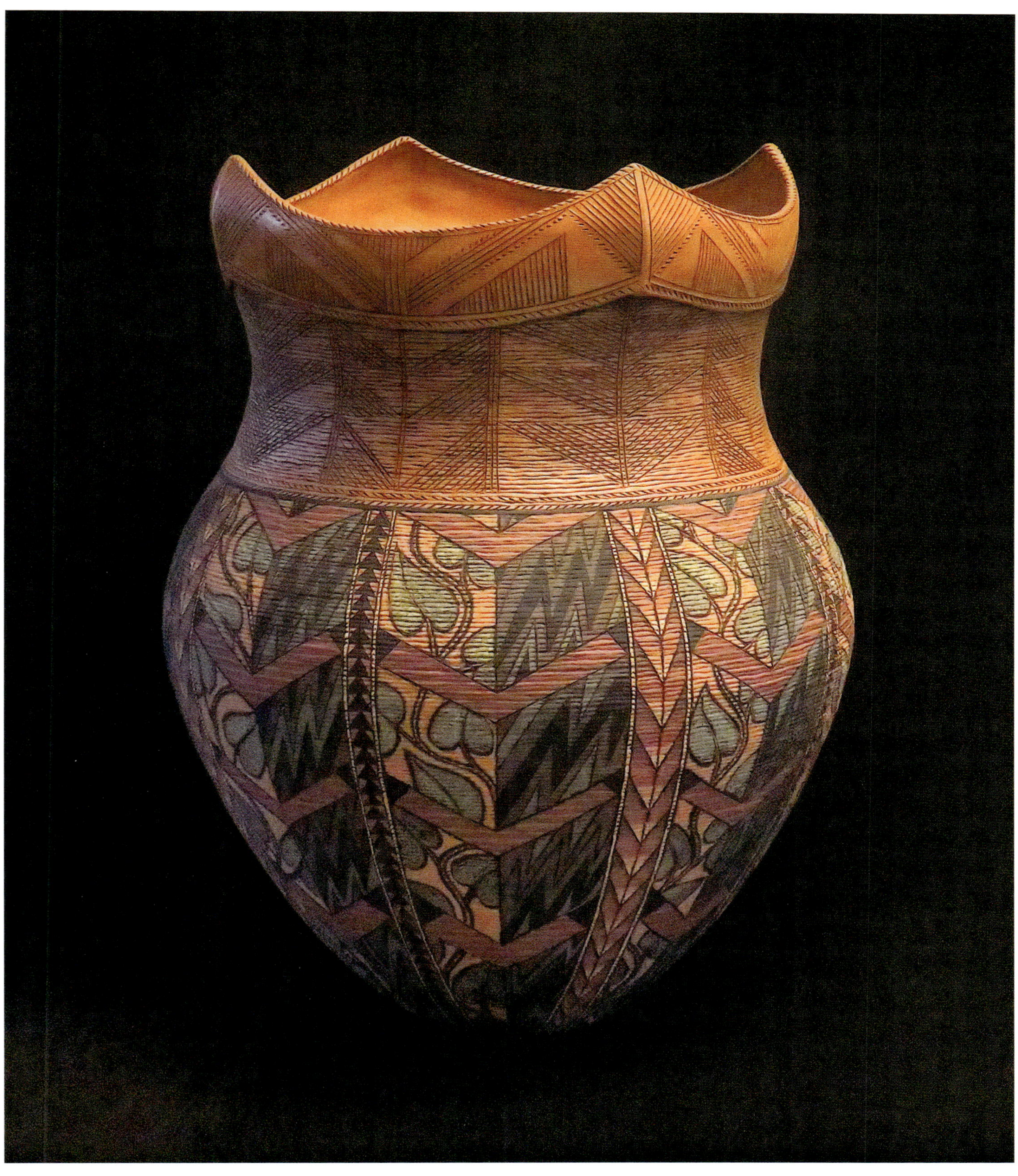

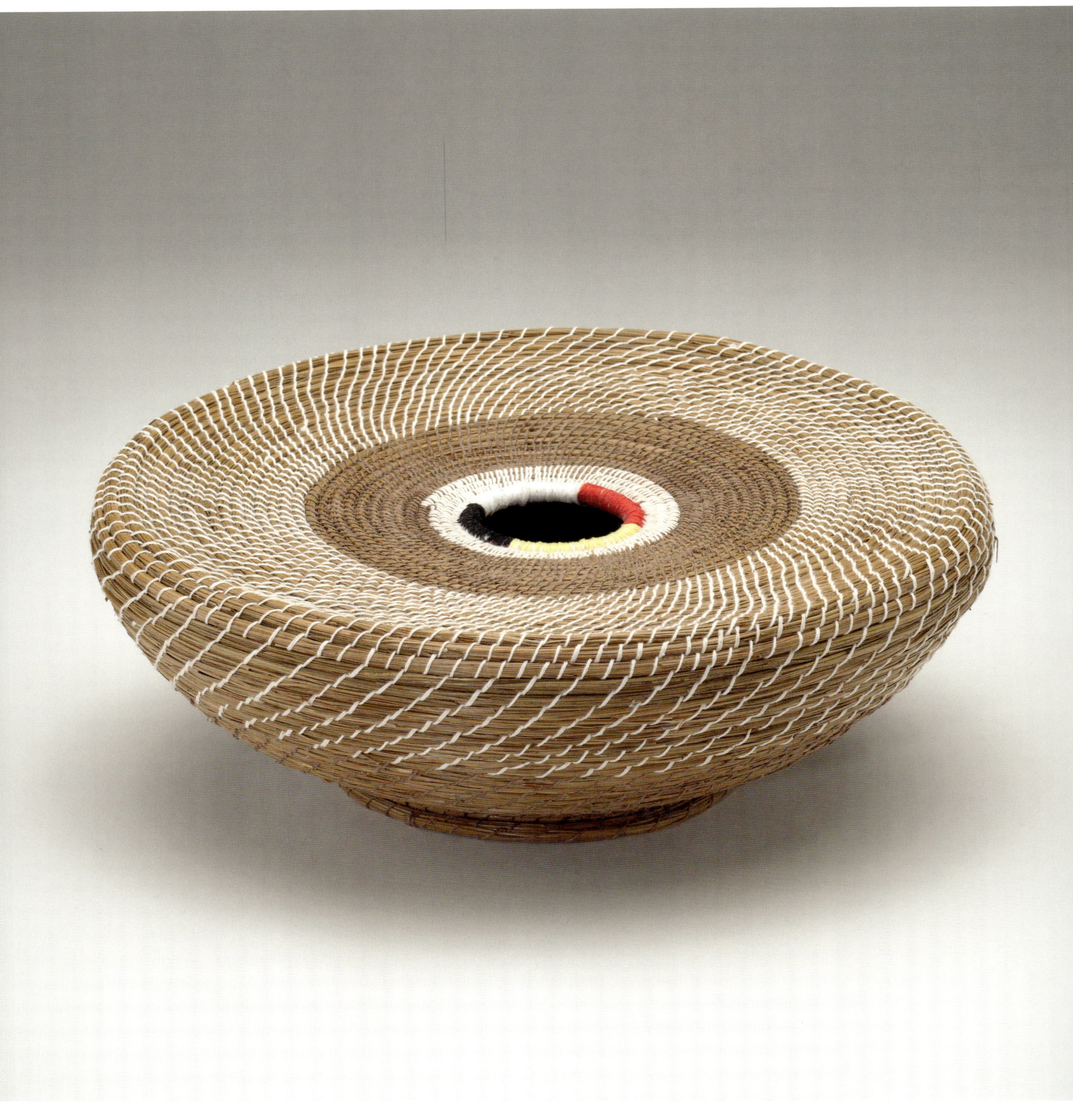

Gloria Tara Lowery
Lumbee, 1944–2020
Seed Basket, 2014
Longleaf pine needles
H. 6 × Diam. 16 in.
Collection of the Museum of the Southeast American Indian

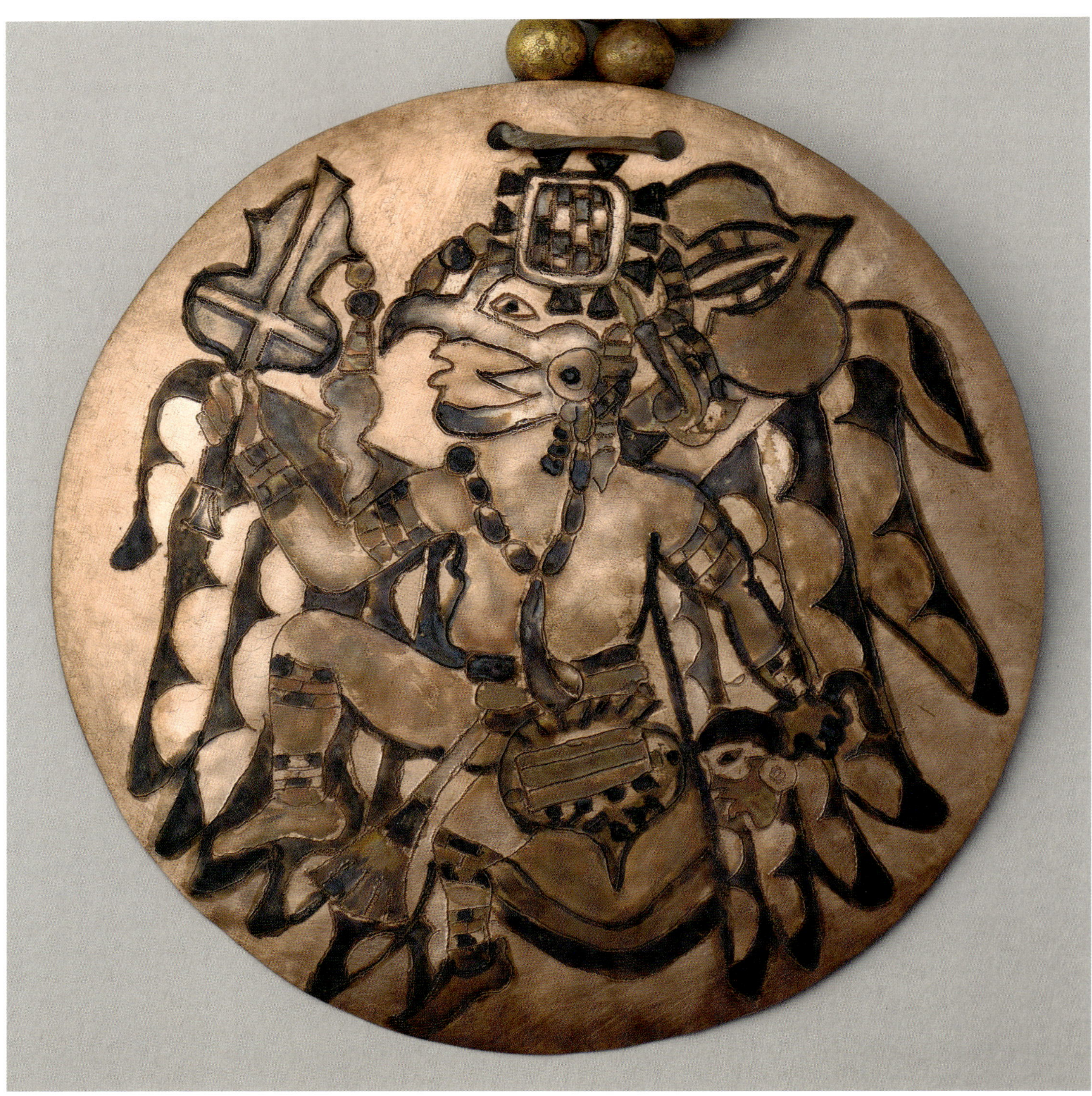

Harlen Chavis Jr.
Lumbee
Mississippian Gorget, 2022
Copper and artificial sinew
H. 22 × W. 5½ in.
Collection of the Museum of the Southeast American Indian

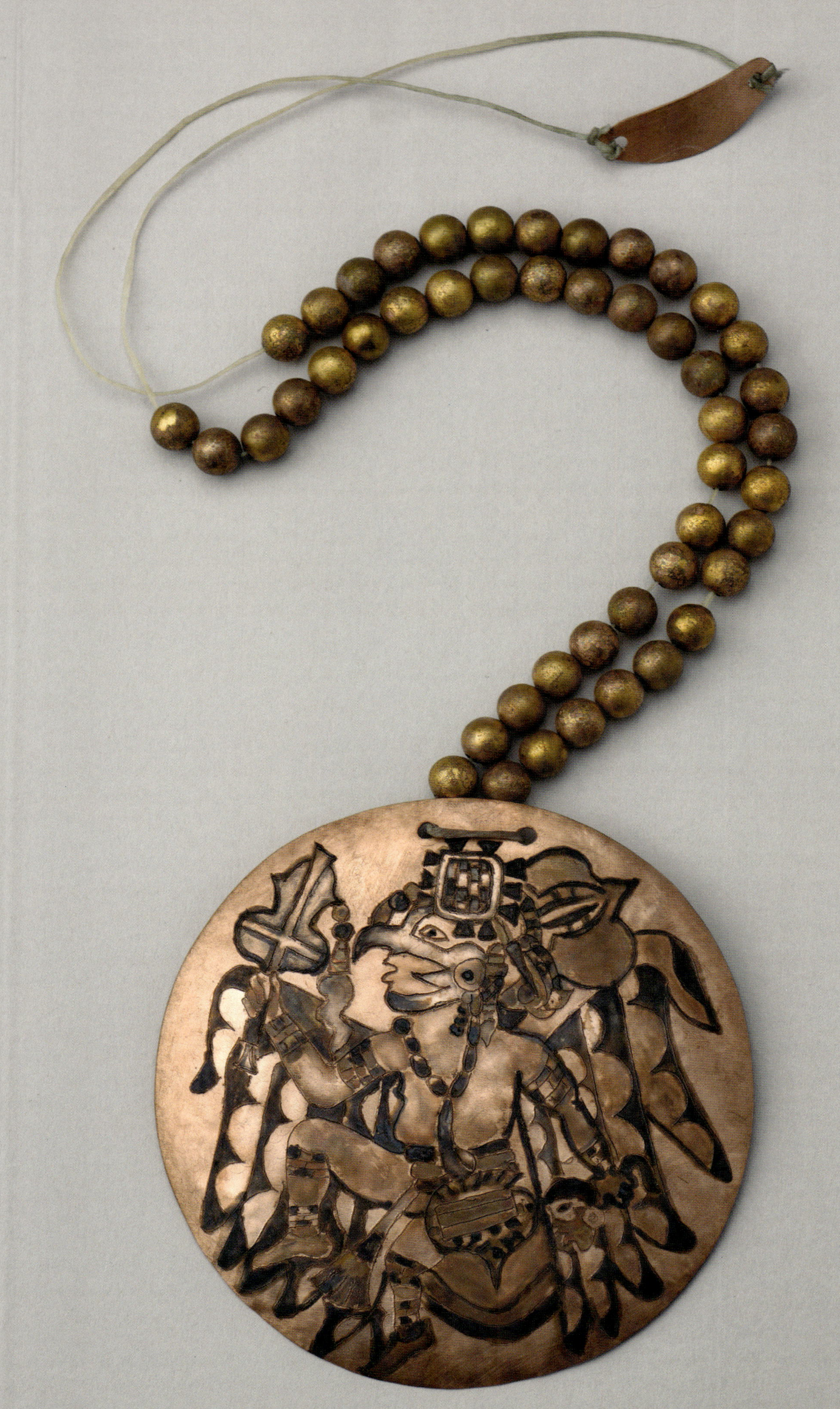

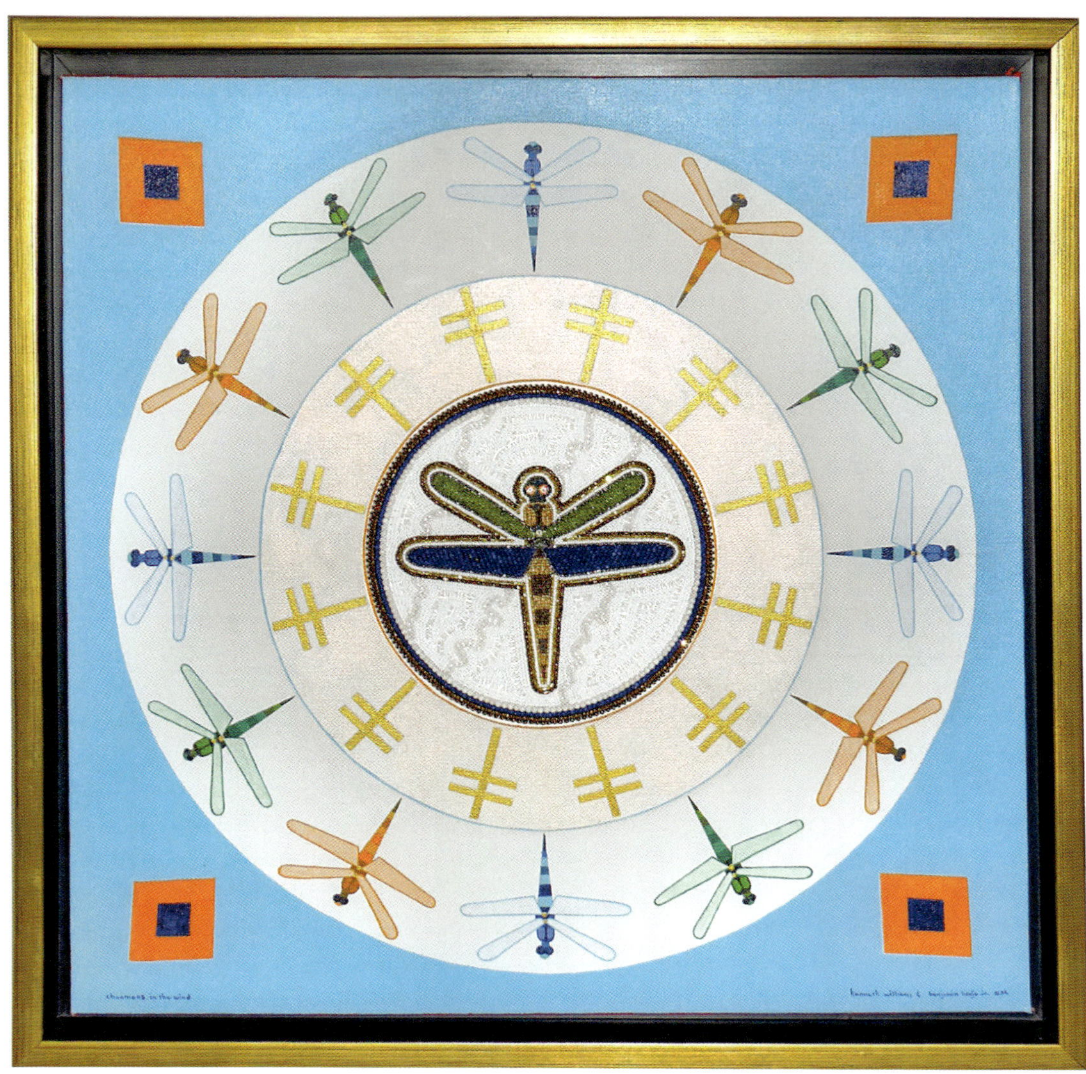

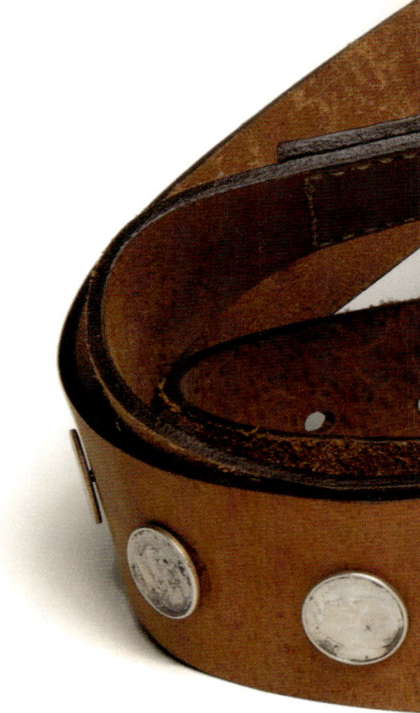

Benjamin Harjo Jr.
Seminole/Absentee Shawnee, 1945–2023
Kenneth Williams Jr.
Northern Arapaho/Cattaraugus Seneca, born 1983
Charmers in the Wind, 2022
Acrylic, canvas, 24K gold-plate beads, vintage and contemporary glass beads,
jade, lapis, white coral beads, and Austrian crystals
H. 22½ × W. 22½ × D. 2 in. (frame)
Courtesy of Ken Williams Jr. and Barbara Harjo

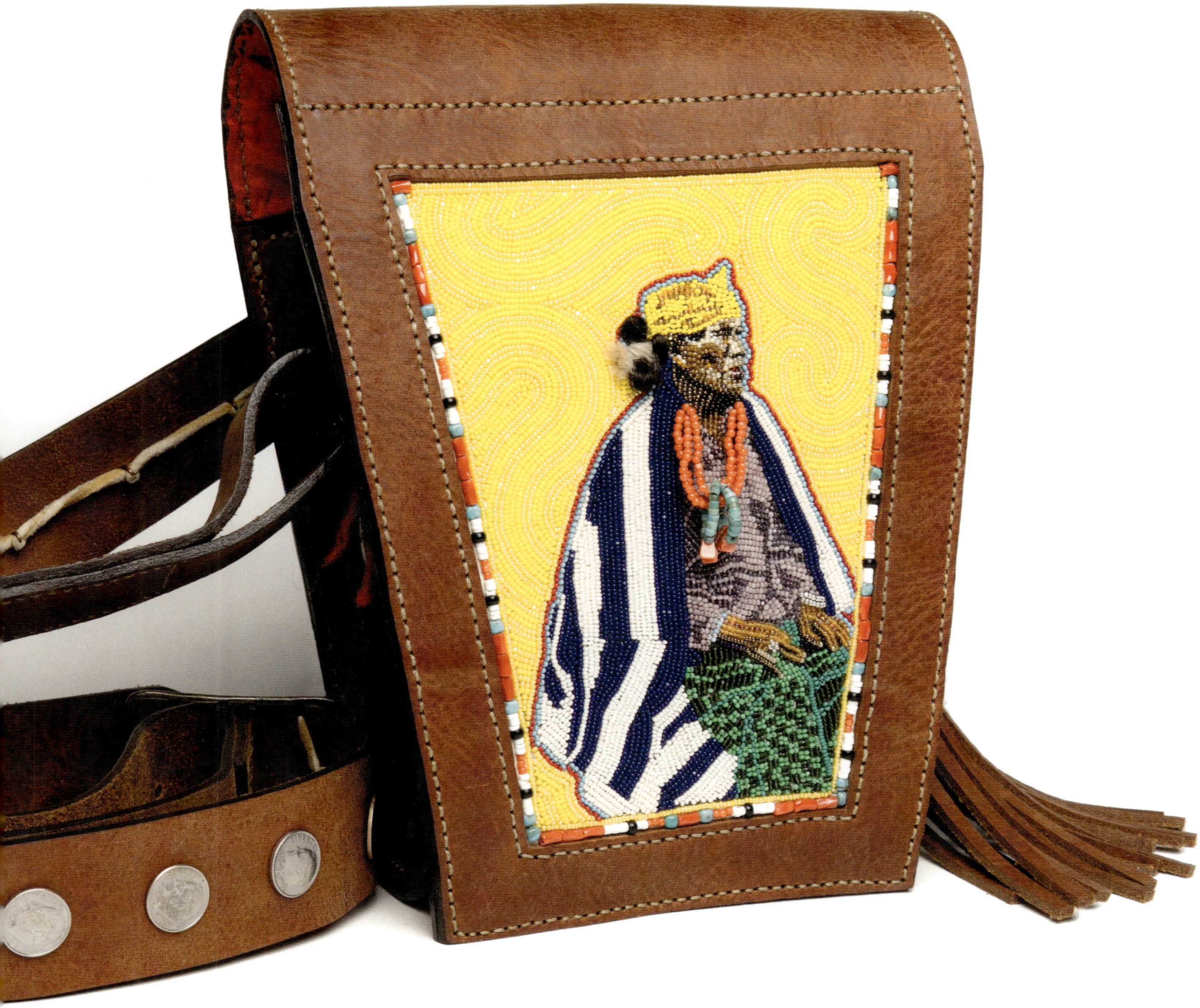

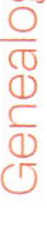

Kenneth Williams Jr.
Northern Arapaho/Cattaraugus Seneca, born 1983
Orlando Dugi
Navajo
Bandolier Bag, no date
Leather, glass, silk, shell, copper, and wool
H. 34 × W. 9 in.
Collection of the Wheelwright Museum of the American Indian, 2019.11.001

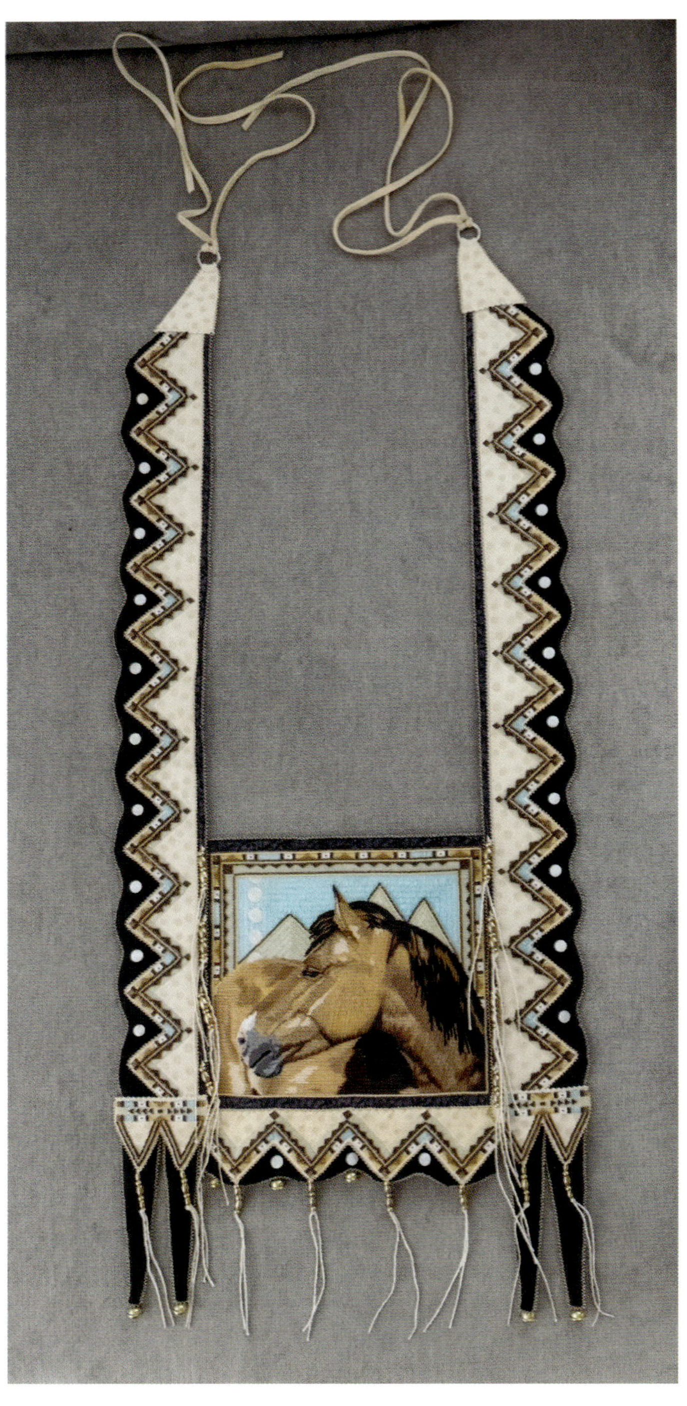

ABOVE

Jackie Larson Bread*
Blackfeet Nation, born 1960
Blackfeet Horse Collar, 2022
Beadwork and traditional painting
on buckskin and wool cloth, with brass
and mother-of-pearl accents
H. 48 × W. 19 in.
Courtesy of the artist
** The exhibition includes a similar work by this artist.*

OPPOSITE

Martha Berry
Cherokee Nation, born 1948
When the Highlands Met the Mounds, 2019
Glass seed beads, wool "Graham of Montrose
Ancient" clan tartan, cotton, silk, wool yarn
(to the extent possible, all materials are authentic
to the late 18th century)
H. 36 × W. 16 × D. 2 in.
Courtesy of the artist

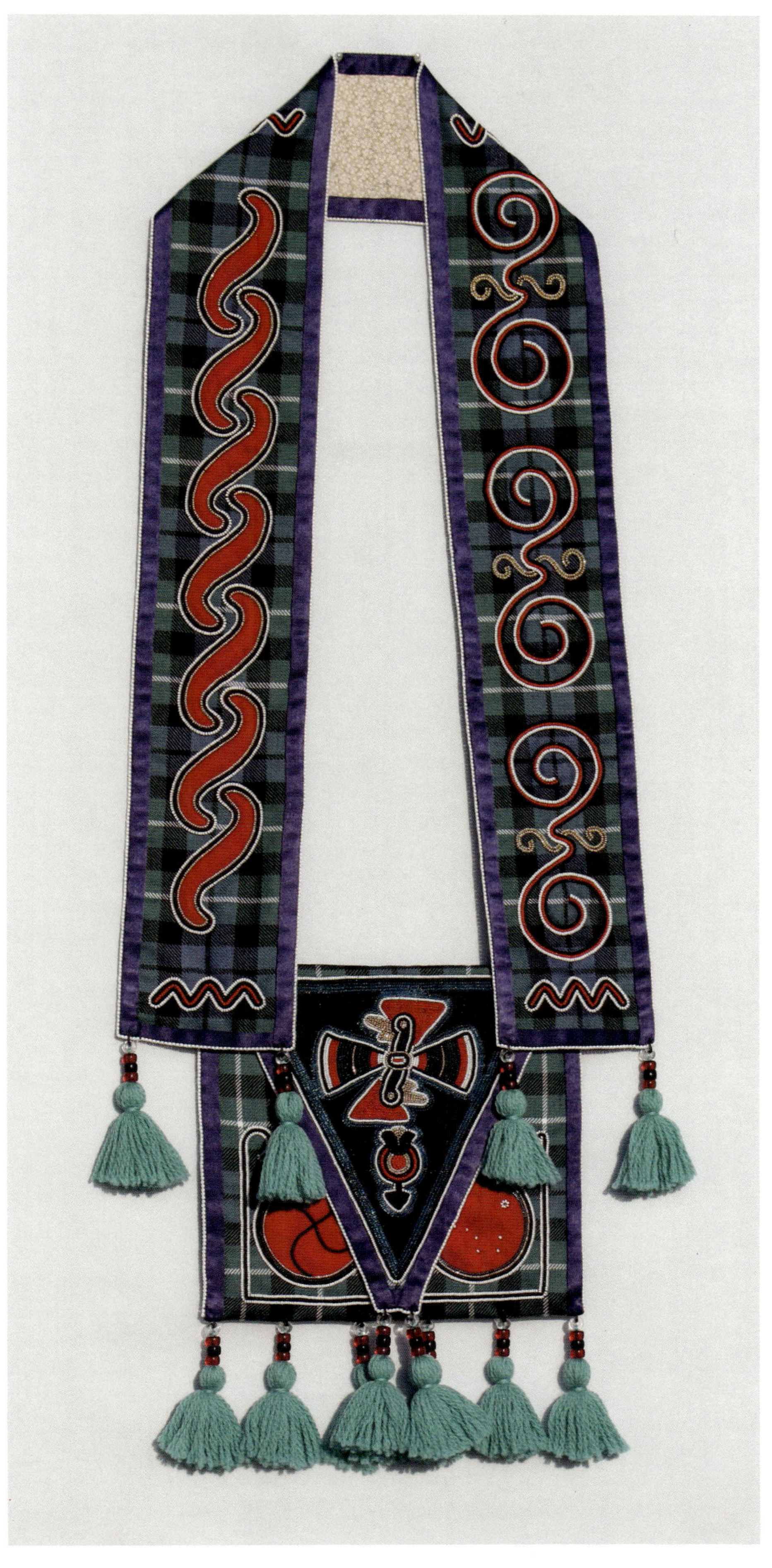

89

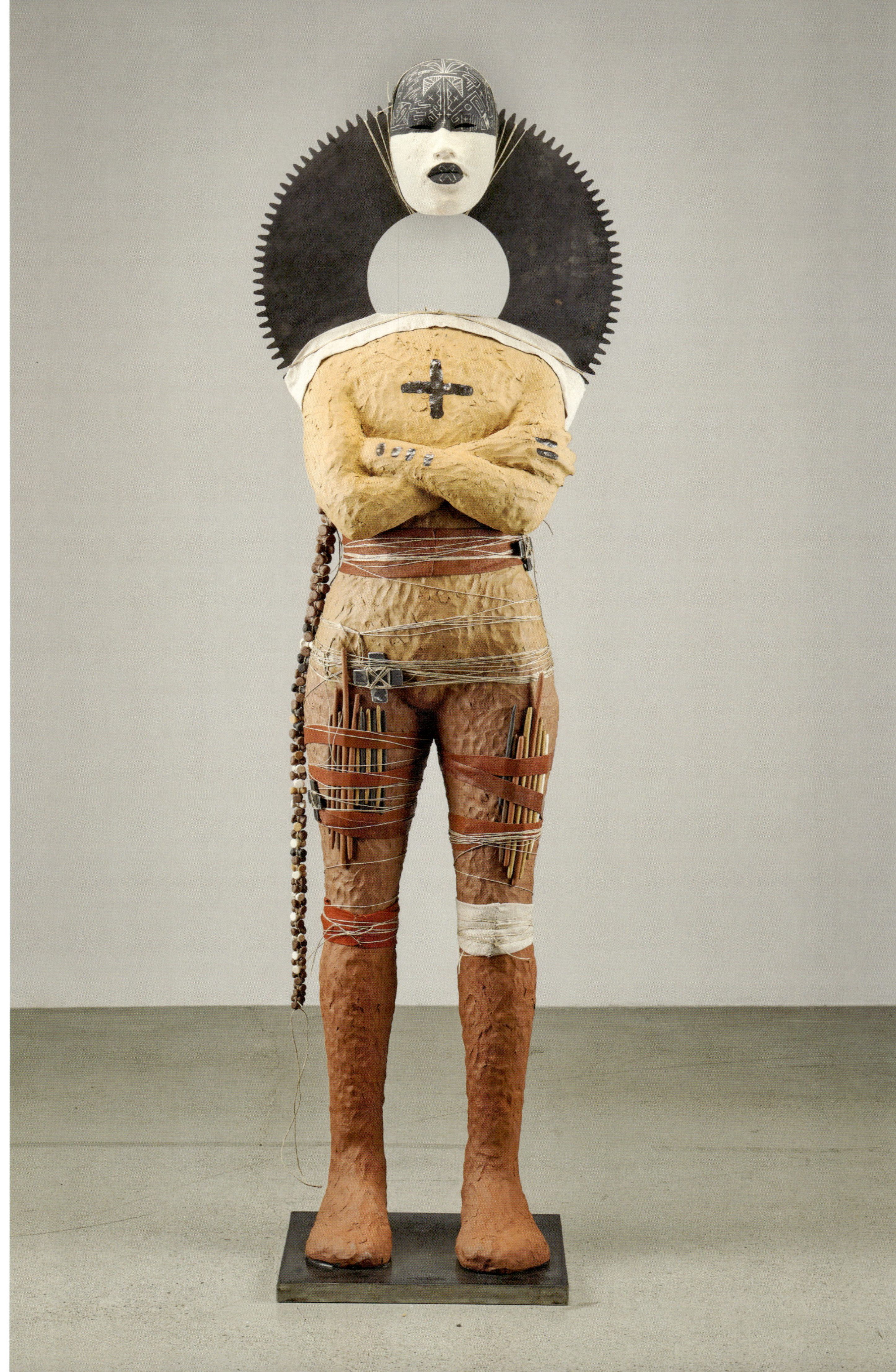

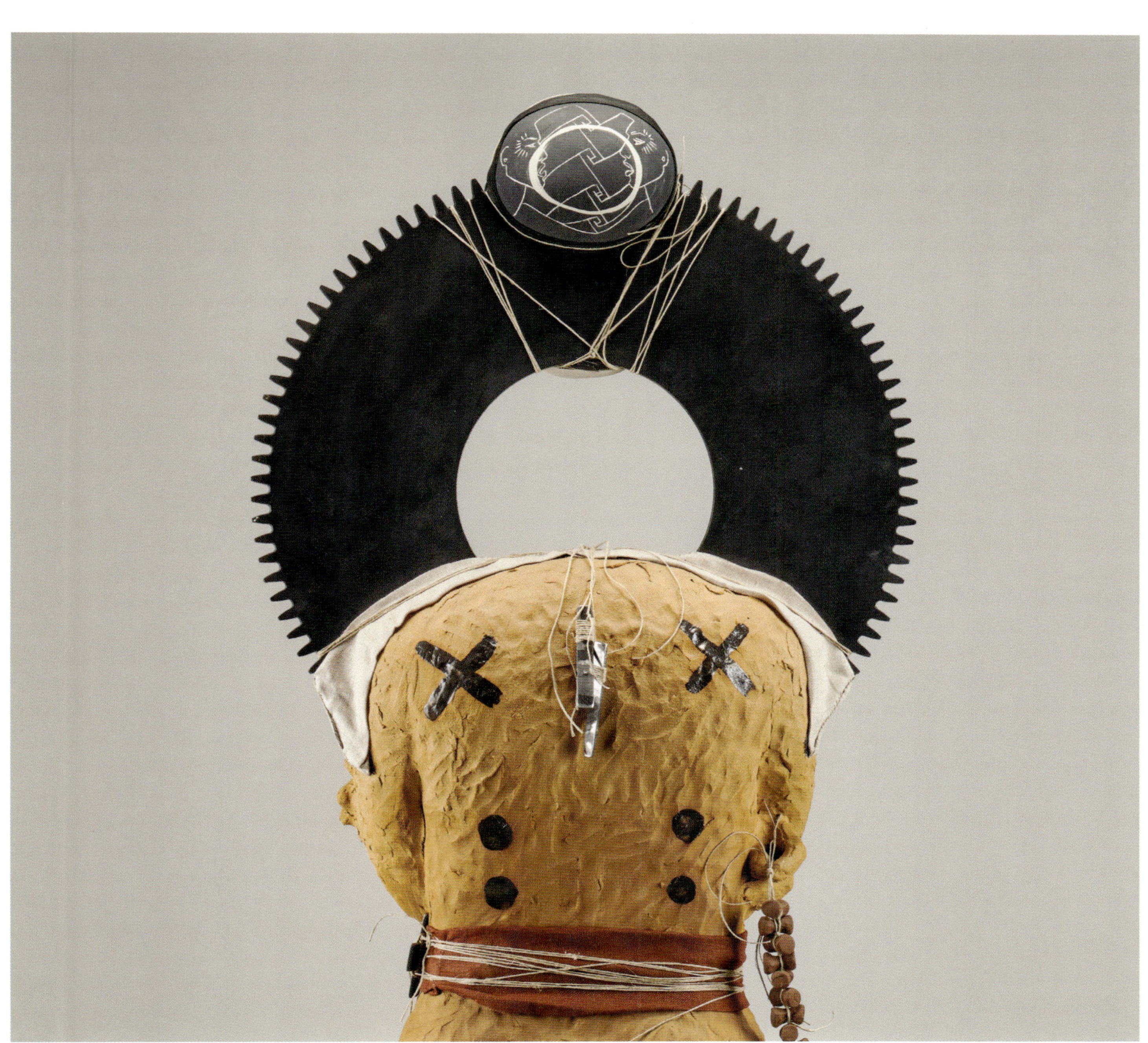

Rose B. Simpson
Santa Clara Pueblo, born 1983
Root I, 2019
Ceramic, glaze, linen, jute string, steel, and leather
H. 70 × W. 20½ × D. 16 in.
Rennie Collection, Vancouver

Cherish Parrish
Pottawatomi/Ottawa/Matchi-be-nash-she-wish, born 1989
The Next Generation – Carriers of Culture, 2018
Black ash
H. 23 × W. 14 × D. 17 in.
Collection of Michigan State University Museum

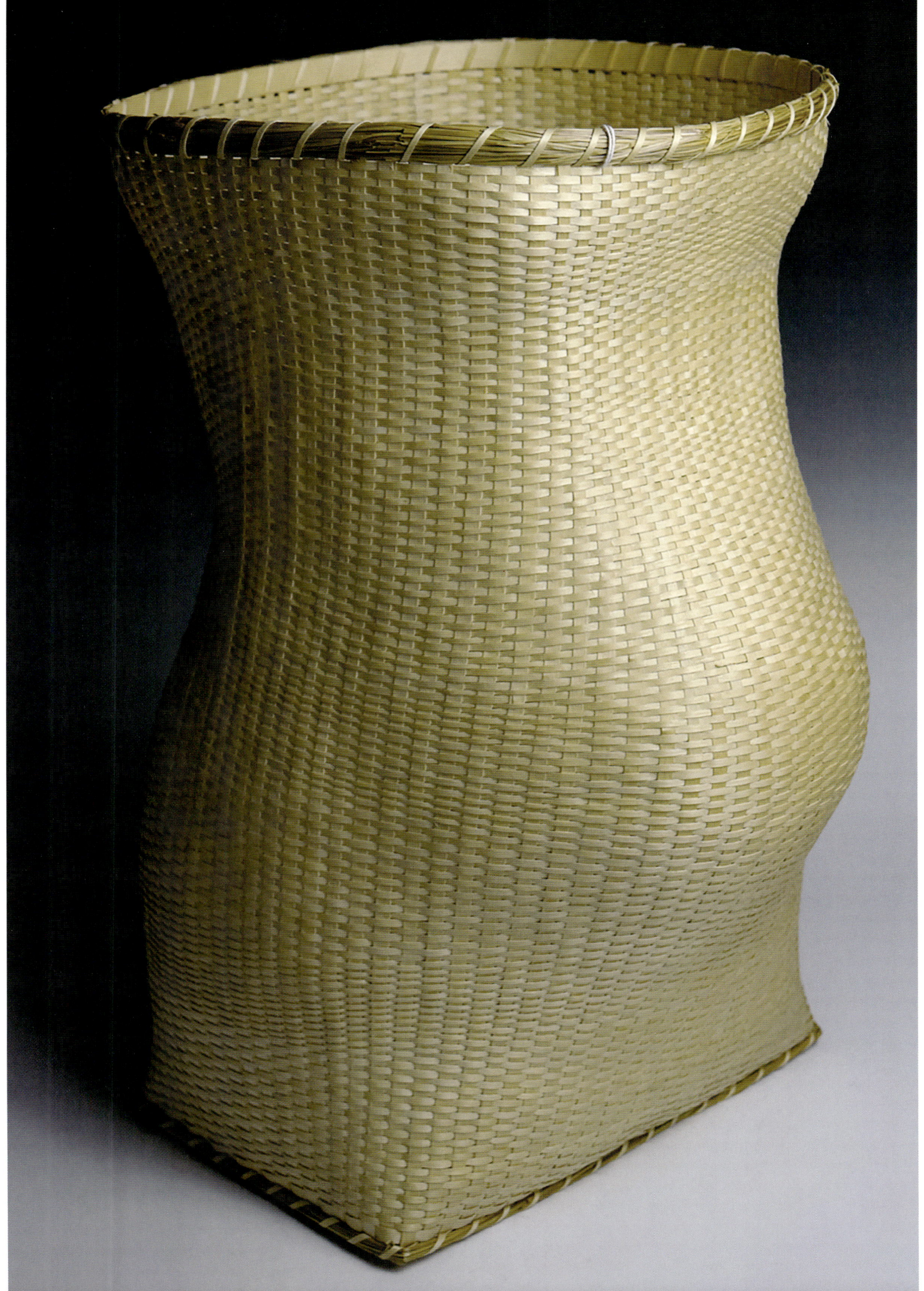

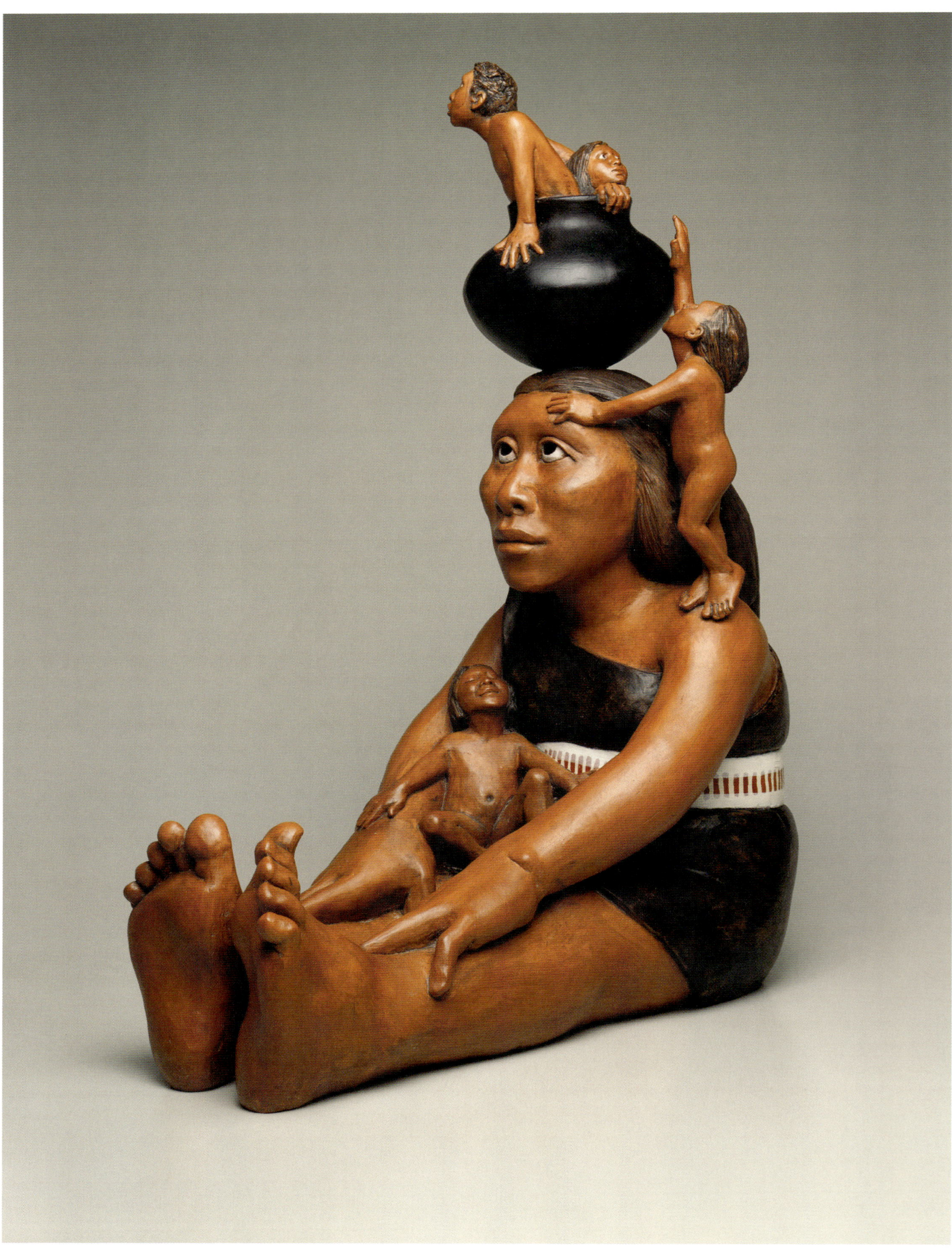

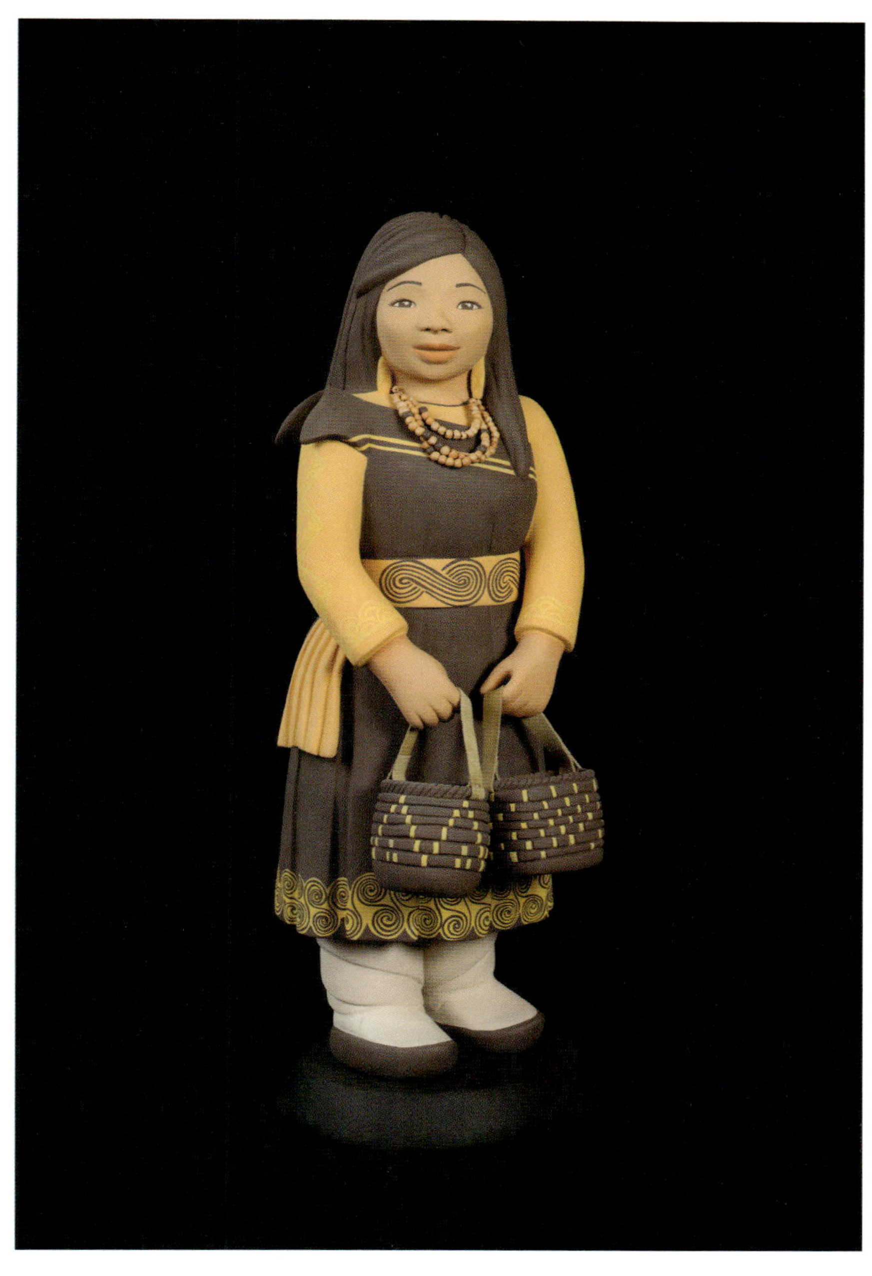

OPPOSITE
Roxanne Swentzell
Santa Clara Pueblo, born 1962
Making Babies for Indian Market, 2004
Clay and pigment
H. 23½ × W. 8½ × D. 17 in.
Brooklyn Museum, Gift in memory
of Helen Thomas Kennedy, 2004.80

ABOVE
Kathleen Wall
Pueblo of Jemez, born 1972
Holding Her Culture, 2022
Clay
H. 28 × W. 10 × D. 11 in.
Private collection

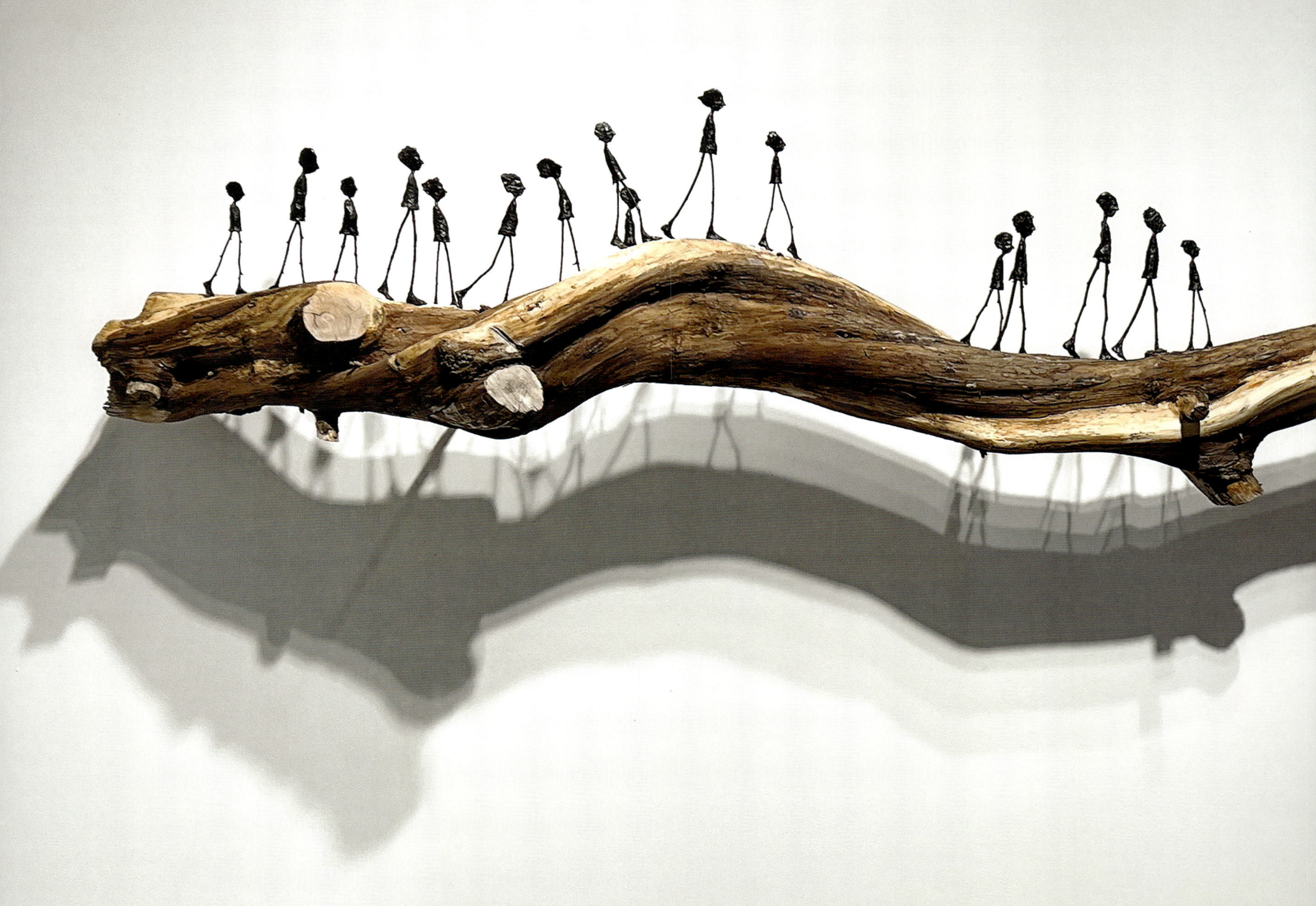

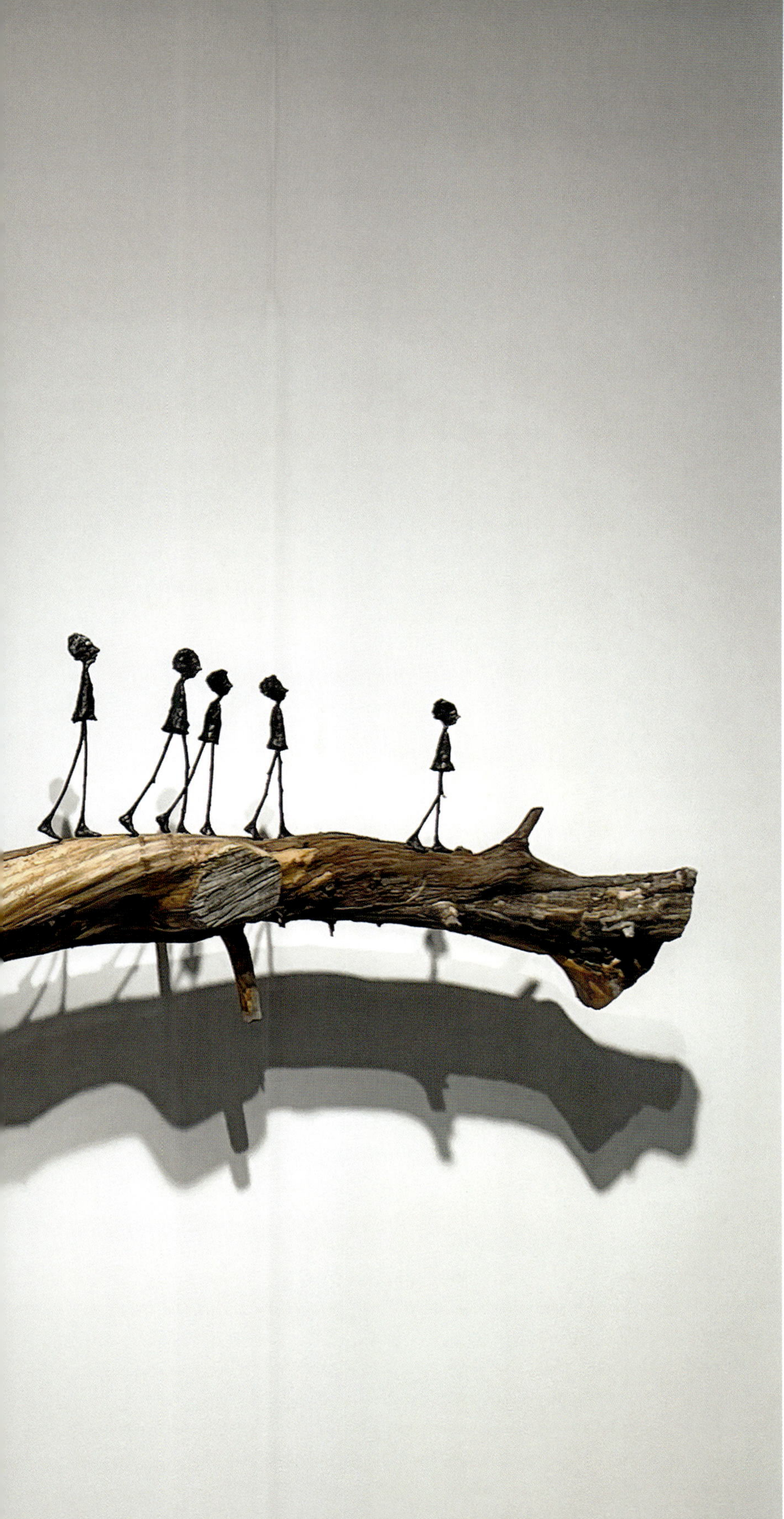

Holly Wilson
Delaware Nation, born 1968
Bloodline, Keeper of the Seeds, 2021
Unique cast bronze with patina, cedar, and steel
H. 30 × W. 98 × D. 15 in.
Courtesy of the artist

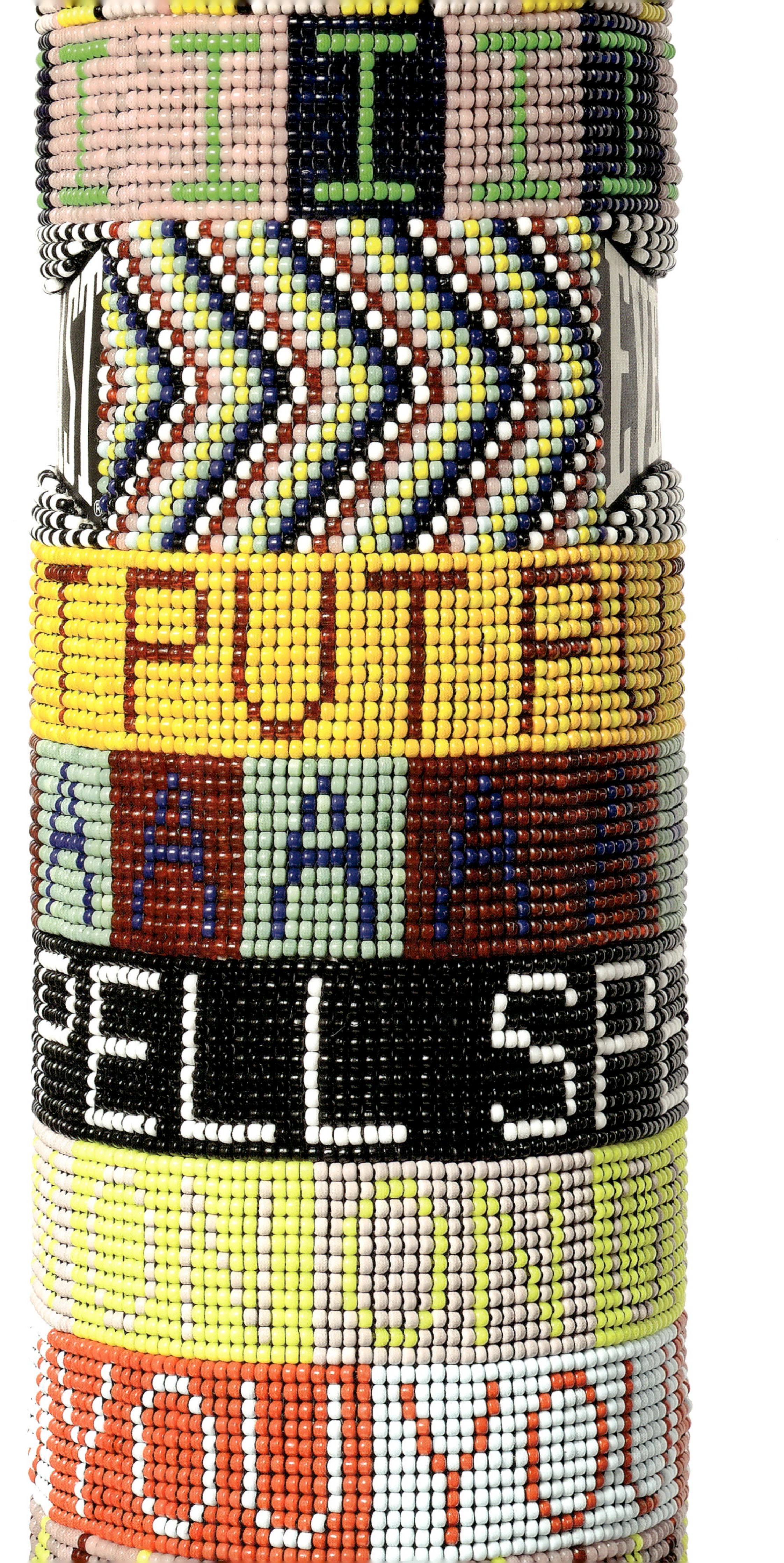

Encoded Commentary

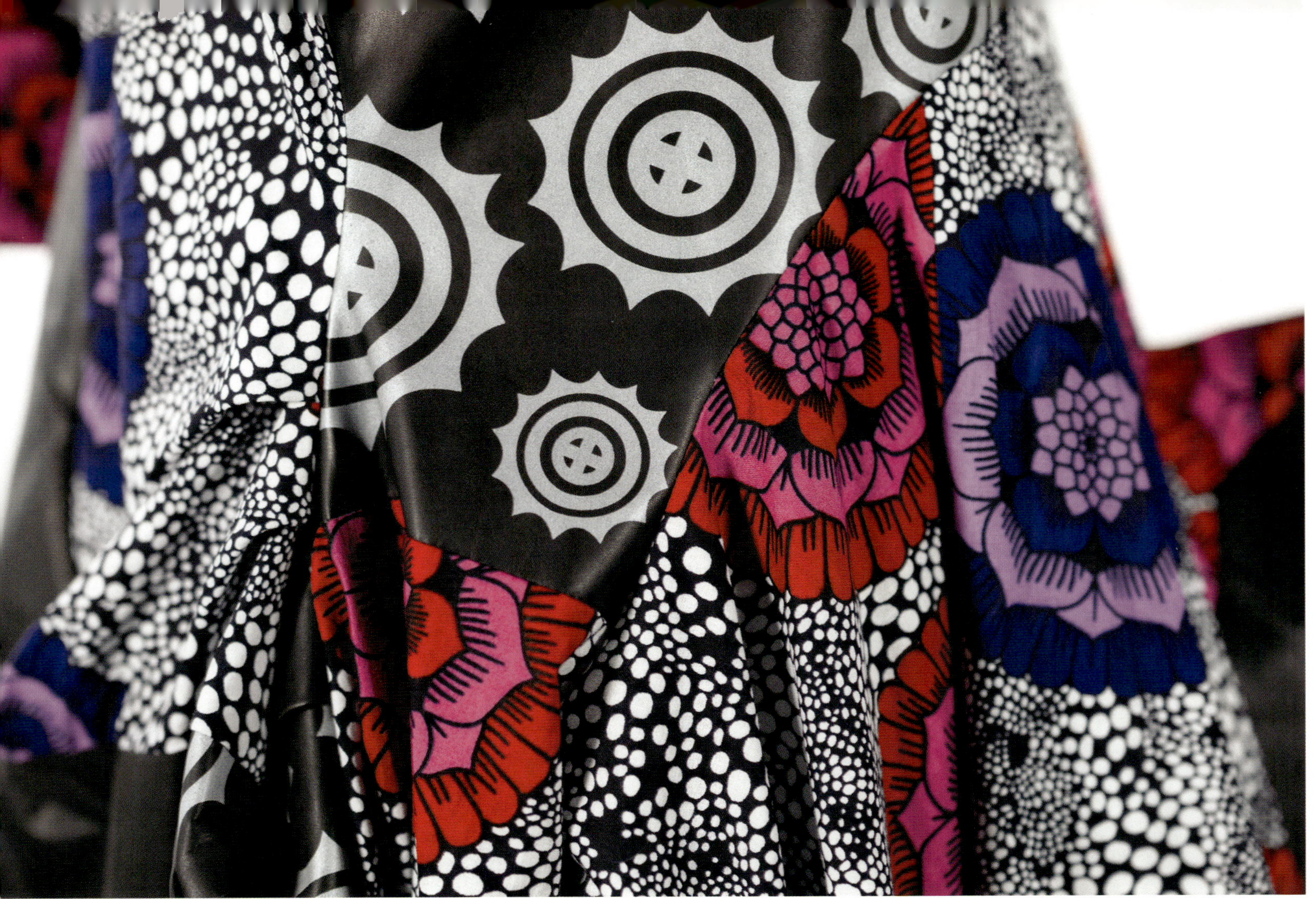

Native art holds power and is empowering in its ability to communicate intellectually. Through their creativity, Indigenous artists offer a wide spectrum of complex ideas and topics, sometimes nuanced, sometimes explicit, for the viewer to unpack and understand. The viewer brings to the conversation their own knowledge, points of reference, and even emotional intelligence. Where the two meet is where the discourse happens. In foregrounding culturally and aesthetically pleasing compositions, perplexing abstraction, or enigmatic meaning, Native artists have the ability through their work to elicit conversations around difficult histories, impart authenticity, heal, educate, make meaningful emotional connections, change perceptions, confront stereotypes, and most of all inspire. Native artists invite viewers to tease out the intended depth of meaning in each object.

A master of commentary and influential storytelling through his figurative ceramics, Virgil Ortiz (Cochiti Pueblo) devotes a significant part of his creativity to narrating the history of the 1680 Pueblo Revolt (p. 109). He imagines a 2180 revolution that would reconcile this past, weaving together history and possibility, confronting viewers with both past and future. On his website Ortiz states, "All my work is based on educating globally about the 1680 Pueblo Revolt. For over two decades, I've incorporated this subject matter into my work and art mediums. It is an awakening of the truth, and education about our history and actual events; reviving social commentary in my traditional clay works is recording a timeline of past and current events."[1]

Interdisciplinary artist Jeffery Gibson (Mississippi Choctaw) produces unexpected commentary through his sculptural, embellished punching bags (p. 115). There are layers of inspiration behind this series: personal therapy, Native powwow regalia, and pop culture. In his work Gibson follows themes that critique social issues around indigeneity, identity, race, class, sexuality, and gender. In a 2019 interview, he explained,

When I put my work together, I use text to sometimes address specific audiences, generally it's available to everybody to interpret and to be subjective with, but I do sometimes choose to speak specifically to other Native Indigenous people. When I showed the first punching bag it was 2012, and I was shocked to see how much viewers really connected with what the punching bag represented. People have told me many stories about things that they have been challenged by, things that they've

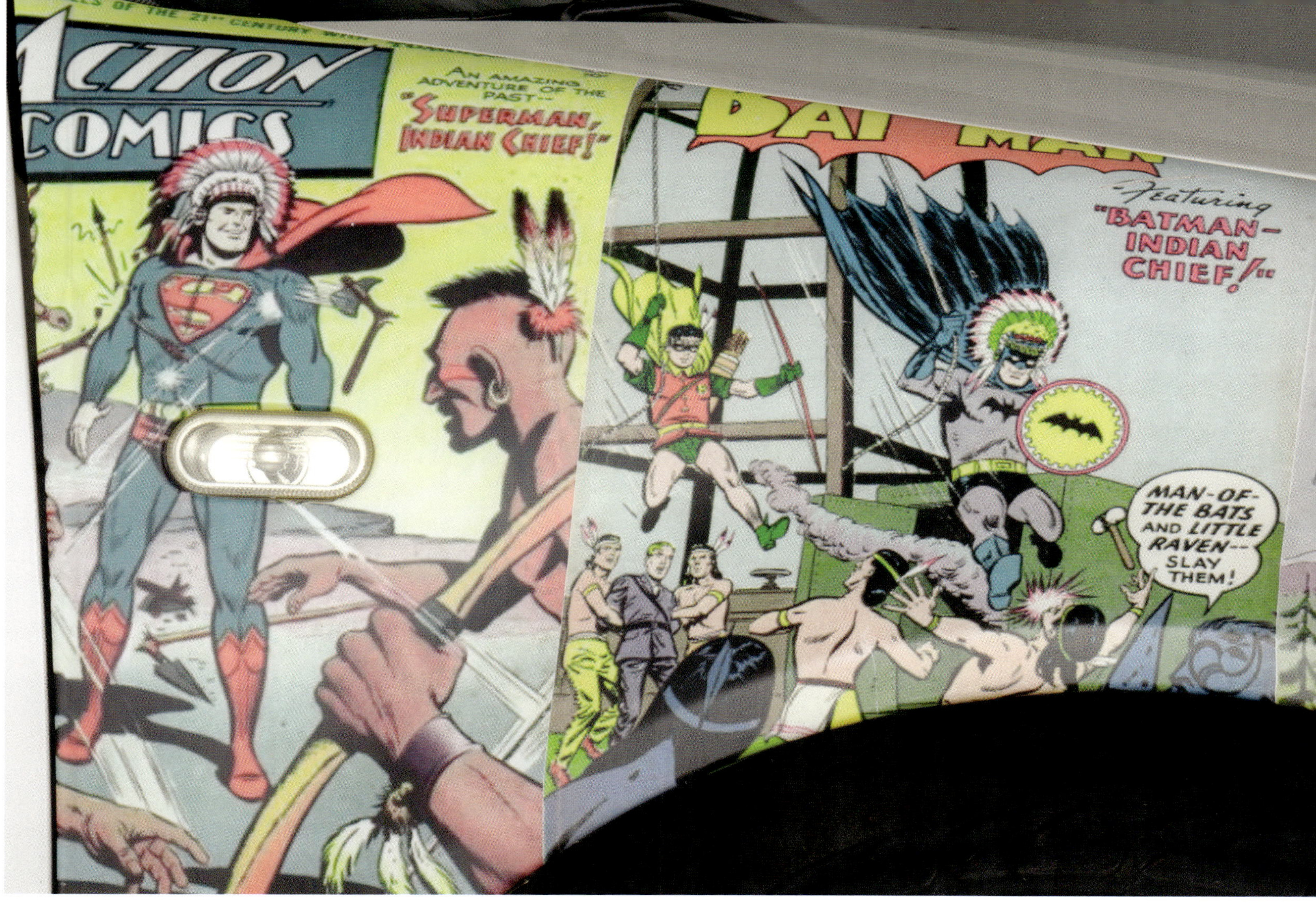

overcome, relationships and power imbalances within those relationships, so the fight, I think, and learning how to maybe even fight ethically fairly using materials that may not be our fists or may not be guns but maybe it's more thought and words, has been what's really pushed the series to continue.[2]

1   Virgil Ortiz, "Revolt 1680/2180: Runners + Gliders," virgilortiz.com, accessed June 24, 2023, https://www.virgilortiz.com /revolt-1680-2180-press-page.

2   MacArthur Foundation, "Jeffrey Gibson, Visual Artist | 2019 MacArthur Fellow," accessed July 24, 2023, YouTube video, 2:50, https://youtu.be /l7bKeGcpqXQ.

PAGE 98: Detail of image on page 115

OPPOSITE: Detail of image on page 112

ABOVE: Detail of image on page 127

Marie Watt
Seneca Nation, born 1967
Acknowledgment: Indigenous Land, Pachamama, Story Circle, 2020
Cast bronze, cedar, LP Unito blankets, patches, and embroidery floss
H. 45 × W. 28 × D. 28 in.
North Carolina Museum of Art, Purchased with funds from the
Matrons of the Arts and with additional funds from various donors,
by exchange, 2021 (2021.10/a–aa)

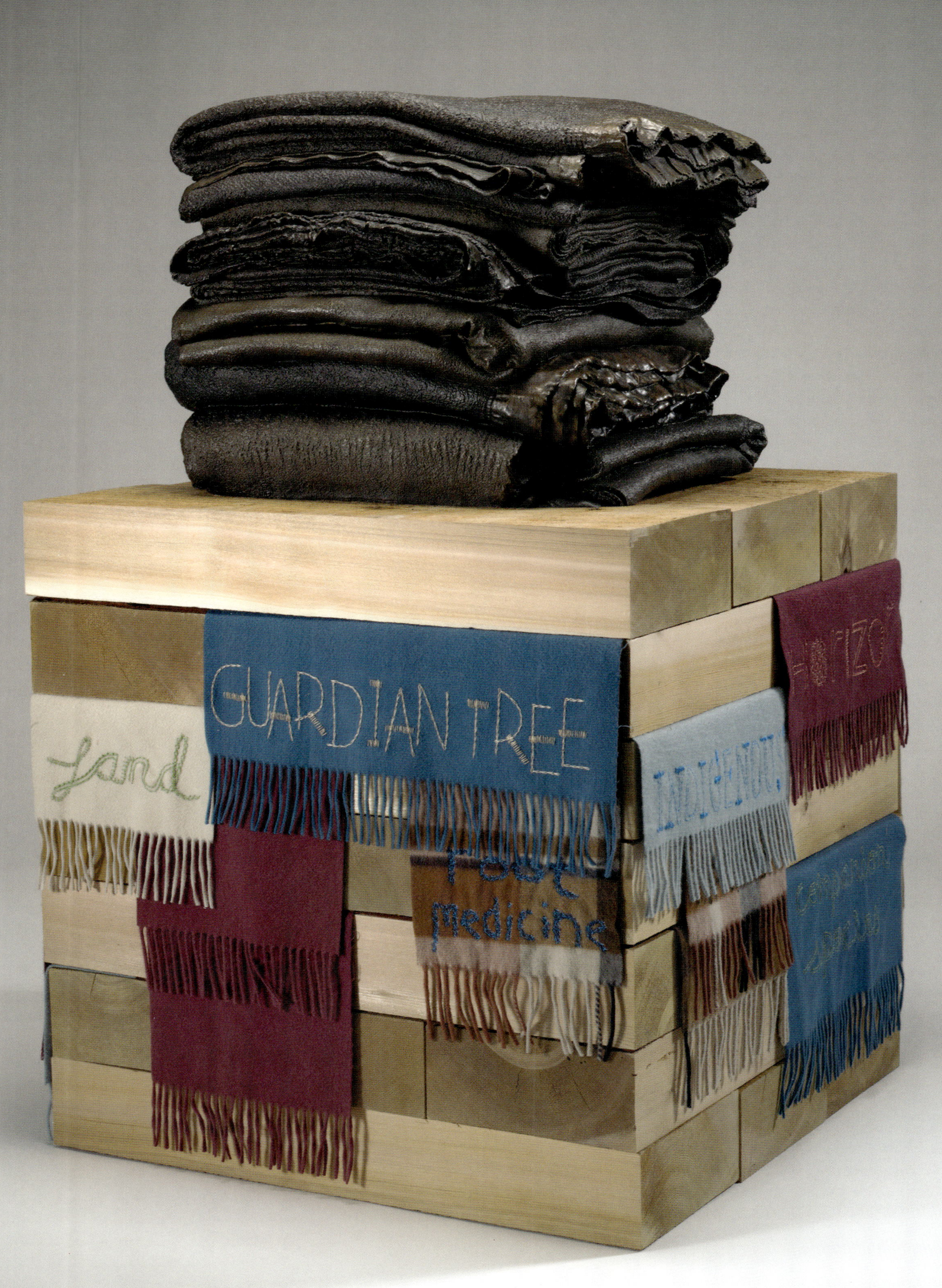

GUARDIAN TREE
Land
HORIZO
INDIGENOU
root
medicine

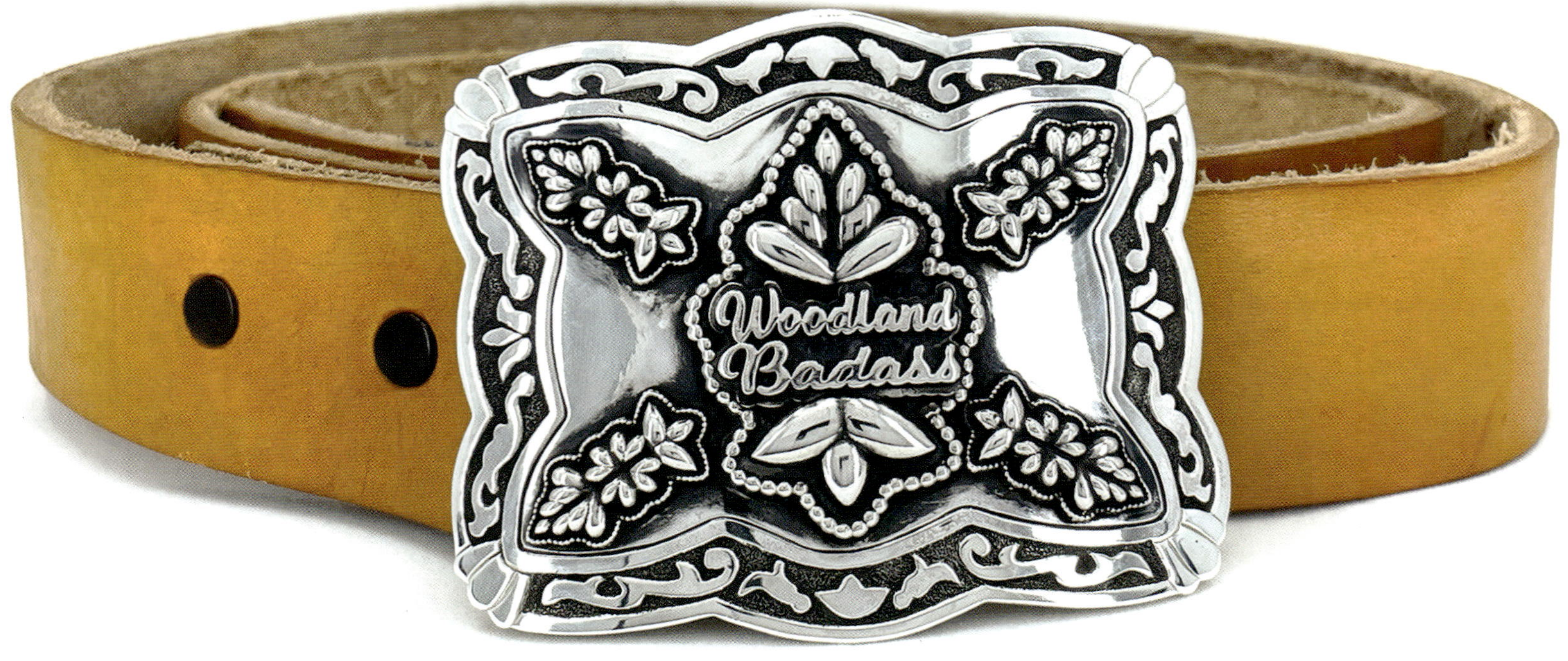

ABOVE
Jodi Webster
Ho-Chunk Nation/Prairie Band Potawatomi Nation
Badass Buckle, 2022
Sterling silver
H. 1 × W. 3⅛ × D. ½ in.
Courtesy of the artist

OPPOSITE
Gabriel Frey
Passamaquoddy
Gal Frey
Passamaquoddy
Wapi-kuhkukhahs/Snowy Owl Basket, 2022
Black ash, leather, glass beads, and metal
H. 12 × W. 7 × D. 4 in.
Collection of the Maine Historical Society

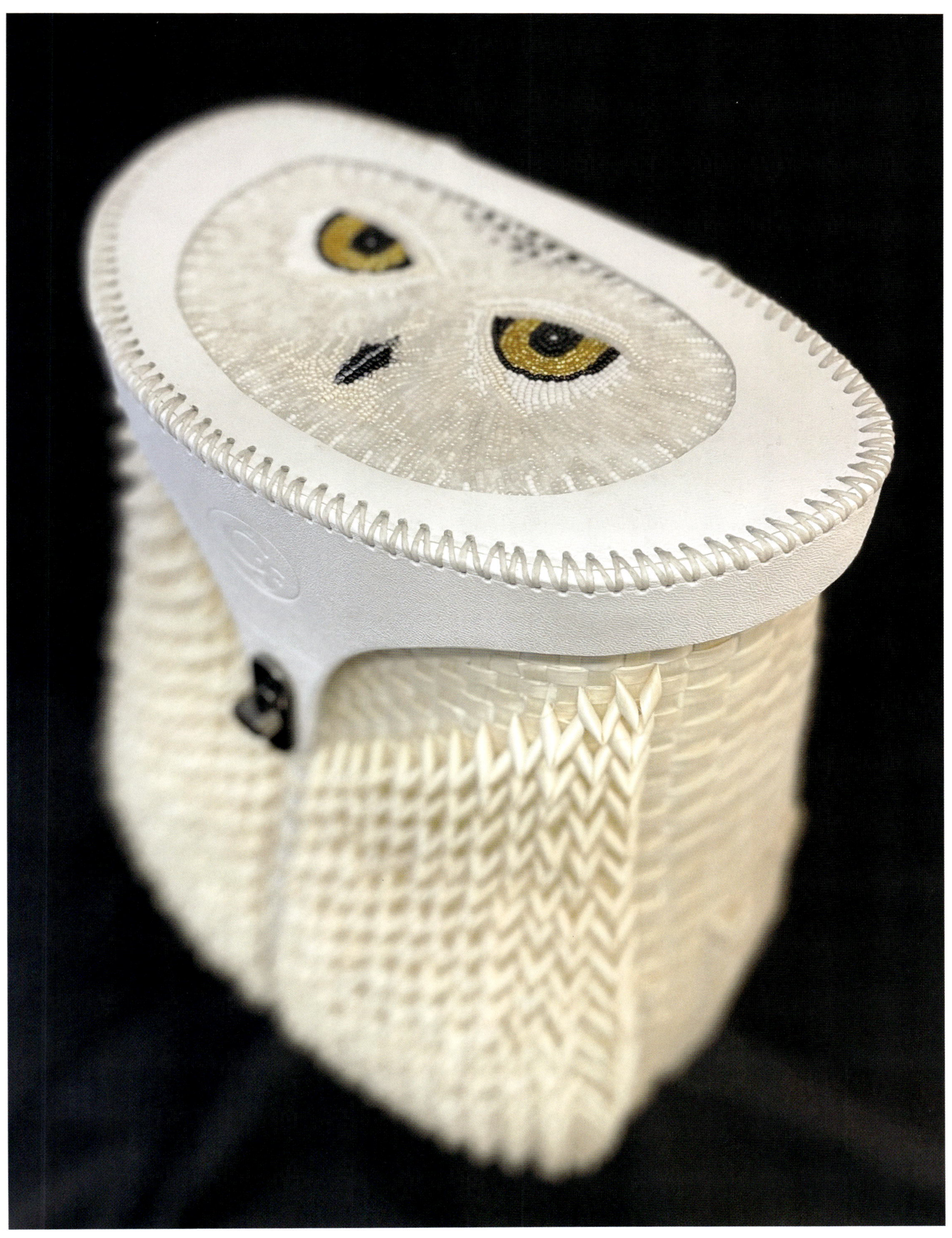

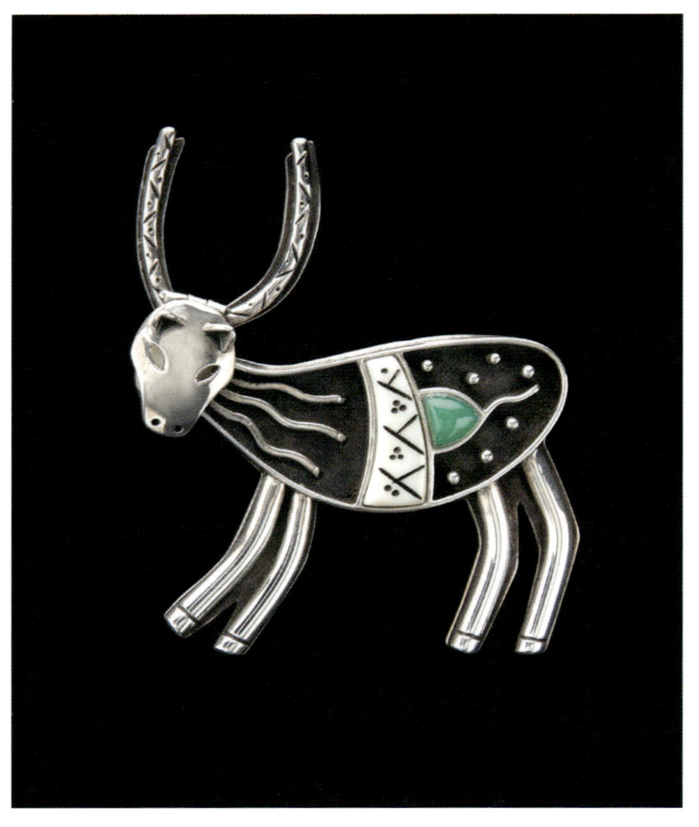
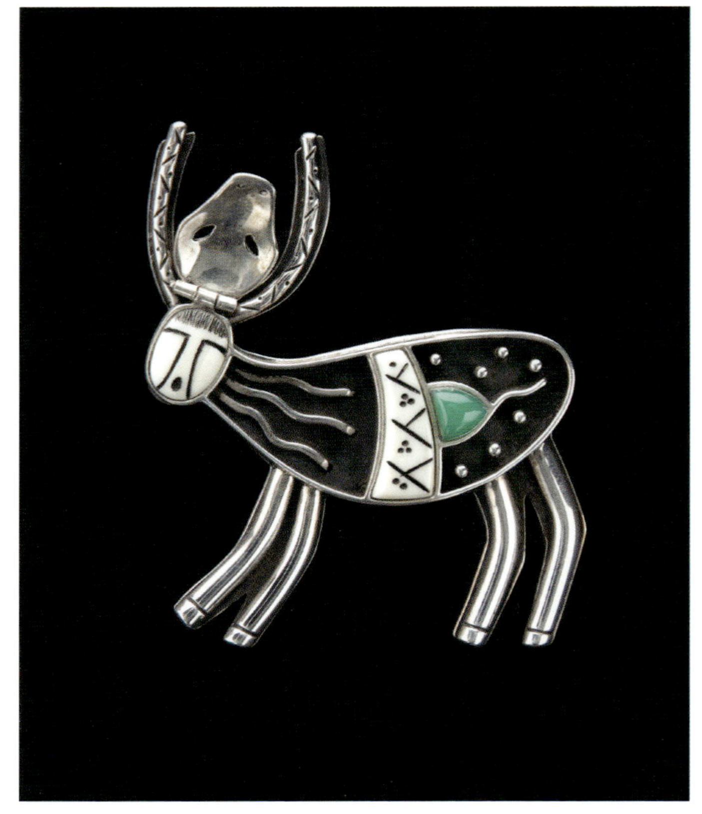
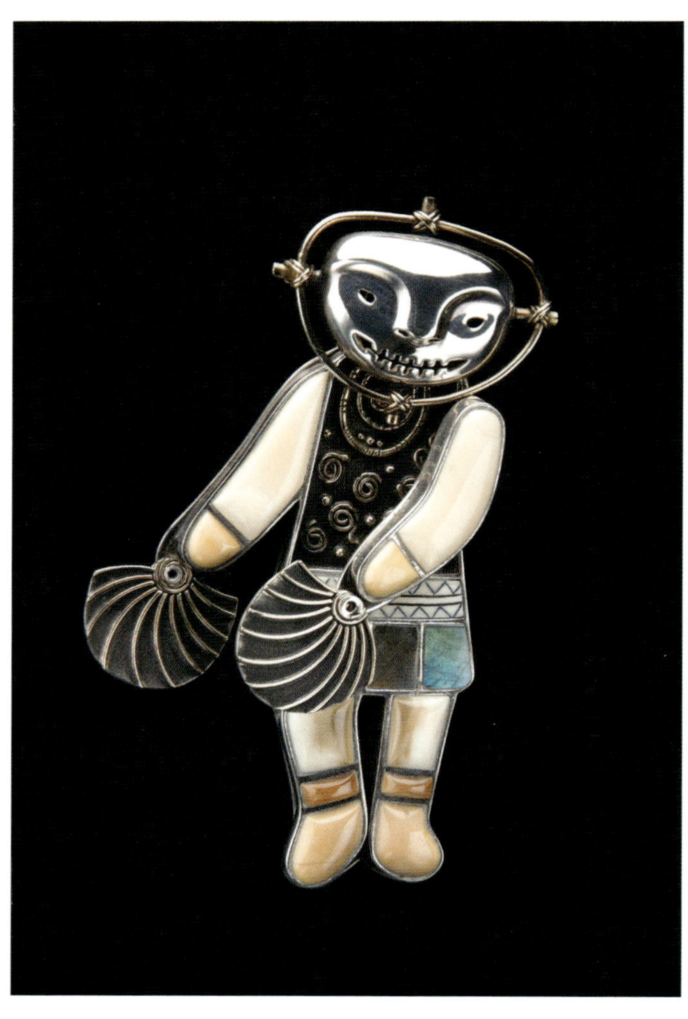
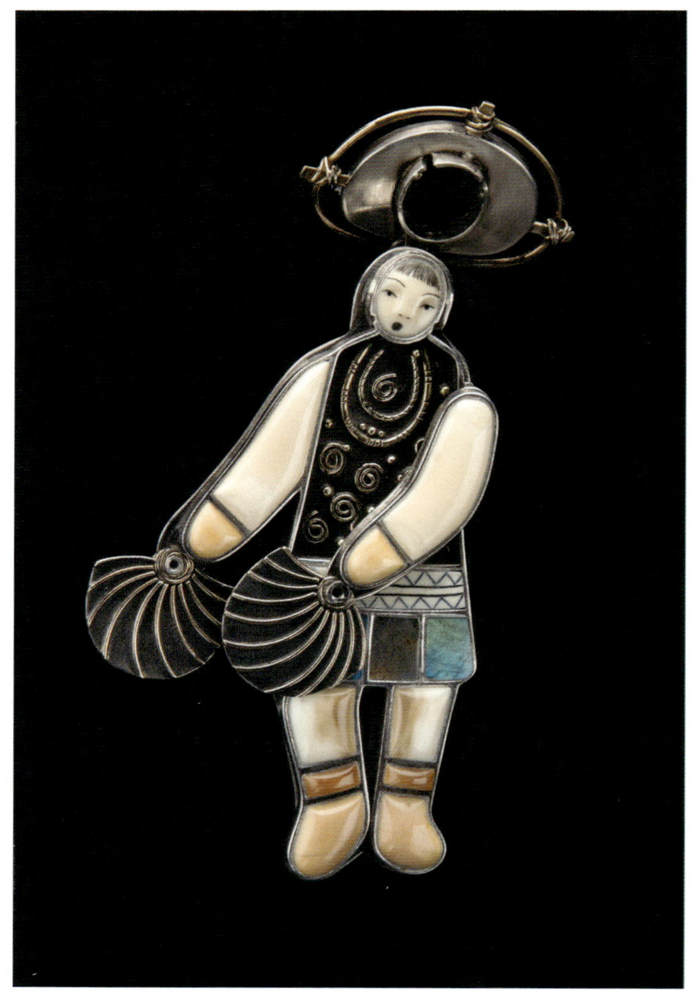

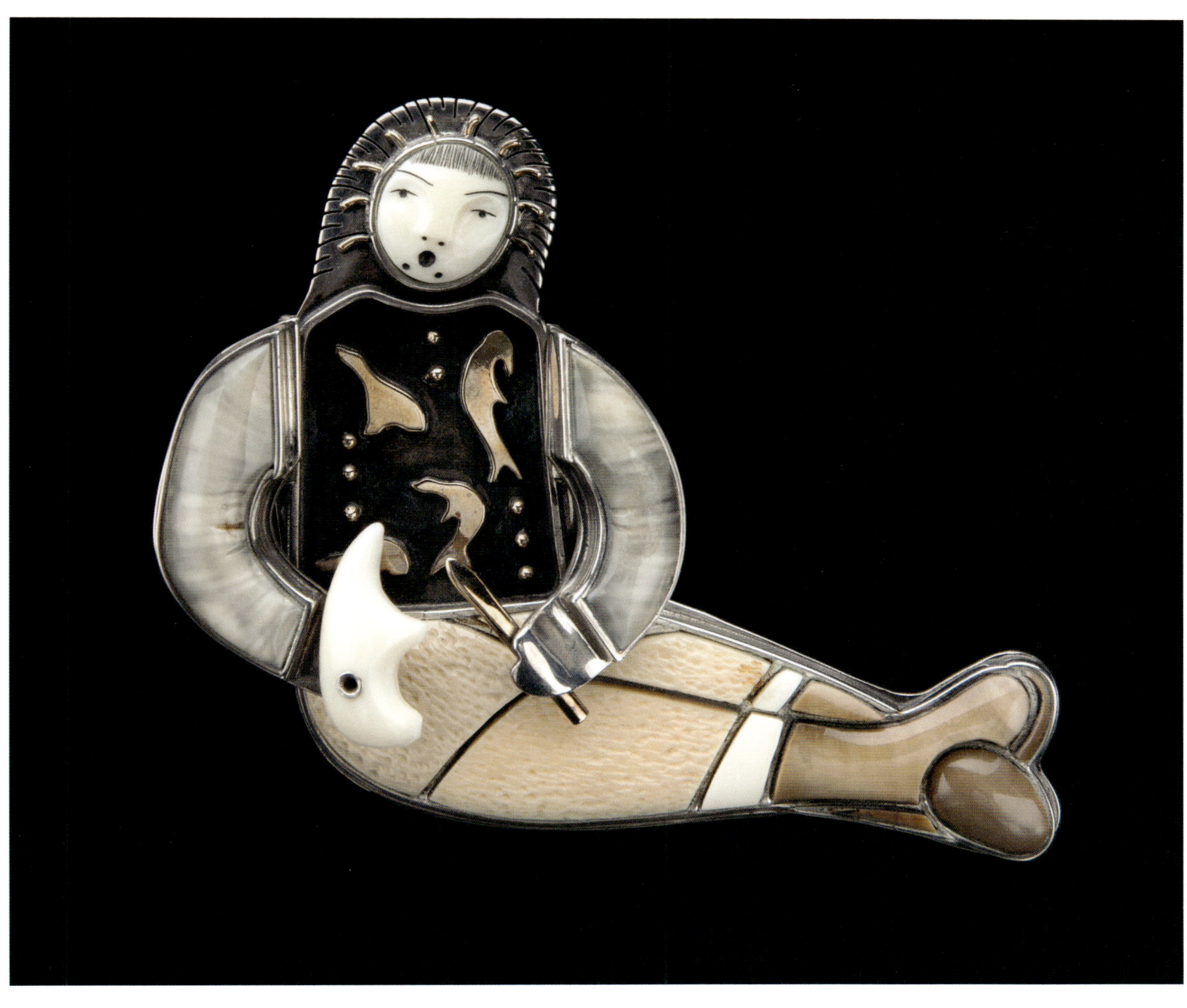

Denise Wallace
Chugach/Sugpiaq/Alutiiq, born 1957

TOP LEFT
Untitled Brooch (Caribou), 1992
Sterling silver, chrysoprase, and fossil ivory
H. 2½ × W. 2¼ × D. ½ in.
Collection of the Wheelwright Museum of the
American Indian, 2014.26.111

BOTTOM LEFT
Untitled Brooch (Yupik Dancer), 1997
Sterling silver, gold, fossil ivory, and spectrolite
H. 3¾ × W. 2¼ × D. 7/16 in.
Collection of the Wheelwright Museum of the
American Indian, 2014.03.054

ABOVE
Untitled Brooch (Figure with Seal Body), 1994
Sterling silver and fossil ivory
H. 2⅝ × W. 3⅜ × D. 3/4 in.
Collection of the Wheelwright Museum of the
American Indian, 2022.03.052

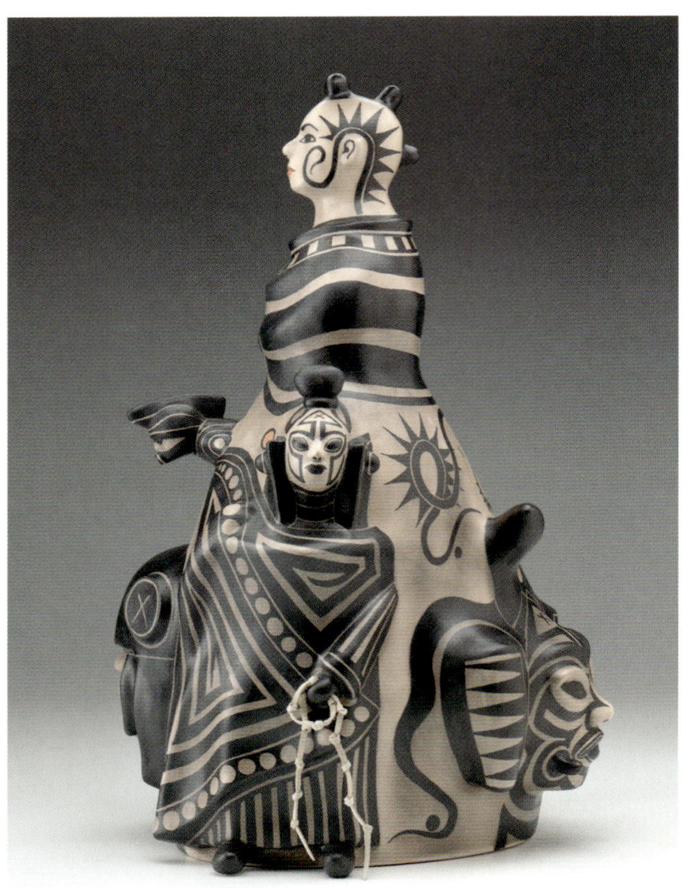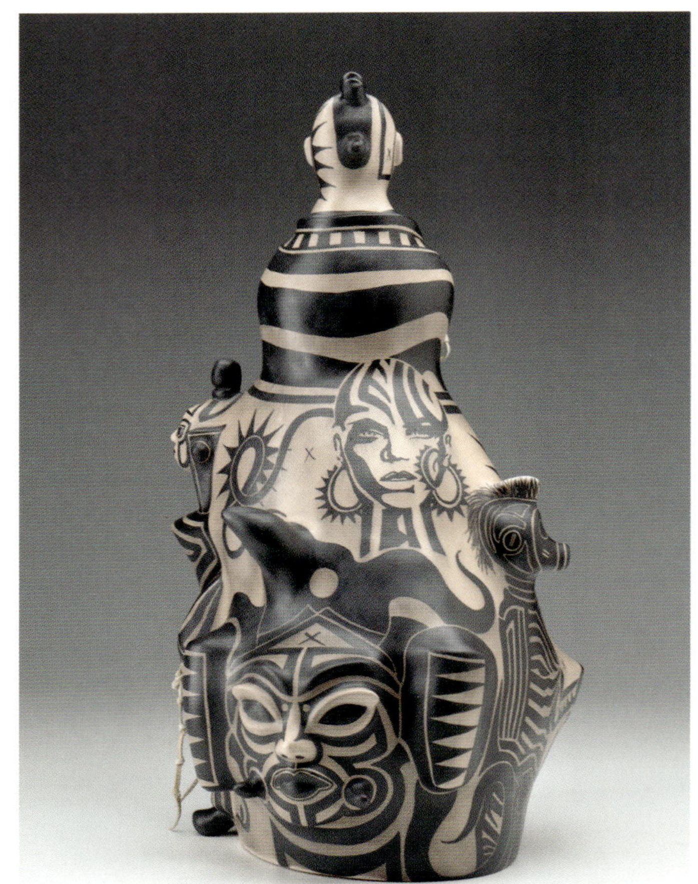

Virgil Ortiz
Cochiti Pueblo, born 1969
Convergence, Defenders Descend from Portal to Pueblo, 2023
Cochiti red clay, white clay slip, red clay slip, and black pigment (wild spinach plant)
H. 28½ × W. 19 × D. 18 in.
North Carolina Museum of Art, Gift of Alan and Benjamin King, Jeffrey Childers
and Onay Cruz Gutierrez, Joyce Fitzpatrick and Jay Stewart, Valerie Hillings and
B. J. Scheessele, Marjorie Hodges and Carlton Midyette, Stefanie and Douglas Kahn,
Bonnie and John Medinger, Mindy and Guy Solie, Cathy and Jim Stuart, Libby and Lee
Buck, Liza and Lee Roberts, 2023 (2023.16.1)

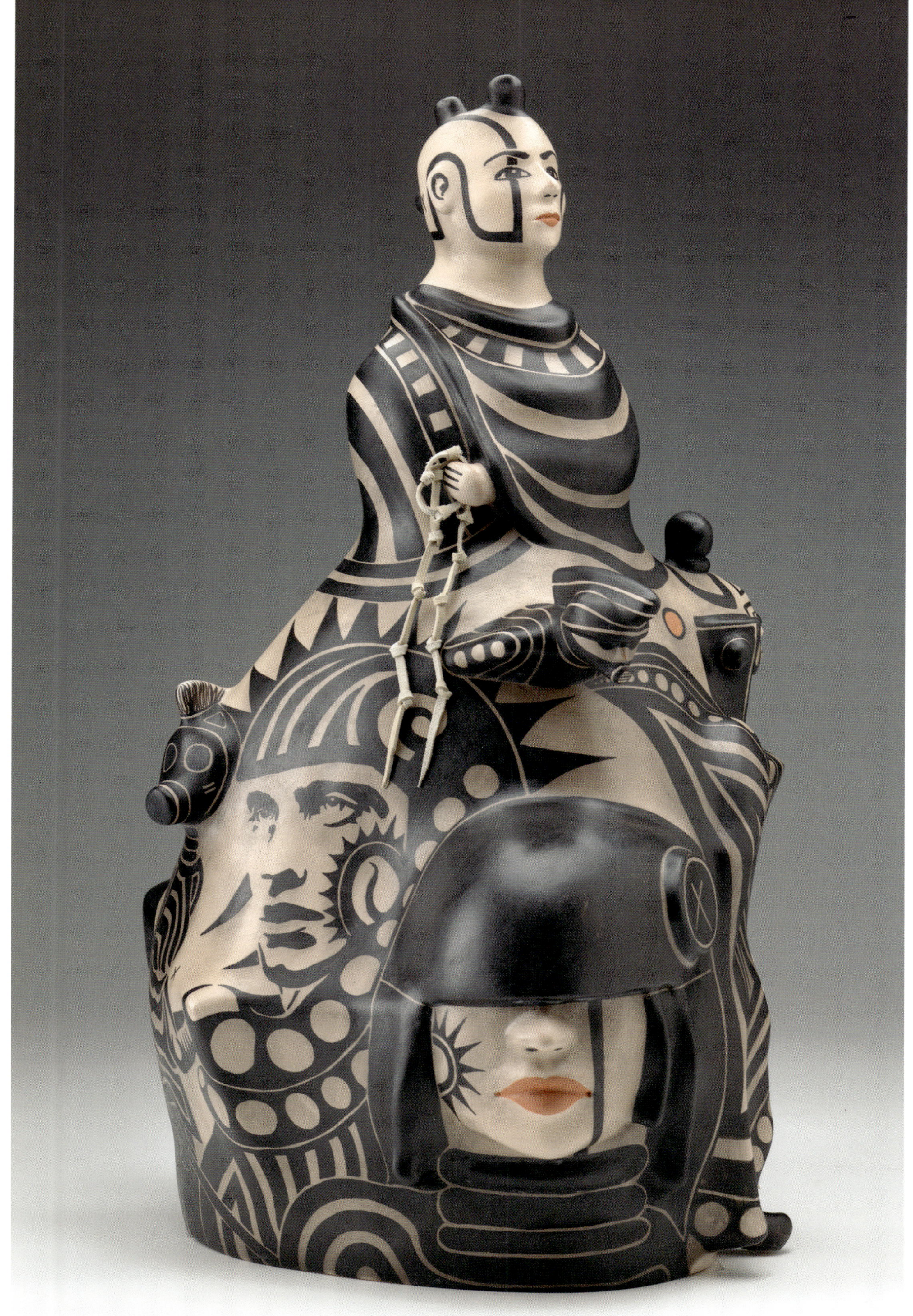

Laura Walkingstick
Cherokee

LEFT
1920s Cherokee Woman, 2021
Cornhusk, wood, cloth, and beads
H. 13¾ × W. 7 × D. 4 in.
Courtesy of the artist

RIGHT
Self-Portrait, 2021
Cornhusk, wood, cloth, and beads
H. 11½ × W. 5 × D. 4 in.
Courtesy of the artist

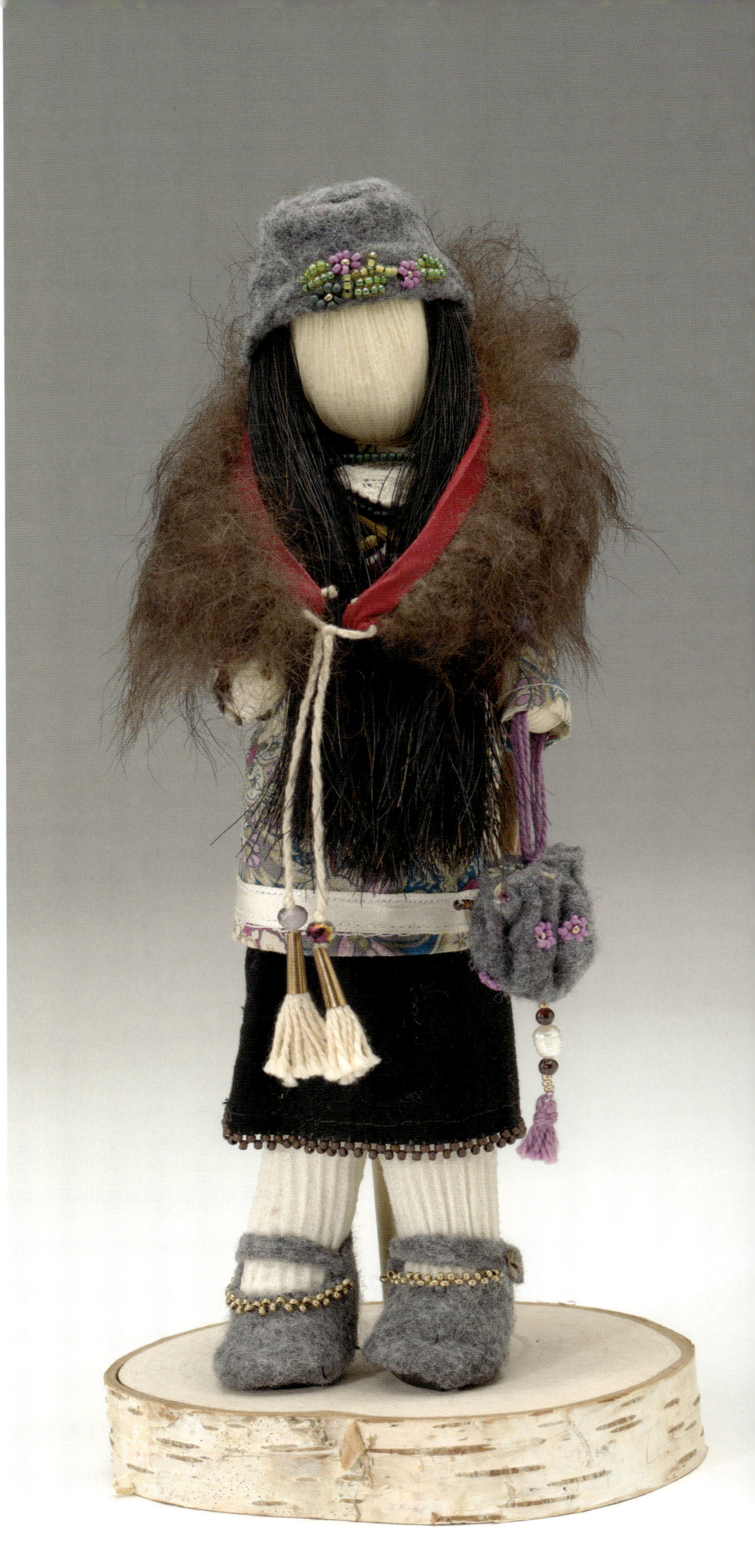

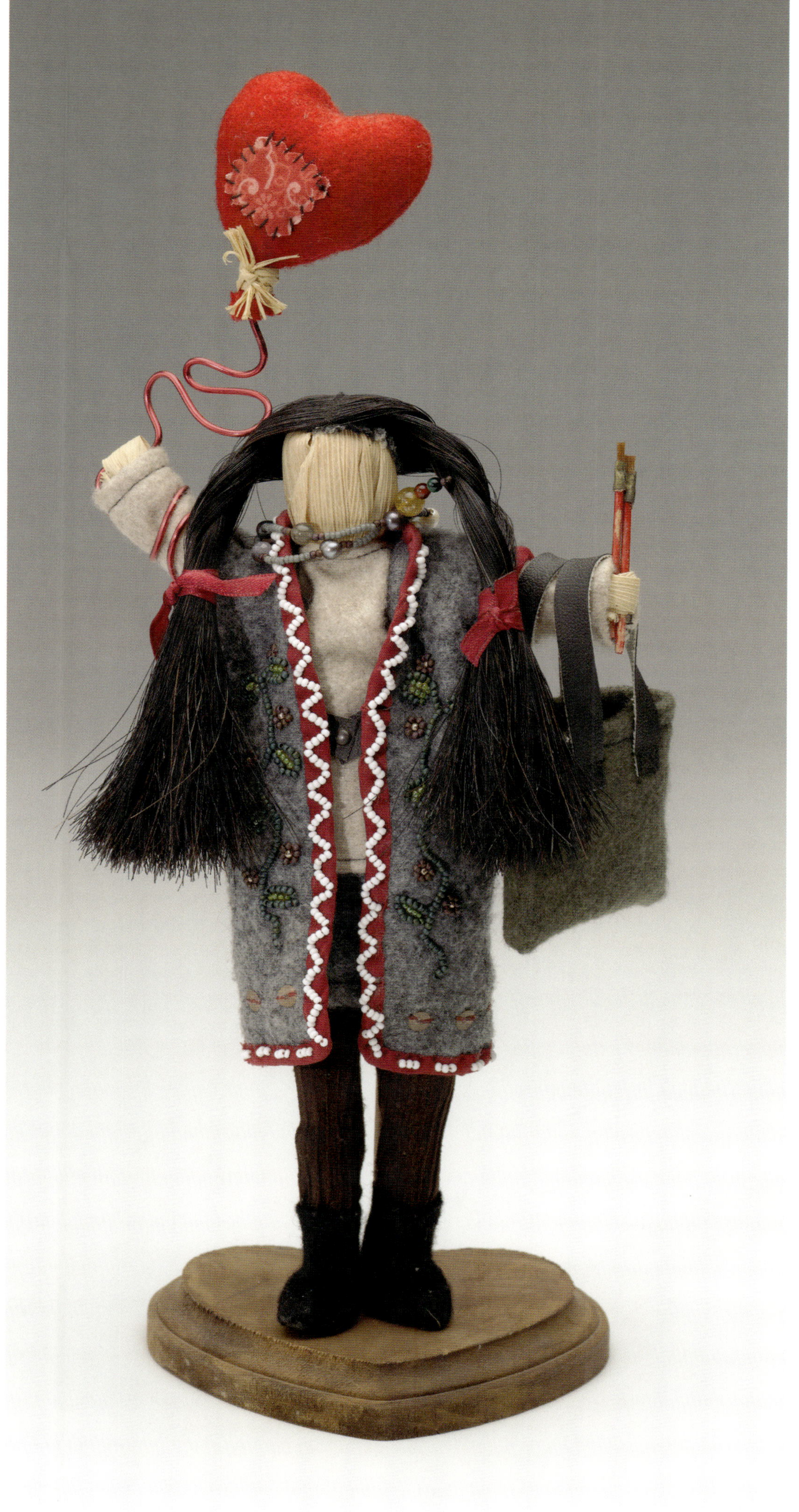

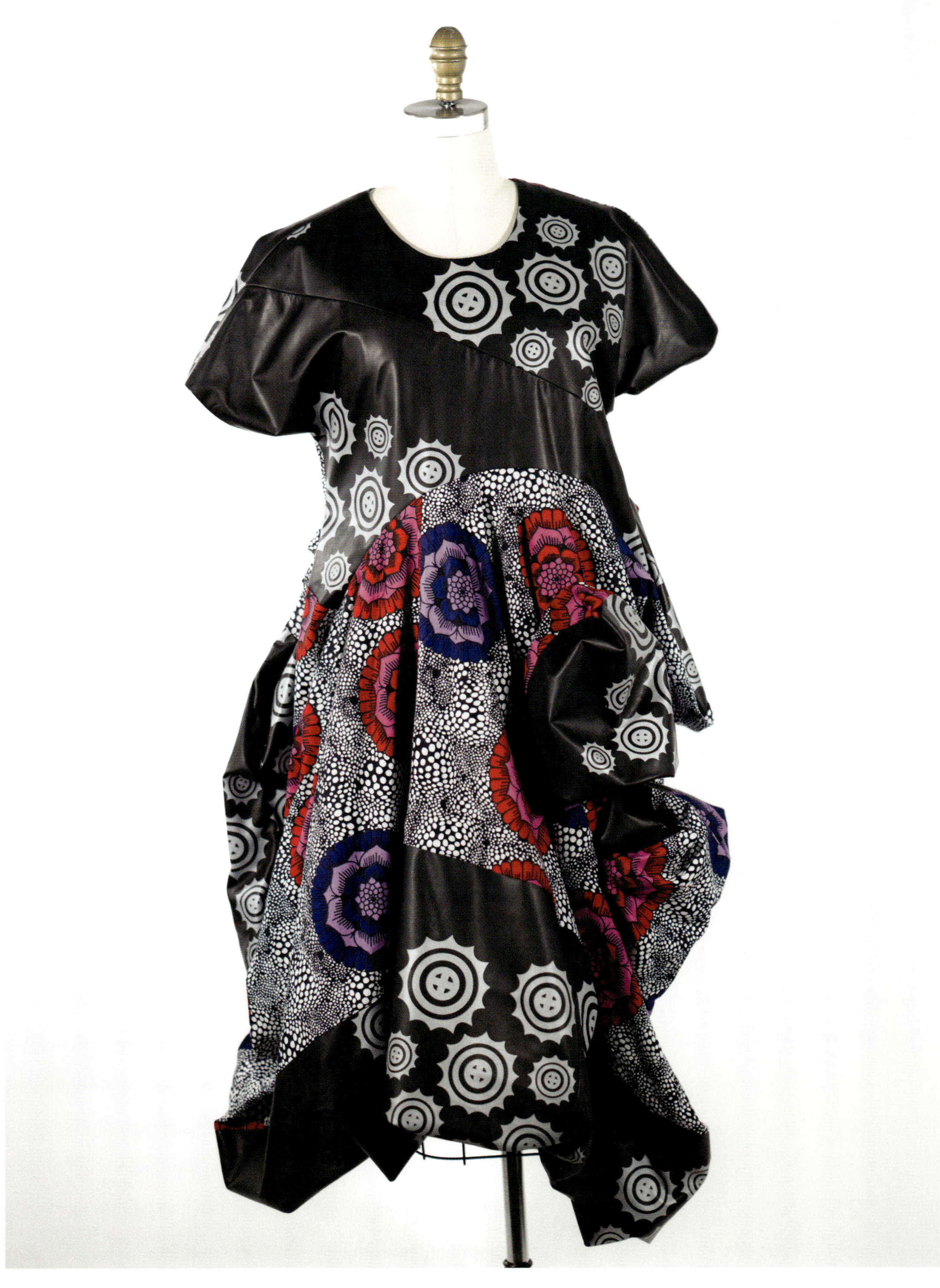

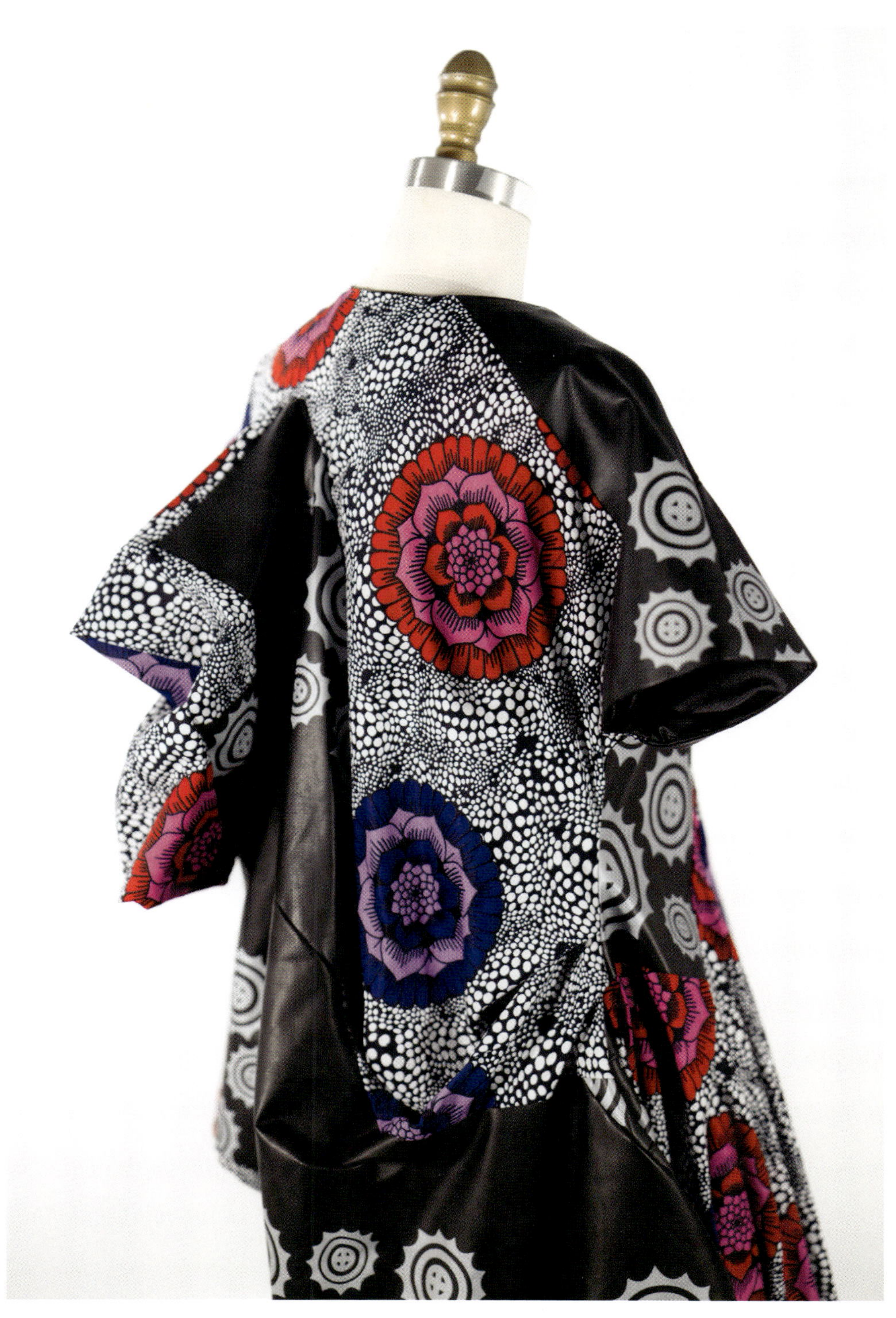

Leslie A. Deer
Muscogee (Mvskoke) Nation of Oklahoma
Equilibrium, 2022
Leather and cotton
H. 47 × W. 46 in.
Courtesy of the artist

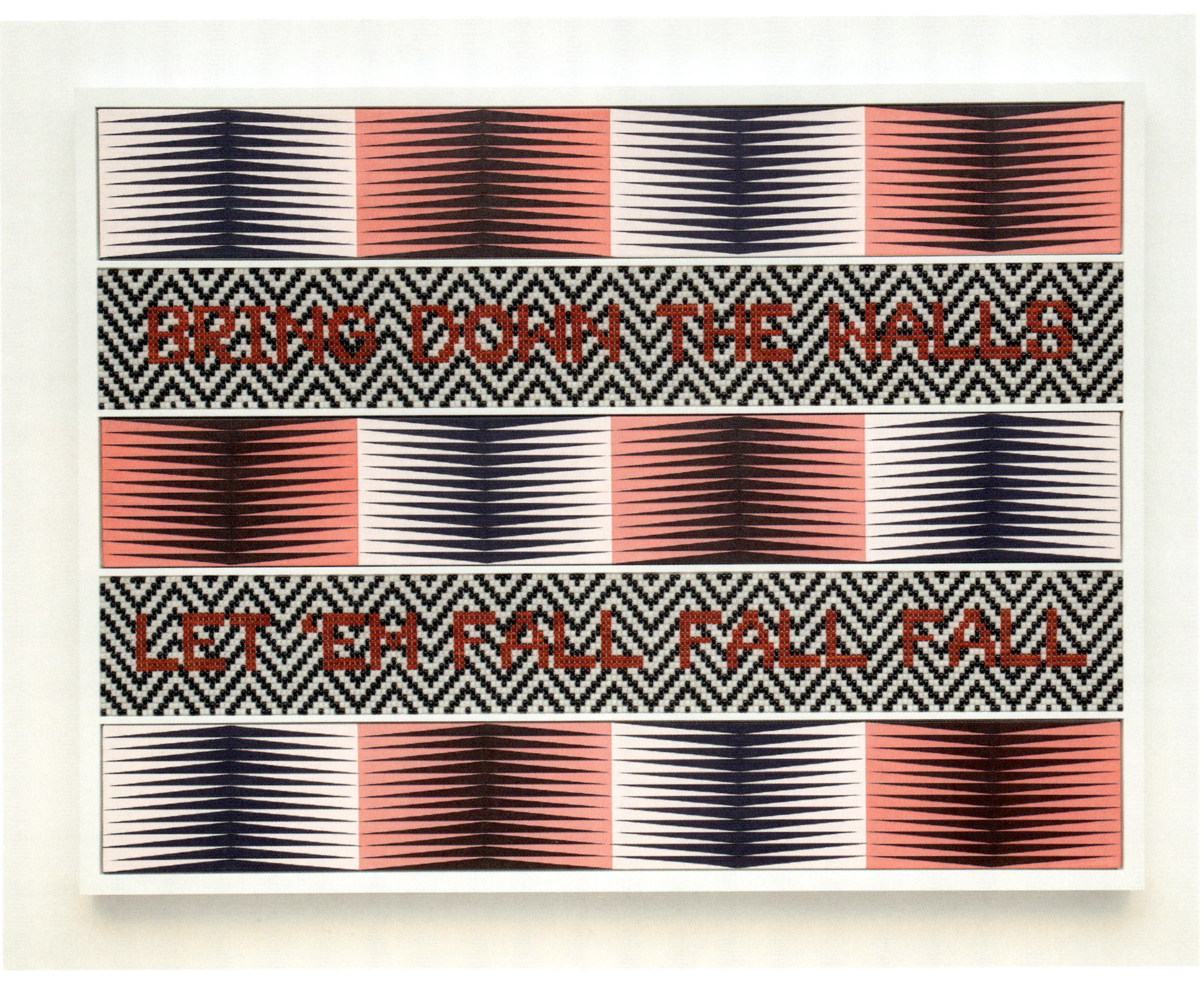

Jeffrey Gibson
Mississippi Choctaw, born 1972

ABOVE
Bring Down the Walls, Let 'Em Fall Fall Fall, 2020
Acrylic on canvas, glass beads, and artificial sinew
inset into wood frame
44 × 56 in.
The Gutierrez Collection, Raleigh, NC

OPPOSITE
I Put a Spell on You, 2015
Repurposed punching bag, glass beads,
artificial sinew, and steel
H. 40 × W. 14 × D. 14 in.
Nasher Museum of Art, Duke University,
Museum Purchase

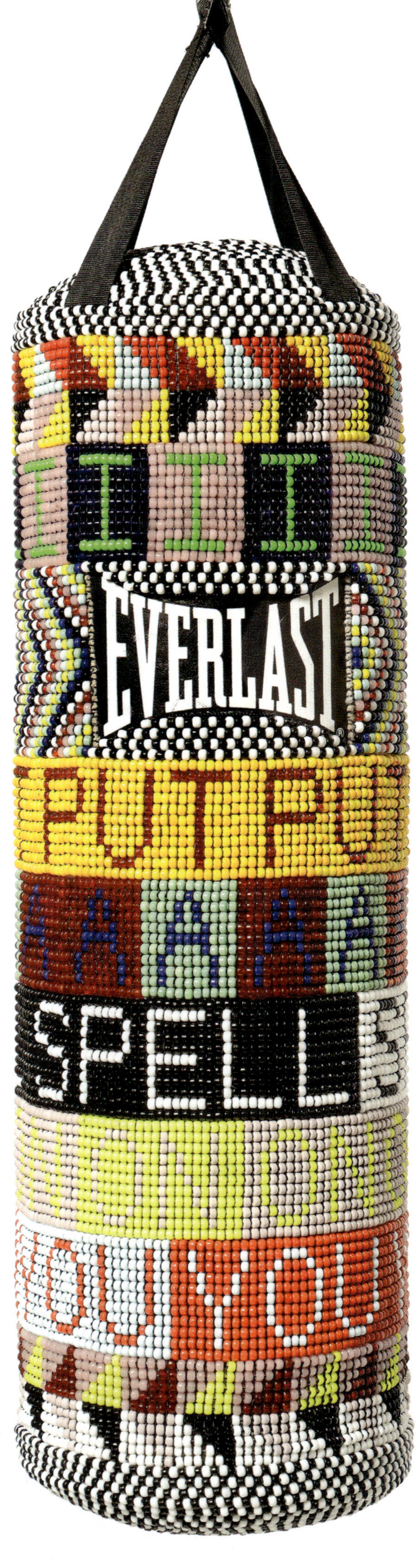EVERLAST
SPELL

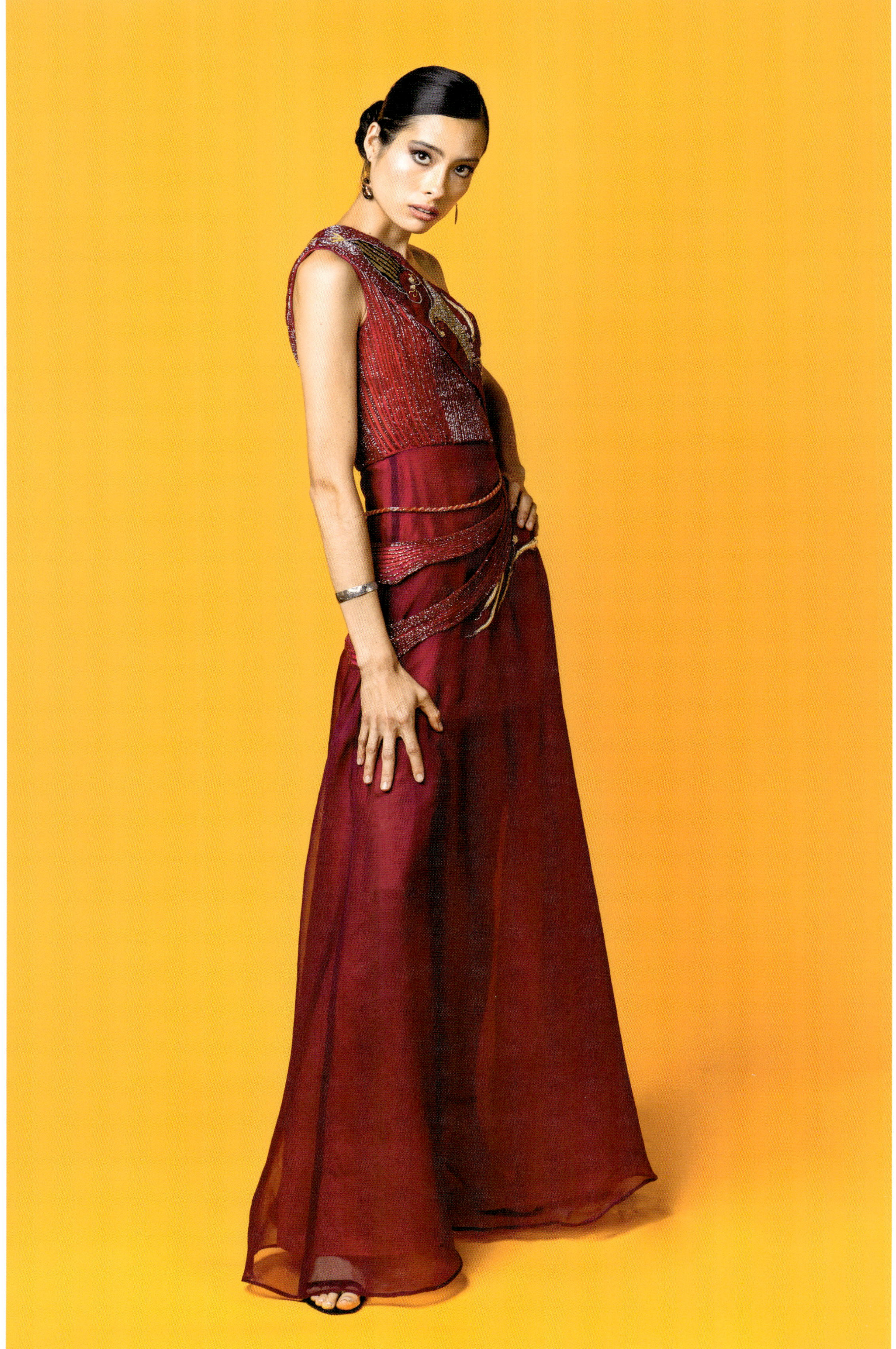

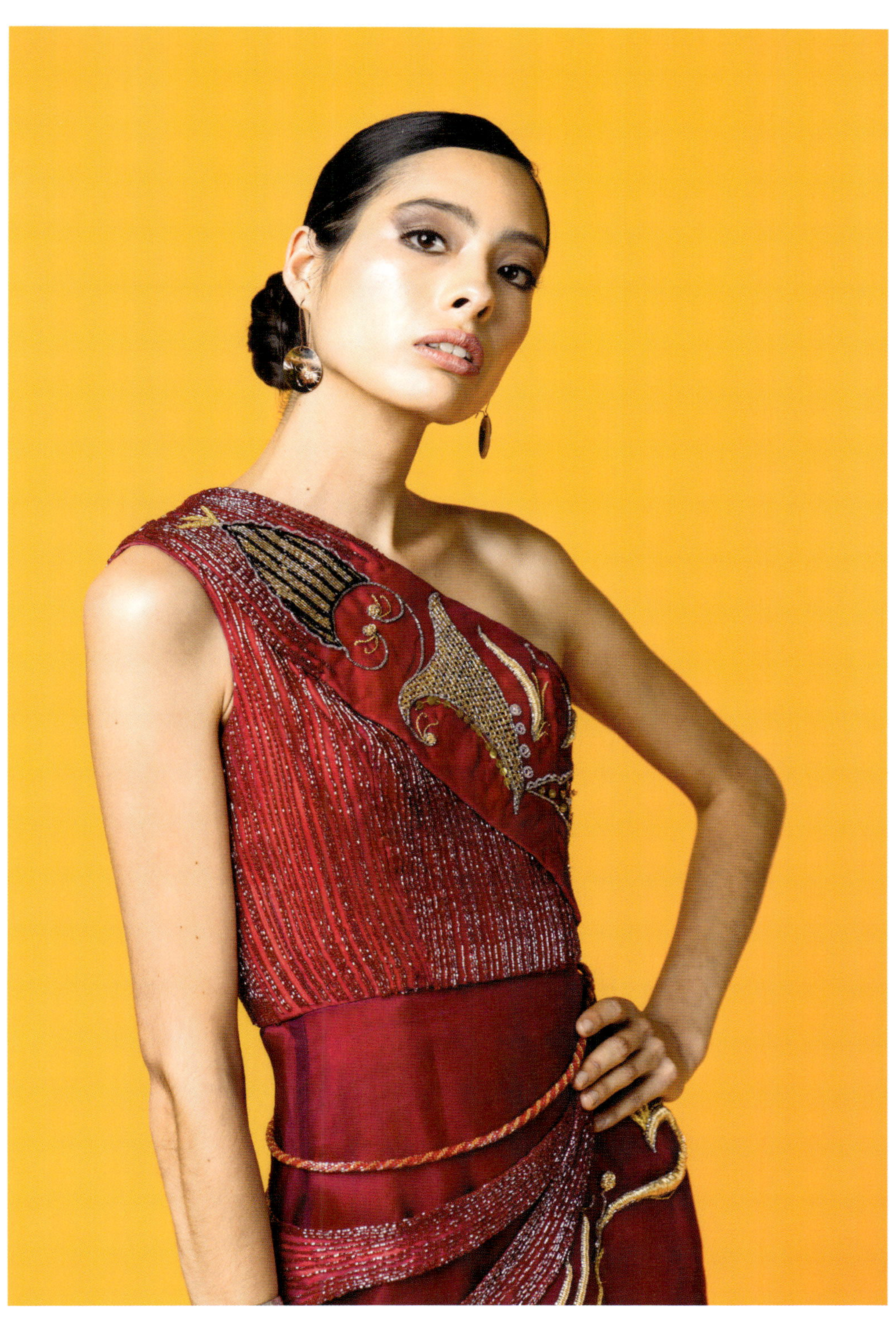

Orlando Dugi
Navajo
Red Cochineal Gown, Red Collection, 2015–2016
Silk organza, silk charmeuse, glass beads, gold bullion,
sequins, and built-in corset boning structure
H. 50 × W. 30 × D. 5 in.
Courtesy of the artist
Jewelry on model by Jennifer Younger (Tlingit)

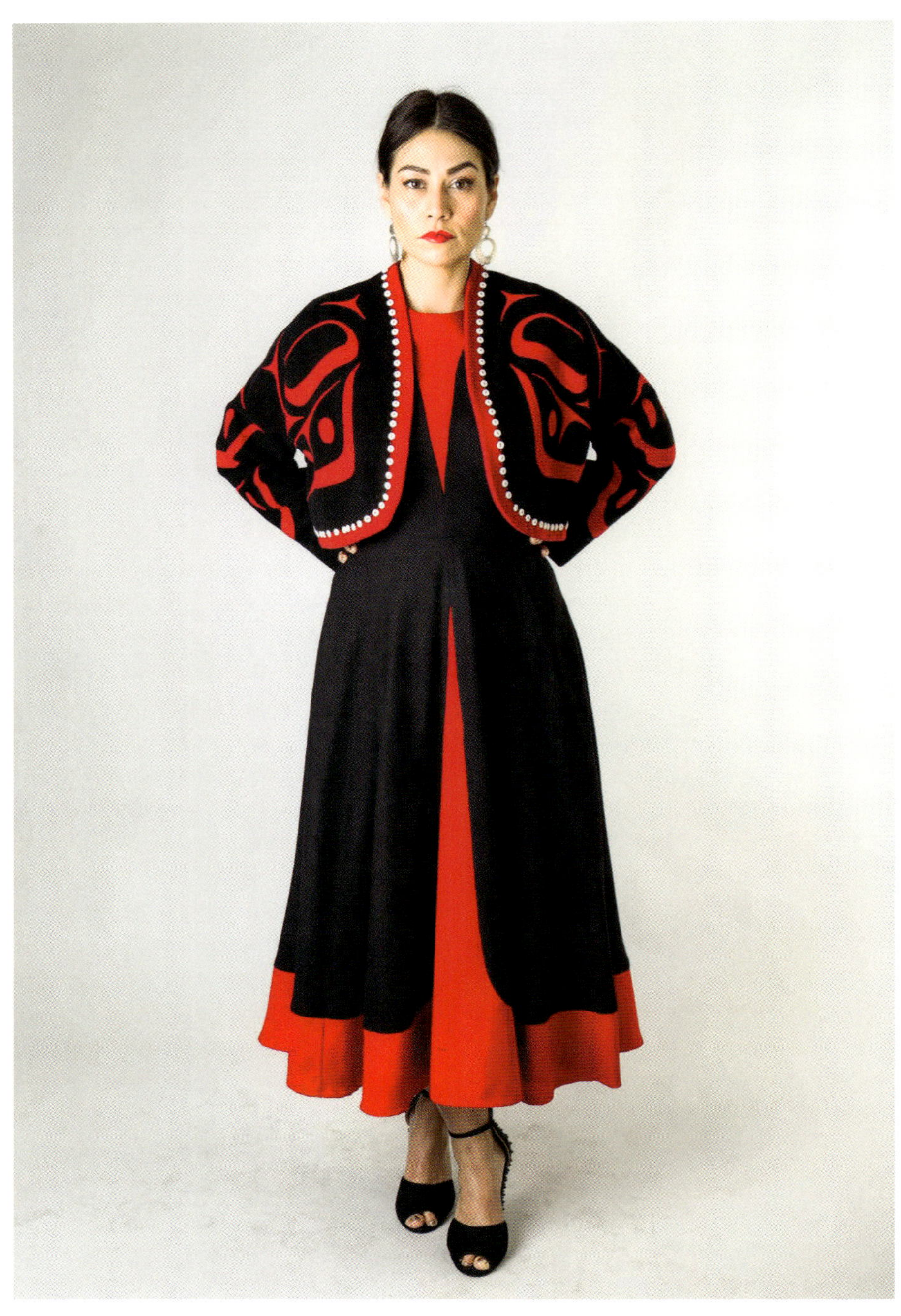

Dorothy Grant
Haida, born 1955
Eagle Bolero with T-Form Dress, 1989
Cashmere and mother-of-pearl
Dimensions variable
Courtesy of the artist

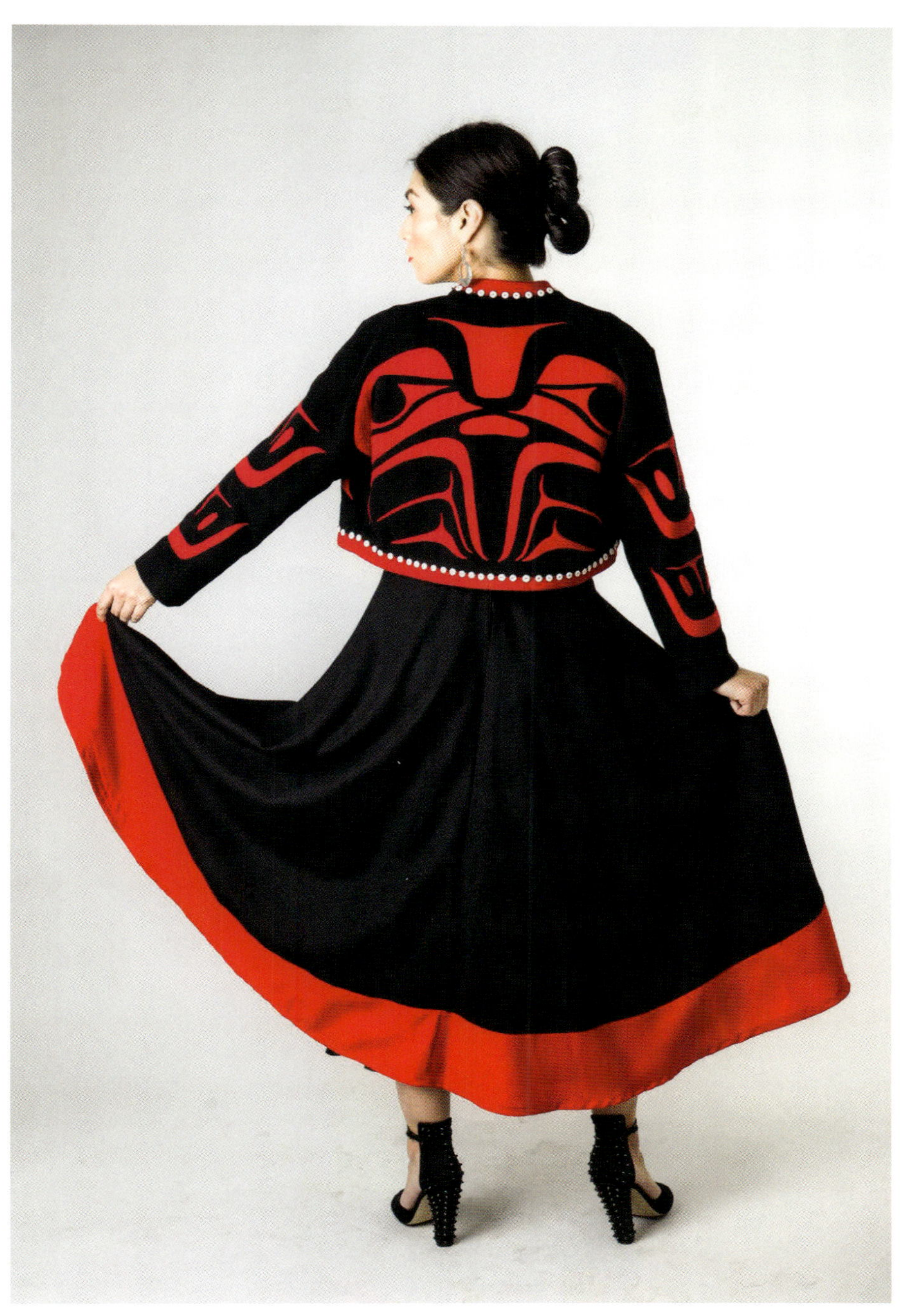

119

Dorothy Torivio
Acoma Pueblo, 1946–2011
Jar, 1994
Clay and paint
H. 8¹³⁄₁₆ × 8 in.
Denver Art Museum: Gift of Virginia Vogel Mattern, 2003.1261

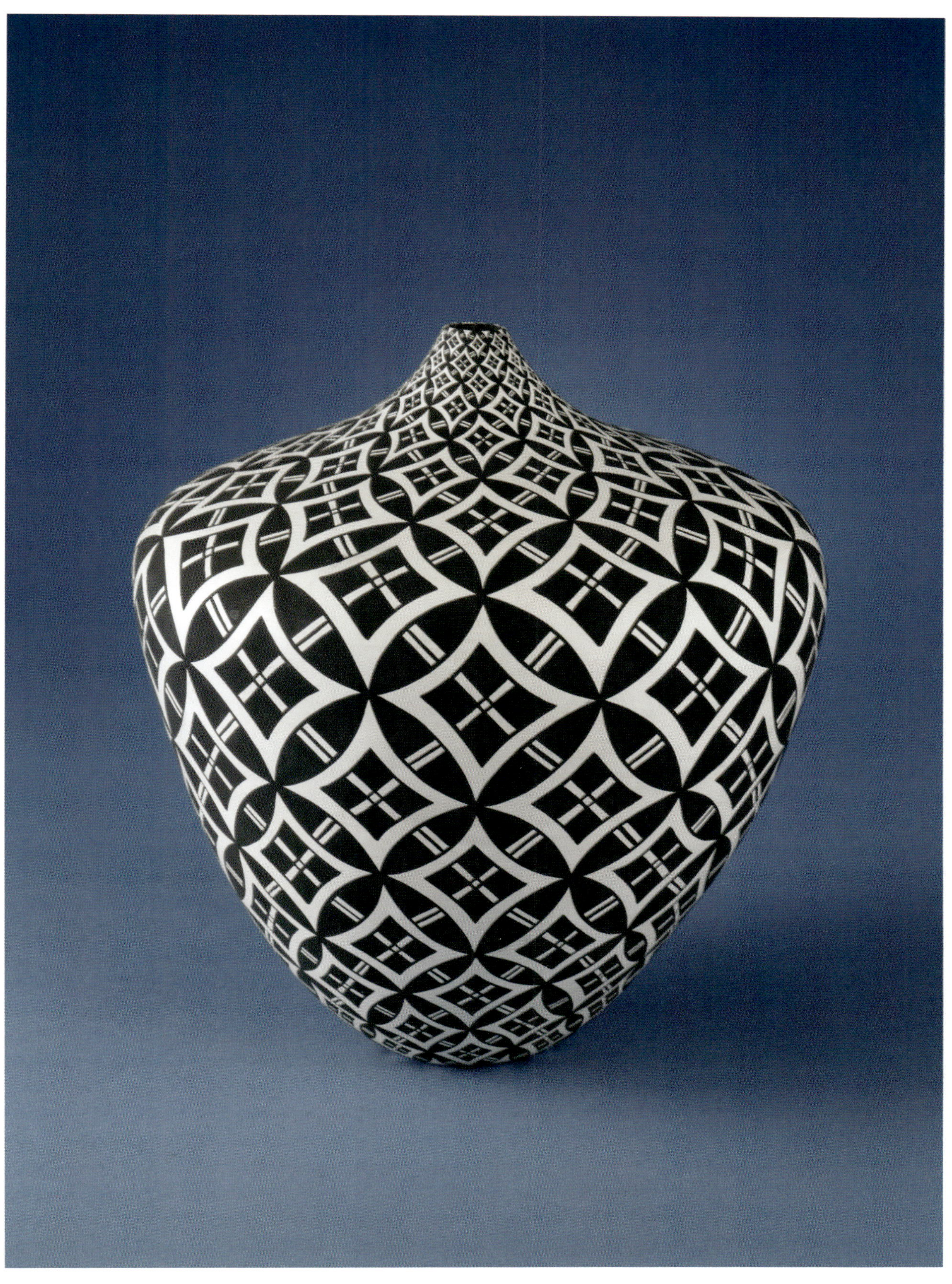

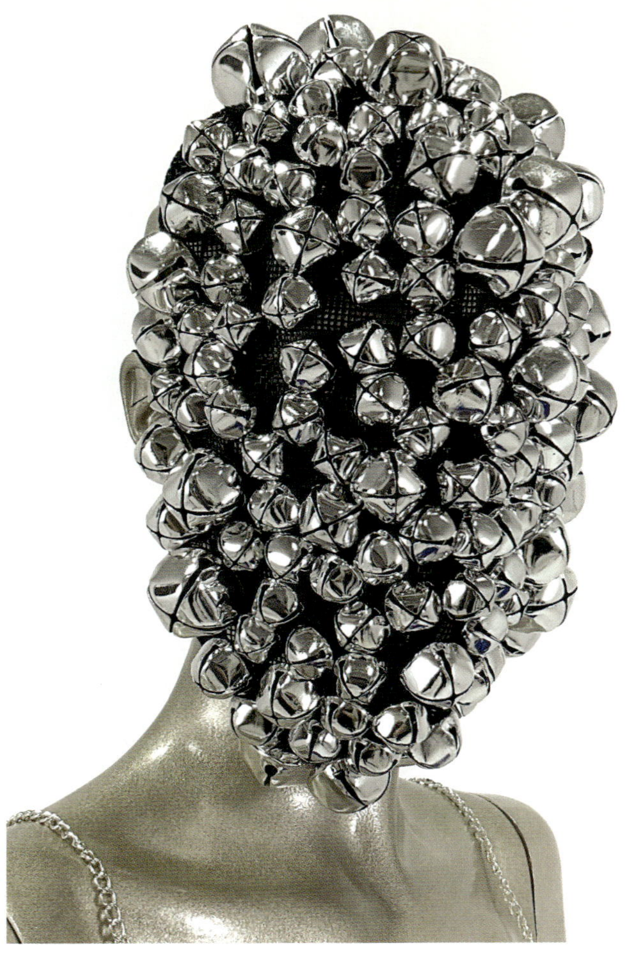

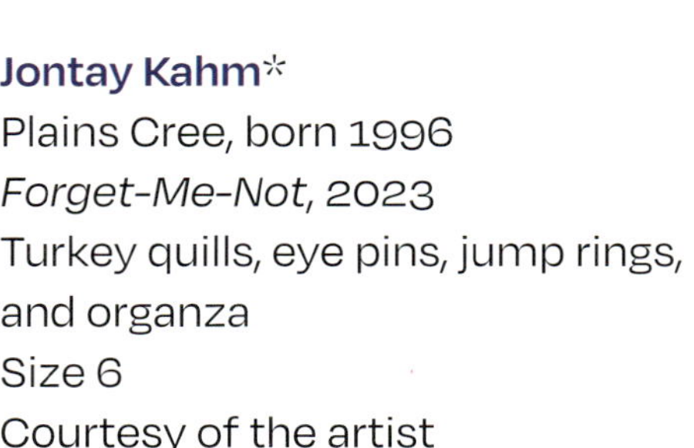

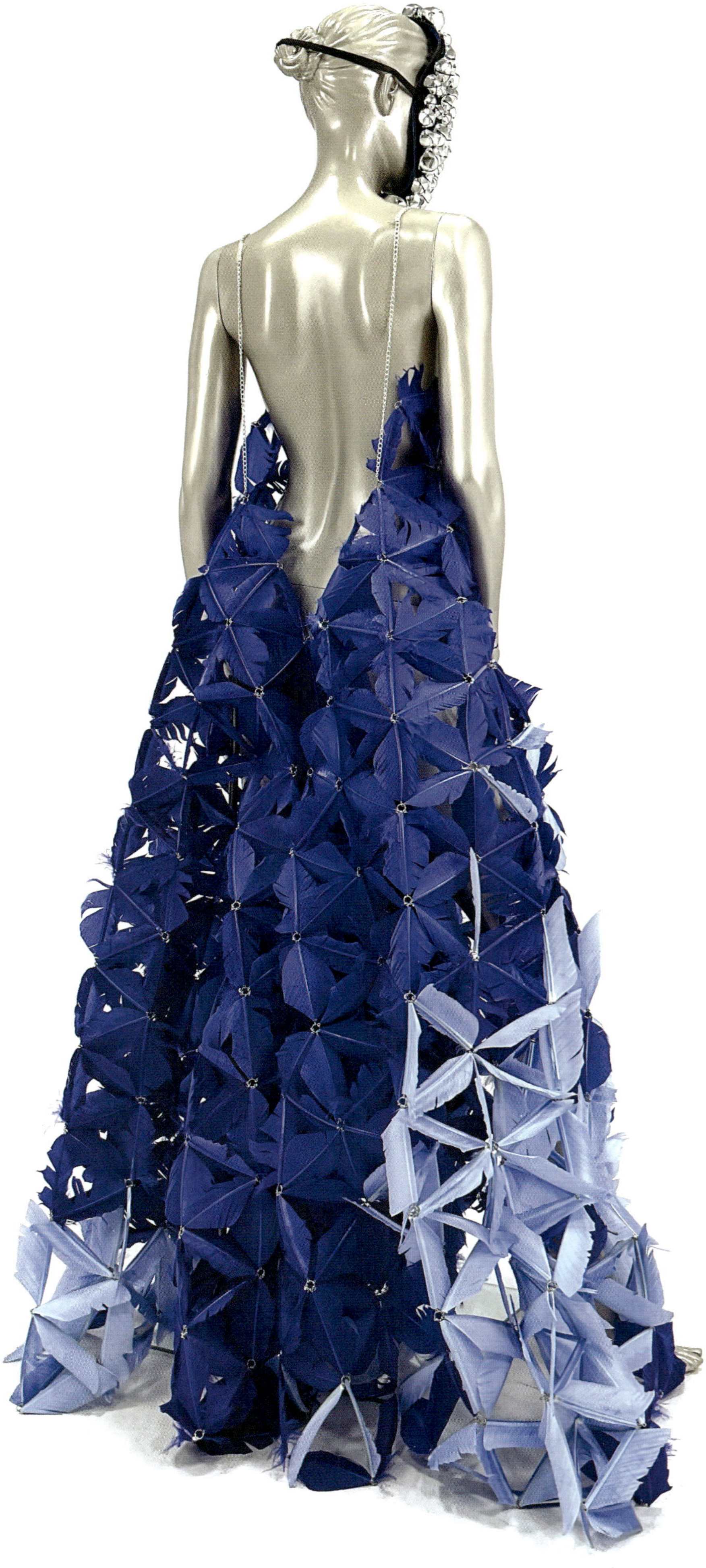

Jontay Kahm*
Plains Cree, born 1996
Forget-Me-Not, 2023
Turkey quills, eye pins, jump rings,
and organza
Size 6
Courtesy of the artist

* *The exhibition includes a similar work by this artist.*

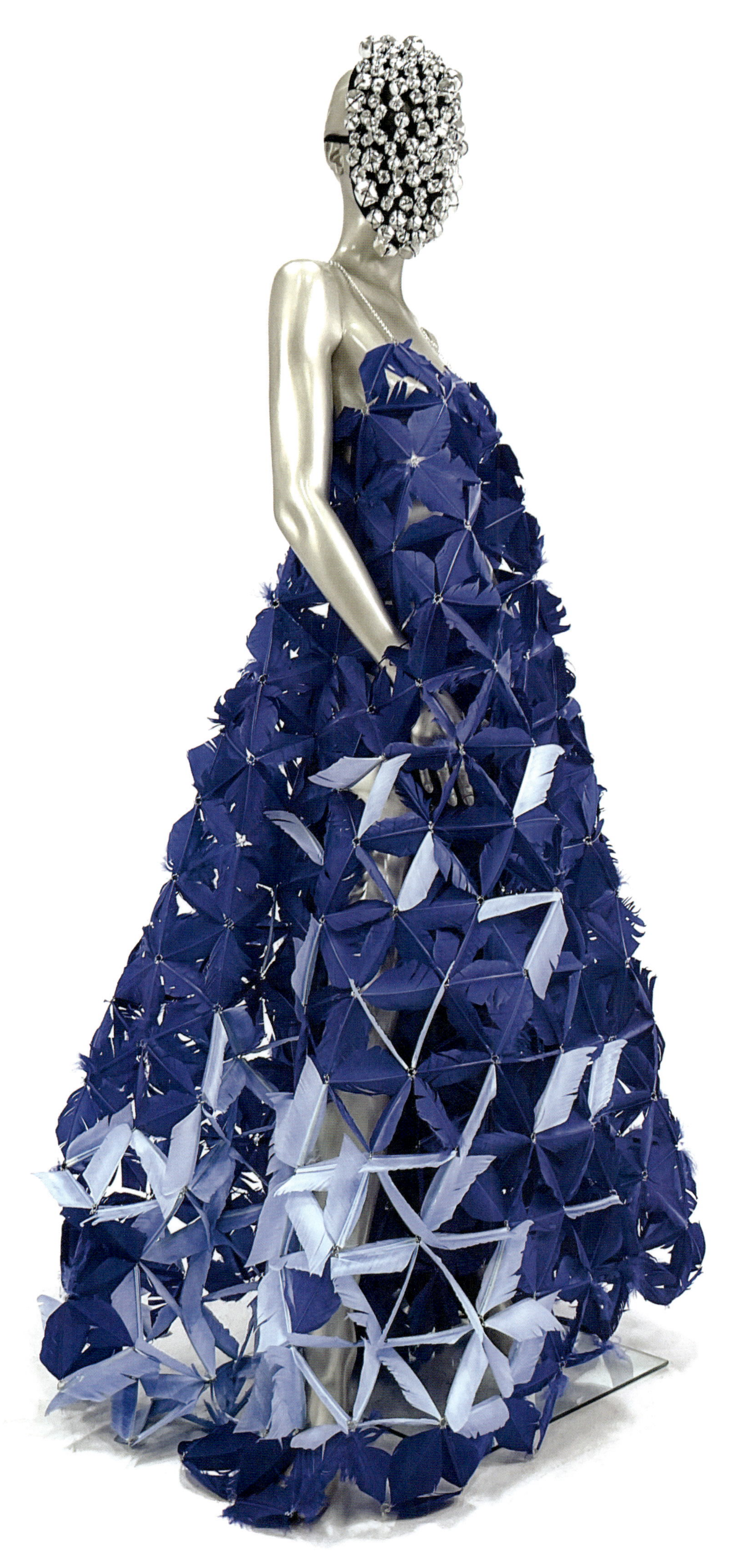

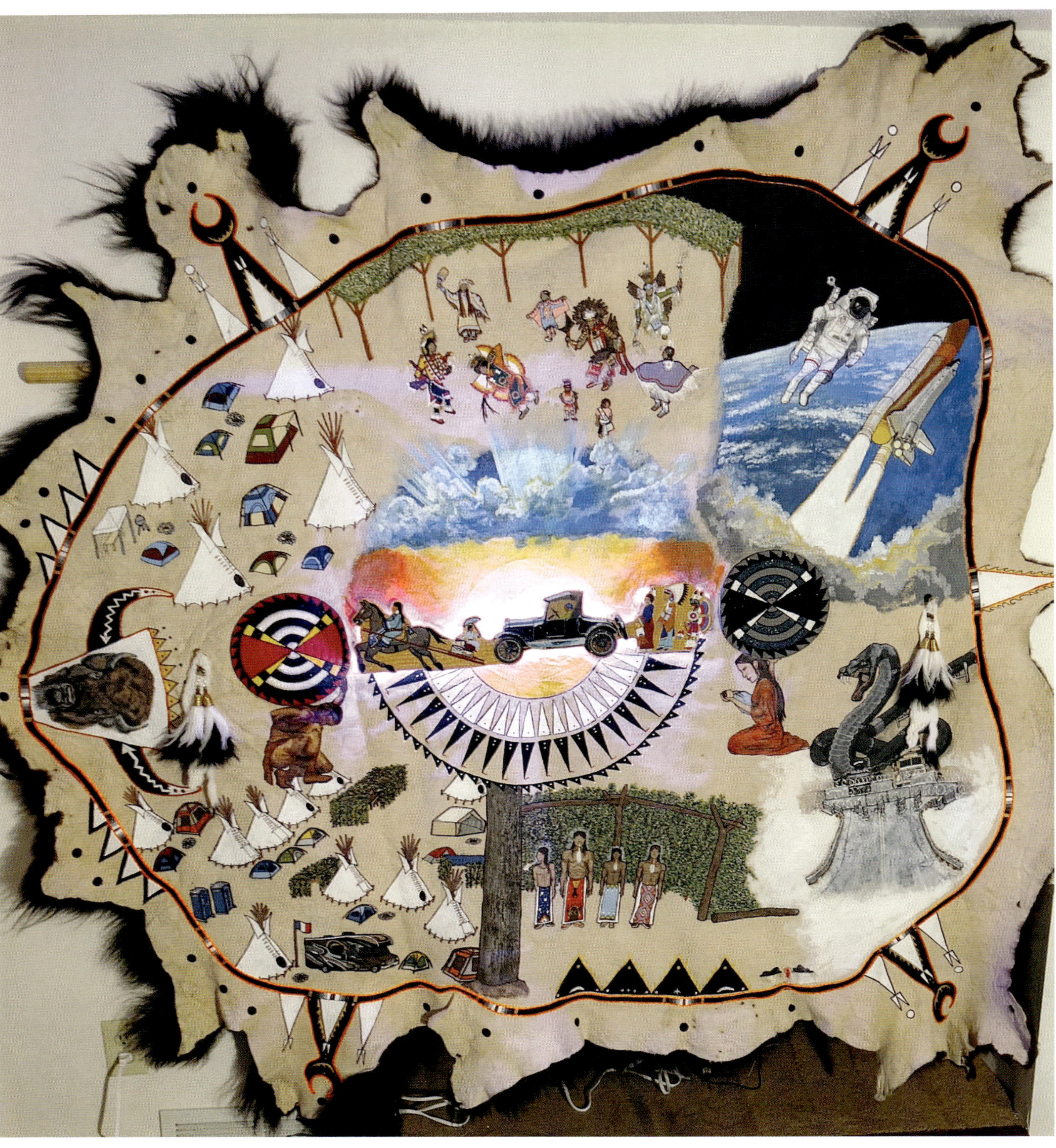

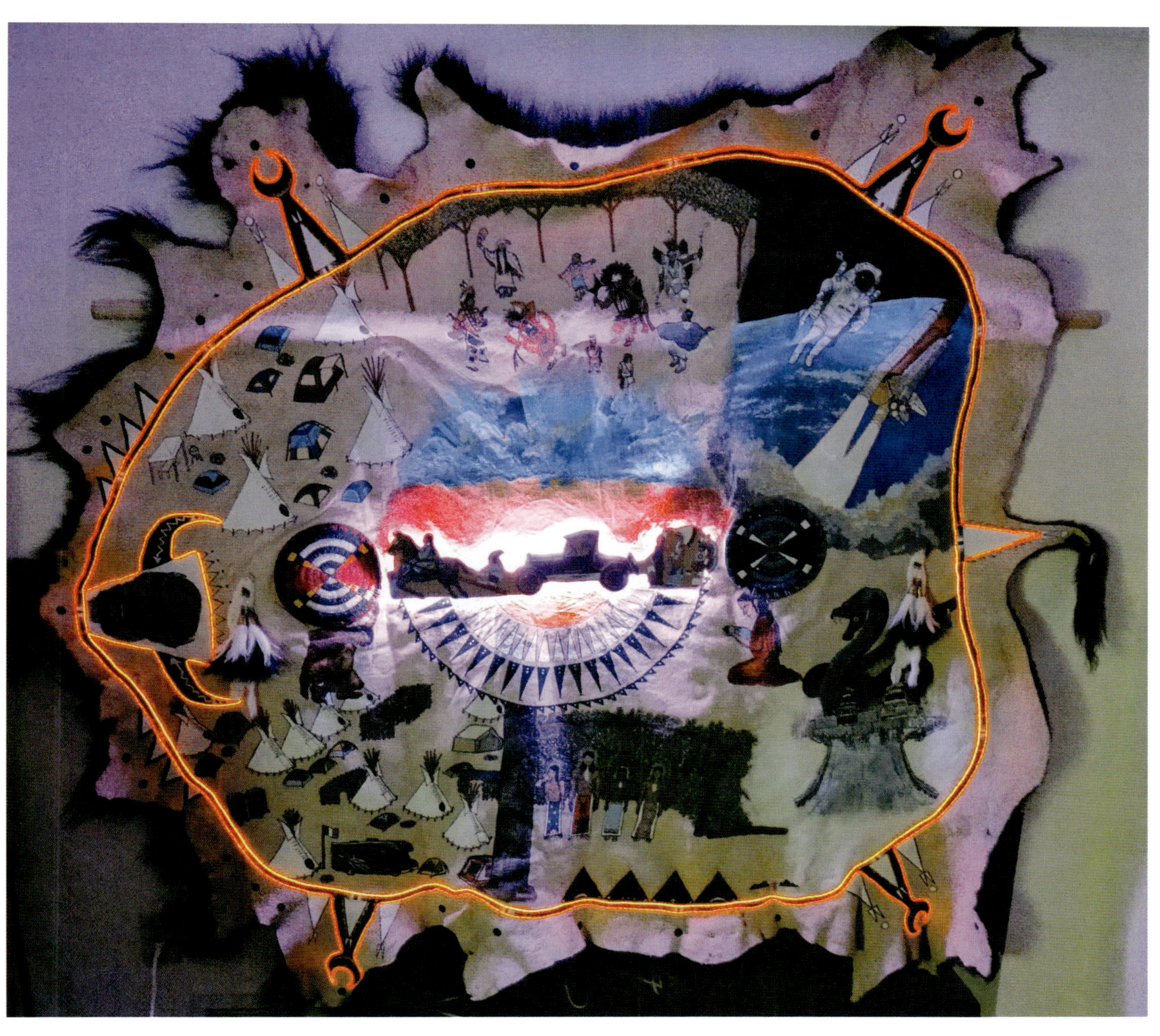

Dallin Maybee
Northern Arapaho/Seneca, born 1974
Buffalo Robe, no date
Buffalo hide, acrylic paint, and beads
Dimensions variable
Courtesy of the artist

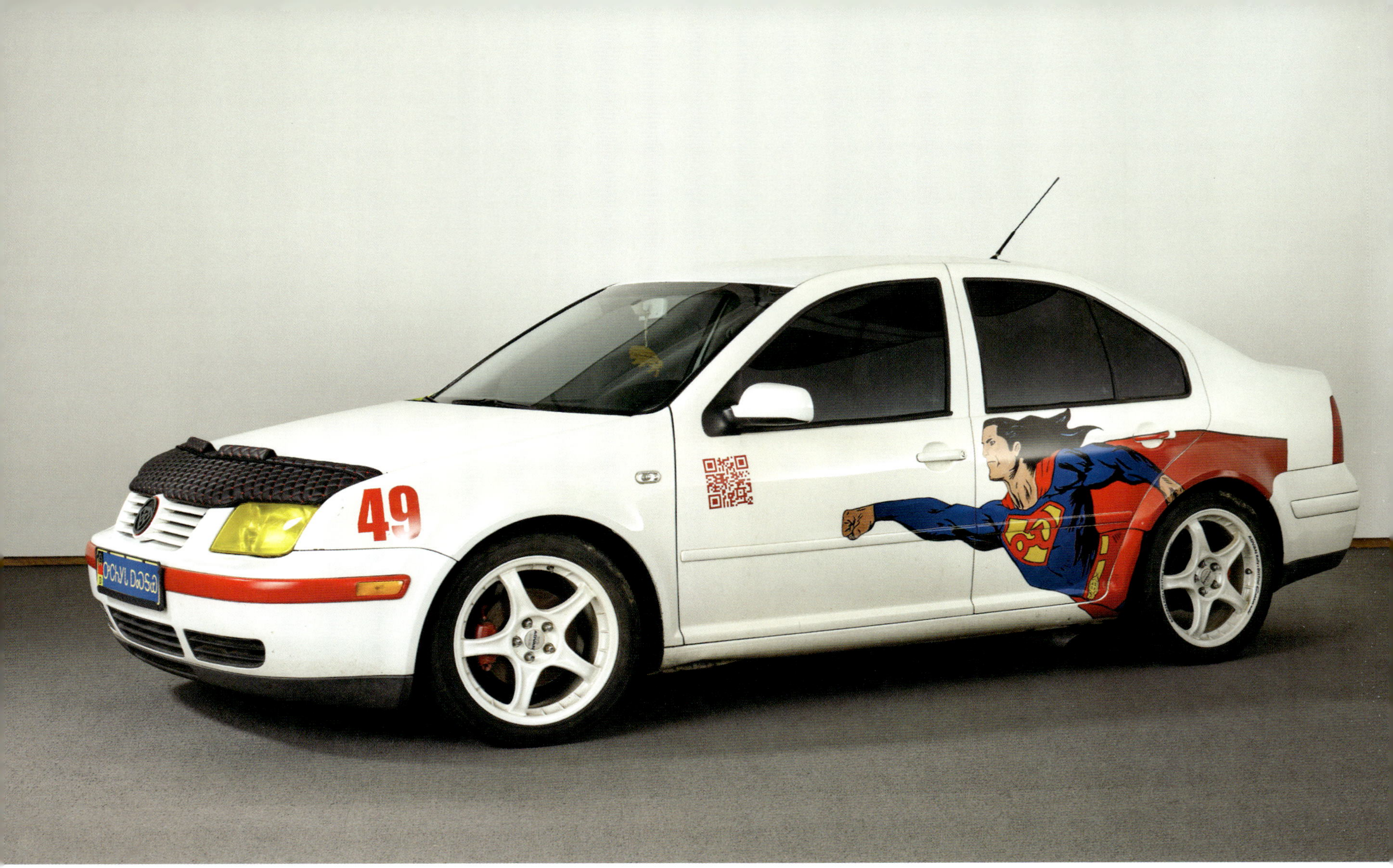

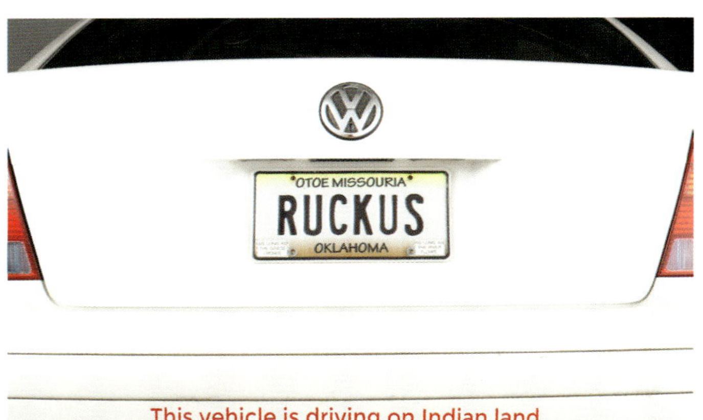

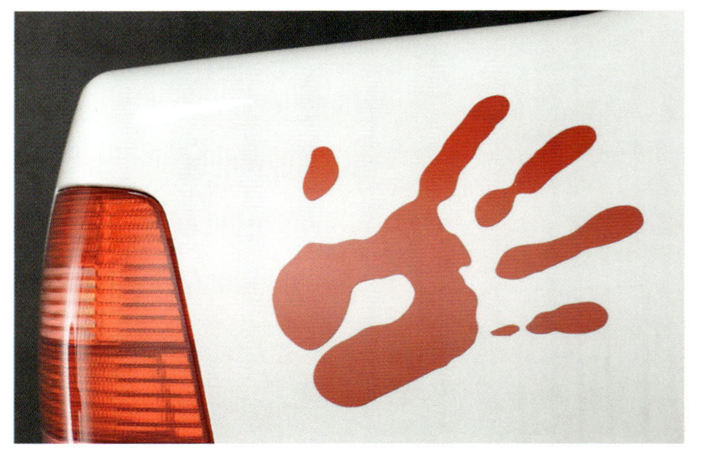

Tom Farris
Otoe-Missouria/Cherokee Nation, born 1978
Shifting Paradigms Übermensch, 2022
Restored 2001 Volkswagen Jetta
H. 59 × W. 68 × D. 174 in.
Courtesy of the artist

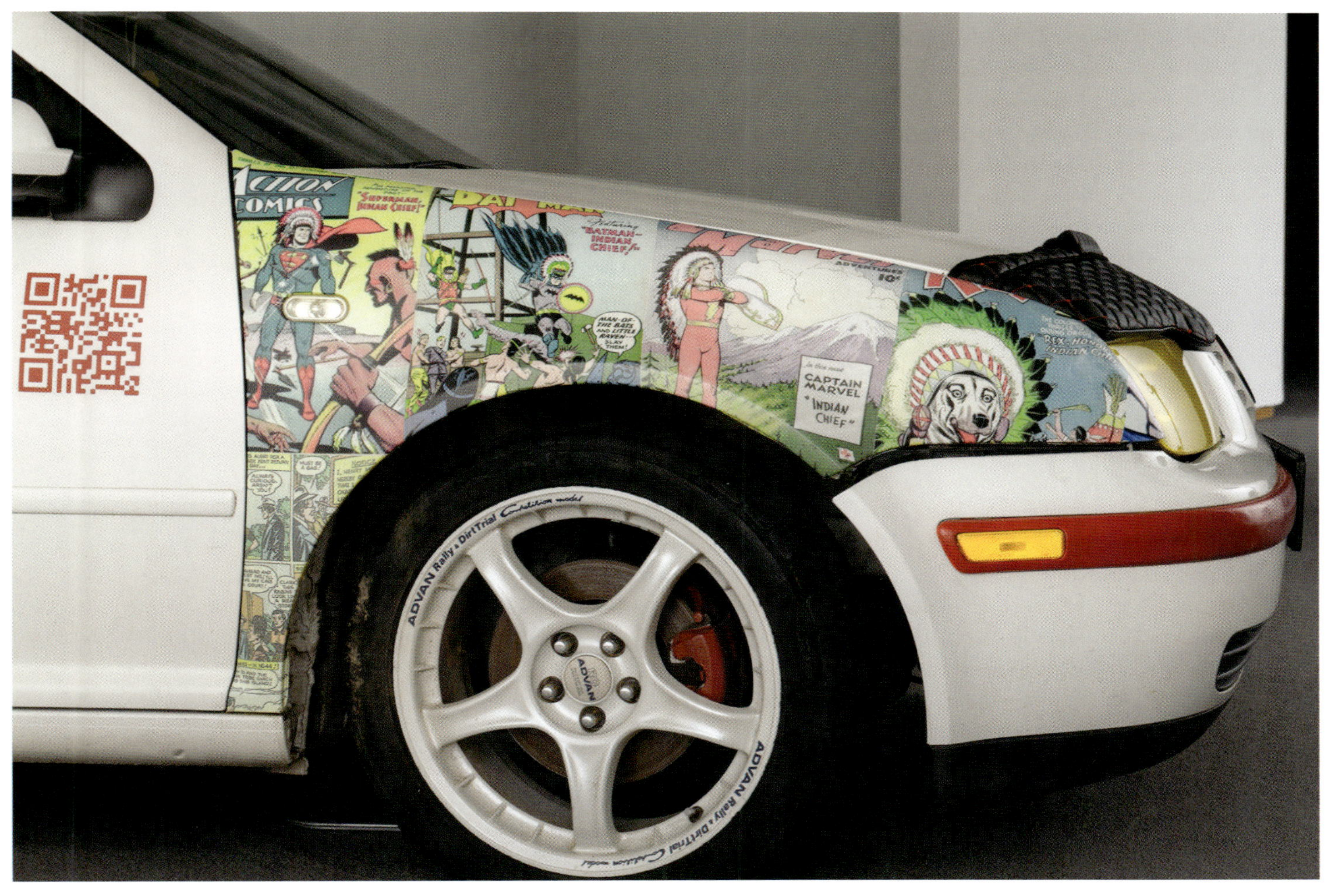

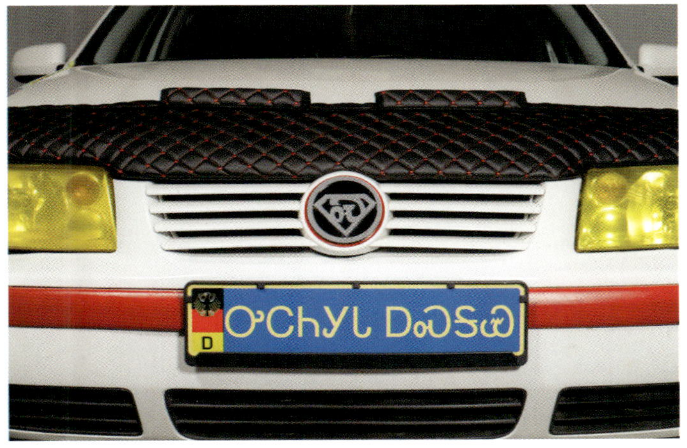

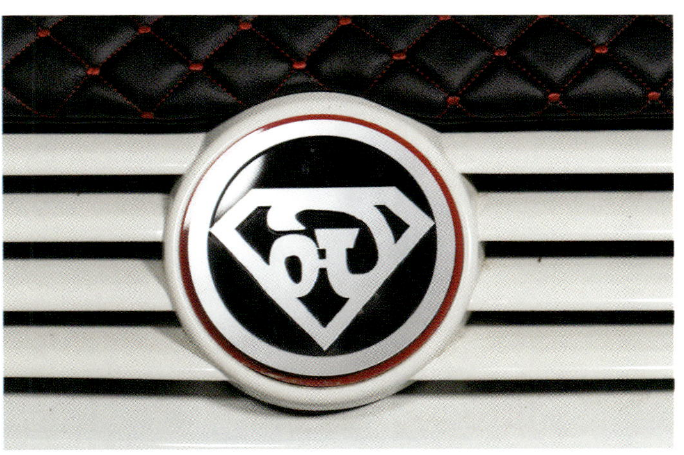

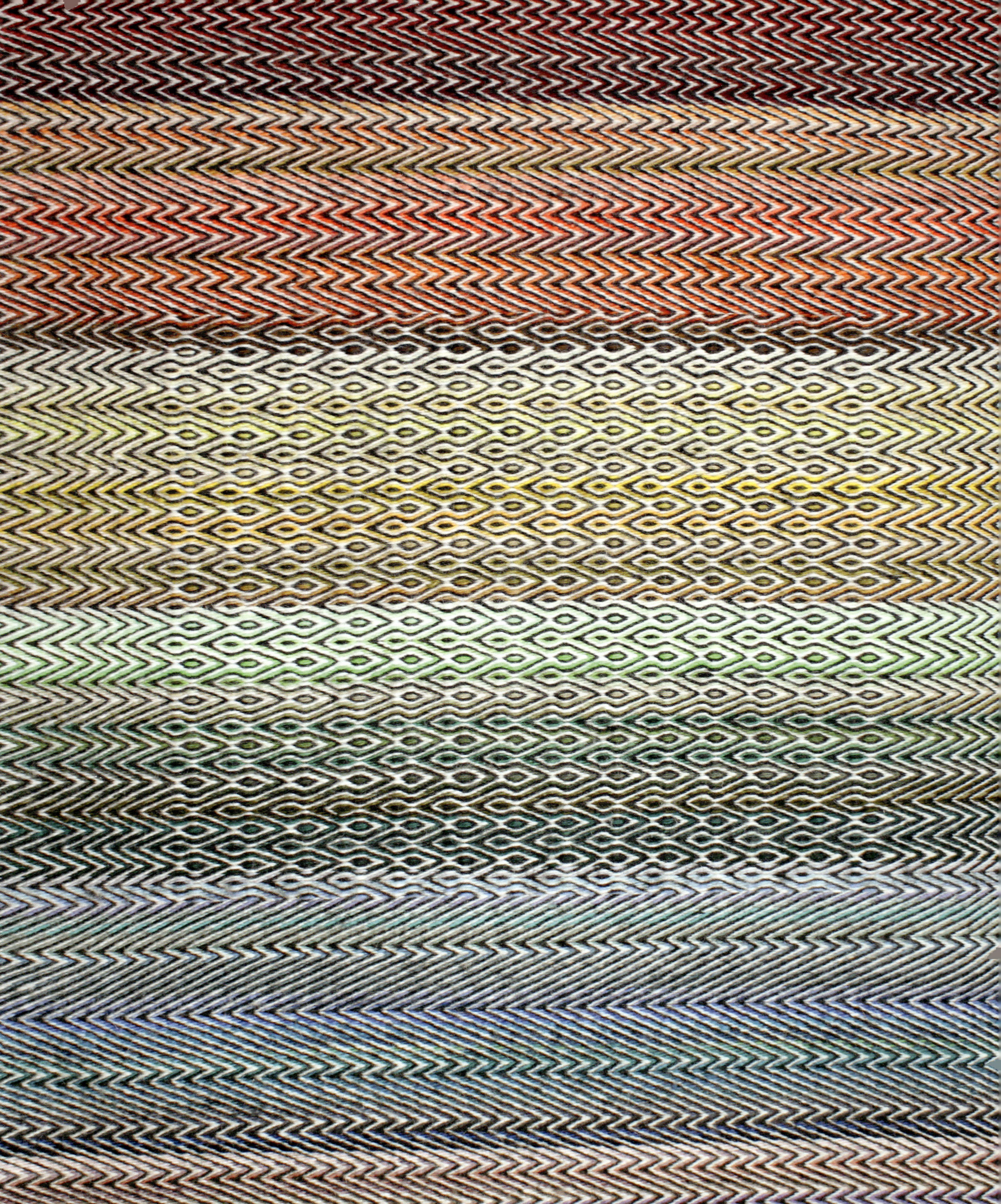

Revival and
Evolution

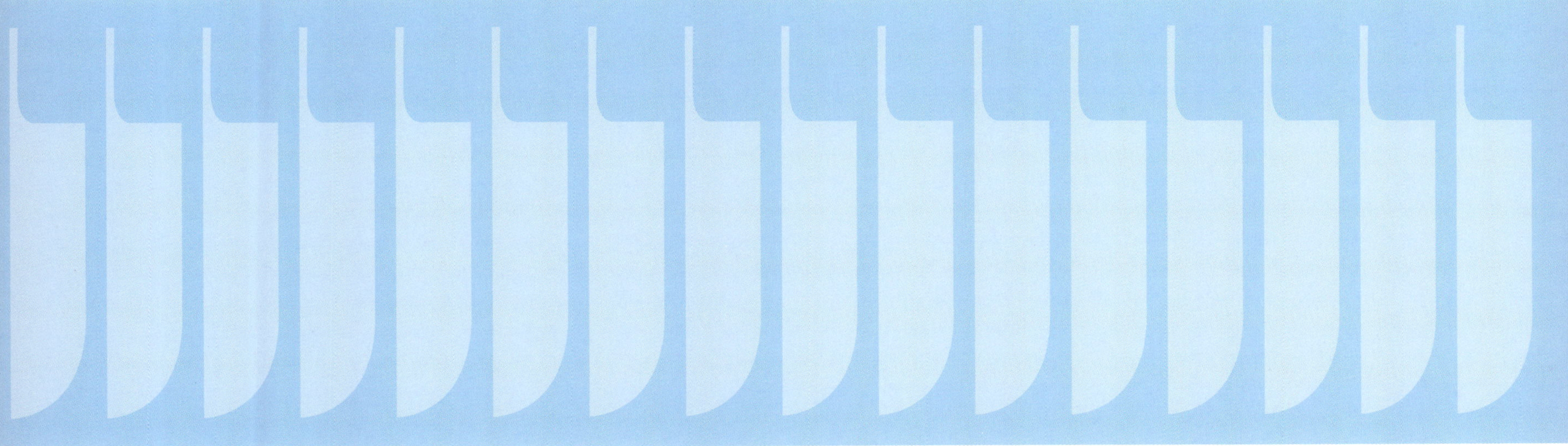

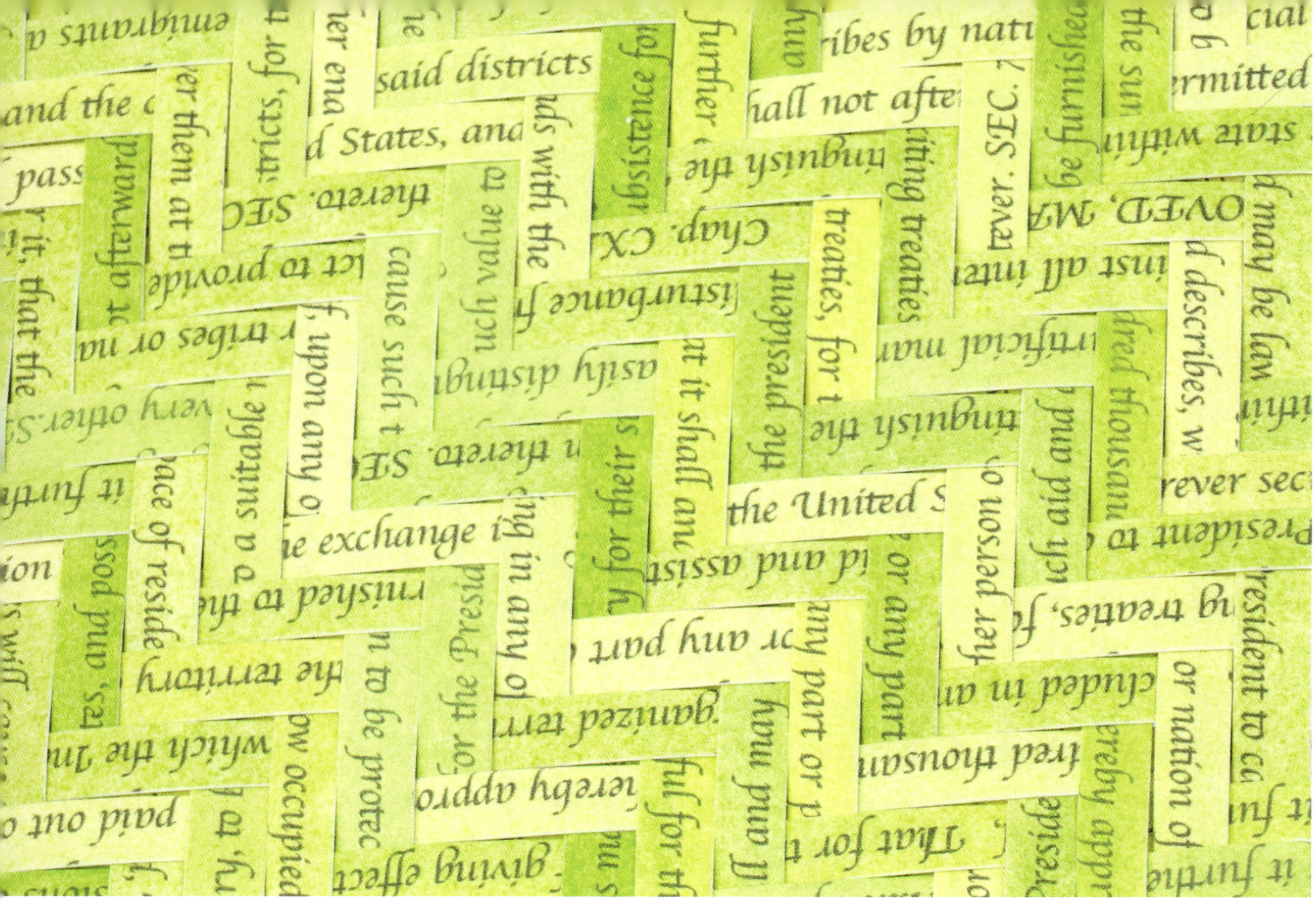

THERE IS A PERCEPTION that traditional American Indian arts have continued to exist and thrive despite indelible changes among the people who make them. This is not true. The survivance of artistic traditions is nothing less than a miracle. Particularly in the late nineteenth and twentieth centuries, varying laws and conditions in every Native community jeopardized the freedom to create art, limited or denied access to natural materials, suppressed identity and culture, and even enforced the absolute repression of artistic expression. In spite of this, as long as the people survived, they found ways to fight for their artistic practices to survive as well.

At the same time, a new kind of Native art developed to fulfill an unexpected demand from tourists with idealized visions of the past. Using the transcontinental railroad and later automobiles on roads like Route 66, Easterners went west to experience and romanticize Native societies. These visits fueled a tourist market in which Native peoples sold their art at railroad stations and roadside stands. Careful not to publicly share and compromise the purpose and meaning of sacred objects, Indigenous artists developed strategic tropes to create "authentic" Native art. Commercial pieces such as Tuscarora raised-beadwork pincushions, Cochiti storyteller pottery, and Navajo weavings with decorative designs appealed to non-Native buyers. The legacy of this history created an ongoing market for Native art; although void of true cultural and sacred representation, it made a place for authentic art to flourish later on, helping to spark a revival among Native artists.

It is important to remember that the **revival** of Native art was not solely dependent on the tourist market. The visceral need of humans to create art exceeds any suppression imposed by those in power. The immersion in artistic practice and the spiritual communion inherent in the process of artmaking act to solidify Native identity, reinforce knowledge, and maintain relationships among community and kin. It allows the creation of cultural objects required for ceremonies, rites of passage, and prayer. Making these objects was and continues to be essential to the lives of Indigenous peoples.

When Chase Earles (Caddo) was a boy, he went with his family out west, where he discovered and fell in love with Pueblo pottery. Years later he connected with Jeri Redcorn (Caddo), who in the 1990s had researched and singlehandedly **revived** the old style of Caddo pottery. She called this time "a journey with her ancestors." Under Redcorn's tutelage Earles found his passion for pottery in his own ancestry.

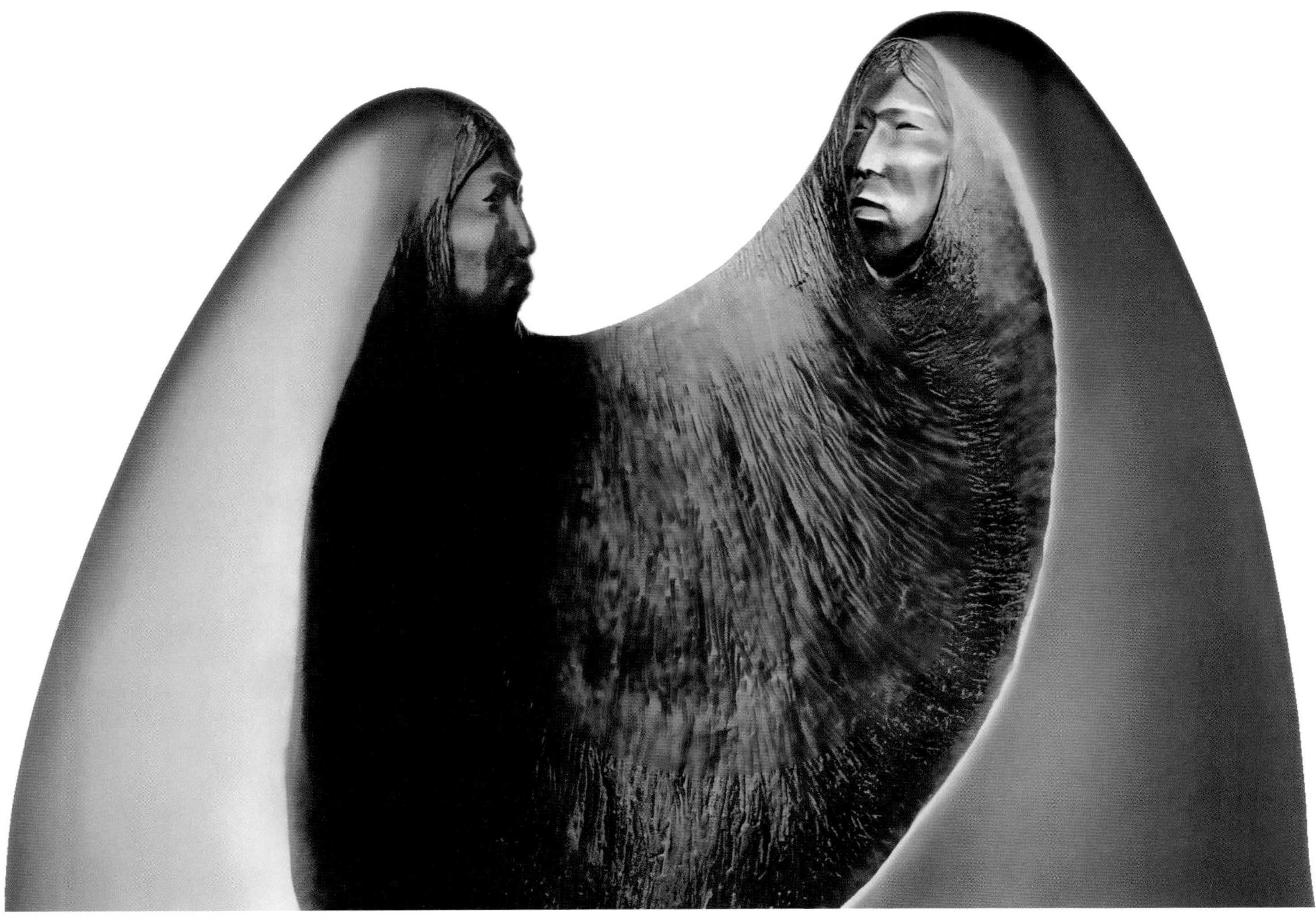

Today, Earles is a master potter committed to creating in the same way his ancestors did. He begins his process digging clay along the riverbanks of Oklahoma. He stays as close to traditional methods as he can, cleaning the clay and preparing it by adding temper such as sand, river mussel shells, or animal bone. He then coils his pieces into traditional forms like tripod vessels (p. 133) and burnishes them by wetting areas of the surface and rubbing them smooth with a river stone. He leaves them to dry before using tools to carve ancient Caddo motifs, such as the sun and moon, everlasting fire, and serpents found in Caddo cosmology. Earles then fires his pottery in a low-burning wood fire pit. The results are the same pottery his ancestors created—with a dark, high-gloss finish and contrasting designs. His commitment to keeping his process as traditional as possible is his way of honoring his ancestors.

Raven Halfmoon (Caddo Nation) is also a ceramist. Like Earles, she is inspired by the traditional Caddo pottery revival sparked by Jeri Redcorn. Unlike him, Halfmoon creates large-scale, textured, and thickly painted sculptures that are unique to her identity and personal interests (p. 134). Halfmoon's surrealist designs present figures of women and horses that are commanding, formative, and seeped in the Caddo world view.

Her work is an **evolution** of Caddo pottery; she follows the tradition of working with clay but evolves the form and meaning to represent the individuality of a modern Caddo woman with a powerful voice. "I create work that is large and powerful. I build sculptures that demand to be heard and experienced. My artwork exists to break the mold of the romanticized Native American stereotype and to simply say: We are still here, and we are powerful."

PAGE 128: Detail of image on page 158

OPPOSITE: Detail of image on page 154

ABOVE: Detail of image on page 142

Chase Earles
Caddo, born 1976
Horse Tripod, 2014
Clay and mussel shell
H. 22 × W. 19 × D. 15
Loan from National Cowboy & Western Heritage Museum

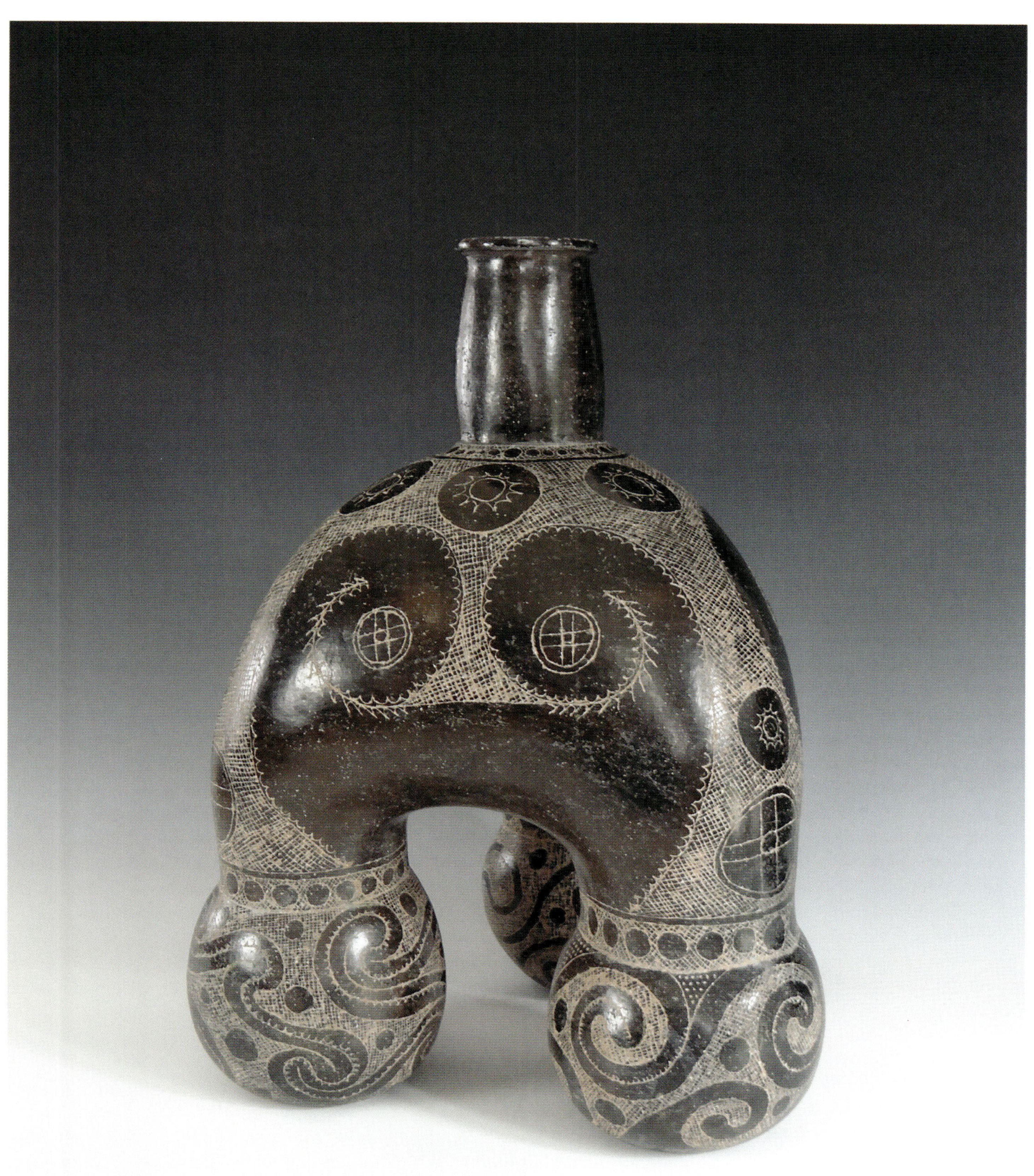

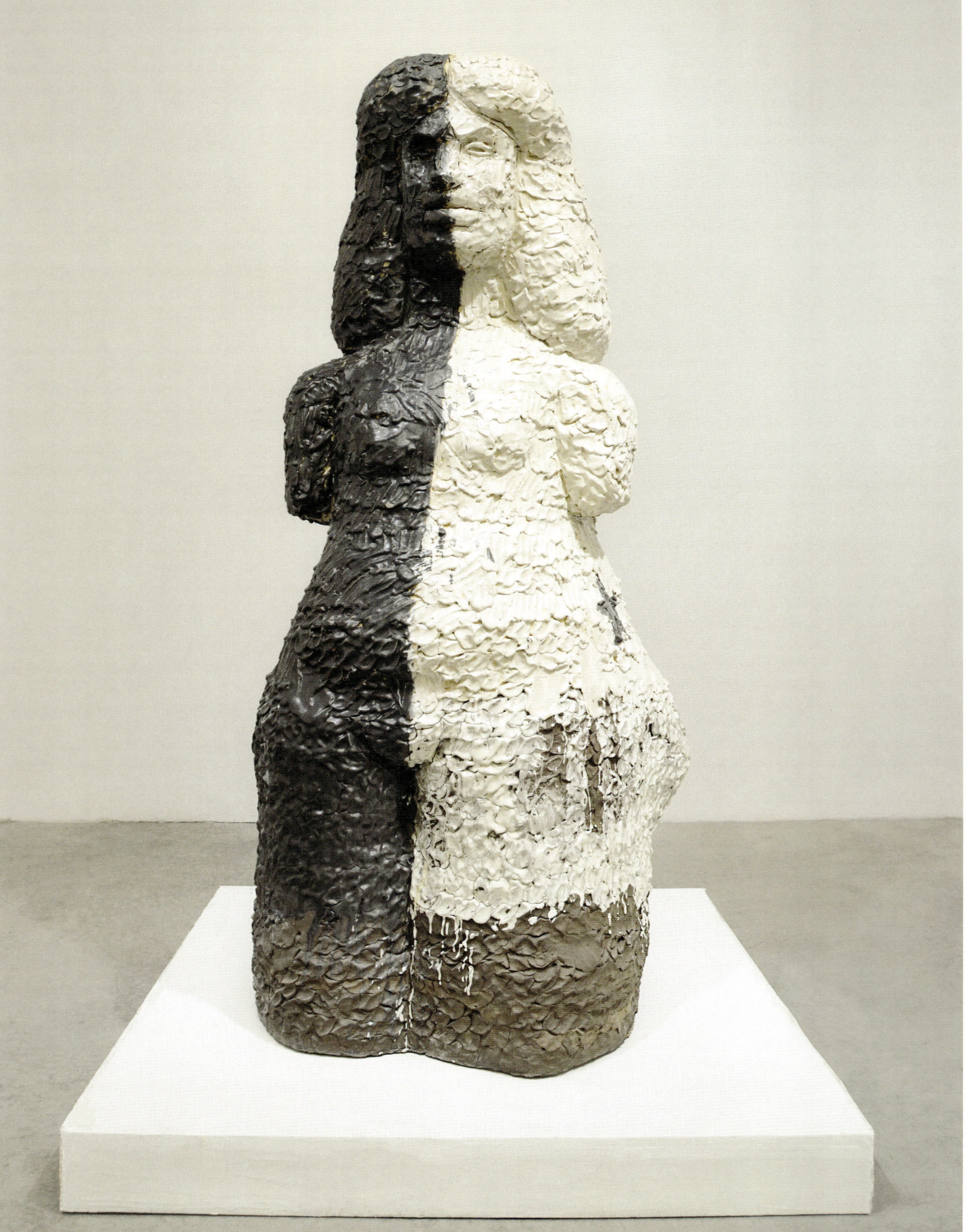

Raven Halfmoon
Caddo Nation, born 1991
Soku & Nish (Sun & Moon – Caddo), 2022
Ceramic and glaze
H. 72 × W. 38 × D. 40 in.
Courtesy of Kouri + Corrao Gallery

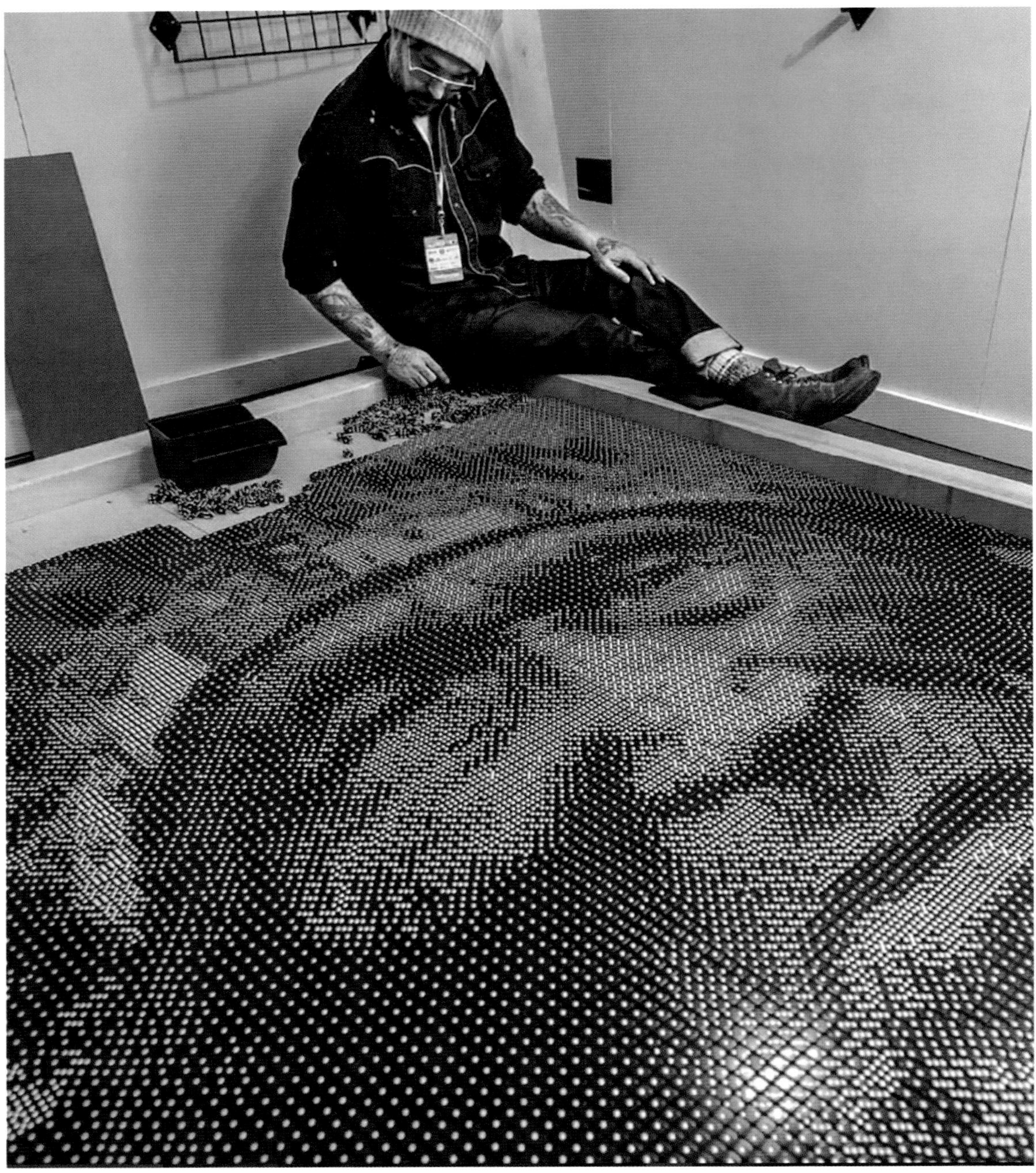

Steven Paul Judd creating mosaic portrait *He Dog* (2022, 16,402 dice, dimensions variable, Private collection),
Courtesy of the artist

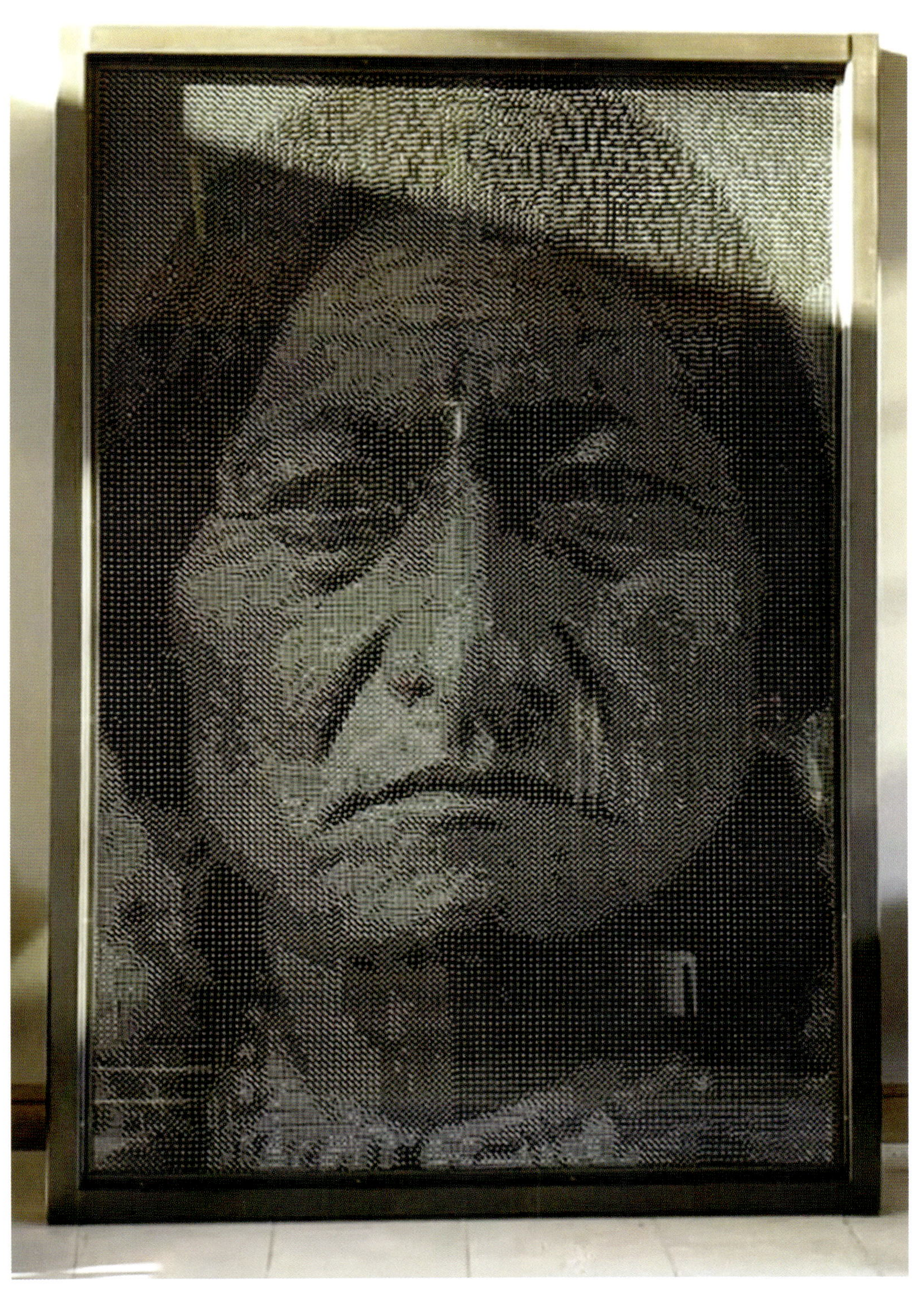

Steven Paul Judd*
Kiowa/Choctaw
Sitting Bull, 2019
20,068 dice
9 × 6 ft.
Private collection

** The exhibition includes a similar work by this artist.*

Peter B. Jones
Onondaga, born 1947
New Indian – Portrait Jar, 2010
Clay, pigment, sinew, copper, and wood
H. 12 × W. 9 × D. 10 in.
Longyear Museum of Anthropology, Colgate University,
Museum purchase, NA2010.104

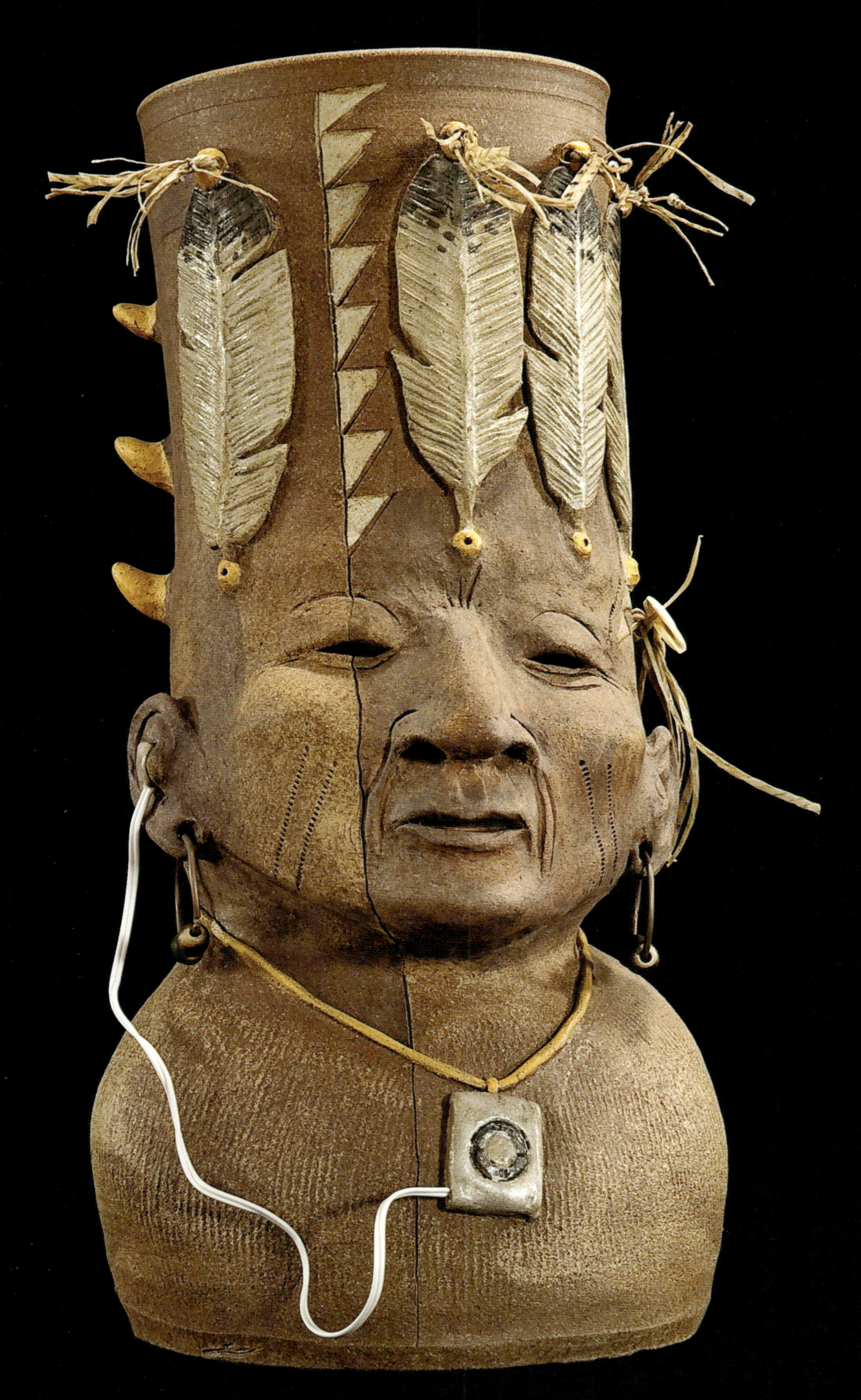

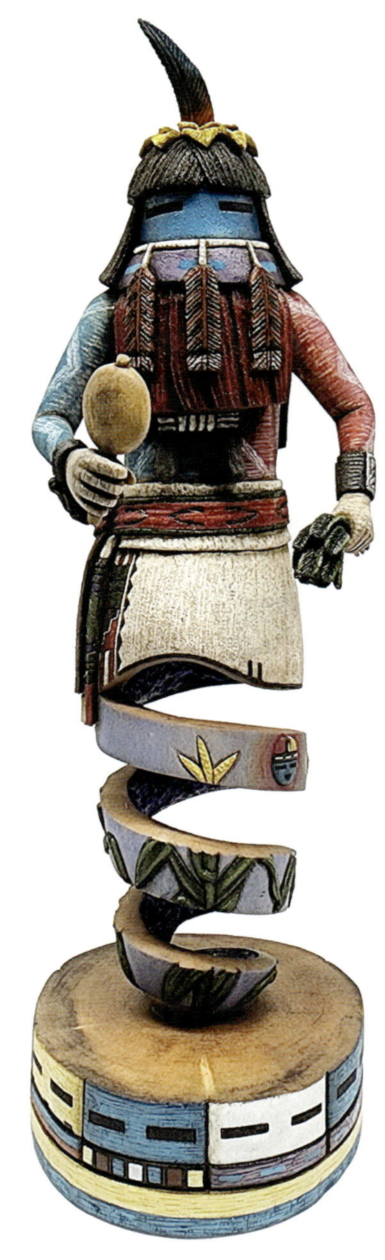

Renferd Koruh
Hopi/Tewa, born 1984

A Time of Harvest, 2023
Aged cottonwood root and acrylic paints
H. 13 × W. 4 × D. 4½ in.
Courtesy of the artist

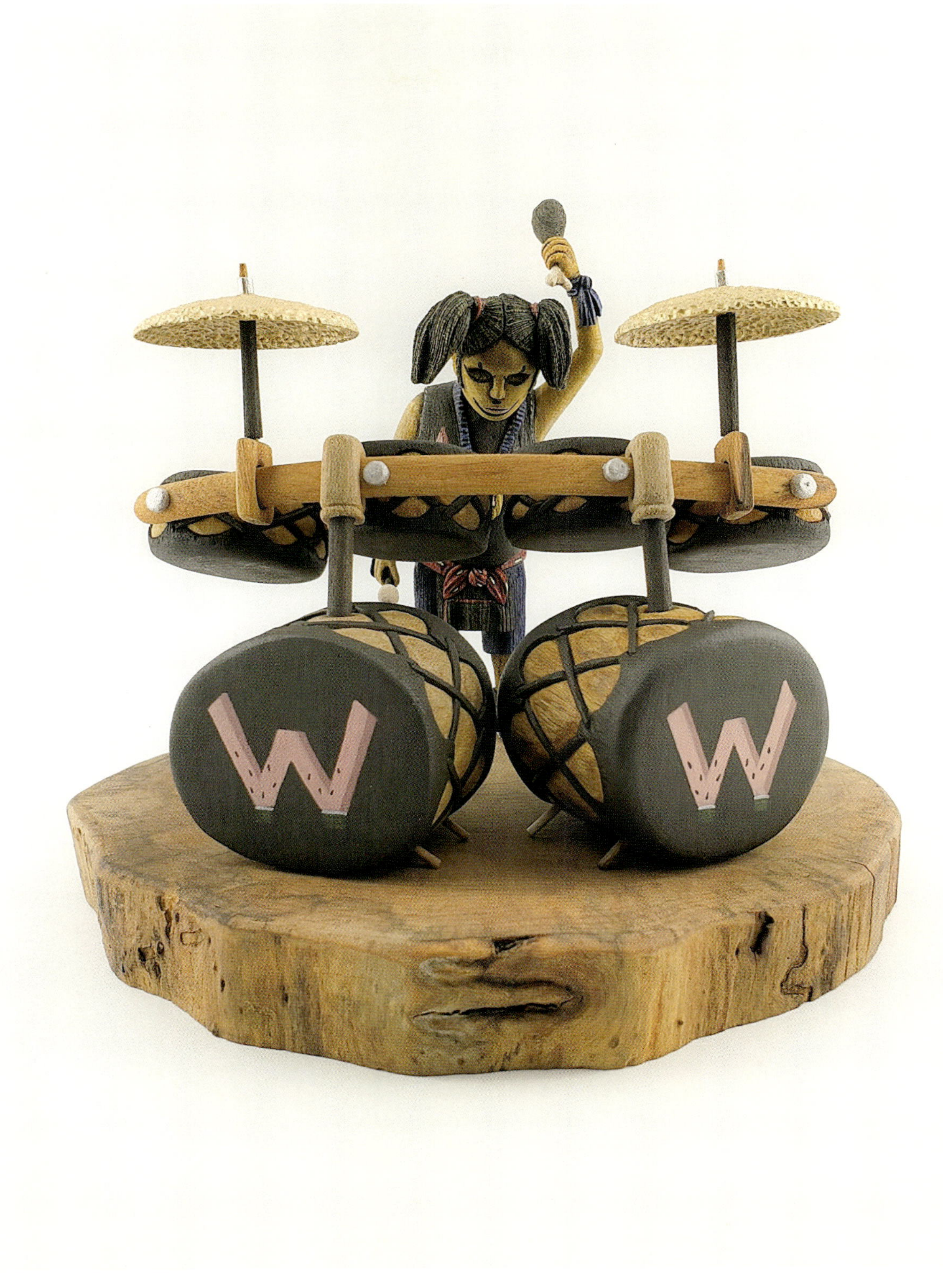

The Watermelon Tour – Encore, 2023
Aged cottonwood root and acrylic paints
H. 7 × W. 9 × D. 9 in.
Courtesy of the artist

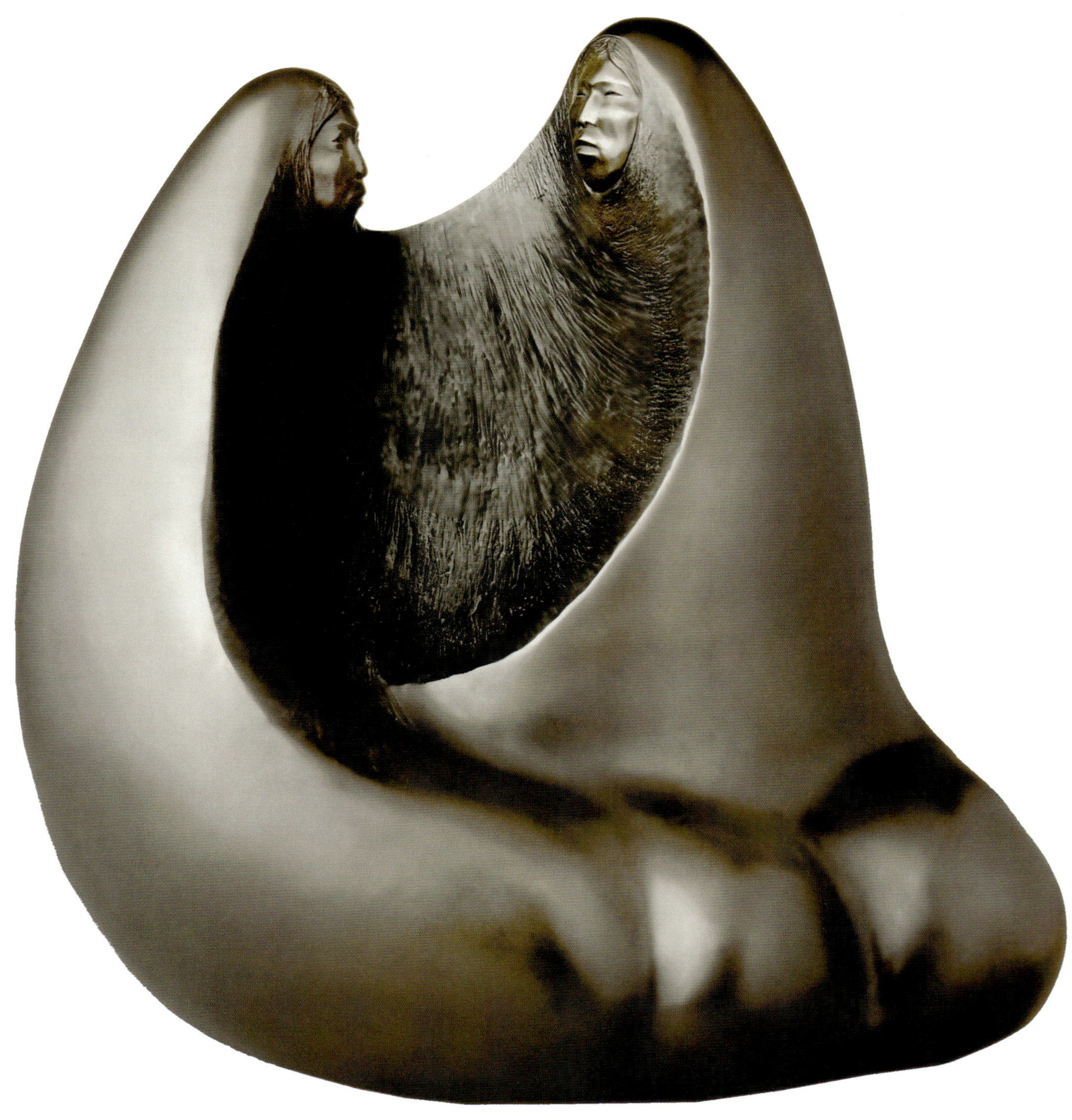

Allan Houser

Fort Sill Apache, 1914–1994

ABOVE
Camp Talk, 1979
Bronze
H. 23½ × W. 22½ × D. 21½ in.
Courtesy of Allan Houser Inc.

OPPOSITE
Reverie, 1981
Bronze
H. 24½ × W. 23 × D. 12½ in.
Courtesy of Allan Houser Inc.

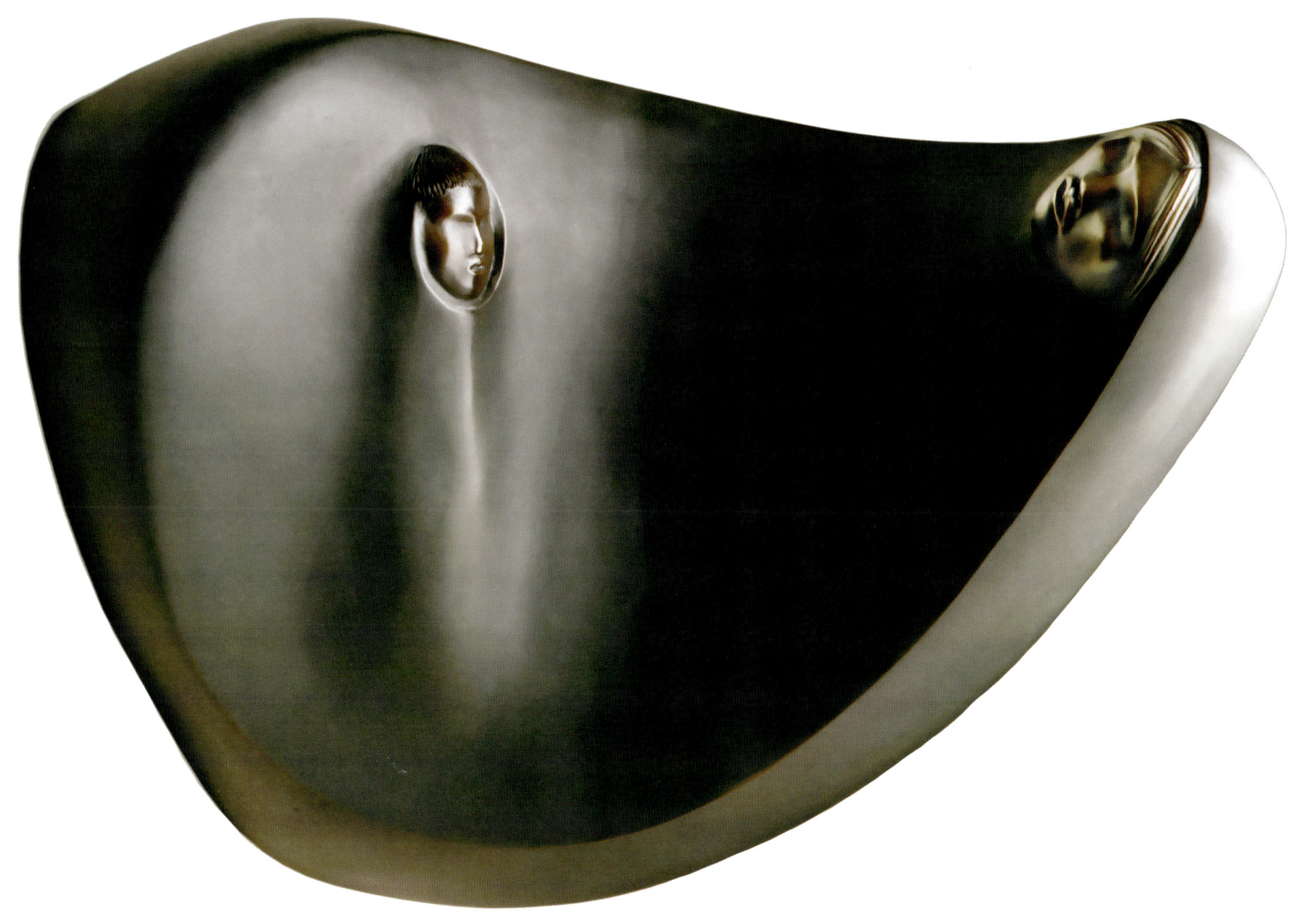

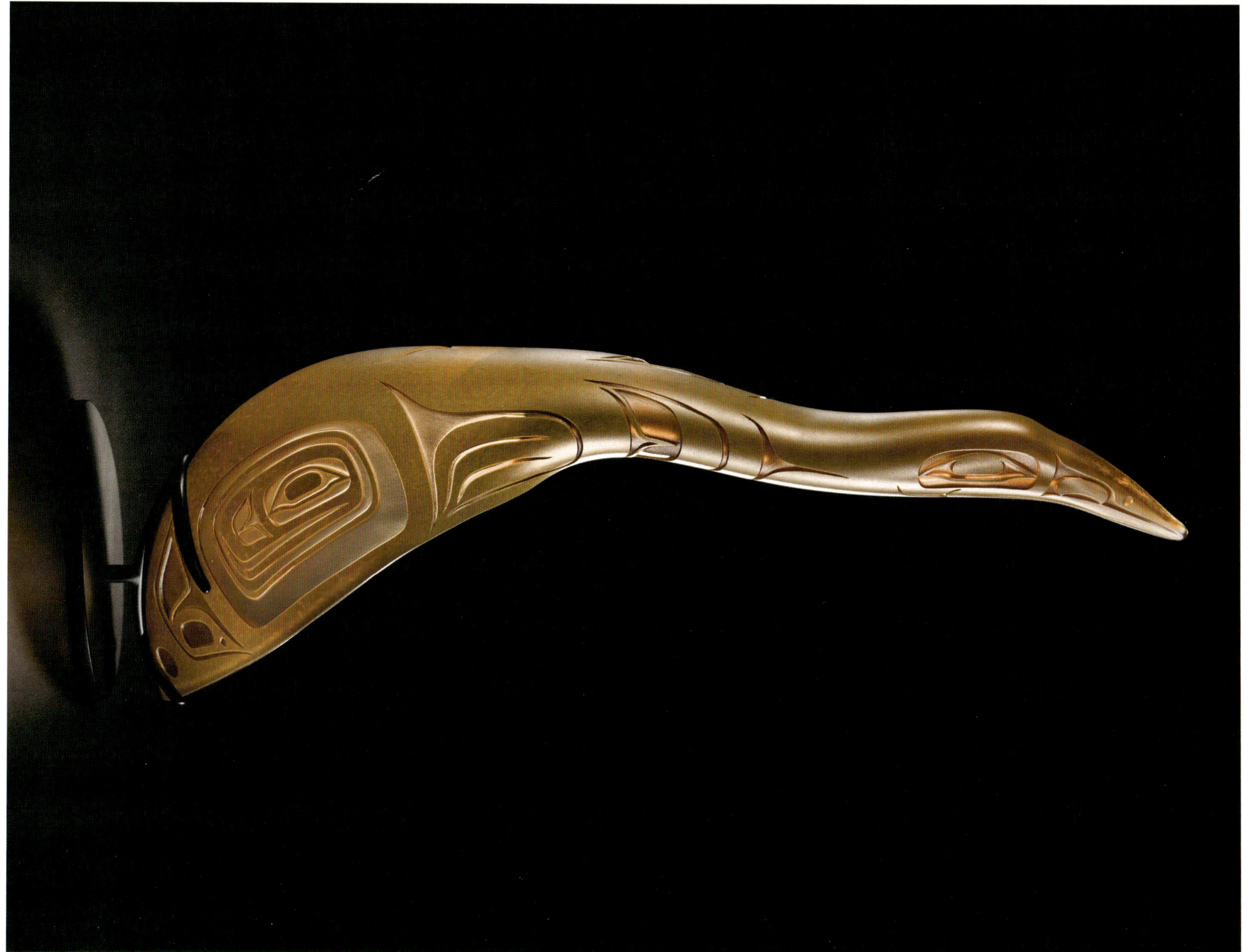

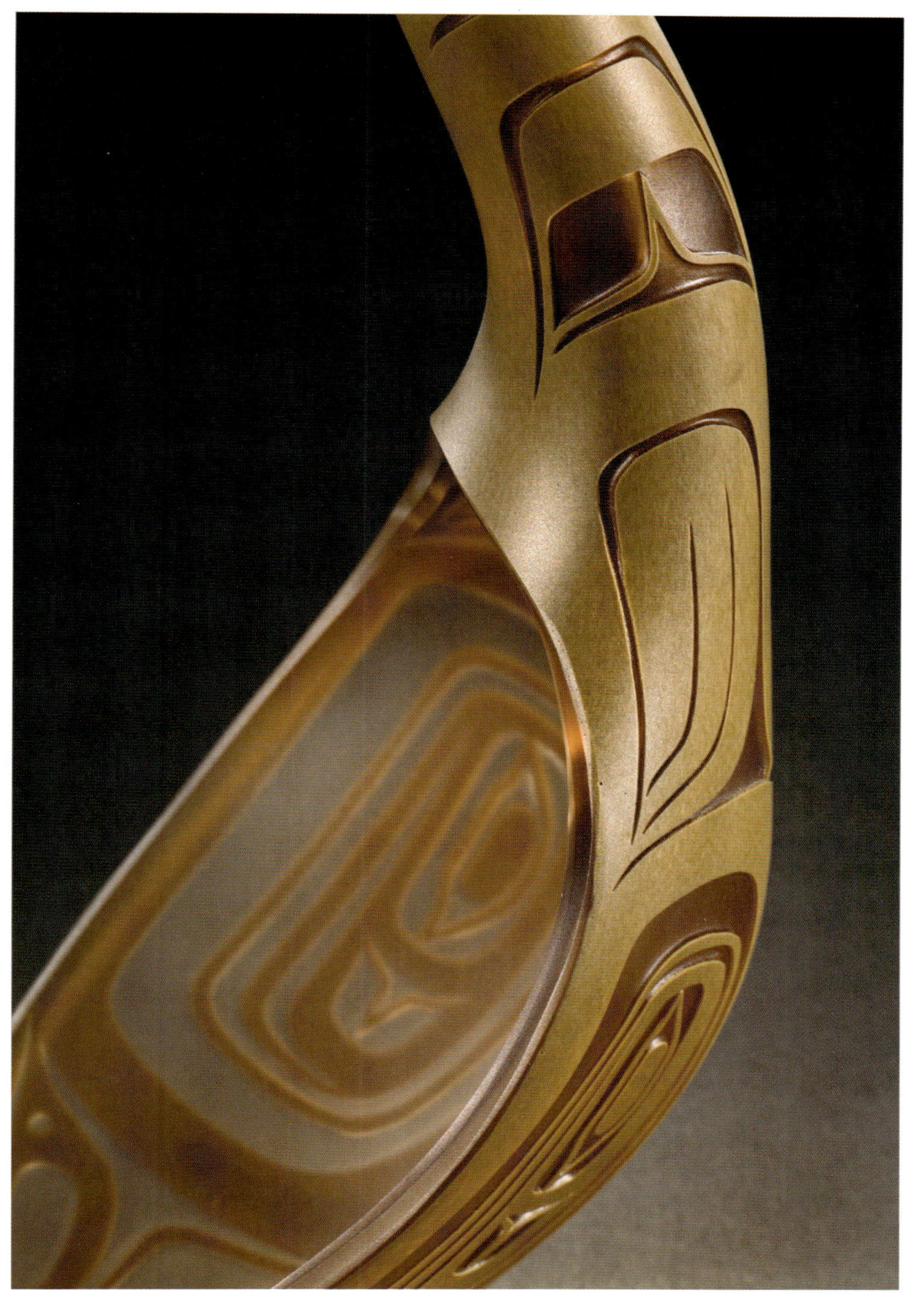

Preston Singletary
Tlingit, born 1963
Raven Ladle, 2014
Blown and sand-carved glass
H. 23½ × W. 6¾ × D. 8¼ in.
Collection of Mina Levin and Ronald Schwarz

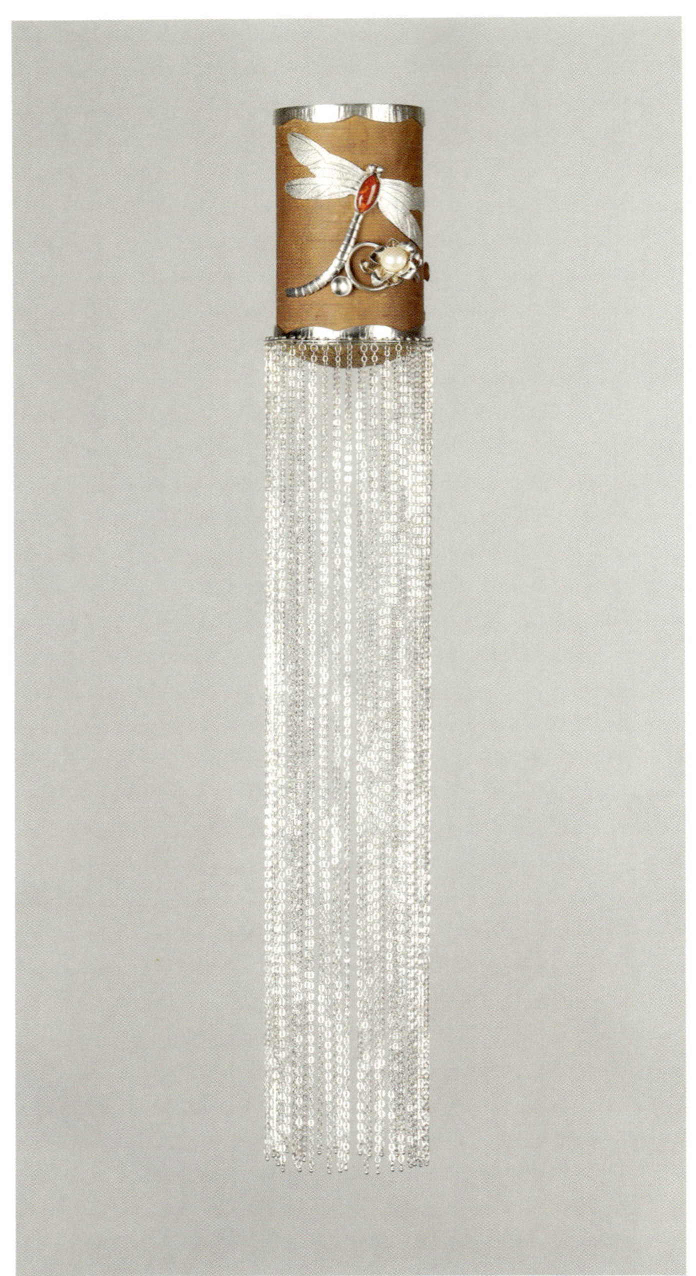

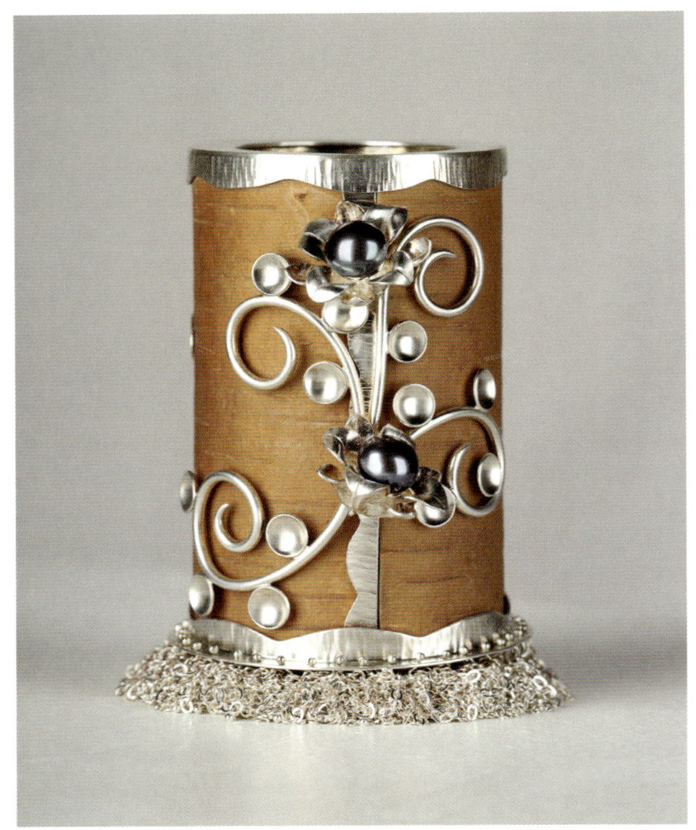

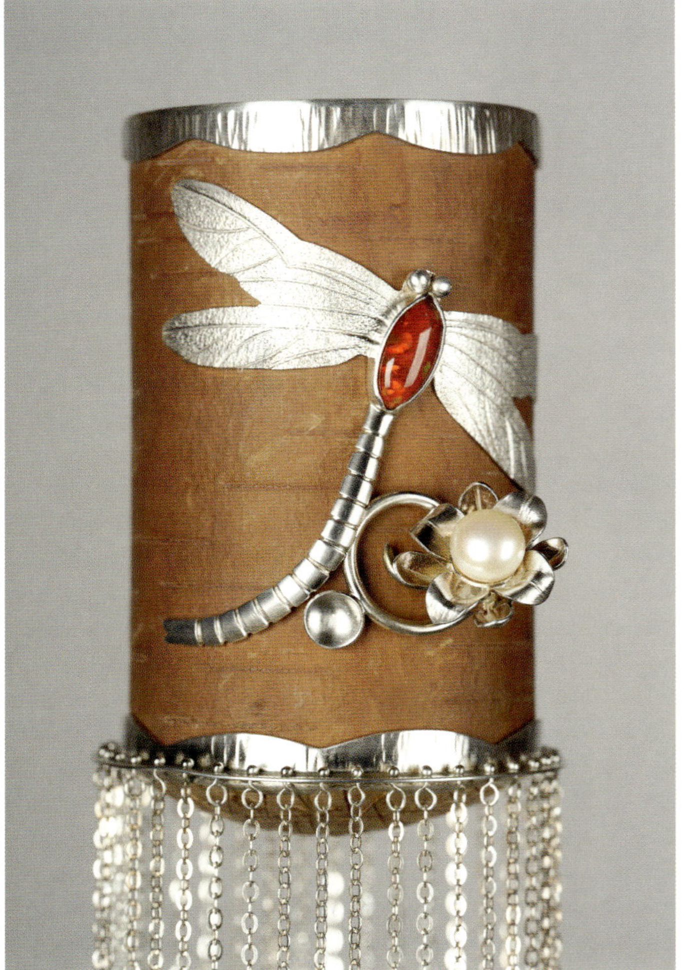

Wanesia Misquadace
Fond du Lac Band of the Ojibway, born 1971
Vessel, 2021
Birchbark, silver, and stones
H. 14 × W. 6 × D. 6 in.
Courtesy of the artist

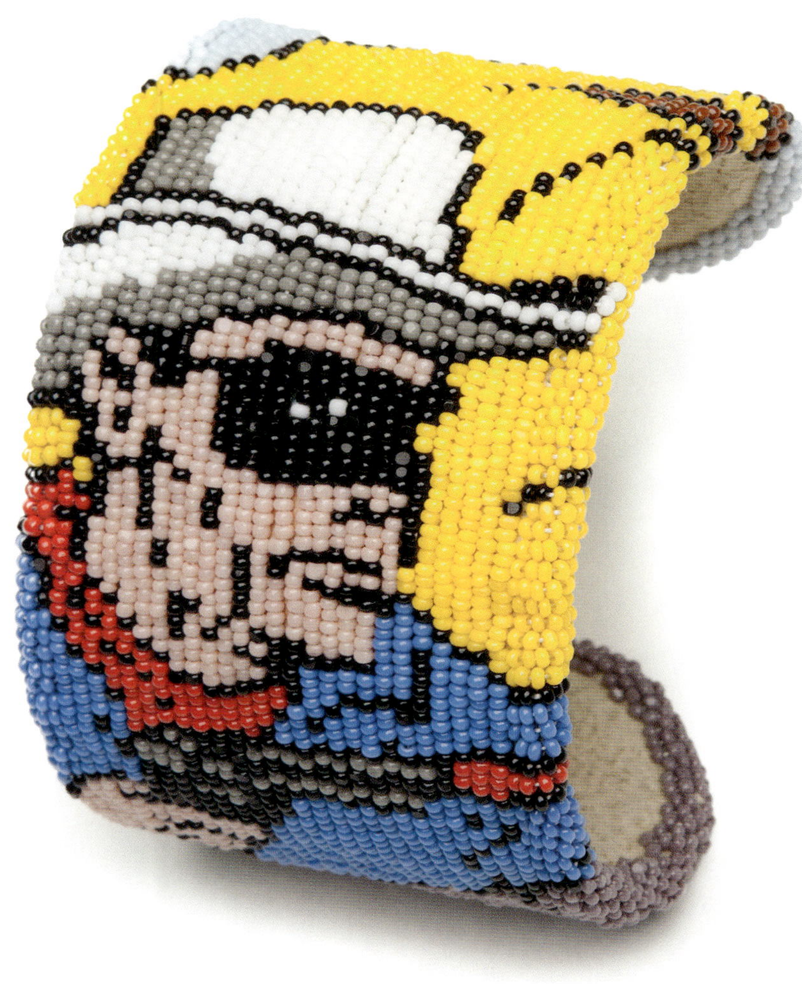

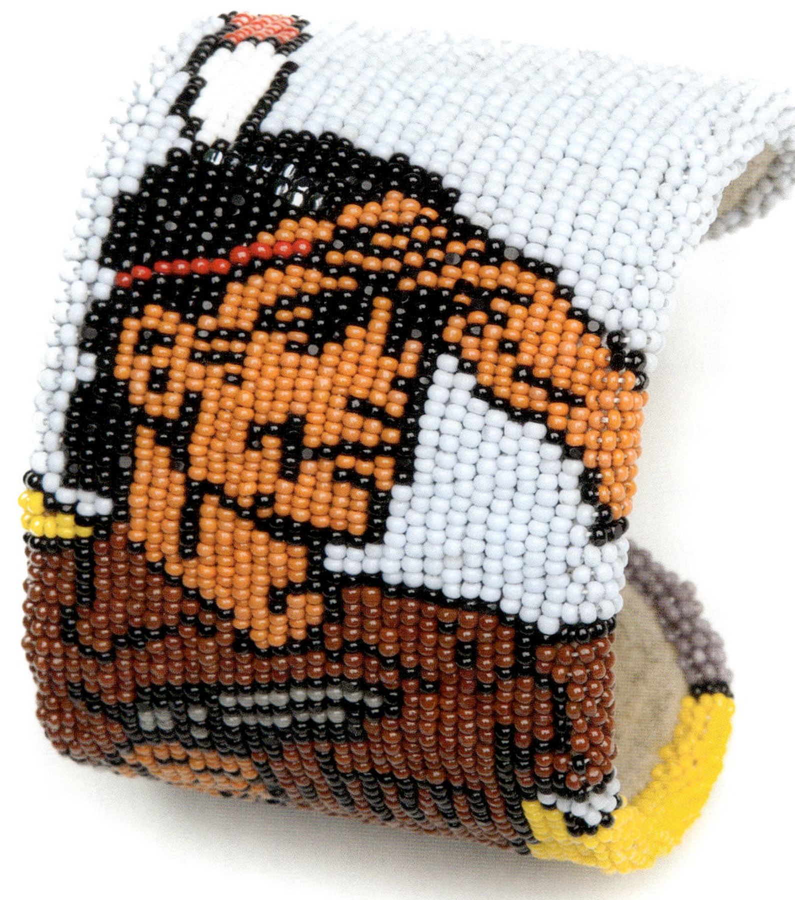

Marcus Amerman
Choctaw, born 1959
Lone Ranger and Tonto Cuff Bracelets, 1999
Glass beads, leather, and thread
H. 2 × W. 2⅞ × D. 2¼ in.
H. 2 × W. 2⅝ × D. 2¼ in.
Philbrook Museum of Art, Tulsa, Oklahoma,
Gift of Don and Rita Newman, 2009.5.1 and
2009.5.2

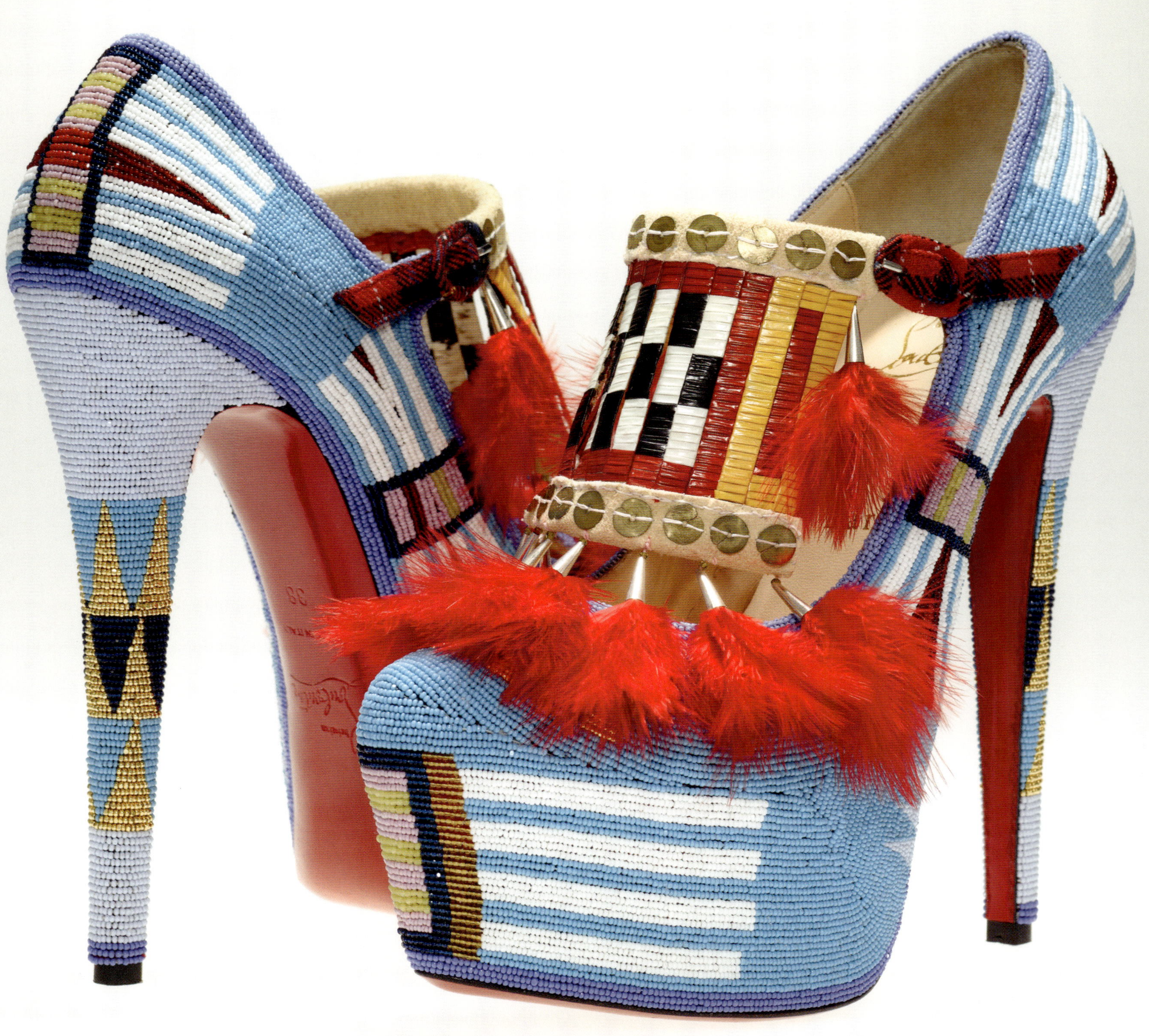

Jamie Okuma
Luiseño/Shoshone e-Bannock/Wailaki/Okinawan, born 1977
Adaptation II, 2012
Shoes designed by Christian Louboutin, leather, glass beads, porcupine quills,
sterling silver cones, brass sequins, and chicken feathers
each H. 8⅝ × W. 3¼ × D. 9³⁄₁₆ in.
Lent by the Minneapolis Institute of Art, Bequest of Virginia Doneghy, by exchange

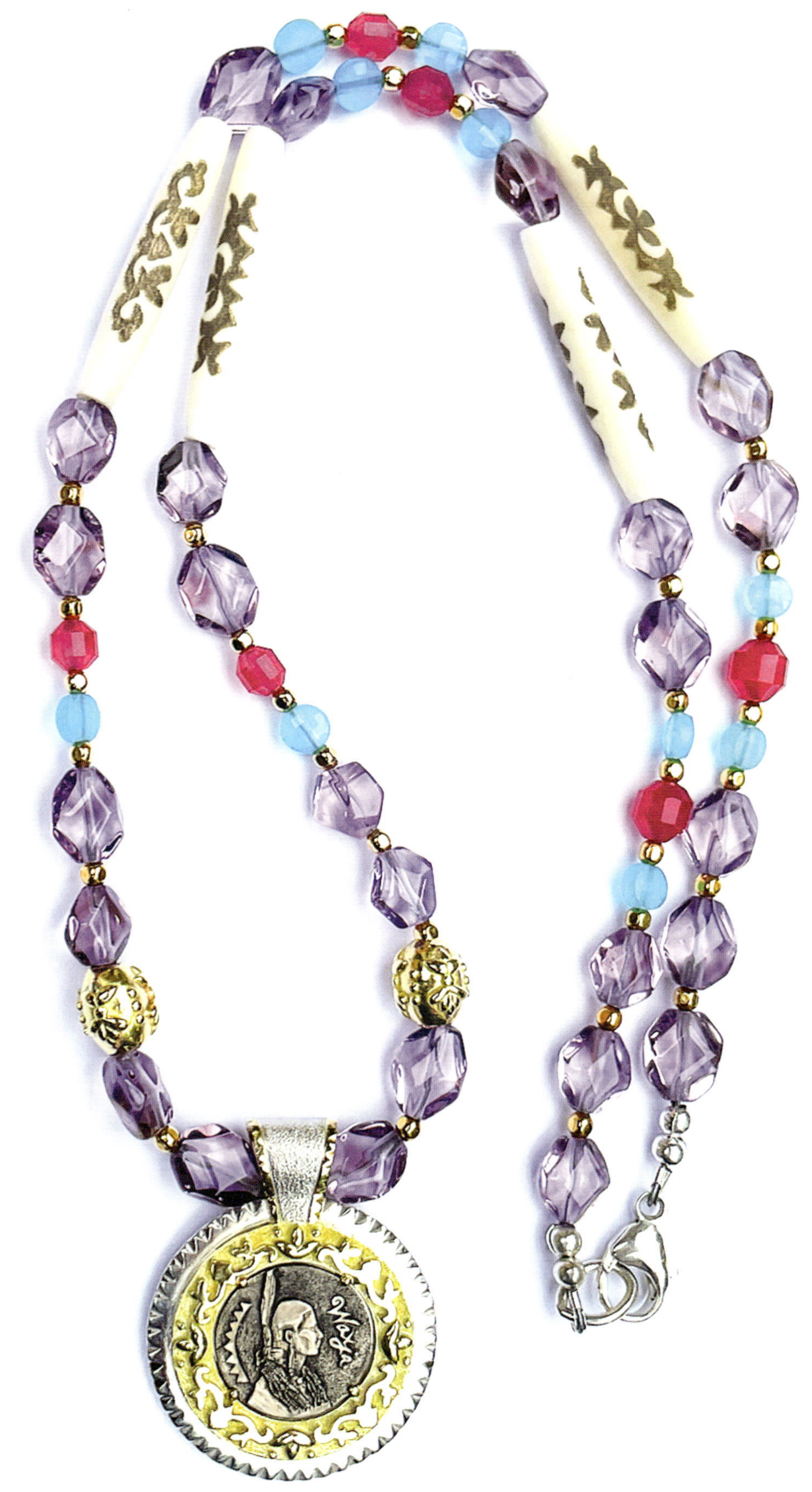

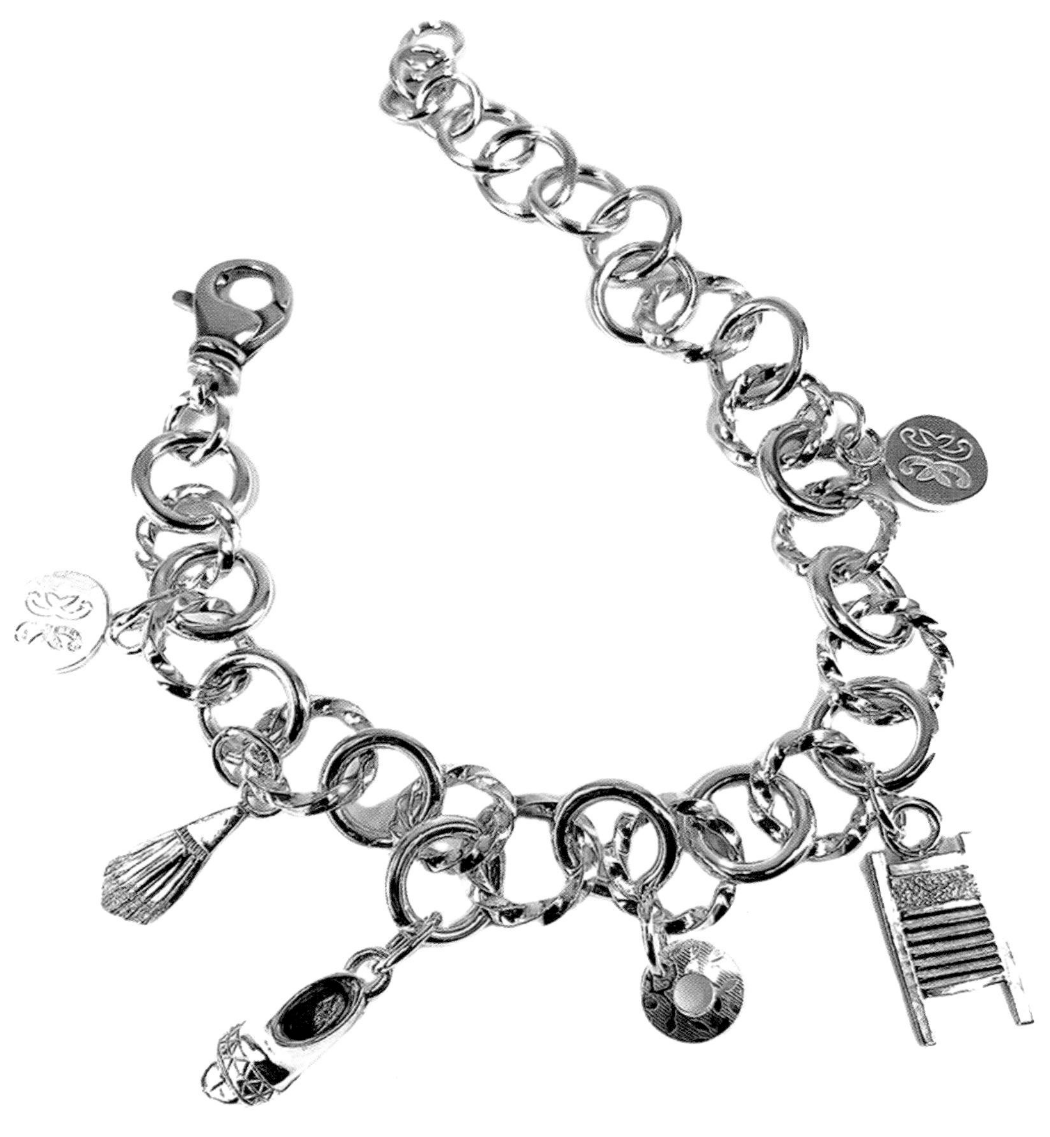

Jodi Webster
Ho-Chunk Nation/Prairie Band Potawatomi Nation

OPPOSITE
Commemorating Ho-Chunk Female Chiefs, 2022
Hand-engraved 1964 Canadian dime (colonizer
removed), 18K gold rim and beads, amethyst,
custom-etched bone bead, amazonite, and quartz
H. 14½ × W. 3 × D. ⅜ in.
Courtesy of the artist

ABOVE
Charmed, 2023
Sterling silver
H. 9½ × W. 1¾ × D. ½ in.
Courtesy of the artist

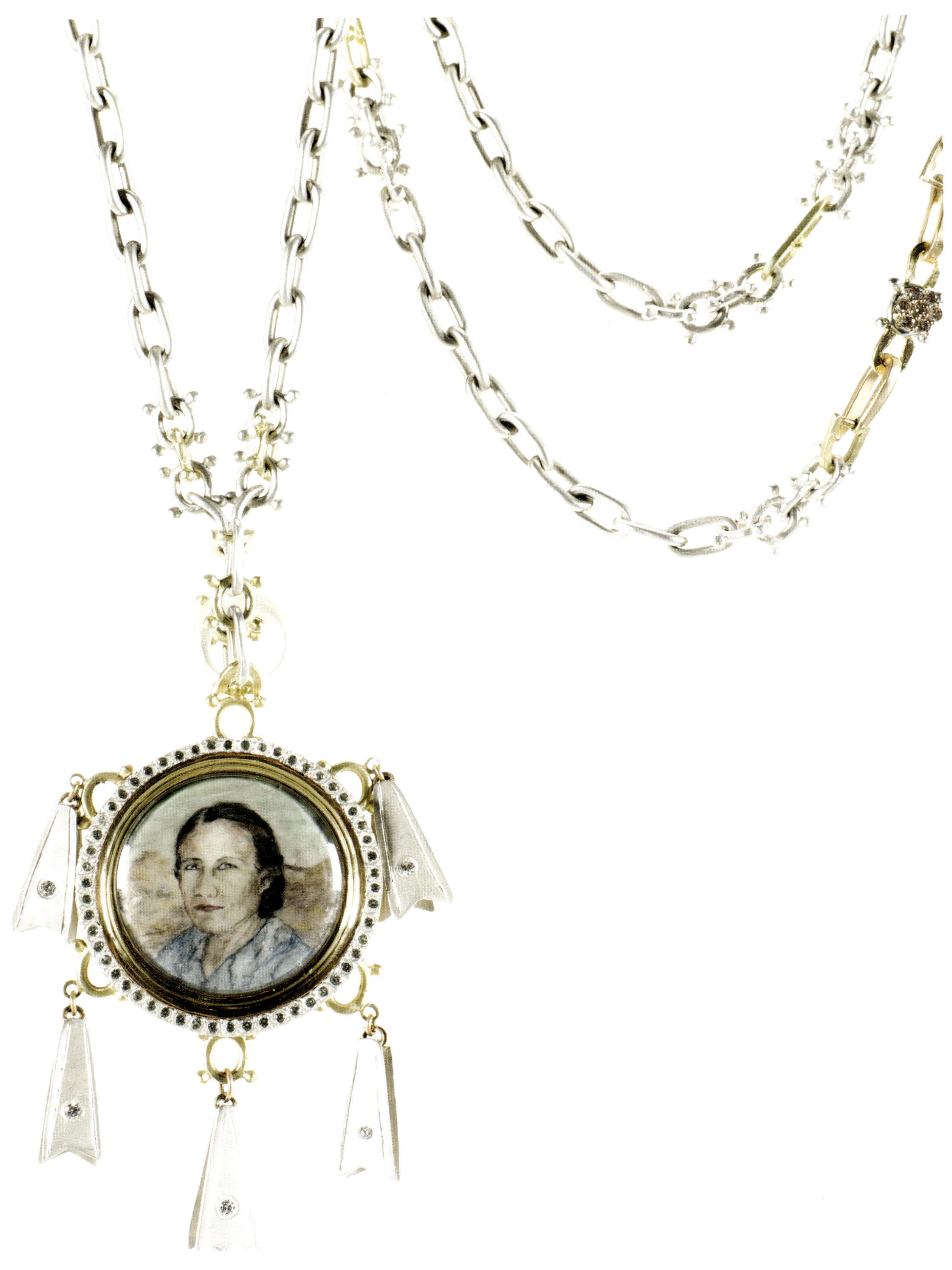

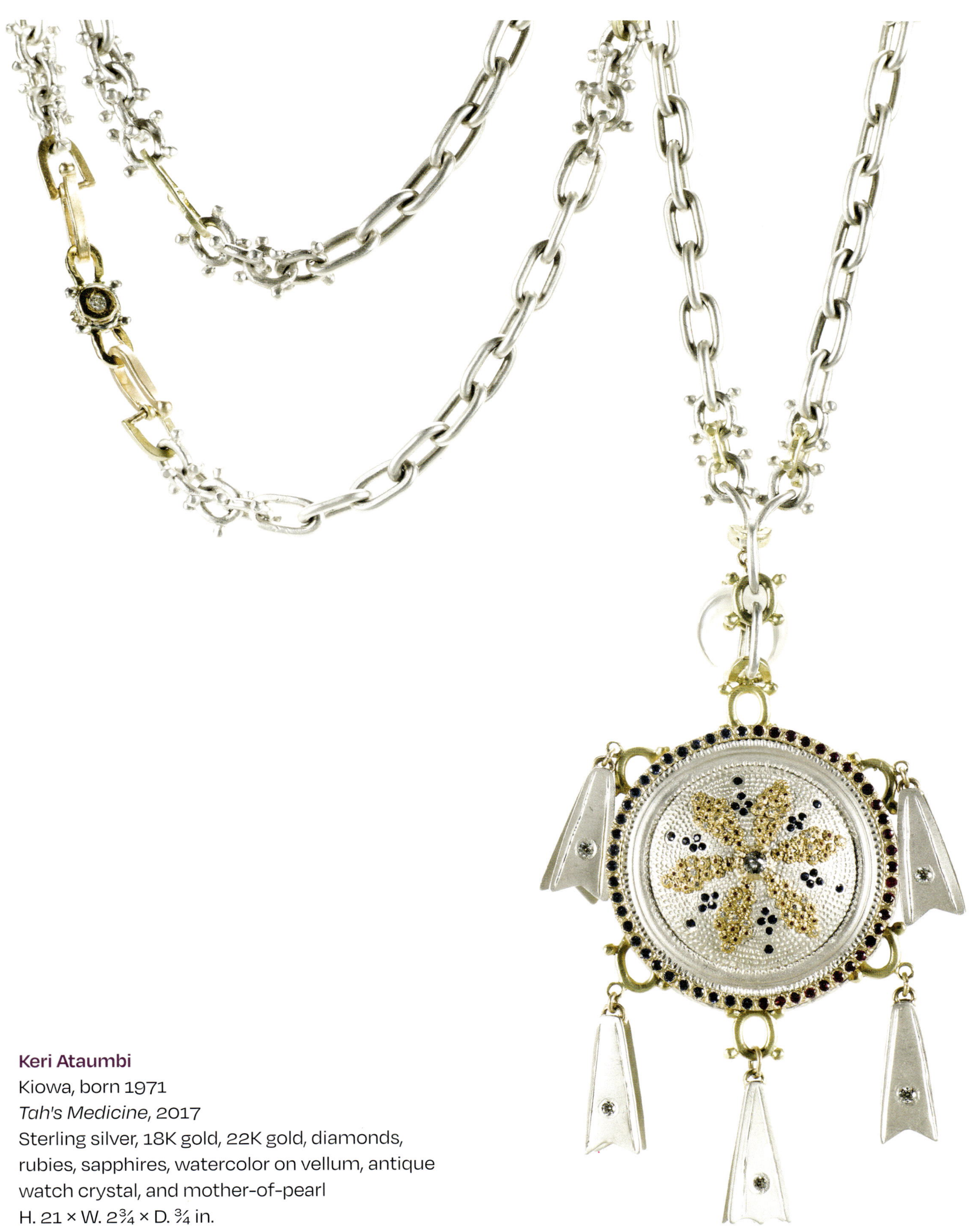

Keri Ataumbi
Kiowa, born 1971
Tah's Medicine, 2017
Sterling silver, 18K gold, 22K gold, diamonds,
rubies, sapphires, watercolor on vellum, antique
watch crystal, and mother-of-pearl
H. 21 × W. 2¾ × D. ¾ in.
Courtesy of the artist

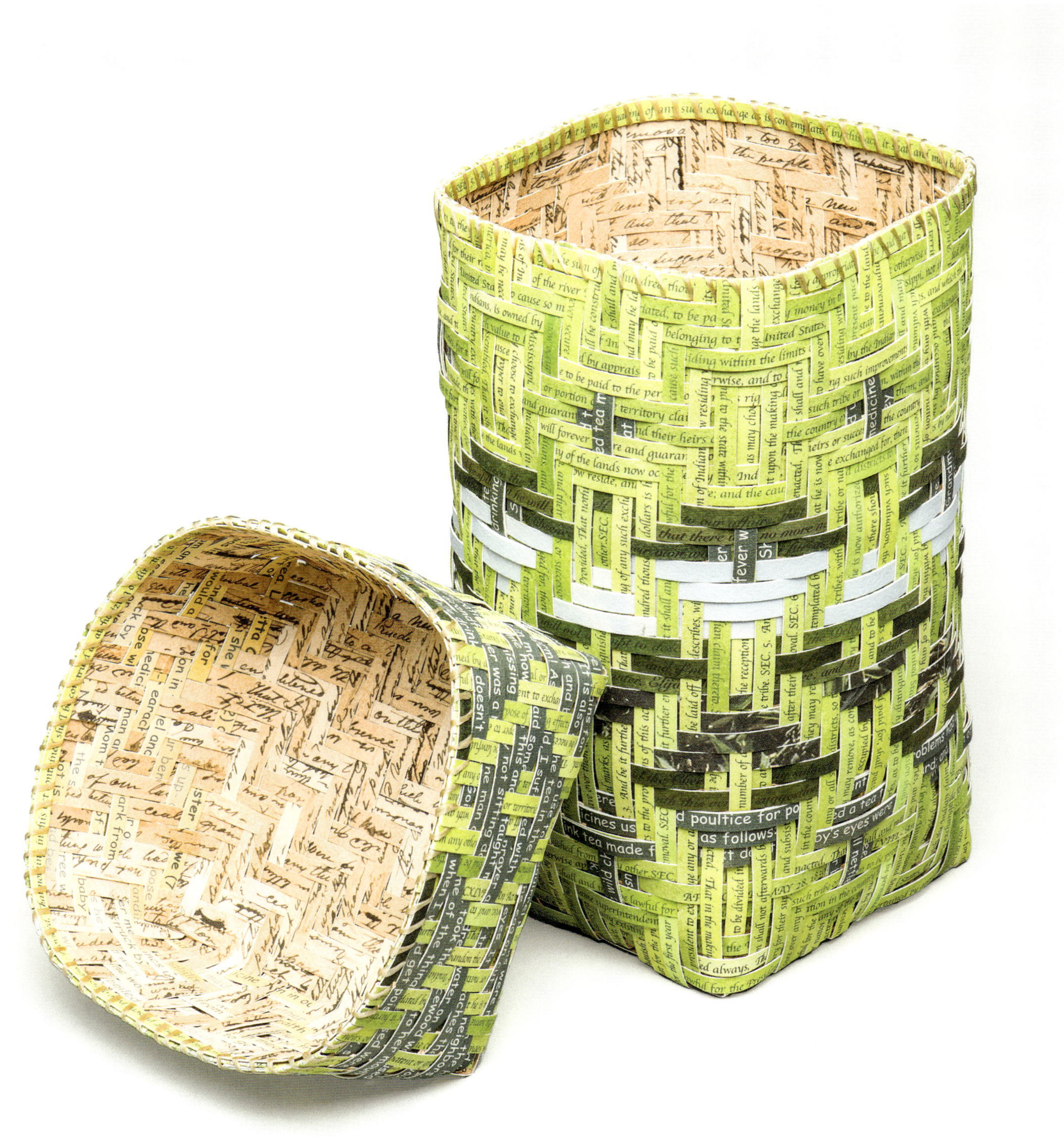

Shan Goshorn
Eastern Band Cherokee, 1957–2018
Home Land, 2016
Arches watercolor paper splints printed with archival inks and acrylic paint
H. 9½ × W. 6 × D. 6 in.
Collection of Asheville Art Museum, Purchased with additional funds provided
by 2016 Collectors' Circle members Gail and Brian McCarthy, 2017.02.01

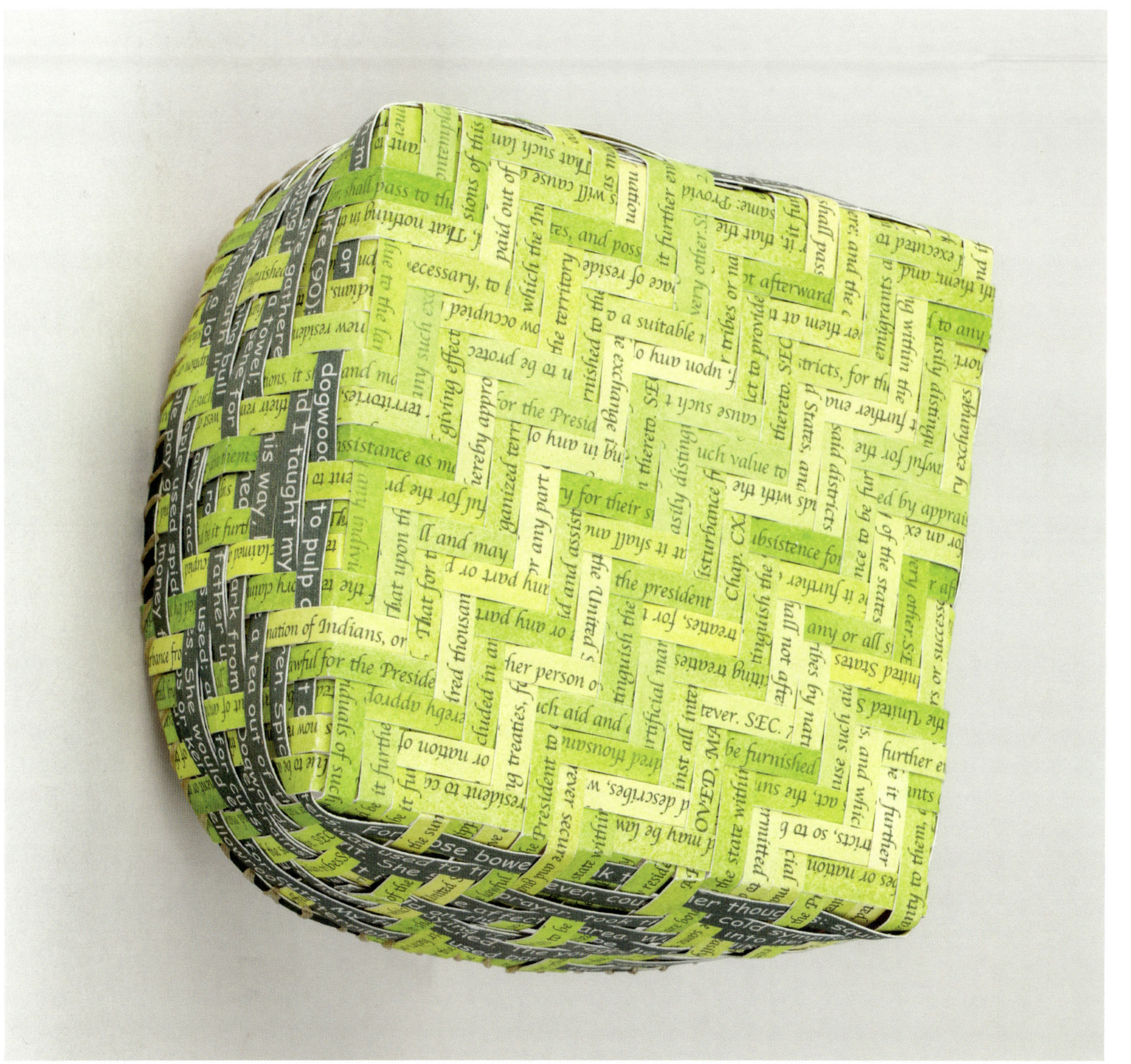

Melissa S. Cody*
Navajo Nation, born 1983
Deep Brain Stimulation, 2011
Wool warp, weft, and selvedge cords and aniline dyes
H. 40 × W. 30¾ in.
Minneapolis Institute of Art, The Patricia and Peter
Frechette Endowment for Art Acquisition, 2012.26
** The exhibition includes a similar work by this artist.*

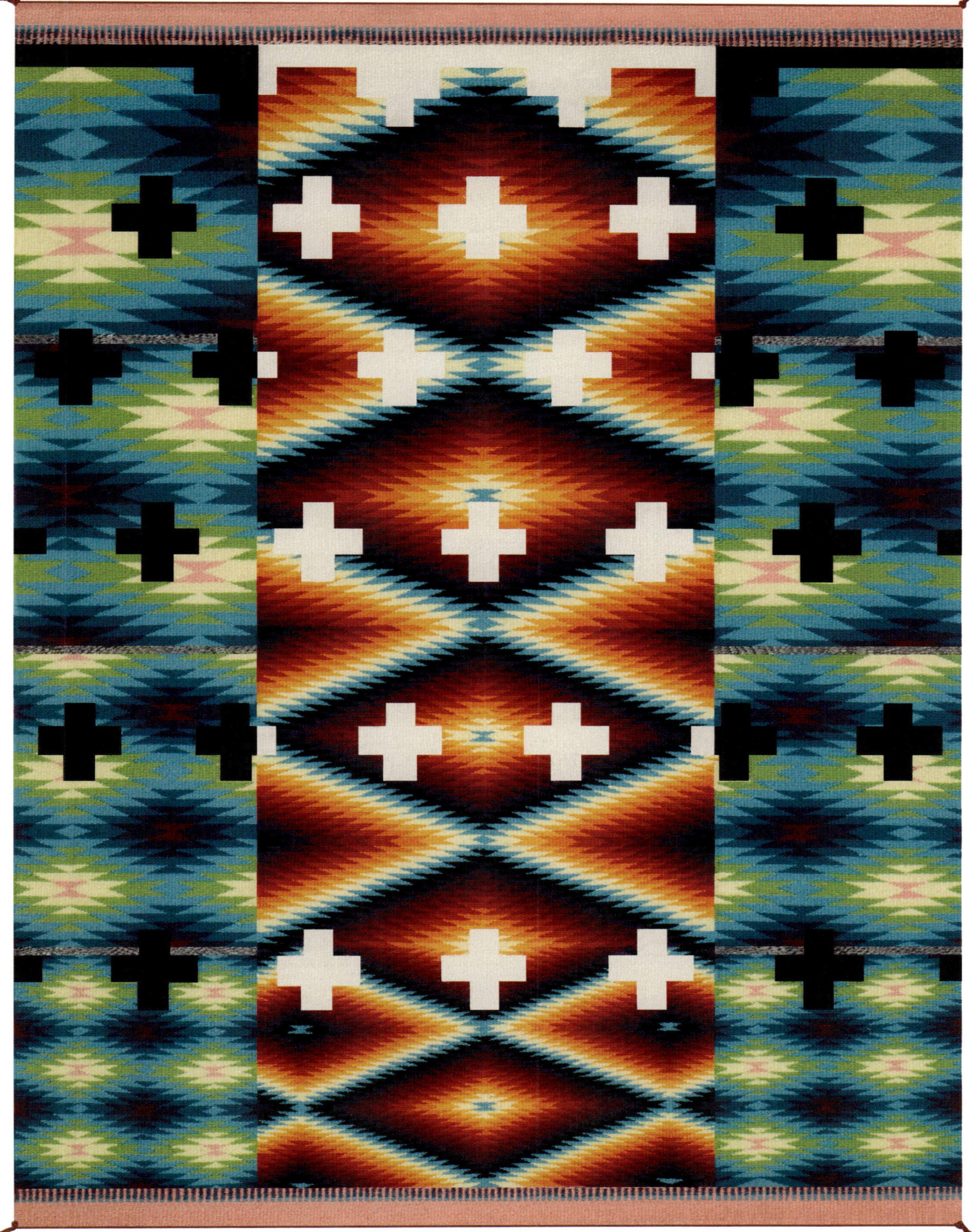

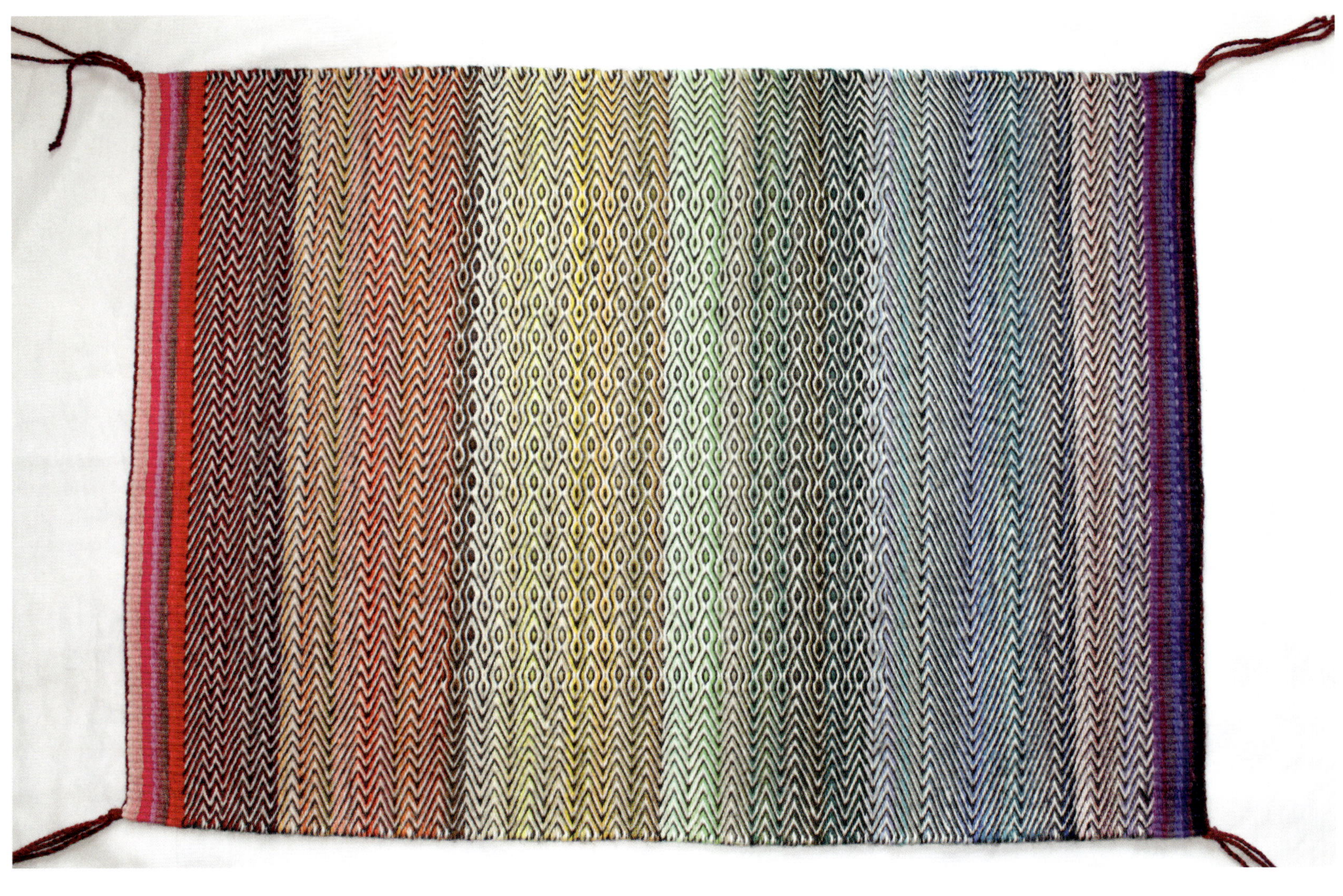

Venancio Aragon*
Navajo Nation, born 1985

ABOVE
Horned Toad and Lightning Twill, 2023
Wool/mohair weft, wool warp, and natural and
synthetic dyes
25 × 33 in.
Courtesy of the artist
** The exhibition includes a similar work by this artist.*

OPPOSITE
Rainbow Wedge, 2023
Wool/mohair weft, wool warp, and natural and
synthetic dyes
24 × 33 in.
Courtesy of the artist

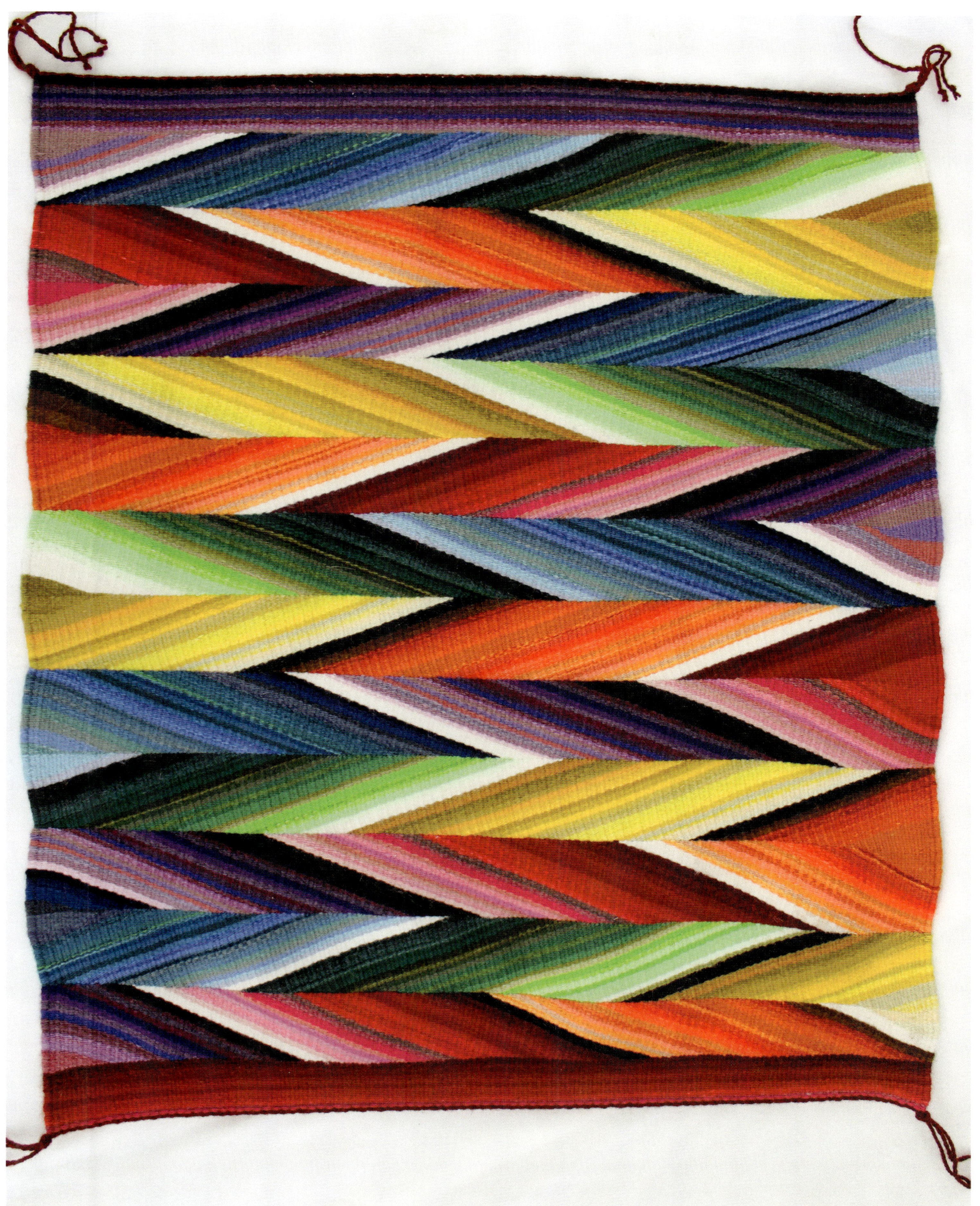

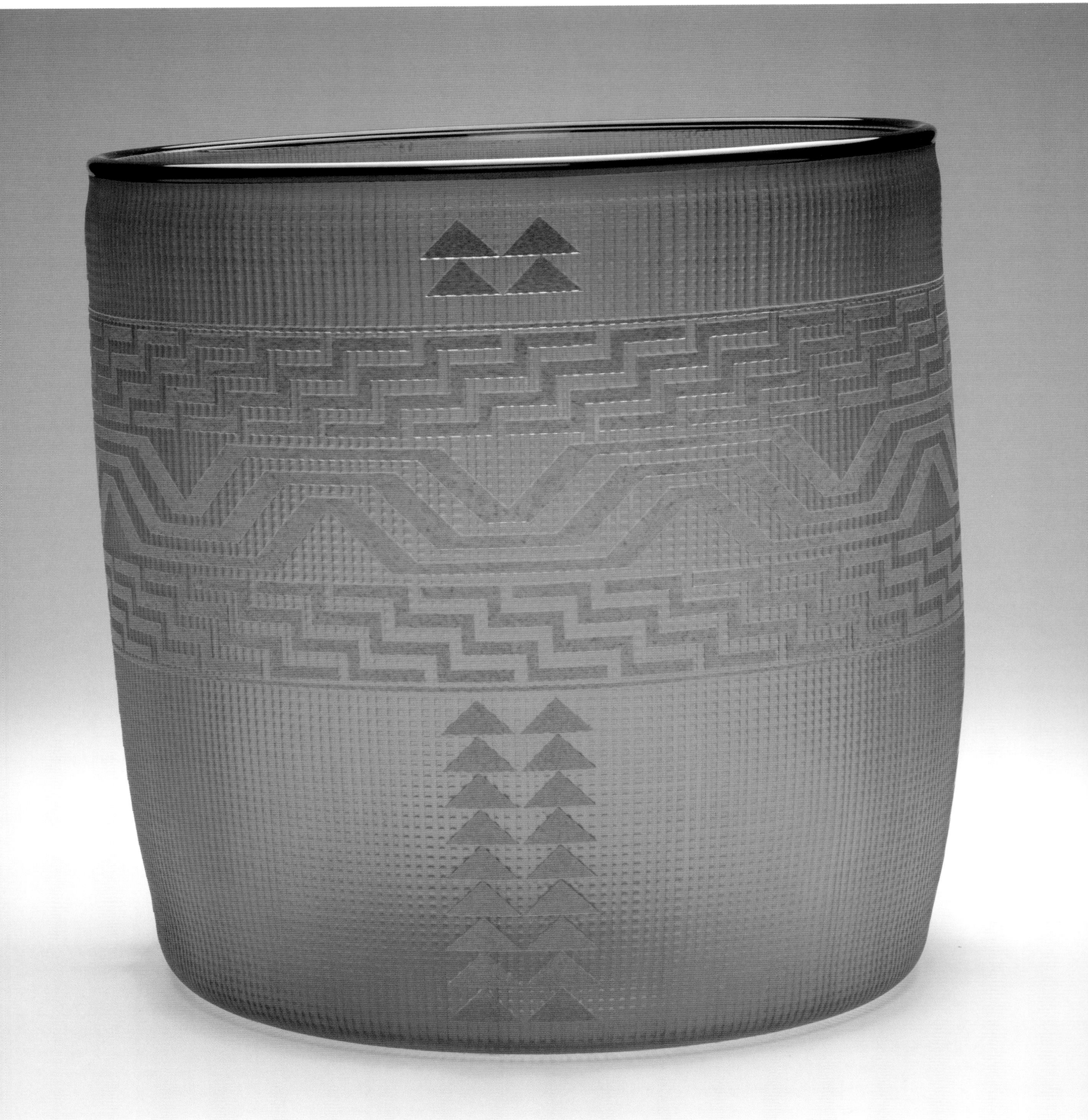

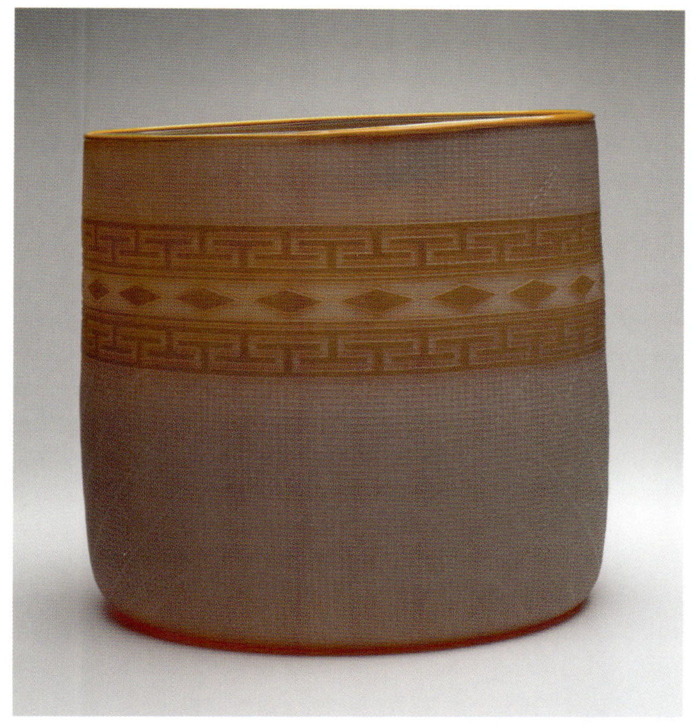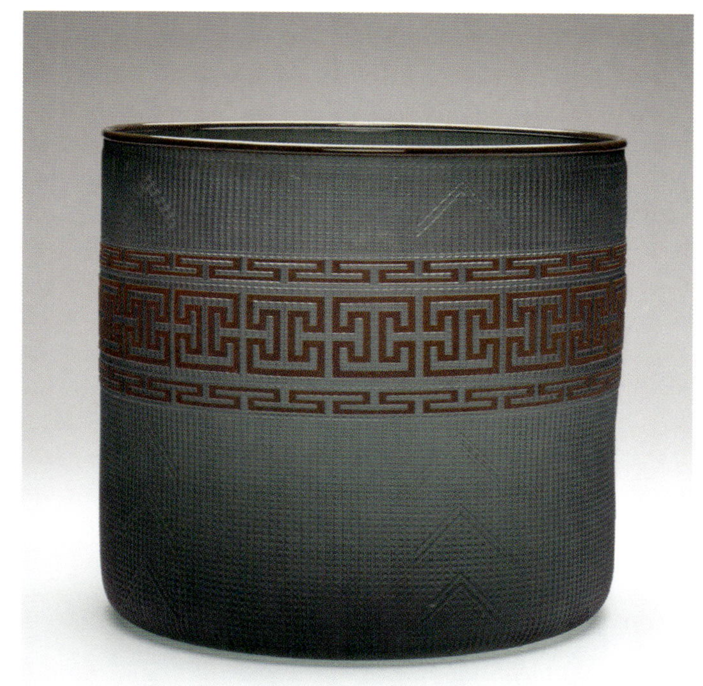

Preston Singletary
Tlingit, born 1963

OPPOSITE
Tlingit Basket, 2012
Blown and sand-carved glass
H. 18 × W. 18½ × D. 18½ in.
North Carolina Museum of Art, Gift of Mr. and
Mrs. G. Wallace Newton, 2023 (2023.5.1)

ABOVE LEFT
Saffron Tlingit Basket, 2016
Blown and sand-carved glass
H. 19 × W. 20½ × D. 19½ in.
North Carolina Museum of Art, Gift of Mr. and
Mrs. G. Wallace Newton, 2023 (2023.5.3)

ABOVE RIGHT
Spruce Green Tlingit Basket, 2016
Blown and sand-carved glass
H. 18 × W. 18½ × D. 18½ in.
North Carolina Museum of Art, Gift of Mr. and
Mrs. G. Wallace Newton, 2023 (2023.5.2)

Maria Martinez
San Ildefonso Pueblo, 1887–1980
Julian Martinez
San Ildefonso Pueblo, 1885–1943
Bowl, circa 1942–1943
Polished blackware pottery with matte paint
H. 6¼ in.
North Carolina Museum of Art, Gift of Dr. and Mrs. John R. Lambert, 1978 (G.78.21.1)

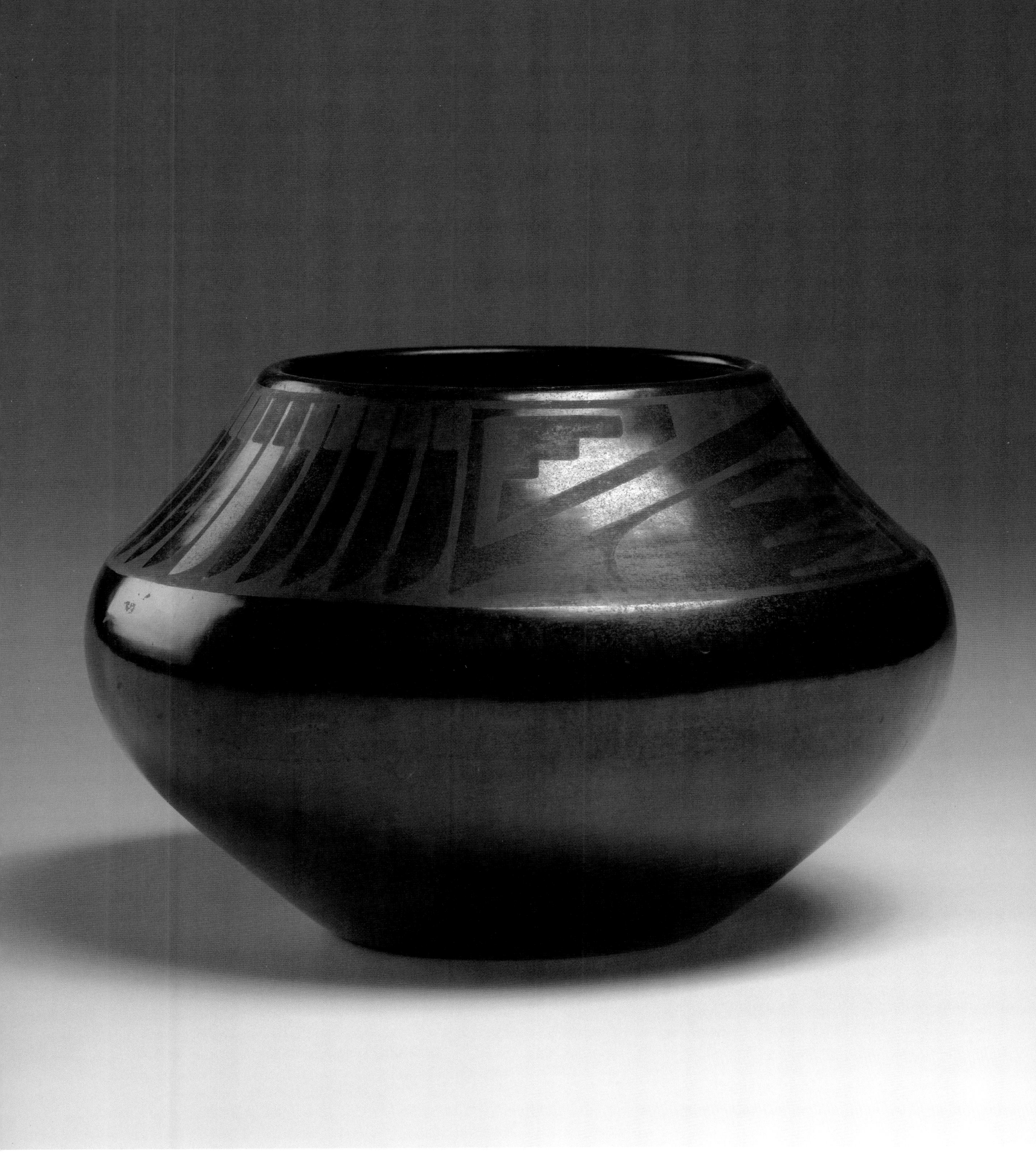

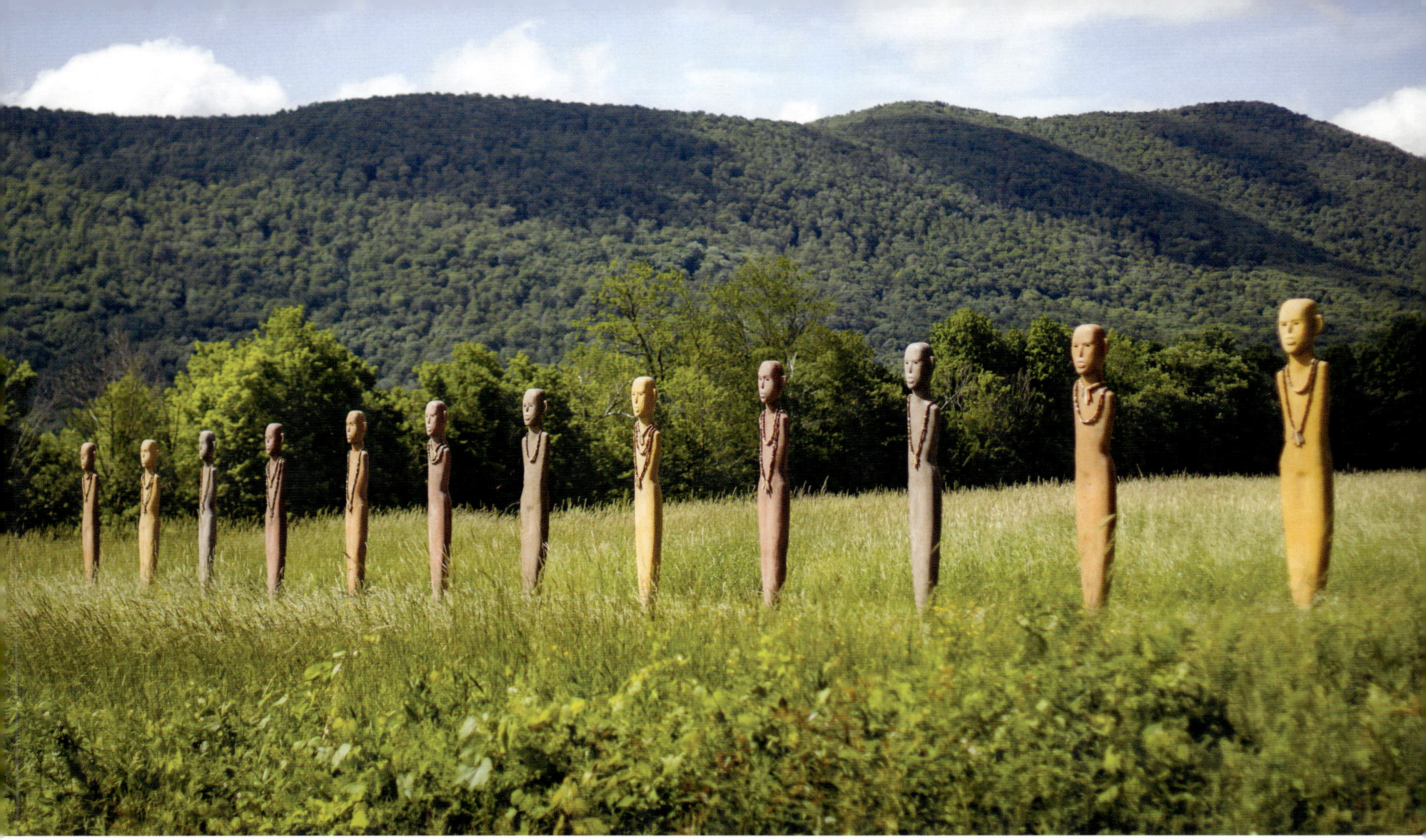

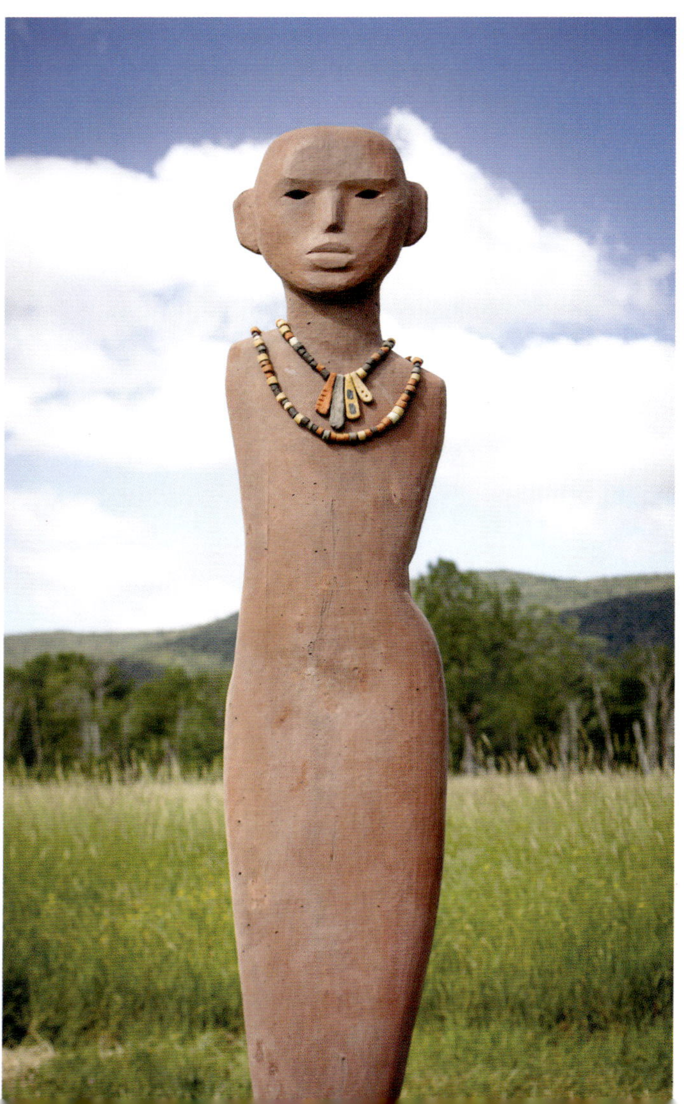

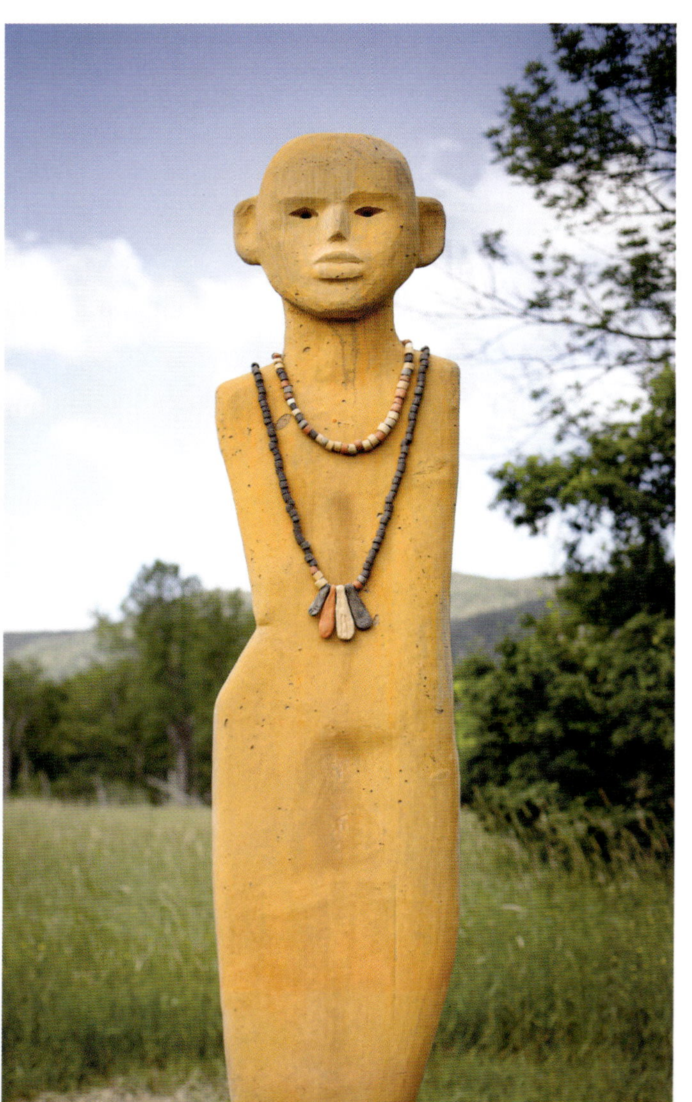

Rose B. Simpson
Santa Clara Pueblo, born 1983
Counterculture, 2022
Dyed concrete, steel, clay, and cable
Dimensions variable
Commissioned by Art & the Landscape, a program
of the Trustees, Massachusetts; Courtesy of the
artist, Jessica Silverman, San Francisco, and Jack
Shainman Gallery, New York

Rose Simpson is deeply wise. She is generationally wise. Listening to her speak can make one feel as if she is a conduit of knowledge and wisdom from peoples, places, and spaces that have come before. She is a calm, artistic, methodical, and philosophic force. This force can be seen and felt in one of her most compelling creations, *Counterculture*. In this work Simpson draws from her cultural understanding of the ancestors' presence in Native peoples' everyday lives and leans into the natural relationship between the living and their ancestors. The figures that compose *Counterculture* serve as ancestral representatives in the landscape—a physical presence of those who cannot be seen. They are witness to their living relations and understand, as Simpson says, living people are "ancestry in the making ... We were given this line, and this heritage, and this story to continue."[1] The figures also represent those who were silenced by colonial powers and stand distinctly to empower and unlock these generationally silenced voices. According to Simpson, they remind us that "we are not independent, that the inanimate are watching, and that we are responsible not only to the present but to the ancestral spirits that inhabit a particular place."[2]

The ground that *Counterculture* stands on in the Ann and Jim Goodnight Museum Park is sacred ground. The land is the ancestral home of the Occaneechi Band of the Saponi Nation, who still occupy this area. Part of the mission of the North Carolina Museum of Art is to share the artistic heritage of North Carolina's people. *Counterculture* helps to unlock that story on the Museum campus. The hallowed figures invite Native peoples to share our experiences and the importance of our existence across the state in a voice of solidarity and celebration. Behind each *Counterculture* ancestral figure stand legions of Indian peoples who have called North Carolina home for thousands of years. Before them stand the living generations—the survivors, descendants, Indigenous of our time—open to sharing this space, this time, and this experience with you. *Counterculture* is a welcome conduit for sharing traditions, evolutions, and cultural meanings in the art of Native peoples in North Carolina and throughout the land with all who are open and willing.

1   *Art in the Twenty-First Century*, season 11, "Rose Simpson in 'Everyday Icons,'" April 7, 2023, video, 13:40, https://art21.org/watch /art-in-the-twenty-first-century/s11/rose-b-simpson-in-everyday-icons.

2   Rose B. Simpson, quoted in "Rose B. Simpson: Counterculture," Whitney Museum of American Art, accessed September 1, 2023, https://whitney.org/exhibitions/rose-simpson-counterculture.

Artist Biographies

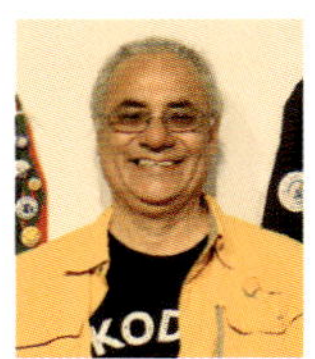

Marcus Amerman (Choctaw) is a bead artist, painter, fashion designer, and multimedia and performance artist. He was taught traditional beadwork techniques at age ten by his aunt. He also credits bead artists of the Plateau region as influential. He received a BFA at Whitman College and studied at the Institute of American Indian Arts (IAIA). Amerman is known for his highly realistic beadwork images with political and socially conscious themes and his photorealistic portraits of historical figures and pop icons. His artworks are in the collections of the National Museum of the American Indian, American Museum of Natural History, Heard Museum, and Museum of Arts and Design, among others.

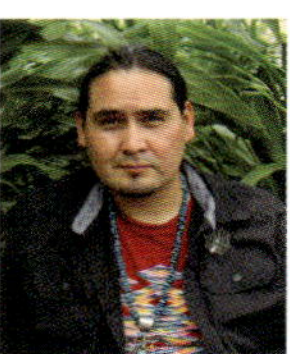

Venancio Aragon (Navajo Nation) holds degrees in cultural anthropology and Native American studies. Prior to becoming a full-time artist, he worked for the National Park Service. His interest in archaeology, anthropology, and art led him to revive portions of the Diné weaving repertoire in danger of being lost. Aragon was a 2020 Native American Artist Fellow at the School for Advanced Research in Santa Fe. His textiles were part of the exhibitions *Color Riot! How Color Changed Navajo Textiles*, *COLOR: The Beauty and Science of Color*, and *Tangible/Intangible*. He lives and works in Farmington, New Mexico, where he continues to promote Diné weaving as a form of decolonial expression.

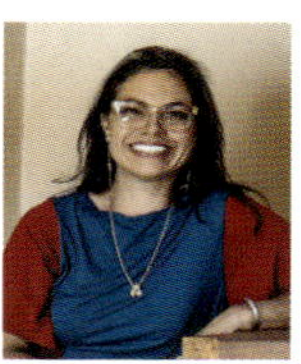

Keri Ataumbi (Kiowa), raised on the Wind River Reservation in Wyoming, was exposed to both traditional Native American aesthetics and contemporary art theory and practice from an early age. Her Kiowa mother ran a trading post and her Italian American father is famous for his bronze sculptures. Ataumbi attended Rhode Island School of Design before moving to Santa Fe in 1990. She worked as a landscape designer while attending the IAIA and received a BFA in painting with a minor in art history from the College of Santa Fe. She lives and works in the Cerrillos Hills outside Santa Fe.

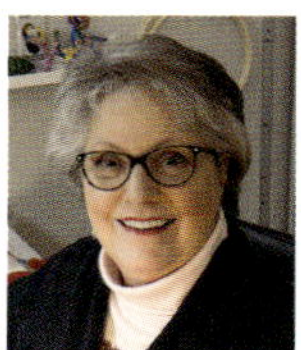

Martha Berry (Cherokee Nation) began creating traditional Cherokee beadwork in the 1980s. At that time there were no classes or books on the subject. She taught herself by studying both historic artifacts and photographs. Berry creates bandolier bags, ceremonial sashes, belts, knee bands, purses, and moccasins. When possible, she uses materials, techniques, styles, and designs authentic to early 19th-century Cherokee beadwork. In 2013 the Cherokee Nation designated Berry a Cherokee National Treasure for her work in preserving and perpetuating the art of traditional Cherokee beadwork. Berry, who resides in Dallas, divides her time between research, creating beadwork, and teaching.

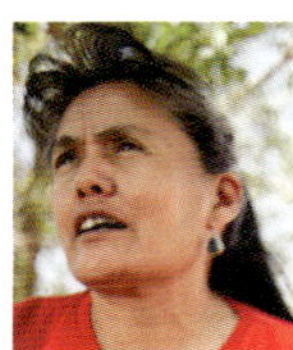

Sally Black (Navajo) is part of a family of artists renowned for reviving Navajo basketry. She is the eldest daughter of famed rug weaver and basketmaker Mary Holiday Black. She began weaving when she was eight years old in her childhood home on Douglas Mesa. Black is known for her precision and clean, innovative designs that incorporate traditional and pictorial motifs. She has received many Best of Show and Best of Class awards. She lives in Monument Valley and has taught workshops throughout the country.

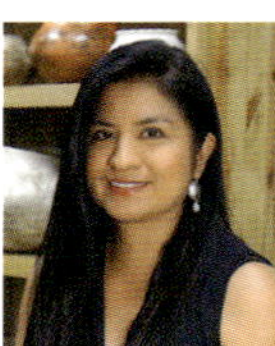

Joanna Underwood Blackburn (Chickasaw Nation) creates sculpture and pottery that is inspired in part by tribal life ways and ancient designs of the Southeast. She earned a BFA in graphic design from the University of Oklahoma, where she was introduced to ceramic sculpture. This sparked her interest in researching Chickasaw pottery, which she has helped revitalize. Blackburn has created large-scale bronzes of her pottery and other works for the Chickasaw Nation. Her artwork is in the collections of the First Americans Museum, Crocker Art Museum, National Museum of the American Indian, and Office of the Ambassador of the Chickasaw Nation to the US.

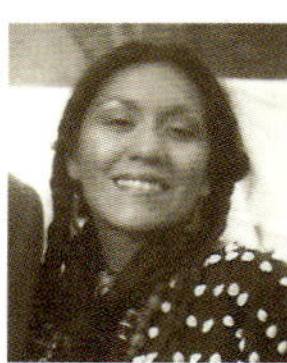

Debra Box (Southern Ute) is an artist in beadwork and parfleche (painted rawhide containers) and more recently sterling silver jewelry. She began her career making period attire for herself and her husband. Her creations are known for their impeccable craftsmanship. She received recognition as most promising artist at the 1988 Santa Fe Indian Market and an NEA grant to work with the Museum of Indian Arts and Culture, among other awards. Box has been commissioned to make works for major motion pictures, including *Dances with Wolves*. Her artwork is in the collections of the National Museum of the American Indian and Denver Art Museum.

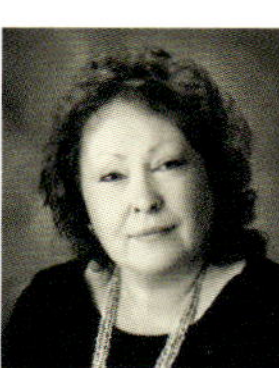

Jackie Larson Bread (Blackfeet Nation) was born and raised on the Blackfeet Reservation in Montana. Her grandmother's exquisite beadwork inspired her to a career making beaded works of art. Bread attended the IAIA, where she developed illusionary pictorial beadwork, currently the focus of her work. She also creates traditional Plains ledger art, delicate Blackfeet florals, and bold Blackfeet geometric designs. Her work is in the National Museum of the American Indian and has received over 100 awards, including Best of Show twice at the Santa Fe Indian Market. She has brought traditional beadwork into the twenty-first century with a color palette and techniques that are unique and innovative.

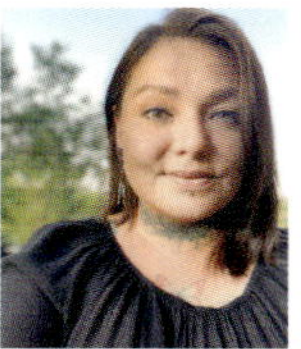

Millie Bridwell (Cheyenne River Sioux) specializes in a cherished art among her peoples: star quilts. She is entirely self-taught and has been making star quilts for almost ten years. She likes to think outside the box—incorporating designs within the star and making each quilt unique—as well as include traditional aspects of her Lakota culture. Each is hand quilted using the traditional method of needle and thread. Bridwell believes that behind every star quilt, there is a story to be shared. It is with great love and passion that she conveys that story through her artistry.

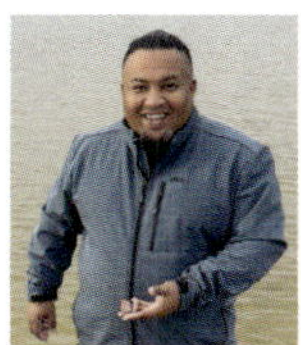

Harlen Chavis Jr. (Lumbee) takes inspiration from his ancestors to create jewelry and other metal art that honors their memory and brings awareness of the rich Indigenous heritage of his people. He considers the artifacts prevalent in his community part of his ancestral inheritance and incorporates the pottery designs, shell engravings, and stamp work into contemporary representations on engraved gorgets, cuffs, and other large statement pieces. In addition to the repeating scrolls, intersecting lines, and checked stamped patterns found on ancestral works, he also includes a style of portraiture to bring forward depictions of ancestral artists.

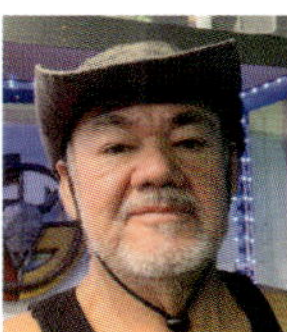

Steven Chrisjohn (Oneida) comes from the Oneida Nation of upstate New York, which is one of the six nations that forms the Iroquois Confederacy. Themes he's used in the past and his new body of work have been inspired by his own culture and ancient cultures around the globe. While studying ancient art from all over the world, Chrisjohn realized the further we go back the more similar it all looks. He believes nature has a role in all art, historic and prehistoric. These are qualities he tries to convey in his own work, which he creates using old and new techniques, such as carving, sculpting, sketching, painting, and jewelry making.

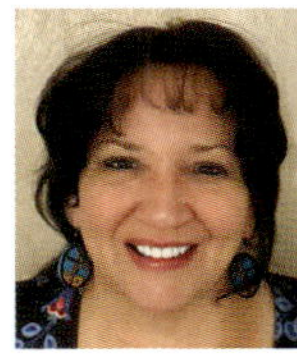

Kelly Church (Ottawa/Pottawatomi/Matchi-be-nash-she-wish) comes from an unbroken line of black ash basketmakers and works with fibers of forests in Michigan to create weavings that share issues affecting us all. Her work tells stories of her experiences as a culture bearer, teacher, Native woman, artist, activist, and part of her community and family. She received her AFA from the IAIA and her BFA from the University of Michigan. She is nationally recognized and the recipient of numerous awards, including the 2018 National Heritage Fellowship, NMAI's Artist Leadership Program, and Community Spirit Award from First Peoples Fund.

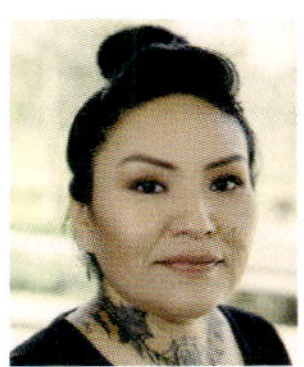

Melissa S. Cody (Navajo Nation) received a BA in studio arts and museum studies from the IAIA. A fourth-generation Navajo weaver, she creates tapestries often associated with the Germantown Revival, named after government wool from Germantown, PA, that was supplied to the Navajo during the time of the Long Walk. Working on a Navajo loom, Cody recombines traditional patterns into sophisticated geometric overlays and haptic color schemes. She has exhibited at the Stark Museum of Art, Museum of Contemporary Native Arts, Navajo Nation Museum, Heard Museum, and National Gallery of Canada. Cody's work is in the Minneapolis Institute of Art's and the Stark's collections.

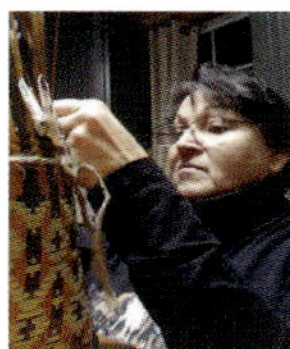

Vivian Garner Cottrell (Cherokee Nation) has been weaving double-walled Cherokee baskets of honeysuckle and buckbrush with her mother since she was thirteen years old. Mother and daughter were recognized as Cherokee National Treasures in 1995 and 1993 respectively. Relying on basketmaking knowledge, Cottrell began weaving rivercane baskets. Every fall and winter, she weaves white oak, rivercane, honeysuckle, and buckbrush in a continual process. Cottrell uses natural dyes of black walnut and bloodroot for weaving patterns in each basket. To her, basket weaving is easy; it is the preparation of the natural materials that is labor intensive. The outcome, however, is very satisfying.

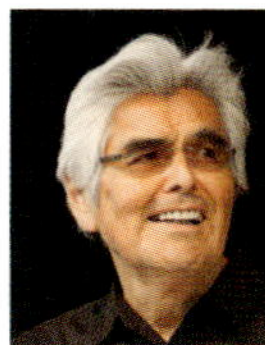

Robert Davidson (Haida) is an artist interested in perpetuating Haida cultural expression, including song, dance, and ceremony. Surrounded by a well-known artist family (his great-grandfather was famed Haida artist Charles Edenshaw), he began carving at fourteen and later attended the Vancouver School of Art. Davidson is considered a leading figure in the revival of Haida art. His work is in the collections of the National Gallery of Canada, Vancouver Art Gallery, Canadian Museum of History, and Southwest Museum. He has received many honors, including an Indspire Award.

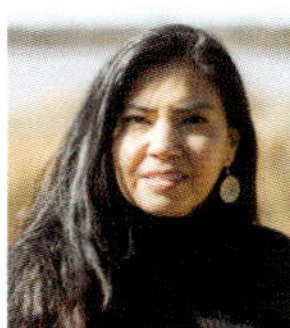

Leslie A. Deer (Muscogee [Mvskoke] Nation of Oklahoma) is an apparel designer. She utilizes intricate appliqué, bright color combinations, curvilinear lines, and traditional iconography to create modern clothing inspired by designs from Muscogee culture. Deer hopes her creations, like traditional songs or stories, help carry her culture and history forward. Various organizations and people, including the National Museum of the American Indian and Joy Harjo, 23rd poet laureate of the United States, own her work. "The designs and motifs I use enable me to share part of my people's culture."

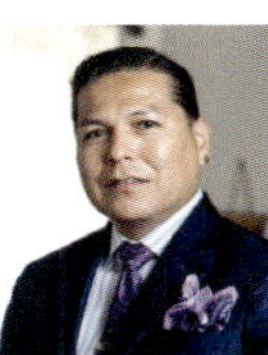

Orlando Dugi (Navaho), designer, leads the made-to-order fashion brand Orlando Dugi located in Santa Fe, New Mexico. Dugi's designs are elegant, timeless, and intricate, often involving many hours of hand-embroidery and embellishing.

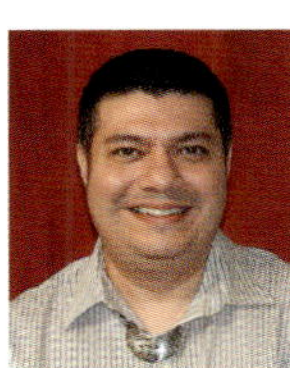

Chase Earles (Caddo) was born in Oklahoma and attended the Savannah College of Art and Design. His purpose, and the voice behind his art, is to revive and reintroduce his tribe's prolific pottery tradition to the world, as it had almost been lost. He creates traditional and modern interpretations of his ancestral pottery in order to educate the public and his own people of their cultural identity. His work is in museum collections throughout the country, including the Dallas Museum of Art, Minneapolis Institute of Art, Milwaukee Art Museum, Crystal Bridges Museum of American Art, Eiteljorg Museum, and Gilcrease Museum.

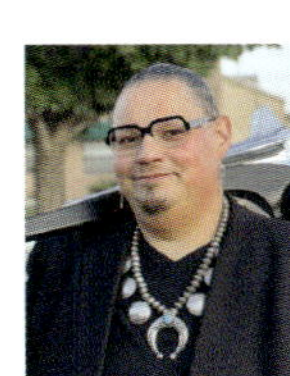

Tom Farris (Otoe-Missouria/Cherokee Nation) draws from his culture and the lifelong influence of American Indian art to create his works. He has a great deal of experience in the business of American Indian Art, most recently as the manager of FAMstore at First Americans Museum. As an artist, Farris has participated in nationally acclaimed art shows including the Santa Fe Indian Market, where he was recognized with the Creativity Award in 2015. He has exhibited at the National Museum of the American Indian, and his work is in the collections of the Heard Museum, Sherwin Miller Museum of Jewish Art, Eiteljorg Museum, and Sam Noble Museum.

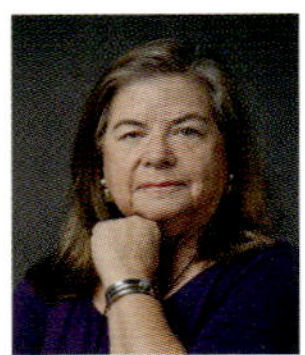

Anita Fields (Osage) creates works of clay and textile that reflect the world view of her Native culture. Her practice explores the complexities of cultural influences and intersections of balance and chaos found within our lives. Textured layers and distorted writing reference the complex layers and distortion of truths found in the written history of Indigenous cultures. Fields creates narratives that ask viewers to consider other ways of seeing and being in an effort to understand our shared existence. Fields's work is in collections including the Minneapolis Institute of Art, Museum of Contemporary Native Arts, Crystal Bridges Museum of American Art, Heard Museum, and National Museum of the American Indian.

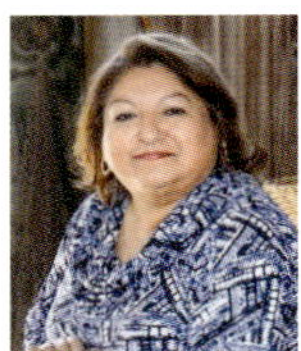

Sue Fish (Chickasaw/Choctaw) earned her associate degree from East Central University and has worked for the Chickasaw Nation and American Indian Institute. She is currently administrative manager for the First Americans Museum in Oklahoma City. Fish's passion for basketmaking began thirty years ago when she was introduced to basketry by her cousin Betty Dodd. She serves as vice president of the Oklahoma Native American Basketweavers Association. Her artworks are on display at Artesian Art Gallery, Chickasaw Nation Homeland Affairs, and the Chickasaw Cultural Center. Fish has received the Chickasaw Nation Silver Feather Award and was inducted into the 2023 Chickasaw Hall of Fame.

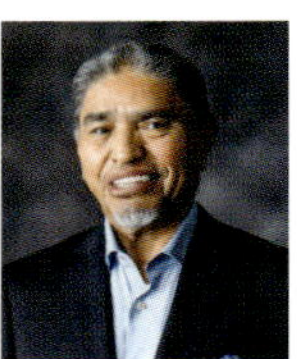

Cliff Fragua (Pueblo of Jemez) is from the Cornstalk Clan, his mother's clan. His father's clan is the Badger Clan. He did not grow up on Jemez but was born in Albuquerque, New Mexico. As a product of the Relocation Program, he spent most of his childhood in St. Louis and San Francisco. He comes from a family of potters, artists, and farmers. Fragua's forte is stone sculptures, and he also works in bronze, clay, glass, and two-dimensional arts. He attended the IAIA in 1973–75, where Allan Houser was his sculpture instructor. His studio is called Singing Stone Studio.

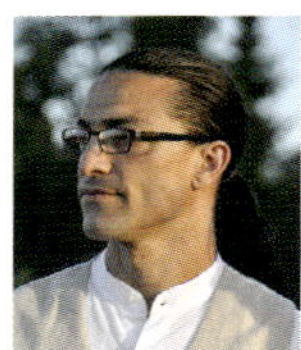

Gabriel Frey (Passamaquoddy) is a basketmaker whose family has been making traditional black ash baskets for over thirteen generations. He specializes in utility baskets, such as pack baskets, market baskets, and purses. Maintaining the traditional knowledge of Wabanaki basketmakers is an important aspect of his artistic process. Culture, family traditions, his personal experiences, and hopes for the future are embodied within each basket. He says, "I work towards perfecting the function and form of the traditional baskets while evolving each basket to reflect my personal style." For him, creating functional Wabanaki baskets is a platform to connect people to place.

Gal Frey (Passamaquoddy) is an accomplished basketmaker who learned skills from renowned artist Sylvia Gabriel. Frey in turn taught her sons Jeremy and Gabriel in all aspects of the basket-weaving tradition. She has won awards at the Santa Fe Indian Market and the Heard Museum Guild Indian Fair.

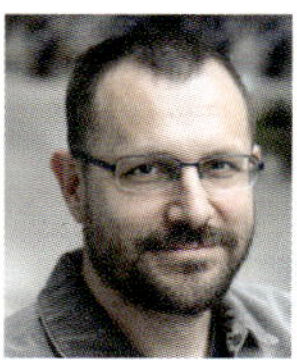

Jeremy Frey (Passamaquoddy) is a descendant of a long line of Native weavers. He learned Wabanaki techniques from his mother and by apprenticing at the Maine Indian Basketmakers Alliance. Working with customary materials such as brown ash and sweetgrass, Frey introduces new materials and forms while maintaining a strong connection to traditional practice. Frey won Best of Show at the Santa Fe Indian Market in 2011 and Heard Museum Guild Indian Fair and Market in 2011 and 2015. Frey's work is in the collections of the Art Institute of Chicago, Smithsonian American Art Museum, Portland Museum of Art, and Virginia Museum of Fine Arts.

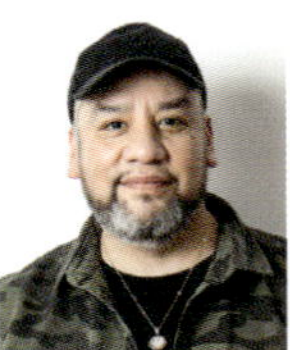

Jeffrey Gibson (Mississippi Choctaw) grew up in major urban centers in the United States, Germany, Korea, and England. He received his BFA in painting from the School of the Art Institute of Chicago (1995), and his MFA in painting from the Royal College of Art, London (1998). He is a citizen of the Mississippi Band of Choctaw Indians and is half Cherokee. He is currently an artist in residence at Bard College and lives and works near Hudson, New York.

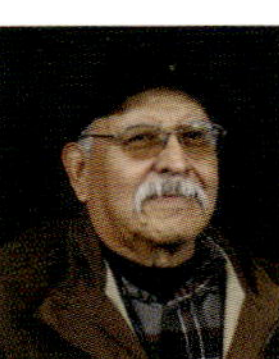

Bill Glass Jr. (Cherokee Nation of Oklahoma) is a ceramist and recognized Cherokee National Treasure. He received his art education from Central State University (Edmond, OK) and the IAIA. In 2001 he established Glass Studio with his son, Demos. They collaborate on welded steel and clay sculptures for public art commissions. Glass's ceramics are in the collections of the National Museum of the American Indian, IAIA Alumni Museum, Atlanta History Center, and Heard Museum. According to Glass, "I work with the clay but not to totally dominate it, letting its spirit coincide with mine."

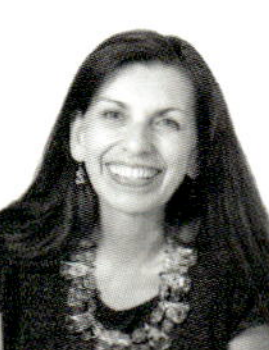

Shan Goshorn (Eastern Band Cherokee) was a multimedia artist whose work addresses human rights issues specific to Native people. Her intricate baskets are in many museum collections, including the National Museum of the American Indian, Museum of Contemporary Native Arts, Minneapolis Institute of Art, Surgut Art Museum, and Nordamerika Native Museum. Goshorn's painted photographs were exhibited in Italy, France, England, South Africa, and China. Goshorn received, among others, two United States Artist Fellowships, a Smithsonian Artist Research Fellowship, and a SWAIA Discovery Fellowship, during which she researched historical documents and baskets to inform her own work.

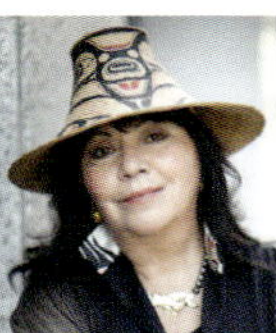

Dorothy Grant (Haida) is a fashion designer and traditional Haida artist. A sense of Haida identity is the creative force behind her fashion labels Feastwear and Dorothy Grant. Born into the Raven Clan in Hydaburg, Alaska, and raised in Ketchikan, she began sewing clothes at thirteen and later made regalia for Haida dance groups. She graduated from Helen Le'Feaux School of Fashion Design in Vancouver and began merging Haida art and fashion. Her Haida-inspired clothing has since appeared around the world on fashion runways, the red carpet, and in museum collections. In 2015 Grant received the Order of Canada for her contributions to the fashion industry.

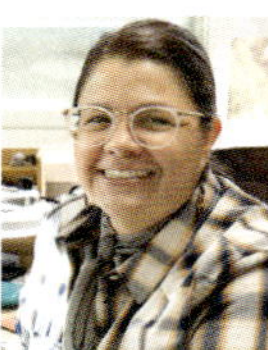

Teri Greeves (Kiowa) was raised on the Wind River Reservation in Wyoming, where her mother owned and ran a trading post. After graduating from UC Santa Cruz, Greeves began her career as a beadwork artist, winning Best of Show at the Santa Fe Indian Market in 1999. Recognition for her beadwork includes a feature in PBS's *Craft in America*, the Dobkin Fellowship from the School of American Research, and a 2016 USA Fellowship in Traditional Arts. Greeves's work is included in the collections of the National Museum of the American Indian, British Museum, Heard Museum, Brooklyn Museum, and Museum of Arts and Design. Greeves lives in Santa Fe, New Mexico.

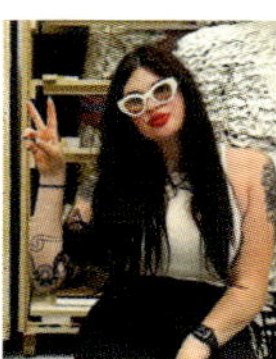

Raven Halfmoon (Caddo Nation) is from Norman, Oklahoma. She attended the University of Arkansas, where she earned a double bachelor's degree in ceramics/painting and cultural anthropology. Her work has been featured in multiple exhibitions throughout the US as well as internationally. A recent finalist for the Burke Award at the

Museum of Arts and Design in New York, Halfmoon is currently based in Norman, Oklahoma. Previously she worked as a long-term resident at the Archie Bray Foundation for the Ceramic Arts in Helena, Montana.

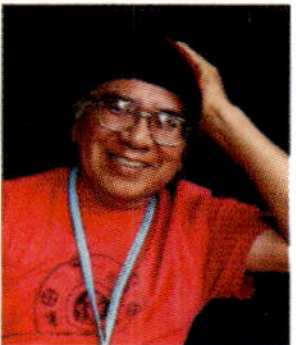

Harry Hank (Inupiaq) is a baleen basketmaker who learned weaving techniques from his mother, Marilyn Hank. His grandparents Carl and Eunice Hank were well-known weavers and are listed in the book *Baleen Basketry of the North Alaskan Eskimo* (1983). Hank is recognized for two distinctive styles: a wide weft woven with more ease and a very fine weft that achieves a detailed, tightly woven basket. His baskets have been compared favorably with the works of Andrew Oenga and Joshus Sakeagak. He is skilled in carving finials for the lids of his baskets. His favorite motifs are walrus, bear, and seal heads and a whale fluke. He currently resides in Anchorage.

Benjamin Harjo Jr. (Seminole/Absentee Shawnee) was inspired by comic books as a very young child. He studied painting, printmaking, color design, and drawing at IAIA under Seymour Tubis, who became a mentor and lifelong friend. In printmaking he found freedom and experimentation and began to see texture and pattern in everything. After graduating from IAIA in 1966 and a tour in Vietnam with the US Army, Harjo studied under J. Jay McVicker at Oklahoma State University and earned a BFA. He worked as a self-employed, self-promoting artist beginning in 1974.

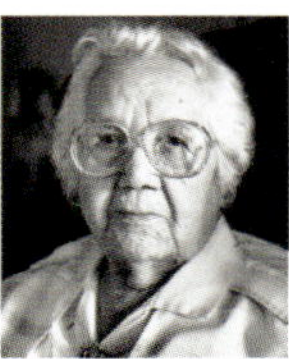

Georgia Harris (Catawba) was an influential potter who used traditional forms and molding and firing techniques. She helped her grandmother and mother make pottery after watching her elders for years. She later passed her knowledge to younger Catawba potters. Her commitment to quality elevated Catawba pottery from tourist ware to works of art that are studied and collected. She was named an NEA National Heritage Fellow in 1997, the year of her death.

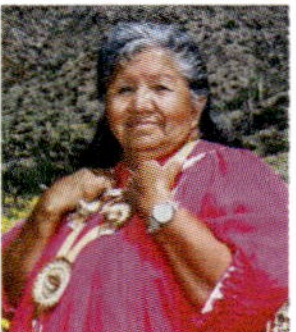

Evalena Henry (San Carlos Apache) is a master basket weaver who learned the craft from her mother, herself a well-regarded basketmaker. Henry is recognized especially for her ceremonial baskets and her burden baskets, used during the Sunrise Dance in Apache girls' coming-of-age ceremonies. She has taught workshops at the Taos Art Institute and many reservations. She's received fellowships from the National Endowment for the Arts and School of American Research as well as numerous awards.

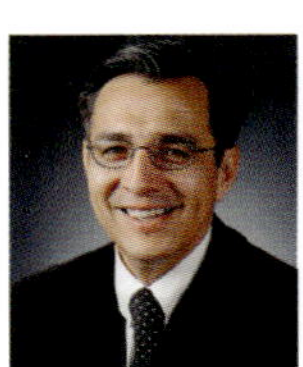

Emil Her Many Horses (Oglala Lakota) is an artist and a curator at the Smithsonian Institution's National Museum of the American Indian (NMAI), where he served as the lead curator of its inaugural permanent exhibition. He is trained in traditional beadwork, quillwork, and doll making, having studied as a teenager with Alice Fish and women influenced by her on South Dakota's Rosebud Sioux Reservation. His work is in the collections of the Eiteljorg Museum, Plains Indian Museum, NMAI, and Autry Museum of the American West.

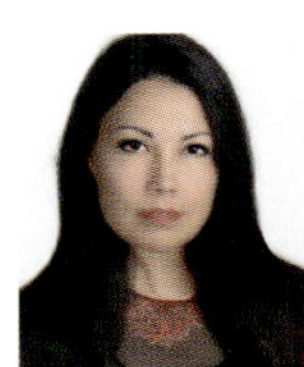

Rhonda Holy Bear (Lakota) spent her formative years on the Cheyenne River Sioux/Lakota Indian Reservation in South Dakota and in Chicago, where she researched the work of her Plains Indian ancestors in the Field Museum. Her innovative transitional art figures, a combination of sculpture and traditional techniques, have elevated the prominence of Plains Art figures in contemporary Native American art. Her work has been featured in the Art Institute of Chicago, Field Museum, Metropolitan Museum of Art, and National Museum of the American Indian.

Her Lakota name is "Wakah Wayuphika Win" (Making with Exceptional Skills Woman).

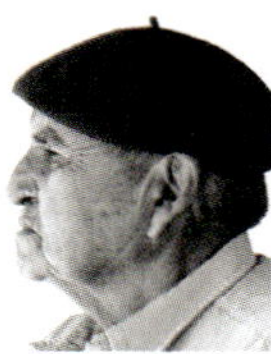

Allan Houser (Fort Sill Apache) is best known for his sculptural work, but his legacy of drawings and paintings is equally rich. He worked in a variety of media and styles, from dramatic realism to abstraction. From 1962 to 1975, Houser was an influential teacher at the IAIA. His work is in the collections of three different museums of the Smithsonian Institution, the Centre Pompidou, and the British and Japanese royal collections. He received the inaugural exhibition at the National Museum of the American Indian in 2004 and was the featured artist of the 2002 Winter Olympics in Salt Lake City.

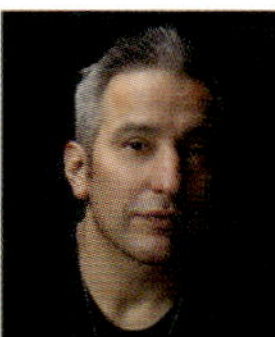

Kenneth Johnson (Muscogee/Seminole), who attended the University of Oklahoma, is a jeweler and sculptor renowned for art crafted from precious metals, gemstones, bronze, and carved stone. He received Best in Show at the Mvskoke Art Market in 2022 for the necklace *Songs of the Fourth World* as well as first place in sculpture and Best Mvskoke Artist in 2023. His artwork has graced prominent red-carpet events, including the Grammys and Spirit Awards. Johnson has created custom jewelry for distinguished figures, including US Supreme Court justices Sandra Day O'Connor, Ruth Bader Ginsburg, and Sonia Sotomayor.

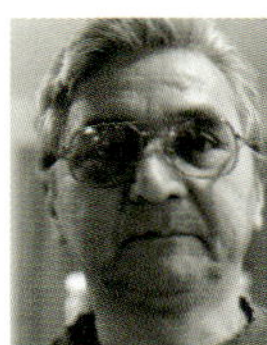

Peter B. Jones (Onondaga) is a sculpture artist and potter. He attended the IAIA and studied under Otellie Loloma (Hopi). He is credited with contributing to the revival of Six Nations ceramic art. His early creations commented on Native social and political issues, and his later artworks are reminiscent of traditional, pit-fired Iroquois pottery. Jones's work is collected by private individuals and museums internationally. He has a pottery studio on the Cattaraugus Territory in New York.

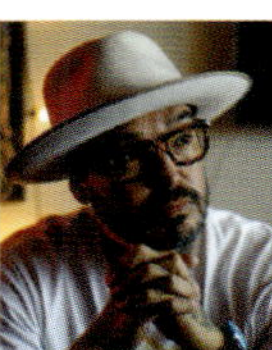

Steven Paul Judd (Kiowa/Choctaw) is an artist and filmmaker based in Oklahoma City. He participated in the Disney/ABC writing fellowship program in Los Angeles in 2008 and was a staff writer for the Disney XD series *Zeke and Luther* before transitioning to visual art and filmmaking. Self-taught, Judd works across media, creating paintings, murals, mosaics, street art, posters, stickers, and T-shirt designs. His work disrupts American Indian stereotypes, often using humor, and reinterprets Native imagery through a pop culture lens. He has received a United States Artists fellowship and several Emmy nominations.

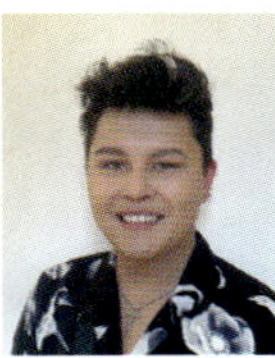

Jontay Kahm (Plains Cree), born in Saskatchewan, Canada, is pursuing a BFA in studio arts with an emphasis on fashion design from the IAIA. Previously, he attended Blanche Macdonald and Marist College. He emphasizes movement and sculpts characteristics of hybrid human-animal spiritual experiences into his work. Kahm incorporates his Plains Cree cultural heritage by taking subtle elements of ceremonial regalia and expressing them through a contemporary perspective. By making garments that evoke a spiritual awakening, Kahm creates an atmosphere that transports individuals to somewhere otherworldly.

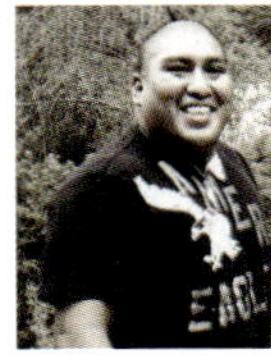

Renferd Koruh (Hopi/Tewa) is from Polacca, Arizona. His passion for art stems from observing family members creating; he began to carve at ten. He graduated from the IAIA in 2005 with a degree in studio arts. Through his work he conveys meaning, stories, and tradition to younger generations so they may value the knowledge and express it in their own way. Equally important to Koruh is using what he learned at school to guide and support Native youth on the reservation. Koruh believes art is for the community as much as for individuals immersed in the art market. For him, positive and spiritual energy is created and resides in every piece.

Chalmers Locklear (Lumbee) creates gourd vessel art. He paints Native symbolism and motifs as well as themes from nature on his gourds. He also creates limited-edition painted feather art. Locklear's work is in private collections across the US and in the collection of the Museum of the Southeast American Indian in Pembroke, North Carolina.

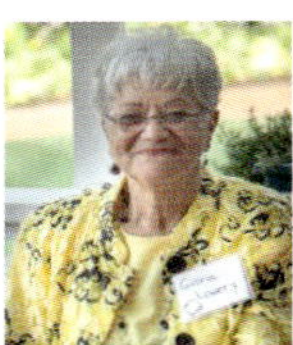

Gloria Tara Lowery (Lumbee) was a North Carolina teacher and artist who worked in watercolor, acrylics, pine needles, and other mixed media. She earned a BA and MA in art education at UNC Pembroke. She was an arts educator in Robeson County and an Indigenous rights activist. Her works are in the collection of the Museum of the Southeast American Indian and have been shown across North Carolina. She used her art to connect to her Native ancestors and to celebrate the landscape of Robeson County.

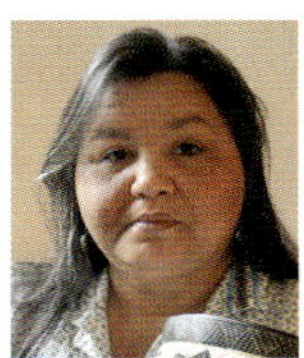

Senora Lynch (Haliwa-Saponi) etches designs in her own style onto the surface of traditional pottery she creates using the hand-coiling method. She began making pottery as a teenager after seeing ancient pottery sherds and working with tribal elders in a pottery class. Lynch's designs depict the stories and beliefs of the Haliwa-Saponi peoples, using Native symbols and motifs to convey a narrative. She etches turtles, lizards, bowls, and bears onto her pottery made of red and white clay. Her work is in the North Carolina Museum of History and the National Museum of the American Indian as well as on the UNC–Chapel Hill campus. She was awarded the NC Folk Heritage Award in 2007.

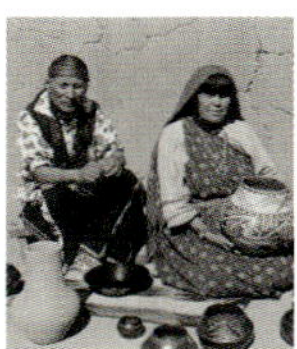

Maria Martinez and **Julian Martinez** (San Ildefonso Pueblo) are renowned for innovations in their ancestral blackware tradition. Partly inspired by the discovery of ancient Pueblo black-on-black sherds excavated in New Mexico's Pajarito Plateau region, they redeveloped the technique. Maria shaped and polished vessels, Julian painted designs, and together they perfected the complex firing process. When first revived, their now iconic black-on-black technique diverged from the polychrome pottery widely produced by Pueblo artisans.

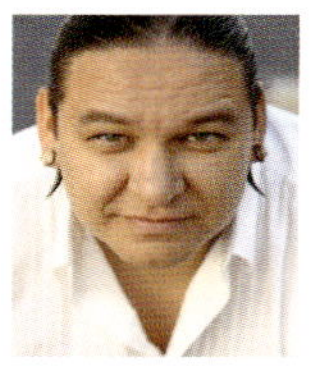

Dallin Maybee (Northern Arapaho/Seneca) is an accomplished artist, public speaker, performer, and currently the assistant director of development at the Native American Rights Fund in Boulder, Colorado. He holds a JD from the Sandra Day O'Conner College of Law with an emphasis in federal Indian law. His work can be found in private collections and museums, including the National Museum of the American Indian, Autry Museum of the American West, Heard Museum, and Portland Art Museum. Awards include Best of Show ribbons at the Santa Fe Indian Market (2007), Cherokee Art Market (2020), Hodinöhsö:ni' Art Show (2021), and Tesoro Indian Market (2021).

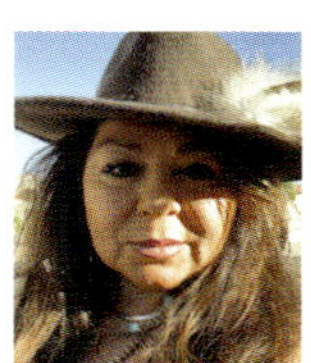

Wanesia Misquadace (Fond du Lac Band of the Ojibway) earned a BFA from the IAIA and an MFA from the University of Wisconsin–Madison. She is a silversmith who also incorporates basketry, beadwork, and photography in her practice. Misquadace uses the traditional technique of birch bark biting to create designs in her work, preserving and bringing awareness to this dying art form. She is an assistant professor of metals and Indigenous arts at Arizona State University and has shown her work at the Museum of Arts and Design and the Tweed Museum of Art.

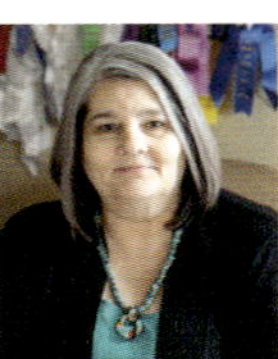

Katrina Mitten (Miami Tribe of Oklahoma) is an award-winning artist who has been beading for over forty-five years. She practices traditional Great Lakes embroidery-style native beadwork through the study of family heirlooms, museum collections, and practice. She says, "My teachers are the beadworkers of the past." The imagery she creates is inspired by the world around her. Her works have been acquired by the Miami Tribe, national museums, and private collectors. Mitten has been a corporate lecturer, contributed to elementary-, secondary-, and university-level educational programs, and is featured in documentary films.

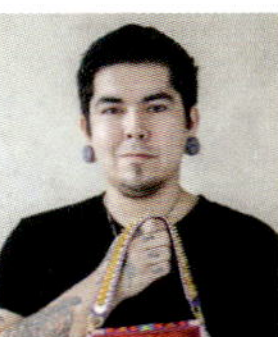

Elias Jade Not Afraid (Apsaalooké Nation) is a bead artist who combines traditional techniques with contemporary fashion and punk aesthetics to keep Crow culture alive while pushing boundaries and sparking the interest of younger tribal members. Not Afraid was born and raised on the Crow Indian Reservation in Montana. He began producing beadwork at age twelve by examining, taking apart, and reassembling beaded items made by his great-grandmother. His work is in the collections of the Field Museum, Heard Museum, Minneapolis Institute of Art, Smithsonian, and Metropolitan Museum of Art. He shares tutorials of traditional techniques on social media.

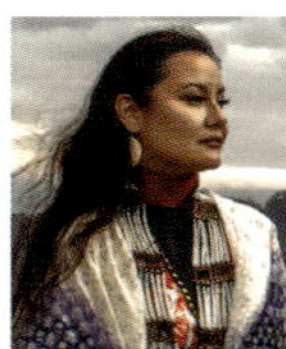

Jamie Okuma (Luiseño/Shoshone e-Bannock/Wailaki/Okinawan) is a member of the La Jolla band of American Indians in Southern California, where she lives and works. She creates one-of-a-kind pieces of wearable art and designs ready-to-wear fashions. After high school, she took graphic design classes at Palomar College and attended the IAIA, and from age eighteen she has been a professional artist. Okuma has received a combined seven Best of Show awards from the Heard and Santa Fe Indian markets. Her work is in the collections of the Minneapolis Institute of Art, Nelson-Atkins Museum of Art, Denver Art Museum, and National Museum of the American Indian.

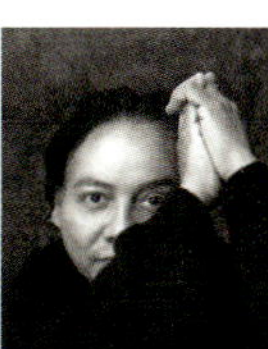

Virgil Ortiz (Cochiti Pueblo) remains influenced by his grandmother and mother, renowned potters. His forty-year career extends across media and boundaries, challenging societal expectations. Ortiz fuses his Pueblo culture with sci-fi, fantasy, and apocalyptic themes, yielding thought-provoking, futuristic imagery. He teaches Pueblo history by telling the story of the 1680 Pueblo Revolt with a cast of superheroes he's created through a series of works, including jars, busts, and live actors. Ortiz's works are in the Stedelijk Museum 's-Hertogenbosch, Fondation Cartier pour l'art contemporain, Smithsonian Institution, Virginia Museum of Fine Arts, Minneapolis Institute of Art, Denver Art Museum, and the NCMA.

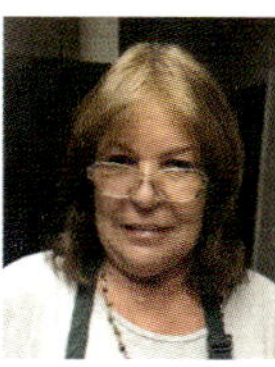

Jane Osti (Cherokee) is an artist, educator, and Cherokee National Treasure. She began making wheel-thrown pottery and sculptures while attending Northeastern State University, where she graduated with a BFA and MA in science education. Award-winning Cherokee potter Anna Mitchell introduced Osti to Southeastern pottery. Osti studied with Mitchell and now teaches students to create pottery in the tradition of the Southeast woodlands. Osti is a veteran of museum shows and Indian markets. She's earned numerous awards, and her work is in museum collections around the nation. Osti says she has been blessed to have amazing teachers who have helped her connect to the clay.

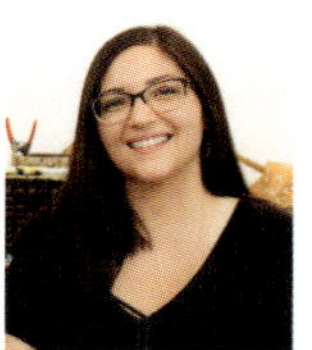

Cherish Parrish (Pottawatomi/Ottawa/Matchi-be-nash-she-wish) is a sixth-generation weaver of black ash baskets, which she learned to make from her mother, Kelly Church. She weaves in the freeform tradition and around molds using black ash bark she harvests from Michigan wetlands. Parrish has participated in the Michigan Traditional Arts Apprenticeship Program and the Smithsonian Folklife Festival. She won Best of Show at the 2012 Eiteljorg Museum Indian Market and more recently has shown her work at the Grand Rapids Art Museum and SAIC Galleries in Chicago.

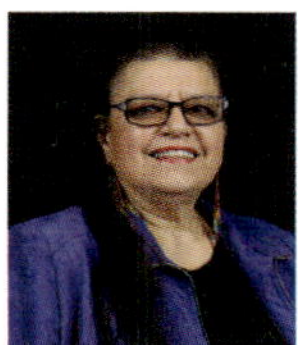

Lisa Rutherford (Cherokee Nation) balances her creative time between clay arts and textile arts, including pottery, sculpture, eighteenth-century clothing, feather capes, Southeast appliqué beadwork, and twined textiles. She has been making ancestral-style pottery since 2005 and began making historic clothing to wear while demonstrating her art, which led to her career as a living history interpreter as well as artist. She creates historic clothing for museum exhibitions, specializing in feather capes. In 2018 she was named a Cherokee National Treasure by the Cherokee Nation for her work in preserving and promoting Cherokee pottery and culture.

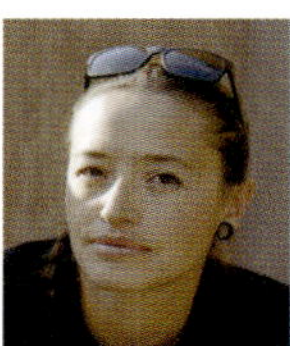

Rose B. Simpson (Santa Clara Pueblo) has a BFA from the IAIA and an MFA in ceramics from the Rhode Island School of Design. She has enjoyed solo exhibitions at the ICA Boston, Fabric Workshop and Museum, Nevada Museum of Art, SCAD Museum of Art, Benton Museum of Art, and Wheelwright Museum of the American Indian. Simpson's work is held in numerous museum collections, including the Hirshhorn Museum and Sculpture Garden, Los Angeles County Museum of Art, Denver Art Museum, Solomon R. Guggenheim Museum, MCA Chicago, Museum of Fine Arts, Boston, Portland Art Museum, and SFMOMA. She is represented by Jessica Silverman, San Francisco, and Jack Shainman Gallery, New York.

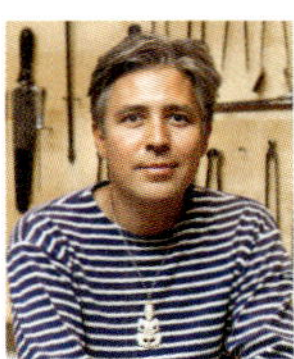

Preston Singletary (Tlingit) attended Pilchuck Glass School and then worked at the studio of Benjamin Moore, where he developed his own work. His glass sculptures contain themes of Tlingit mythology and traditional designs and use music to shape a contemporary perspective of Native culture. Forty years of working with elders has put him in a position of being a keeper of cultural knowledge, while he forges new directions in materials and concepts of Indigenous arts. Singletary's works are included in the Museum of Fine Arts, Boston, Seattle Art Museum, British Museum, National Museum of the American Indian, and the NCMA.

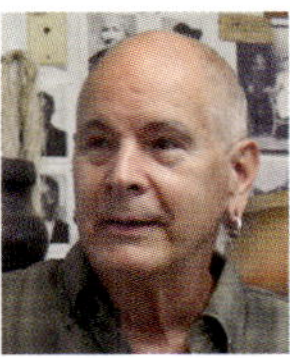

Richard Zane Smith (Wyandot Nation of Kansas) is a ceramic artist who earned a BFA at Meramec Community College and studied at the Kansas City Art Institute. He's active in Wyandot/Wendat language and culture revitalization and spent seven years teaching Wyandot language and storytelling in the Wyandotte public schools. He holds pottery workshops for First Nations peoples, teaching bow making, rattle making, and other Indigenous art forms. Smith's dream is to see all Indigenous art traditions restored. He has work in major museums and books and is an Indian Arts and Crafts Board–certified Indian artisan.

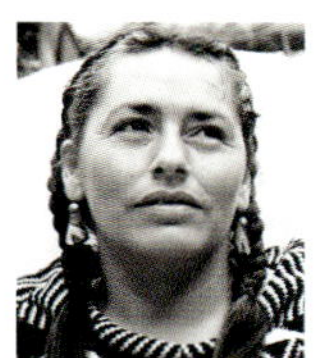

Roxanne Swentzell (Santa Clara Pueblo) is a clay and bronze sculptor who comes from a family of artists, including uncle Michael Naranjo. She took classes at the IAIA during high school and attended the Portland Museum Art School. Swentzell uses traditional techniques, such as layering coils of clay, and creates figures that reflect a range of human experiences. Her work is in many museum collections, including the National Museum of American Indian Art, British Museum, Denver Art Museum, and Nelson-Atkins Museum of Art. She received an honorary doctorate from the IAIA in 2018. She runs the nonprofit Flowering Tree Permaculture Institute to promote Indigenous ways of knowing.

Dorothy Torivio (Acoma Pueblo) was a potter known for her well-balanced shapes and dramatic painted designs. She learned how to build thin-walled, steeply sloped pots from her mother-in-law, Lolita Concho. She was considered one of Acoma's finest potters in the 1970s. In the early 1980s, she started covering her pots with repeating geometric, eye-dazzler designs derived from classic Acoma patterns. She soon began exhibiting her work in international venues. Torivio earned countless awards at shows and markets and was included in an exhibition at the National Museum of Women in the Arts.

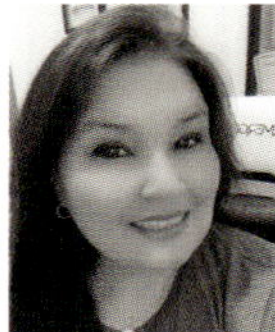

Laura Walkingstick (Cherokee) is a cloth and cornhusk doll maker and creates narrative sculptures using acrylic, clay, wood, metal, and cloth. She is an enrolled member of the Eastern Band of Cherokee Indians from the Qualla Boundary of North Carolina, where she was born and currently lives. She received an AFA and BFA at the IAIA and an MA in counseling and art therapy at Southwestern College in Santa Fe. She is an instructor at the John C. Campbell Folk Art School, teaching cornhusk doll making. Her work is in the Museum of Contemporary Native Arts, Museum of the Southeast American Indian, and Mountain Heritage Center.

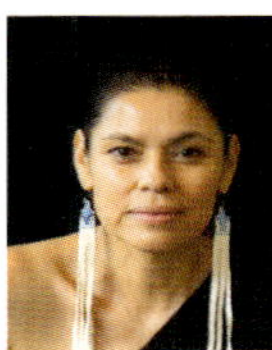

Kathleen Wall (Pueblo of Jemez) carries on the matrilineal tradition of being a clay artist as passed down from her grandmother and mother. She began by making storytellers; her work then took on more figurative qualities. Numerous exhibitions and art shows have featured her pottery and her whimsical clay figurines. She has won multiple awards and fellowships. Even as her work transcends the art form taught to Kathleen in her youth, she remains grounded in tradition. Wall continues embracing her connection to clay while exploring other mediums. Her recent works intertwine clay sculptures and acrylic paint on wood panels to create cohesive objects. Her current mixed-media works center on land and identity.

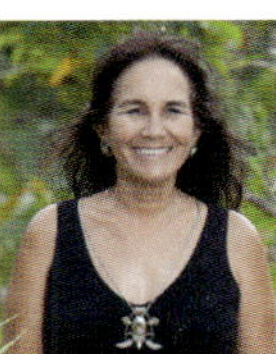

Denise Wallace (Chugach/Sugpiaq/Alutiiq) studied at the IAIA in the late 1970s. After graduating, she and her husband, Samuel, remained in Santa Fe creating and selling work from their studio and gallery. The content of her jewelry remains planted in the rich stories and customs of the Native peoples of arctic Alaska, stories that deal with themes of healing, growth, nature, and transformation. Wallace utilizes mechanical components and materials like silver, gold, semiprecious stones, and scrimshawed, fossilized bone to join old traditions and stories with newly envisioned interpretations. She maintains an international following and resume of international exhibitions and exchanges.

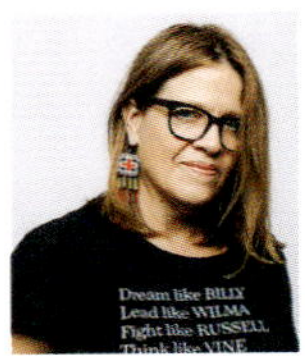

Marie Watt (Seneca Nation) is a citizen of the Seneca Nation with German-Scots ancestry, which informs her work and process deeply. She weaves into her sculptures her own experiences as a Seneca woman, including indigenous design techniques. She has a BS from Willamette University, an AFA from the IAIA, and an MFA from Yale University. Watt's work has been in numerous exhibitions, including the Pennsylvania Academy of the Fine Arts, Denver Art Museum, and Crystal Bridges Museum of American Art. Her works are held in many collections, including the Metropolitan Museum of Art, National Gallery of Canada, Smithsonian American Art Museum and Renwick Gallery, and the NCMA. She currently lives in Portland, Oregon.

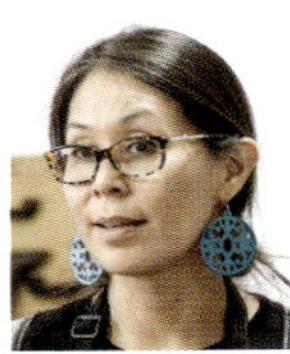

Jodi Webster (Ho-Chunk Nation/Prairie Band Potawatomi Nation) holds degrees in graphic design, a BFA in painting/drawing, and an MFA in jewelry/metals. Her jewelry echoes designs of the Great Lakes region. Webster's techniques range from fabrication by hand to the modern use of CAD software and a 3-D printer. Her utilization of technology counters the stereotypes ascribed to Native American art/jewelry. She explains, "Just as my ancestors acquired and used the most innovative supplies (glass beads, metal, silk, and printed fabrics), I, too, am using the most current tools to adorn, heal, celebrate, and interpret myself culturally."

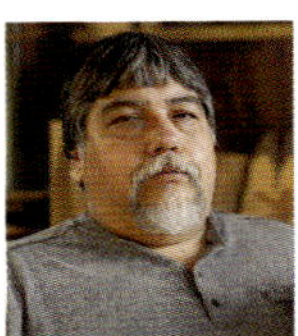

Billy Welch (Snowbird Cherokee) grew up in the Snowbird Community, where he learned to carve. He is self-taught but was influenced by his grandmothers, both basketmakers. They showed him how they made different natural dyes out of roots to create color for their baskets, techniques Welch now uses for his masks. Welch has sold sets of masks to multiple museums and tribal programs. With his wife, Debbie, he has owned the store Hunting Boy Woodcarving for over ten years. He also teaches Native arts and crafts at Robbinsville High School in Graham County, North Carolina, in hopes of keeping traditions and customs alive.

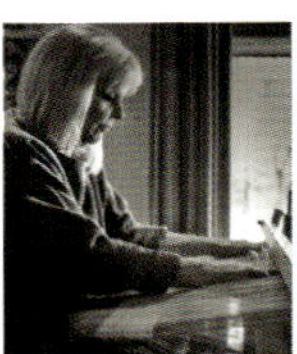

Margaret Roach Wheeler (Chickasaw/Choctaw) has merged her fine arts education with her Native American heritage to weave contemporary clothing based on American Indian costumes. The spirit of her great-great-great-great grandmother Mahota flows through her contemporary designs. Wheeler's hand-woven garments have won major awards in North American Indian markets. Her works have appeared in exhibitions at and are in the collections of the Metropolitan Museum of Art, Portland Art Museum, Indianapolis Museum of Art, and Eiteljorg Museum. She was an artist in residence at the National Museum of the American Indian and voted into the Chickasaw Hall of Fame.

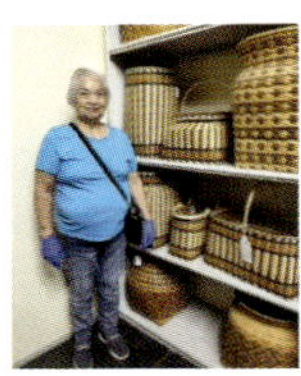

Maidena Welch Wildcatt (Cherokee) of the Big Cove Community in Cherokee, North Carolina, is a white oak basketmaker renowned for her intricate designs and narrow-cut splints. She learned basket weaving from her mother, Agnes Wolfe Welch, and has been making baskets for more than sixty years. She enjoys weaving the unbroken friendship design and her mother's design using narrow strips. Her family, first her father and now her brothers James and Joe, help her make and dye the splints she uses. Her brother Charlie helps make the handles for her baskets.

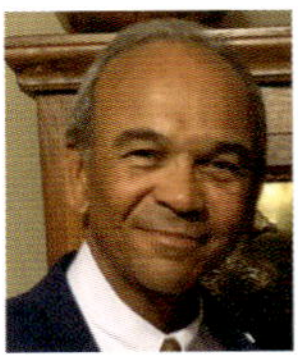

Dennis Michael Wilkins (Lumbee) is a North Carolina–based stone and wood carver. He's been honing his skills since 1981. He carves what he sees in rough stone and wood, and as he works a story usually begins to develop. These stories are of the Creator, family, clan, tribe, nation, and environment. When the story is clear to Wilkins, the sculpture is ready for completion. Wilkins has won many first place and best of show awards. He has shown and demonstrated his art at numerous pow-wows, shows, and galleries. His most memorable exhibition to date was during Lumbee Days at the National Museum of the American Indian.

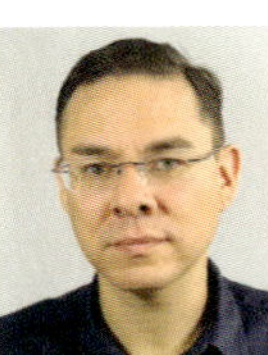

Kenneth Williams Jr. (Northern Arapaho/Cattaraugus Seneca) has been a bead worker since he was five years old. Coming from a strong line of beadwork artists on his matrilineal side, he has found it important to maintain and uphold his family's traditional teachings while always looking ahead to the future through his works. Williams describes the work he does as contemporary traditional. He lives and works in Santa Fe, New Mexico.

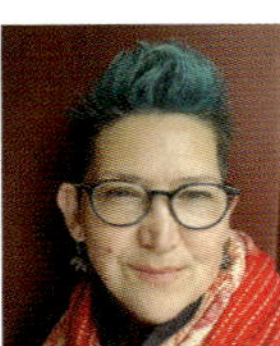

Holly Wilson (Delaware Nation) is a multidisciplinary artist who creates figures as her storytellers, interweaving stories of the sacred and precious and capturing moments of our day, vulnerabilities, and strengths. Wilson invites viewers to see their connection to her personal narratives of family and Lenape history. She uses bronze, paint, encaustic, photography, clay, and glass as layers of meaning, with depth and sensitivity, and her figures serve as vessels for memory. Wilson holds a BFA (ceramics), MA (ceramics), and MFA (sculpture). Exhibiting since the 1990s, she has works in private, public, and museum collections.

Works in the Exhibition

Marcus Amerman
Choctaw, born 1959
Lone Ranger and Tonto Cuff Bracelets, 1999
Glass beads, leather, and thread
H. 2 × W. 2⅞ × D. 2¼ in.
H. 2 × W. 2⅝ × D. 2¼ in.
Philbrook Museum of Art, Tulsa, Oklahoma,
Gift of Don and Rita Newman, 2009.5.1 and
2009.5.2

Marcus Amerman
Choctaw, born 1959
Warriors of Snaketown, 2010
Glass
H. 14¾ × W. 8 × D. 8 in.
Courtesy of the artist

Marcus Amerman
Choctaw, born 1959
Preston Singletary
Tlingit, born 1963
Deerman of the Hopewell, 2010
Glass
H. 24½ × W. 12 × D. 5 in.
Courtesy of the artists

Venancio Aragon✳
Navajo Nation, born 1985
Untitled, 2023
Weaving
Dimensions variable
Courtesy of the artist

Keri Ataumbi
Kiowa, born 1971
Tah's Medicine, 2017
Sterling silver, 18K gold, 22K gold, diamonds,
rubies, sapphires, watercolor on vellum,
antique watch crystal, and mother-of-pearl
H. 21 × W. 2¾ × D. ¾ in.
Courtesy of the artist

Martha Berry
Cherokee Nation, born 1948
When the Highlands Met the Mounds, 2019
Glass seed beads, wool "Graham of
Montrose Ancient" clan tartan, cotton,
silk, wool yarn (to the extent possible,
all materials are authentic to the late
18th century)
H. 36 × W. 16 × D. 2 in.
Courtesy of the artist

Sally Black
Navajo, born 1959
Untitled, 1979
Coiled sumac, vegetable dyes,
and commercial dyes
H. 4 × Diam. 41¼ in.
Heard Museum Collection, NA-SW-NA-B-20

Joanna Underwood Blackburn
Chickasaw Nation
Water Jar, 2017
Bronze
H. 46 × W. 48 × D. 48 in.
Courtesy of the artist

Debra Box
Southern Ute, born 1956
Box, 2010
Cowhide, pigment, and wool
H. 10½ × W. 20 × D. 13 in.
Denver Art Museum: Native Arts
acquisition fund, 2010.497

Jackie Larson Bread✳
Blackfeet Nation, born 1960
New work created for the exhibition
Courtesy of the artist

Millie Bridwell
Cheyenne River Sioux
Star Quilt, 2023
Cotton
H. 79 × W. 70 in.
Courtesy of the artist

Harlen Chavis Jr.
Lumbee
Mississippian Gorget, 2022
Copper and artificial sinew
H. 22 × W. 5½ in.
Collection of the Museum of
the Southeast American Indian

Steven Chrisjohn
Oneida
Moundbuilder Necklace, 2022
Serpentine, sterling silver, and copper
H. 11 × W. 6¼ in.
Courtesy of the artist

Kelly Church
Ottawa/Pottawatomi/Matchi-be-nash-
she-wish, born 1967
blueberry time, 2015
Black ash, Rit dye, and sweetgrass
H. 10 × W. 11 × D. 11 in.
Courtesy of the artist

Melissa S. Cody✳
Navajo Nation, born 1983
Loaned artwork

Vivian Garner Cottrell✳
Cherokee Nation
One Fire, 2023
Rivercane and black walnut
and bloodroot dyes
H. 11 × W. 9 in.
Courtesy of the artist

Robert Davidson
Haida, born 1946
Eagle Transformation Mask, 1998
Red cedar, pigment, cedar bark, and hair
H. 15 × W. 35⅜ × D. 23 in.
Audain Art Museum Collection,
Gift of Patricia and S. Bruce McLaughlin

Leslie A. Deer
Muscogee (Mvskoke) Nation of Oklahoma
Equilibrium, 2022
Leather and cotton
H. 47 × W. 46 in.
Courtesy of the artist

Orlando Dugi
Navajo
Red Cochineal Gown, Red Collection,
2015–2016
Silk organza, silk charmeuse, glass beads,
gold bullion, sequins, and built-in corset
boning structure
H. 50 × W. 30 × D. 5 in.
Courtesy of the artist

Chase Earles
Caddo, born 1976
Horse Tripod, 2014
Clay and mussel shell
H. 22 × W. 19 × D. 15
Loan from National Cowboy & Western
Heritage Museum

Tom Farris
Otoe-Missouria/Cherokee Nation, born 1978
Shifting Paradigms Übermensch, 2022
Restored 2001 Volkswagen Jetta
H. 59 × W. 68 × D. 174 in.
Courtesy of the artist

Anita Fields
Osage, born 1951
To Know Your People Are Beautiful, 2019
Contemporary Osage wedding coat
with deconstructed images of historical
documents written by US government
agents, traders, and journalists
H. 120 × W. 60 × D. 60 in.
Eiteljorg Museum, Museum purchase from
the Eiteljorg Contemporary Art Fellowship

Sue Fish✳
Chickasaw/Choctaw, born 1957
Choctaw Elbow Basket (Fish Style), 2023
Rivercane dyed with black walnut
H. 18 × W. 14 in.
Courtesy of the artist

Cliff Fragua
Pueblo of Jemez, born 1955
Earth Song, no date
Marble and turquoise
H. 56¾ × W. 21½ × D. 12 in.
Courtesy of the artist

Gabriel Frey
Passamaquoddy
Gal Frey
Passamaquoddy
Wapi-kuhkukhahs/Snowy Owl Basket, 2022
Black ash, leather, glass beads, and metal
H. 12 × W. 7 × D. 4 in.
Collection of the Maine Historical Society

Jeremy Frey
Passamaquoddy, born 1978
Quilted Cedar, 2020
Black ash, cedar bark, sweet grass, and
synthetic dye
H. 19 × W. 10 × D. 4 in.
The Robert and Barbara Buker Collections

Jeffrey Gibson
Mississippi Choctaw, born 1972
Bring Down the Walls, Let 'Em Fall Fall Fall,
2020
Acrylic on canvas, glass beads, and artificial
sinew inset into wood frame
44 × 56 in.
The Gutierrez Collection, Raleigh, NC

Jeffrey Gibson
Mississippi Choctaw, born 1972
I Put a Spell on You, 2015
Repurposed punching bag, glass beads,
artificial sinew, and steel
H. 40 × W. 14 × D. 14 in.
Nasher Museum of Art, Duke University,
Museum Purchase

Bill Glass Jr.
Cherokee Nation of Oklahoma, born 1950
Birdman, 2013
Lizella clay and glazes fired at
Cone 6 oxidation
H. 14 × W. 7½ × D. 6 in.
Courtesy of the artist

Bill Glass Jr.
Cherokee Nation of Oklahoma, born 1950
Southeast Images, 1996
Lizella clay and glazes fired at
Cone 6 oxidation
H. 7¼ × W. 9 × D. 9 in.
Courtesy of the artist

Shan Goshorn
Eastern Band Cherokee, 1957–2018
Home Land, 2016
Arches watercolor paper splints printed
with archival inks and acrylic paint
H. 9½ × W. 6 × D. 6 in.
Collection of Asheville Art Museum,
Purchased with additional funds provided
by 2016 Collectors' Circle members Gail
and Brian McCarthy, 2017.02.01

Dorothy Grant
Haida, born 1955
Eagle Bolero with T-Form Dress, 1989
Cashmere and mother-of-pearl
Dimensions variable
Courtesy of the artist

Teri Greeves
Kiowa, born 1970
"Between Worlds" Beaded Parfleche Vessel,
2016
Rawhide and beads
H. 23 × Diam. 7 in.
Collection of the Art Fund Inc. at the
Birmingham Museum of Art; Gift of
Martha Pezrow, AFI.105.2016

Raven Halfmoon
Caddo Nation, born 1991
Soku & Nish (Sun & Moon – Caddo), 2022
Ceramic and glaze
H. 72 × W. 38 × D. 40 in.
Courtesy of Kouri + Corrao Gallery

Harry Hank
Inupiaq, born 1972
Baleen Basket with Polar Bear Head Finial,
no date
Baleen and ivory
H. 4 × W. 3 × D. 3 in.
Private collection, North Carolina

Benjamin Harjo Jr.
Seminole/Absentee Shawnee, 1945–2023
Kenneth Williams Jr.
Northern Arapaho/Cattaraugus Seneca,
born 1983
Charmers in the Wind, 2022
Acrylic, canvas, 24K gold-plate beads,
vintage and contemporary glass beads,
jade, lapis, white coral beads, and Austrian
crystals
H. 22½ × W. 22½ × D. 2 in. (frame)
Courtesy of Ken Williams Jr. and Barbara
Harjo

Georgia Harris
Catawba, 1905–1997
Indian Head Jar, no date
Earthenware
H. 8½ × W. 10½ × D. 7½ in.
Collection of the Native American Studies
Center, University of South Carolina
Lancaster

   ✳ These works are not illustrated in the catalogue.

Evalena Henry
San Carlos Apache, born 1939
Burden Basket, 1983
Willow or sumac, leather, twine, and
tin cones
H. 13¾ × W. 16¾ in.
Courtesy of the School for Advanced
Research, Indian Arts Research Center
purchase for the permanent collection,
1983

Emil Her Many Horses
Oglala Lakota
Grandma's Favorite, 2022
Size 13 cut-glass beads, tanned hide,
cotton cloth, and brass sequins
H. 28 × W. 11 × D. 11 in.
Courtesy of the artist

Emil Her Many Horses
Oglala Lakota
Traditional Doll, 1989
Size 13 seed beads, tanned deer hide,
wool cloth, bugle beads, silver metallic
beads, and buffalo hide
H. 14 × W. 8 × D. 8 in.
Courtesy of the artist

Rhonda Holy Bear
Lakota, born 1959
The Last Lakota Horse Raid, 1991
Wood (basswood), Native-tanned and
commercial leather, glass beads, pigment,
cotton cloth, hair, dentalium shells, abalone,
German silver, metal cones, brass tacks, and
beads
H. 30 × W. 13 × D. 9 in.
Collection of Joyce Chelberg

Allan Houser
Fort Sill Apache, 1914–1994
Camp Talk, 1979
Bronze
H. 23½ × W. 22½ × D. 21½ in.
Courtesy of Allan Houser Inc.

Allan Houser
Fort Sill Apache, 1914–1994
Reverie, 1981
Bronze
H. 24½ × W. 23 × D. 12½ in.
Courtesy of Allan Houser Inc.

Kenneth Johnson
Muscogee/Seminole, born 1967
"Mother Earth" Turtle, 2023
Silicon bronze cast
H. 20 × W. 17 × D. 3½ in.
Courtesy of the artist

Kenneth Johnson
Muscogee/Seminole, born 1967
Songs of the Fourth World, 2022
Silver, copper, 18K red and yellow gold,
and Mokume Gane layered metal
H. 13 × W. 6 × D. ⅜ in.
Courtesy of the artist

Kenneth Johnson
Muscogee/Seminole, born 1967
Sun Spider Cuff, 2023
Palladium, 24K gold, and sapphire
H. 2½ × W. 2½ × D. 3 in.
Courtesy of the artist

Peter B. Jones
Onondaga, born 1947
New Indian – Portrait Jar, 2010
Clay, pigment, sinew, copper, and wood
H. 12 × W. 9 × D. 10 in.
Longyear Museum of Anthropology, Colgate
University, Museum purchase, NA2010.104

Steven Paul Judd＊
Kiowa/Choctaw
New work created for the exhibition
Commissioned by the North Carolina
Museum of Art

Jontay Kahm＊
Plains Cree, born 1996
Transcendence, 2023
Goose feathers, turkey quills, felt base,
and nylon ribbon
Size 6
Courtesy of the artist

Renferd Koruh
Hopi/Tewa, born 1984
A Time of Harvest, 2023
Aged cottonwood root and acrylic paints
H. 13 × W. 4 × D. 4½ in.
Courtesy of the artist

Renferd Koruh
Hopi/Tewa, born 1984
The Watermelon Tour – Encore, 2023
Aged cottonwood root and acrylic paints
H. 7 × W. 9 × D. 9 in.
Courtesy of the artist

Chalmers Locklear
Lumbee
Cardinal Gourd, 2014
Acrylic on gourd
H. 11 × W. 9½ in.
Collection of the Museum of
the Southeast American Indian

Gloria Tara Lowery
Lumbee, 1944–2020
Seed Basket, 2014
Longleaf pine needles
H. 6 × Diam. 16 in.
Collection of the Museum of
the Southeast American Indian

Senora Lynch
Haliwa-Saponi, born 1963
Woodland People Bowl, 2003
Red and white clay
H. 20 × Diam. 15 in.
Collection of Bobby Brayboy

Maria Martinez
San Ildefonso Pueblo, 1887–1980
Julian Martinez
San Ildefonso Pueblo, 1885–1943
Bowl, circa 1942–1943
Polished blackware pottery with matte paint
H. 6¾ in.
North Carolina Museum of Art, Gift of Dr.
and Mrs. John R. Lambert, 1978 (G.78.21.1)

Dallin Maybee
Northern Arapaho/Seneca, born 1974
Buffalo Robe, no date
Buffalo hide, acrylic paint, and beads
Dimensions variable
Courtesy of the artist

Wanesia Misquadace
Fond du Lac Band of the Ojibway, born 1971
Vessel, 2021
Birchbark, silver, and stones
H. 14 × W. 6 × D. 6 in.
Courtesy of the artist

Katrina Mitten
Miami Tribe of Oklahoma, born 1937
She Shimmers, 2022
Wool, silk ribbon, trade silver, sterling silver,
brain-tanned and smoked deer hide, cotton
print fabric, and size 11 Czech seed beads
Dimensions variable
Courtesy of the artist

Elias Jade Not Afraid
Apsaalooké Nation
Apsaalooké Rosette Earrings, 2023
Smoked deer hide, antique glass seed
beads, ermine tails, and vintage brass
connectors
H. 7 × W. 2¾ in.
Private collection, North Carolina

Jamie Okuma
Luiseño/Shoshone e-Bannock/Wailaki/
Okinawan, born 1977
Adaptation II, 2012
Shoes designed by Christian Louboutin,
leather, glass beads, porcupine quills,
sterling silver cones, brass sequins,
and chicken feathers
each H. 8⅝ × W. 3¼ × D. 9³⁄₁₆ in.
Lent by the Minneapolis Institute of Art,
Bequest of Virginia Doneghy, by exchange

Virgil Ortiz
Cochiti Pueblo, born 1969
*Convergence, Defenders Descend from
Portal to Pueblo*, 2023
Cochiti red clay, white clay slip, red clay slip,
and black pigment (wild spinach plant)
H. 28½ × W. 19 × D. 18 in.
North Carolina Museum of Art, Gift of Alan
and Benjamin King, Jeffrey Childers and
Onay Cruz Gutierrez, Joyce Fitzpatrick
and Jay Stewart, Valerie Hillings and B. J.
Scheessele, Marjorie Hodges and Carlton
Midyette, Stefanie and Douglas Kahn,
Bonnie and John Medinger, Mindy and
Guy Solie, Cathy and Jim Stuart, Libby
and Lee Buck, Liza and Lee Roberts, 2023
(2023.16.1)

Jane Osti
Cherokee, born 1945
Pot, 2023
Ceramic
Dimensions variable
Courtesy of the artist

Cherish Parrish
Pottawatomi/Ottawa/Matchi-be-nash-she-
wish, born 1989
The Next Generation – Carriers of Culture,
2018
Black ash
H. 23 × W. 14 × D. 17 in.
Collection of Michigan State University
Museum

Peedee Artist
Storage Vessel, 1100
Earthenware
H. 20 × W. 15 × D. 15 in.
Collection of the Rankin Museum
of American Heritage

Lisa Rutherford
Cherokee Nation, born 1958
In Times of War (War Chief's Mantle), 2015
Hemp netting, tanned deerskin, wild turkey
feathers, and dyed domestic goose feathers
Dimensions variable
Eiteljorg Museum, Harrison Eiteljorg
Purchase Award, 2015 Indian Market &
Festival

Rose B. Simpson
Santa Clara Pueblo, born 1983
Counterculture, 2022
Dyed concrete, steel, clay, and cable
Dimensions variable
Commissioned by Art & the Landscape, a
program of the Trustees, Massachusetts;
Courtesy of the artist, Jessica Silverman,
San Francisco, and Jack Shainman Gallery,
New York

Rose B. Simpson
Santa Clara Pueblo, born 1983
Maria, 2014
1985 Chevy El Camino
H. 54 × W. 72 × D. 202 in.
Courtesy of the artist

Rose B. Simpson
Santa Clara Pueblo, born 1983
Root I, 2019
Ceramic, glaze, linen, jute string, steel,
and leather
H. 70 × W. 20½ × D. 16 in.
Rennie Collection, Vancouver

Preston Singletary
Tlingit, born 1963
Raven Ladle, 2014
Blown and sand-carved glass
H. 23½ × W. 6¾ × D. 8¼ in.
Collection of Mina Levin and
Ronald Schwarz

Preston Singletary
Tlingit, born 1963
Saffron Tlingit Basket, 2016
Blown and sand-carved glass
H. 19 × W. 20½ × D. 19½ in.
North Carolina Museum of Art, Gift of
Mr. and Mrs. G. Wallace Newton, 2023
(2023.5.3)

Preston Singletary
Tlingit, born 1963
Spruce Green Tlingit Basket, 2016
Blown and sand-carved glass
H. 18 × W. 18½ × D. 18½ in.
North Carolina Museum of Art, Gift of
Mr. and Mrs. G. Wallace Newton, 2023
(2023.5.2)

Preston Singletary
Tlingit, born 1963
Tlingit Basket, 2012
Blown and sand-carved glass
H. 18 × W. 18½ × D. 18½ in.
North Carolina Museum of Art, Gift of
Mr. and Mrs. G. Wallace Newton, 2023
(2023.5.1)

Richard Zane Smith
Wyandot Nation of Kansas, born 1955
tribute to my ancestors, 2022
Hand-dug and processed Oklahoma clay
painted with clay slips
H. 17½ × Diam. 13 in.
Courtesy of the artist

Roxanne Swentzell
Santa Clara Pueblo, born 1962
Making Babies for Indian Market, 2004
Clay and pigment
H. 23½ × W. 8½ × D. 17 in.
Brooklyn Museum, Gift in memory of
Helen Thomas Kennedy, 2004.80

Dorothy Torivio
Acoma Pueblo, 1946–2011
Jar, 1994
Clay and paint
H. 8¹³⁄₁₆ × Diam. 8 in.
Denver Art Museum: Gift of Virginia Vogel
Mattern, 2003.1261

Laura Walkingstick
Cherokee
1920s Cherokee Woman, 2021
Cornhusk, wood, cloth, and beads
H. 13¾ × W. 7 × D. 4 in.
Courtesy of the artist

Laura Walkingstick
Cherokee
Self-Portrait, 2021
Cornhusk, wood, cloth, and beads
H. 11½ × W. 5 × D. 4 in.
Courtesy of the artist

Kathleen Wall
Pueblo of Jemez, born 1972
Holding Her Culture, 2022
Clay
H. 28 × W. 10 × D. 11 in.
Private collection

Denise Wallace
Chugach/Sugpiaq/Alutiiq, born 1957
Untitled Brooch (Caribou), 1992
Sterling silver, chrysoprase, and fossil ivory
H. 2½ × W. 2¼ × D. ½ in.
Collection of the Wheelwright Museum
of the American Indian, 2014.26.111

Denise Wallace
Chugach/Sugpiaq/Alutiiq, born 1957
Untitled Brooch (Figure with Seal Body),
1994
Sterling silver and fossil ivory
H. 2⅝ × W. 3⅜ × D. ¾ in.
Collection of the Wheelwright Museum
of the American Indian, 2022.03.052

 ✳ These works are not illustrated in the catalogue.

Denise Wallace
Chugach/Sugpiaq/Alutiiq, born 1957
Untitled Brooch (Yupik Dancer), 1997
Sterling silver, gold, fossil ivory, and
spectrolite
H. 3¾ × W. 2¼ × D. ⁷⁄₁₆ in.
Collection of the Wheelwright Museum
of the American Indian, 2014.03.054

Marie Watt
Seneca Nation, born 1967
*Acknowledgment: Indigenous Land,
Pachamama, Story Circle*, 2020
Cast bronze, cedar, LP Unito blankets,
patches, and embroidery floss
H. 45 × W. 28 × D. 28 in.
North Carolina Museum of Art, Purchased
with funds from the Matrons of the Arts and
with additional funds from various donors,
by exchange, 2021 (2021.10/a–aa)

Jodi Webster
Ho-Chunk Nation/Prairie Band Potawatomi
Nation
Badass Buckle, 2022
Sterling silver
H. 1 × W. 3⅛ × D. ½ in.
Courtesy of the artist

Jodi Webster
Ho-Chunk Nation/Prairie Band Potawatomi
Nation
Charmed, 2023
Sterling silver
H. 9½ × W. 1¾ × D. ½ in.
Courtesy of the artist

Jodi Webster
Ho-Chunk Nation/Prairie Band Potawatomi
Nation
Commemorating Ho-Chunk Female Chiefs,
2022
Hand-engraved 1964 Canadian dime
(colonizer removed), 18K gold rim and
beads, amethyst, custom-etched bone
bead, amazonite, and quartz
H. 14½ × W. 3 × D. ⅜ in.
Courtesy of the artist

Billy Welch
Snowbird Cherokee, born 1967
Shapeshifter Mask, 2023
Walnut and stain
H. 12 × W. 7 in.
Courtesy of the artist

Margaret Roach Wheeler
Chickasaw/Choctaw, born 1943
Chikasha Issoba, Chickasaw Horse, 2015
Handwoven cotton, glass beads, copper,
and handmade brass bells
H. 37 × W. 25 × D. 25 in.
Courtesy of the artist

Maidena Welch Wildcatt
Cherokee, born 1951
Basket, circa 1990–2000
White oak, bloodroot, and butternut root
H. 14 × W. 14 × D. 6 in.
Museum of the Cherokee Indian, Maidena
Welch Wildcatt Collection, 2011.599

Dennis Michael Wilkins
Lumbee
Fan Bowl, no date
North Carolina soapstone, wood, and beads
H. 4 × W. 11 × D. 25½ in.
Courtesy of the artist

Kenneth Williams Jr.
Northern Arapaho/Cattaraugus Seneca,
born 1983
Orlando Dugi
Navajo
Bandolier Bag, no date
Leather, glass, silk, shell, copper, and wool
H. 34 × W. 9 in.
Collection of the Wheelwright Museum
of the American Indian, 2019.11.001

Holly Wilson
Delaware Nation, born 1968
Bloodline, Keeper of the Seeds, 2021
Unique cast bronze with patina, cedar,
and steel
H. 30 × W. 98 × D. 15 in.
Courtesy of the artist

About the Authors

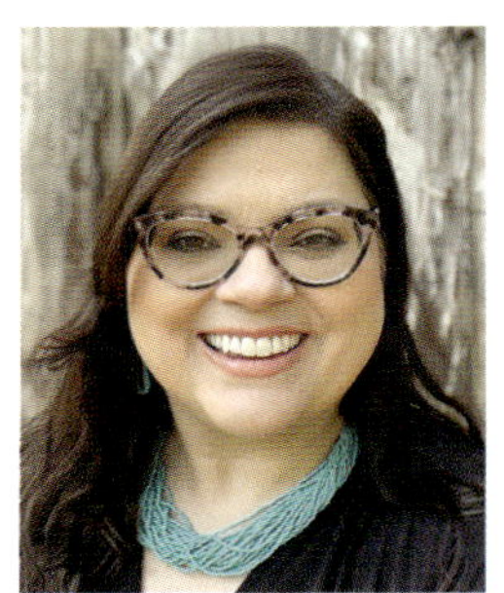

Nancy Strickland Fields (Lumbee), guest curator and lead author, is a member of the Lumbee tribe of North Carolina and has over twenty years of experience focused in museum education, curatorial work, and administration. She has worked at the Museum of Contemporary Native Art, Santa Fe, New Mexico; National Museum of the American Indian, Washington, DC; and American Indian Cultural Center and Museum, Oklahoma City. She is currently the director and curator of the Museum of the Southeast American Indian at the University of North Carolina at Pembroke. Fields is the first Lumbee graduate of the Institute of American Indian Arts (IAIA), where she earned a bachelor's degree in museum studies. She earned her master's degree in history from UNC Wilmington and is currently a doctoral student in the public history program at North Carolina State University. Fields's area of research focuses on Southeastern Native peoples and the American colonial experience.

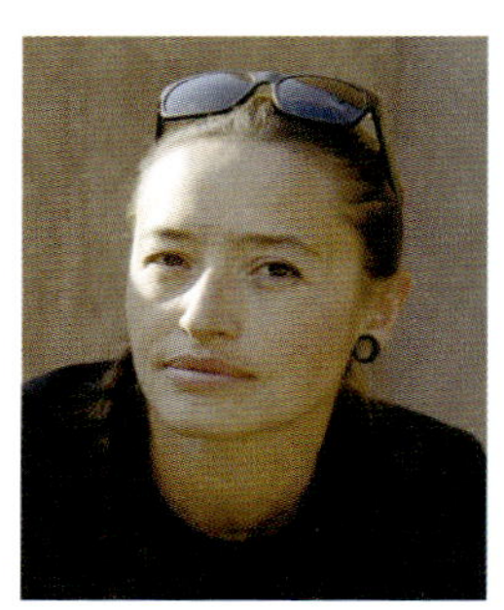

Rose B. Simpson (Santa Clara Pueblo), essay contributor, is a mixed-media artist whose artwork is also featured in *To Take Shape and Meaning*. She received her MFA in creative nonfiction from the IAIA in 2018. She lives and works on her ancestral homelands in New Mexico.

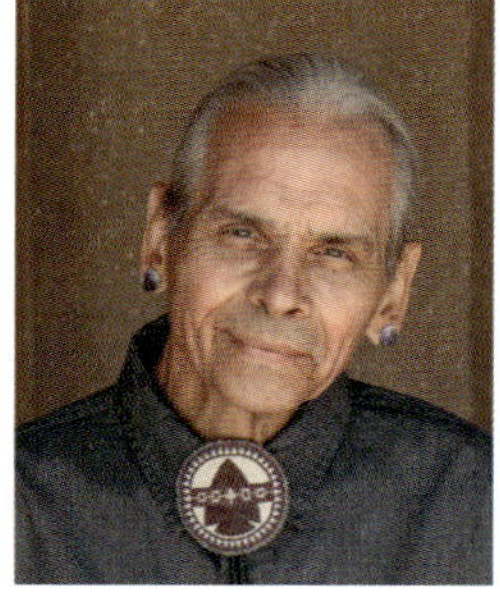

Stephen Fadden (Mohawk), essay contributor, is a traditional storyteller and director of programming at the Poeh Cultural Center and Museum at Pojoaque Pueblo. He earned his bachelor's and master's degrees at Cornell University. Fadden is a former instructor at Santa Fe Community College, where he taught small group communication, anthropology, and art history, and at the IAIA in Santa Fe, New Mexico, where he offered oral history classes.

PAGE 180: Virgil Ortiz (Cochiti Pueblo), *Convergence, Defenders Descend from Portal to Pueblo*, 2023, Cochiti red clay, white clay slip, red clay slip, and black pigment (wild spinach plant), H. 28½ × W. 19 × D. 18 in., North Carolina Museum of Art, Gift of Alan and Benjamin King, Jeffrey Childers and Onay Cruz Gutierrez, Joyce Fitzpatrick and Jay Stewart, Valerie Hillings and B. J. Scheessele, Marjorie Hodges and Carlton Midyette, Stefanie and Douglas Kahn, Bonnie and John Medinger, Mindy and Guy Solie, Cathy and Jim Stuart, Libby and Lee Buck, Liza and Lee Roberts

Photo Credits

cover, 21 Lynch: Collection of Bobby Brayboy; NCMA Photography, Christopher Ciccone

frontispiece, 90–91 Simpson: Renni Collection, Vancouver

vi, 160–61 Singletary: NCMA Photography, Christopher Ciccone

x, 105 Frey/Frey: Collections of Maine Historical Society

xii, 2, 3, 18 Peedee: Collection of the Rankin Museum of American Heritage; NCMA Photography, Christopher Ciccone

4, 171, 178 Simpson: Minesh Bacrania, Courtesy of the artist

7 Simpson: Kate Russell

8 Ataumbi/Okuma: Minneapolis Institute of Art

10, 89 Berry: Courtesy of the artist

11, 38–39 Fields: Courtesy of the Eiteljorg Museum of American Indians and Western Art, Indianapolis

12, 139 Jones: Courtesy of the Longyear Museum of Anthropology, Colgate University

13 Houser: © Chiinde LLC, Courtesy of Allan Houser Inc.

14, 32 Bridwell: NCMA Photography, Christopher Ciccone

16 Not Afraid: Courtesy of the artist

17, 36–37 Greeves: Birmingham Museum of Art

22–23 Welch: Courtesy of the artist

24 Davidson: Courtesy of the Audain Art Museum

25 Chrisjohn: Courtesy of the artist

26, 27 (top) Johnson: Justin Rogers Photography

27 (bottom) Johnson: Wendy McEahern Photography

29 Amerman: Courtesy of the artist, NCMA Photography, Christopher Ciccone

30 Wilkins: Collection of the Museum of the Southeast American Indian; NCMA Photography, Christopher Ciccone

31 Not Afraid: NCMA Photography, Christopher Ciccone

33 Box: Denver Art Museum: Native Arts acquisition fund, 2010.497; Photography © Denver Art Museum

35 Church: Courtesy of the artist

40–41 Glass: Courtesy of the artist

42 Black: Heard Museum Collection; Photograph by Craig Smith

43 Henry: Courtesy of the School for Advanced Research, Photo: Addison Doty

44 Locklear: Collection of the Museum of the Southeast American Indian; NCMA Photography, Christopher Ciccone

46–47 Blackburn: Courtesy of the artist

49 Wheeler: Courtesy of the artist

50, 58–59 Frey: On loan from the Robert and Barbara Buker Collections; Photography by Saygo Studios

52, 70–71 Mitten: Courtesy of the artist

53, 61 Wildcatt: Museum of the Cherokee Indian

55 Hank: NCMA Photography, Christopher Ciccone

56 Amerman/Singletary: Courtesy of the artists; NCMA Photography, Christopher Ciccone

62 Fragua: Courtesy of the artist

63 Fish: Courtesy of the artist

64 Rutherford: Courtesy of the Eiteljorg Museum of American Indians and Western Art, Indianapolis

65 Cottrell: Courtesy of the artist

66–67 Harris: Collection of the Native American Studies Center, University of South Carolina Lancaster

69 Holy Bear: Courtesy of the artist

72–73 Her Many Horses: NCMA Photography, Christopher Ciccone

74, 82 Lowery: Collection of the Museum of the Southeast American Indian; NCMA Photography, Christopher Ciccone

76–77, 96–97 Wilson: Courtesy of the artist

78–79 Simpson: Kate Russell

80 Osti: Courtesy of the artist

81 Smith: Courtesy of the artist

84–85 Chavis: Collection of the Museum of the Southeast American Indian; NCMA Photography, Christopher Ciccone

86 Harjo/Williams: Courtesy of Shiprock Santa Fe

87 Williams/Dugi: Courtesy of the Wheelwright Museum of the American Indian, Santa Fe, Photo: Addison Doty

88 Bread: Paris Bread

93 Parrish: Courtesy of Michigan State University Museum

94 Swentzell: Brooklyn Museum, Gift in memory of Helen Thomas Kennedy, 2004.80; © Roxanne Swentzell

95 Wall: Courtesy of the artist

98, 115 Gibson: Collection of the Nasher Museum of Art at Duke University, Museum purchase, 2015.11.1; © Jeffrey Gibson, Photo by Peter Paul Geoffrion

100, 112–13 Deer: Courtesy of the artist

101, 126–27 Farris: NCMA Photography, Christopher Ciccone

103 Watt: NCMA Photography, Christopher Ciccone and Karen Malinofski

104 Webster: Courtesy of the artist

106–7 Wallace: Courtesy of the Wheelwright Museum of the American Indian, Santa Fe, Photo: Addison Doty

108–9, 180 Ortiz: NCMA Photography, Christopher Ciccone

110–11 Walkingstick: NCMA Photography, Christopher Ciccone

114 Gibson: Courtesy of the artist and Roberts Projects, Los Angeles, Photo: Max Yawney

116–17 Dugi: Courtesy of the artist

118–19 Grant: Courtesy of the artist

121 Torivio: Denver Art Museum: Gift of Virginia Vogel Mattern, 2003.1261; Photography © Denver Art Museum

122–23 Kahm: Courtesy of the artist

124–25 Maybee: Courtesy of the artist

128, 158–59 Aragon: Courtesy of the artist

130, 154–55 Goshorn: © Shan Goshorn Studio, Photo: David Dietrich

131, 142–43 Houser: © Chiinde LLC, Photo courtesy of Allan Houser Inc.

133 Earles: National Cowboy and Western Heritage Museum

134 Halfmoon: Courtesy of the artist and Kouri + Corrao Gallery, Santa Fe

136–37 Judd: Courtesy of the artist

140–41 Koruh: Courtesy of the artist

144–45 Singletary: Russell Johnson

146 Misquadace: Courtesy of the artist

147 Amerman: Philbrook Museum of Art, Tulsa, Oklahoma, Gift of Don and Rita Newman, 2009.5.2; © Marcus Amerman

148, back cover Okuma: Minneapolis Institute of Art

150–51 Webster: Courtesy of the artist

152–53 Ataumbi: Courtesy of the artist

157 Cody: Minneapolis Institute of Art

163 Martinez: NCMA Photography, Christopher Ciccone and Karen Malinofski

164 Simpson: Courtesy of Jessica Silverman Gallery, Photos: Stephanie Zollshan

166 Amerman: Lee Marmon (Laguna/Acoma); Aragon: Courtesy of the artist; Ataumbi: R. de Give; Berry: Courtesy of the artist; Black: Kirstin Roper, © NHMU; Blackburn: Courtesy of the artist; Box: Courtesy of the artist; Bread: Courtesy of the artist

167 Bridwell: Courtesy of the artist; Chavis: Courtesy of the artist; Chrisjohn: Courtesy of the artist; Church: Courtesy of the artist; Cody: Joy Newell; Cottrell: Courtesy of the artist; Davidson: Courtesy of the artist; Deer: Courtesy of the artist; Dugi: G. Marks; Earles: Courtesy of the artist

168 Farris: Courtesy of the artist; Fields: Courtesy of the artist; Fish: Courtesy of the artist; Fragua: Courtesy of the artist; G. Frey: Courtesy of the artist; J. Frey: Courtesy of the artist; Gibson: Andrew Kist; Glass: Courtesy of the artist; Goshorn: © Rosalie Favell

169 Grant: Nadya Kwandibens, Red Works; Greeves: Mary Neiberg; Halfmoon: Courtesy of the artist; Harjo: © Paul Slaughter; Harris: Courtesy of National Endowment for the Arts; Henry: Tom Pich; Her Many Horses: Courtesy of the NMAI; Holy Bear: Courtesy of the artist; Houser: Lee Marmon (Laguna/Acoma); Johnson: Courtesy of the artist; Jones: Courtesy of the artist; Judd: Courtesy of the artist

170 Kahm: Courtesy of the artist; Koruh: Courtesy of the artist; Locklear: Courtesy of the artist; Lowery: Courtesy of UNC Pembroke; Lynch: Courtesy of American Indian Made in North Carolina; Martinez: Photograph by Wyatt Davis, Palace of the Governors Photo Archives (NMHM/DCA), Negative No. 004591; Maybee: Courtesy of the artist; Misquadace: Courtesy of the artist; Mitten: Courtesy of the artist; Not Afraid: Latoya Flowers, Courtesy of the artist

171 Okuma: Courtesy of the artist; Ortiz: Courtesy of the artist; Osti: Courtesy of VisitCherokeeNation; Parrish: Courtesy of Grand Rapids Museum of Art; Rutherford: Courtesy of the artist; Singletary: Courtesy of the artist; Smith: Courtesy of the artist; Swentzell: Julien McRoberts; Walkingstick: Courtesy of the artist

172 Wall: Just Lores; Wallace: Courtesy of the artist; Watt: Sam Gehrke; Webster: Jason S. Ordaz; Welch: Brooks Bennett; Wheeler: Courtesy of the artist; Wildcatt: Courtesy of the artist; Wilkins: Courtesy of the artist; Williams: Courtesy of the artist; Wilson: Courtesy of the artist

179 Fields: Courtesy of the artist; Fadden: Gabriela Campos/The New Mexican

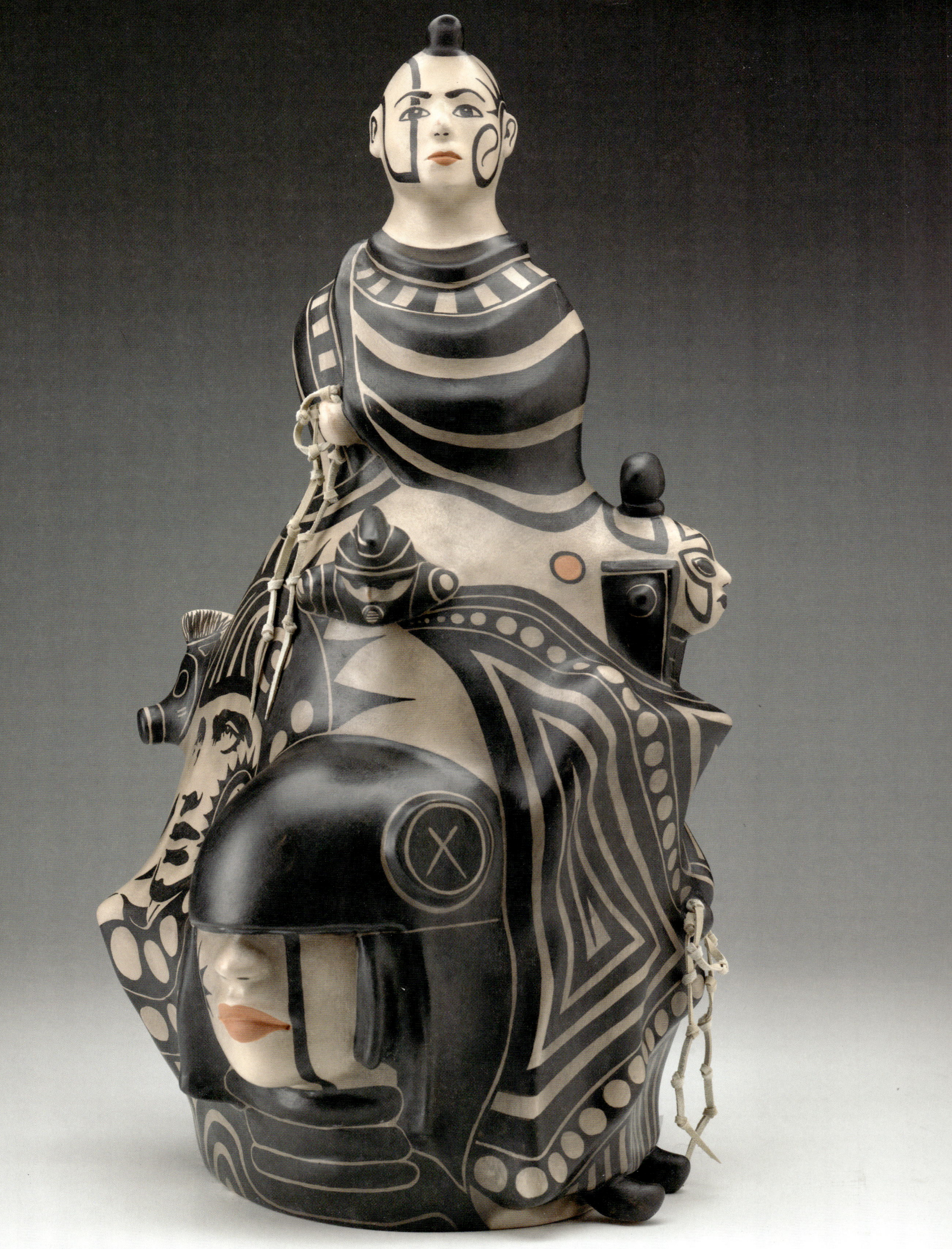